Y0-EAM-997

Garden Gate

The YEAR IN GARDENING

— VOLUME 16 —

AUGUST HOME
PUBLISHING COMPANY

SPECIAL PUBLICATIONS

"Order is the shape
upon which
beauty depends."
—Pearl S. Buck

Garden Gate

Please contact us to find out about other *Garden Gate* products and services:

By Phone: 1-800-341-4769
By Mail: 2200 Grand Avenue, Des Moines, IA 50312
By E-mail: GardenGate@GardenGateMagazine.com

OR VISIT OUR
Web Sites: www.GardenGateMagazine.com
or www.GardenGateStore.com

Copyright 2010 August Home Publishing Co.

"No *winter lasts forever;*
no spring skips its turn."
—Hal Borland

Welcome

You hold in your hands a wealth of information from the pages of *Garden Gate* magazine 2010. Each year the editors bring you great stories about the plants you love, design ideas for your garden and basic how-to information from our test garden, along with tips and questions from our readers, before and after gardens and plans straight from our drawing board. We're here to help you create a beautiful place of your own!

In this new book, not only are all of the year's stories at your fingertips, but we've organized them in an easy-to-access format. Whether you're looking for inspiration from gardens we've photographed or how to plant and care for daylilies, you'll be able to find the information quickly and easily. It's like having the editors of *Garden Gate* in your own back yard.

Each section has its own contents and in the back of the book you'll find an index for the entire book along with zone maps.

So sit back and enjoy a full year of gardening!

Steven

Garden Gate
The Illustrated Guide to Home Gardening and Design

PUBLISHER **Donald B. Peschke**

EDITOR **Steven M. Nordmeyer**

MANAGING EDITOR **Kristin Beane Sullivan**

ART DIRECTOR **Eric Flynn**

ASSOCIATE ART DIRECTOR **Carrie Topp**

SENIOR EDITORS
Luke Miller
Stephanie Polsley Bruner

ASSOCIATE EDITORS
Jim Childs, Deborah Gruca, Sherri Ribbey

SENIOR GRAPHIC DESIGNERS
Kate Corman
Kevin Venhaus

ILLUSTRATOR **Carlie Hamilton**

SENIOR PHOTOGRAPHER **Jack Coyier**

CORPORATE GARDENER **Marcia Leeper**

PRODUCTION ASSISTANT **Minniette Johnson**

VIDEOGRAPHER **Mark A. Hayes, Jr.**

Garden Gate® (ISBN 978-0-9842029-1-1) Garden Gate® is a registered trademark of August Home Publishing Co., 2200 Grand Avenue, Des Moines, IA 50312. © Copyright 2010, August Home Publishing Company. All rights reserved.
PRINTED IN CHINA.

TO ORDER ADDITIONAL COPIES
OF THIS BOOK
VISIT, WRITE OR CALL

www.GardenGateStore.com

Customer Service
P.O. Box 842, Des Moines, IA
50304-9961

800-341-4769
(Weekdays 8 a.m. to 5 p.m. CT)

To learn more about
Garden Gate magazine visit

www.GardenGateMagazine.com

AUGUST HOME®
PUBLISHING COMPANY

Garden Gate contents

The YEAR IN GARDENING VOLUME 16

great plants p. 8

Sunjoy Gold Beret Barberry	10
Blanket Flower	12
Chinese Snowball	16
'Pretty Bonnets' Columbine	18
Delphiniums	20
Euphorbias	24
Flowers of Fall	26
'Hameln' Fountain Grass	30
Gloriosa Daisies	32
Hellebores	34
Impatiens	38
An Iris for Everyone	44
'Red Rocks' Penstemon	48
Peonies	50
Primsoses	54
The Easiest Roses	56
Brilliance Lemon Strawflower	60
Did You Know	62

top picks p. 70

New Plants for 2010	72
Out-of-the-Ordinary Tulips	80
Big, Beautiful Blooms	86
Readers' Favorite Cut Flowers	92
Long-Blooming Perennials	98
Multiseason Showoffs	104

before and after p. 110

Boost Your Curb Appeal	112
This Color Won't Stop	116
Create a Fantastic Fall Entry Garden	120
No Space is Too Small for a Great Garden!	122
Shape Up a Neglected Bed	124

garden design p. 128

The Crowning Glory	130
4 Tips for Fragrance All Year!	136
Let the Sun Shine In!	138
Shape Up Your Garden	142
Cheer Up with Chartreuse	144
What You Need to Know About Fences	148
Create a Charming Cottage Garden Anywhere	152
Six Plants, Three Beds	154
Easy Island Bed	156
A Garden to Explore	158
Accessorizing Your Garden	164
Winter Wonders	166
Summer of Color	170
8 Simple Ideas to Fix This Skinny Back Yard	174
Design Tips for Awkward Corners	178
Nearly No-Care Getaway	180
Fabulous Combos Bring in Spring	182
Did You Know	186

design challenge drawing board p. 188

Make it Easy on Yourself	**190**
Easy to Maintain	**192**
Bring in the Butterflies	**194**
Butterfly Bistro	**196**
Feeding Butterfly Caterpillars and Container Recipe	**198**
Birds, Welcome!	**200**
Bird-Attracting Deck Planting	**202**
How to Tame a Big Space	**204**
Create a Woodland Retreat	**206**
Shady Haven	**208**
Pretty *and* Practical	**210**

Web extra: Throughout the book, you'll find this icon indicating additional tips, videos and information on our Web site. Visit www.GardenGateMagazine.com, click the Web extras button and look for this information in issues 91-96 of *Garden Gate* magazine. And while you're there, be sure to browse the rest of our helpful online content!

all about containers p. 212

Plant Shopping	**214**
How to Wow with Containers	**216**
Container Season is Here!	**222**
Disappointing Containers? Give Them a Makeover!	**226**
Windowboxes	**230**
Pansies in Pots: 3 Cool Looks	**236**
Ever so Exuberant	**238**
Flowery Fall	**239**
Make a Tough Job Easier!	**240**
Did You Know	**242**

index p. 310

gardening basics p. 246

Our Top 10 Tips to Save Money and Time	**248**
Get Started with Spring Cleanup	**250**
Enjoy More Flowers!	**252**
Start Perennials from Seed and Save Money	**256**
Success with Bare-Root Perennials	**258**
Fall is for Planting Cool-Season Vegetables	**262**
What's Your Fall Garden IQ?	**264**
Do Home Remedies Really Work?	**268**
Spring Weed Alert	**270**
9 Bugs to Stop Now!	**274**
Slugging it Out with Slugs	**278**
Is That Critter a Friend or Foe?	**280**
The Best Sprinkler for You and Your Plants!	**282**
Make Over a Stark Patio	**284**
Elegant Ornaments	**288**
Did You Know	**290**
Pests to Watch	**304**
Beneficials to Know	**305**
6 Weeds to Know	**306**
Know Your Zones	**308**

www.GardenGateMagazine.com *the* YEAR IN GARDENING 7

Meet 'Red Rocks' penstemon, a bold perennial for dusty soils, on page 48.

great plants *for* your garden

COLOR YOUR WORLD with some great plants that never fall short in the looks department. Learn about our favorite choices for adding long-lasting flowers or bold foliage to the garden — no matter what the growing conditions. And there's plenty of no-nonsense advice on planting, feeding, watering and pruning to share, too.

Sunjoy Gold Beret Barberry....... **10**	Hellebores................................... **34**
Blanket Flower............................. **12**	Impatiens..................................... **38**
Chinese Snowball........................ **16**	An Iris for Everyone.................... **44**
'Pretty Bonnets' Columbine....... **18**	'Red Rocks' Penstemon.............. **48**
Delphiniums................................ **20**	Peonies... **50**
Euphorbias................................... **24**	Primroses..................................... **54**
Flowers of Fall............................. **26**	The Easiest Roses........................ **56**
'Hameln' Fountain Grass............ **30**	Brilliance Lemon Strawflower... **60**
Gloriosa Daisies........................... **32**	Did You Know.............................. **62**

www.GardenGateMagazine.com *the* YEAR IN GARDENING **9**

PLANTS | EDITOR'S CHOICE

Sunjoy Gold Beret Barberry

Sunjoy Gold Beret barberry
Berberis thunbergii 'Talago'

Type	Shrub
Blooms	NA
Light	Full sun to part shade
Soil	Well-drained
Pests	None serious
Size	6 to 12 in. tall, 18 to 24 in. wide
Hardiness	Cold: USDA zones 4 to 7 Heat: AHS zones 7 to 1

PHOTO: Courtesy of Proven Winners (fall foliage)

Shrubs are great for gardens — they add structure and season-long interest. But they don't have to be mammoth plants to do the job. Take Sunjoy™ Gold Beret barberry. At just 6 to 12 inches tall, this petite shrub's intense foliage color acts as a beacon, drawing your eye to the garden.

FOLIAGE SHOW
Unlike flowering perennials, there's no need to deadhead Gold Beret to get the color you enjoy from spring to fall. Yellow leaves emerge in spring with a hint of red. By summer its sunburn-resistant foliage matures to the yellow-green you see at right. Then by fall the foliage is blushed the rusty orange-red in the inset photo.

SHORT BUT SWEET
Gold Beret is perfect for gardens that are tight on space. Or grow one of these shrubs in a container like the one below. Many of the plants for sale at the garden center are about half size and slow growing, so they won't take over the pot.

You can see why it would be easy to lose a shrub this size in the middle of the border. Keep that gorgeous gold foliage up front where you can see it. With nearby neighbors in the 15- to 18-inch-height range, Gold Beret will be the center of attention.

If there's a path nearby, I've found it helps to provide a low ground cover like the sedum next to the Gold Beret in the photo as a buffer. Barberries have prickly thorns that can grab your clothes.

CARE AND FEEDING
When talk centers around low-maintenance plants, barberries are at the top of the list. Gold Beret is no exception. Give it plenty of sun to keep that glowing foliage color. (It grows fine in part shade, but the habit is looser and the leaves greener.)

Barberries aren't heavy feeders, so a slow-release fertilizer once in spring is plenty. Get a fertilizer with more nitrogen. That's the first number in the analysis and promotes foliage growth.

This may be a small shrub but, with color like this, Gold Beret will have a mighty presence in your garden. □

Hats off to Gold Beret! The key to an interesting container is a variety of shapes and colors, and this grouping has both. There's an upright coreopsis and trailing calibrachoa, but Gold Beret does double duty. It has eye-catching color *and* a solid-looking shape, which gives your eye a place to rest.

A Barberry Sunjoy Gold Beret *Berberis thunbergii* 'Talago' See the information above left

B Calibrachoa *Calibrachoa* Minifamous™ Purple Annual; purple flowers; full sun; 5 to 10 in. tall, 12 to 14 in. wide; heat-tolerant in AHS zones 12 to 1

C Euphorbia *Euphorbia* xmartinii 'Ascot Rainbow' Perennial; variegated foliage; full sun; 20 in. tall and wide; cold-hardy in USDA zones 6 to 9, heat-tolerant in AHS zones 12 to 1

D Coreopsis *Coreopsis* Big Bang™ Galaxy Perennial; semidouble yellow flowers; full sun; 12 to 15 in. tall, 12 to 18 in. wide; cold-hardy in USDA zones 5 to 9, heat-tolerant in AHS zones 9 to 1

E Fountain grass *Pennisetum setaceum rubrum* 'Fireworks' Perennial; purple flowers; full sun; 24 to 30 in. tall and wide; cold-hardy in USDA zones 9 to 10, heat-tolerant in AHS zones 12 to 1

the YEAR IN GARDENING   www.GardenGateMagazine.com

Fall foliage

Mail-order sources

Garden Crossings
www.gardencrossings.com
616-875-6355. *Online catalog*

**Deer Resistant
Landscape Nursery**
www.deerxlandscape.com
800-595-3650. *Online catalog*

PLANTS | SUMMER PERENNIAL

Bright colors, easy care, long-blooming — your garden needs this perennial!

Blanket Flower

BLANKET FLOWER
Gaillardia spp. and hybrids

'Goblin'

Perennial
Flowers in red and yellow bicolor or solids in summer
Full sun
Well-drained soil
No serious pests
6 to 36 in. tall, 12 to 24 in. wide
The hardiest are cold-hardy in USDA zones 3 to 11
Heat-tolerant in AHS zones 11 to 1

Botanical Names

Catmint
  Nepeta racemosa
Daylily
  Hemerocallis hybrids

PHOTOS: Steven Nordmeyer (No more floppy flowers); © Charles Mann (1)

While it's true that not every wildflower can make the transition from meadow to garden very easily, blanket flower is a sure thing. It's cold-hardy, drought-tolerant and colorful.

There are about 30 species of blanket flower; some are annuals and some are perennials. Hybrid perennials, like the ones here, offer up the most variety. But crossing perennial blanket flowers with annual types for a longer bloom time resulted in a shorter life span. So you'll find that many hybrids usually only live for two or three years.

FLOWERS ALL SEASON Flowers start blooming in late spring to early summer and keep going until a hard frost. Your garden will be filled with blooms all summer if you grow blanket flower with other reblooming perennials, such as the daylilies and catmint growing alongside 'Goblin' in photo 1. I like to deadhead blanket flower as the first flushes of blooms fade. It makes the plants look tidier, encourages more blooms and prevents reseeding. And the more flowers there are, the more butterflies visit my garden. As summer turns to fall, let the flowers go to seed so hungry goldfinches have a snack before winter settles in. More than likely, a few seeds will escape the birds' notice, and you'll see new seedlings sprouting in spring. But they probably won't look like the parent plants so you may want to pull them while they're small.

GROWING BASICS Blanket flower thrives on neglect and prefers a poor but well-drained soil. It's extremely tolerant of cold temperatures, too. In fact, many of these colorful perennials are cold-hardy to USDA zone 3.

There's no need for extra watering once blanket flower is established, but it's a good idea to water regularly the first year to help new plants establish a good root system. After that, too much water or even heavy clay soil can cause them to rot.

To provide your blanket flower with just the right amount of nutrients, topdress annually with compost. (Organic matter like this helps with drainage, too.) I find it's easy to toss about an inch on the garden in fall after the foliage has died back. Don't bother with chemical fertilizers during the growing season. They just cause plants to get floppy and grow more foliage than flowers.

Even without fertilizer, some cultivars and species can have such long flower stems that they lean or fall on the ground. "No more floppy flowers" at left offers a simple way to keep the stems standing tall. On the other hand, many of the more recent cultivars have no problem staying upright because their habit is naturally more compact.

Now let's take a look at just which blanket flowers you'll find in the garden center and how you can use them in your garden.

✻ No more floppy flowers This tip from reader Barry Davis of New York helps keep floppy stems standing tall. Use green vinyl-covered wire in a low arch over the clump of plants. The five plants in the photo needed a 2x3-ft. piece. Push the ends into the soil to hold it in place. As the flower stems grow through the squares, they'll stay upright instead of falling into the mulch and mud.

---

12   *the* YEAR IN GARDENING   www.GardenGateMagazine.com

(1) Grow blanket flower with other low-maintenance sun-loving perennials. The purple 'Walker's Low' catmint and yellow 'Stella de Oro' daylily in this garden bloom nearly all summer.

DESIGNING WITH BLANKET FLOWER

Botanical Names

Agave *Agave* spp.
Perennial geranium *Geranium* spp.
Tall sedum *Sedum* spp.

Mail-order sources

High Country Gardens
www.highcountrygardens.com
800-925-9387
Catalog free

Sooner Plant Farm
www.soonerplantfarm.com
Online catalog

Park Seed
www.parkseed.com
800-213-0076

This versatile plant has plenty of sizes, flower colors and shapes to keep things interesting. Go ahead and mix and match cultivars to fit your garden's style — they all have the same cultural needs.

CHOOSE YOUR SIZE With its low-growing foliage, blanket flower is a good choice along this path in photo 2. Clumps of lance-shaped leaves hug the gravel and brick, softening the edge and creating a nice contrast of color, shape and texture. Since the flowers have long stems you can still see through to the plants behind them. Blanket flower cultivars range from 6 to 36 inches tall while flowering. So keep an eye on the plant tags when you're shopping to make sure you're getting the right size for your situation. If you'd like a plant for the front of the border or you don't have a lot of room, check out the list of dwarf cultivars below. These compact plants have shorter flower stems, creating a denser form.

FLOWERS GALORE You can't miss the colorful wall in photo 2. And the green foliage in the garden in front really helps set it off. The blanket flower adds a bright note of color that picks up the yellow of the big variegated agave's leaves and the warm tones of the wall.

Bicolor red and yellow blooms are classic blanket flower colors. But there are plenty of other color choices. You can also find solids and unusual color combinations. Learn more about these cultivars at right.

While all blanket flowers are long-blooming, some cultivars are even more so than others. I've listed these top performers, according to the University of Georgia trials, in the list at right. You have to admit, perennials that bloom for 28 weeks are hard to find — and a couple of these do! Plant these varieties with perennial geranium and tall sedum for three seasons of bloom.

Because blanket flower has a low-growing rosette of foliage, even the tall ones are placed near the front of the border. That way, the leaves get plenty of sunshine and aren't shaded out by taller neighbors. And with your plants close to a path or patio, you'll be able to enjoy them up close — especially if you decide on one of the more fancy flower types, such as fluted Commotion® Frenzy or frilled 'Amber Wheels'.

No matter what shape the petals are, you'll notice more butterflies and hummingbirds dropping by your garden when you grow blanket flower. In fact, blanket flower is so pretty, you might find more than just winged visitors in your garden — your neighbors will want to know where you got this brightly colored beauty! □

— *Sherri Ribbey*

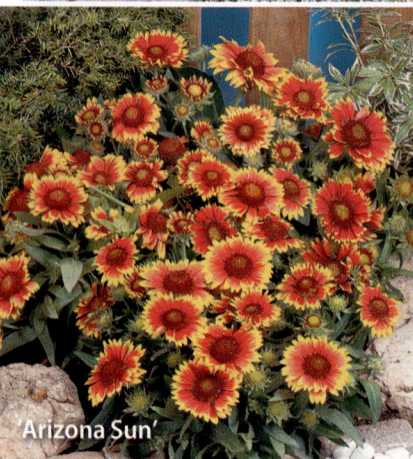

'Arizona Sun'

Dwarf habit You don't need a lot of space for these blanket flowers but they'll sure attract attention.

'Arizona Sun' Red and yellow flowers; 6 to 12 in. tall, 12 to 15 in. wide; cold-hardy in USDA zones 3 to 9, heat-tolerant in AHS zones 9 to 1

'Jazzy Wheeler' Large red and yellow flowers; 10 in. tall, 16 in. wide; cold-hardy in USDA zones 3 to 10, heat-tolerant in AHS zones 10 to 1

'Fancy Wheeler' Deep burgundy center with golden yellow edge; 10 in. tall, 16 in. wide; cold-hardy in USDA zones 3 to 10, heat-tolerant in AHS zones 10 to 1

Goblin ('Kobold') Scarlet red center with yellow edge; 12 in. tall, 15 in. wide; cold-hardy in USDA zones 3 to 10, heat-tolerant in AHS zones 10 to 1

PHOTOS: © Charles Mann (2); courtesy of Benary Seed Company ('Arizona Sun'); courtesy of North Creek Nurseries, Inc. ('Burgundy'); courtesy of Ball Horticultural Company ('Mesa Yellow'); courtesy of Park Seed (Commotion Frenzy)

(2) Plant in groups of three to five. Grouping the flowers together creates a bigger impact and you'll have plenty of flowers to cut and enjoy in a vase, too.

'Burgundy'

'Mesa Yellow'

Commotion Frenzy

Unusual colors
The color palette for blanket flower has expanded in the past few years. Here are some of the newer choices.

'Burgundy' ('Burgunder') Burgundy flowers up to 3 in. across; long stems can flop; 2 to 3 ft. tall, 1 to 2 ft. wide; cold-hardy in USDA zones 3 to 8, heat-tolerant in AHS zones 8 to 1

'Summer's Kiss' Apricot yellow flowers; 18 to 24 in. tall, 12 to 18 in. wide; cold-hardy in USDA zones 5 to 9, heat-tolerant in AHS zones 9 to 1

'Oranges and Lemons' Orange and yellow flowers; 18 to 24 in. tall, 15 to 18 in. wide; cold-hardy in USDA zones 5 to 10, heat-tolerant in AHS zones 10 to 1

Long blooming
Get the most bloom for your buck with these cultivars. The length of time is approximate since weather and garden conditions affect flower production.

'Mesa Yellow' Single yellow flowers for up to 28 weeks; 16 to 18 in. tall, 20 to 24 in. wide; cold-hardy in USDA zones 5 to 10, heat-tolerant in AHS zones 10 to 1

'Georgia Yellow' Single yellow flowers for up to 28 weeks; 18 in. tall, 25 in. wide; cold-hardy in USDA zones 7 to 11, heat-tolerant in AHS zones 11 to 1

Sunburst™ Scarlet Halo Burgundy flowers with yellow tips for up to 24 weeks; 14 to 20 in. tall and wide; cold-hardy in USDA zones 3 to 10, heat-tolerant in AHS zones 10 to 1

Fancy flowers
Single petal flowers aren't the only game in town. Check out these unusual bloom shapes.

Commotion® Frenzy Red and yellow fluted petals; 18 to 24 in. tall, 24 in. wide; cold-hardy in USDA zones 5 to 9, heat-tolerant in AHS zones 9 to 1

'Amber Wheels' Shaggy yellow petals with a red center; 30 in. tall, 18 in. wide; cold-hardy in USDA zones 4 to 9, heat-tolerant in AHS zones 9 to 1

'Fanfare' Fluted red and yellow flowers; 18 to 24 in. tall, 24 in. wide; cold-hardy in USDA zones 4 to 10, heat-tolerant in AHS zones 10 to 1

PLANTS | EDITOR'S CHOICE

Chinese Snowball

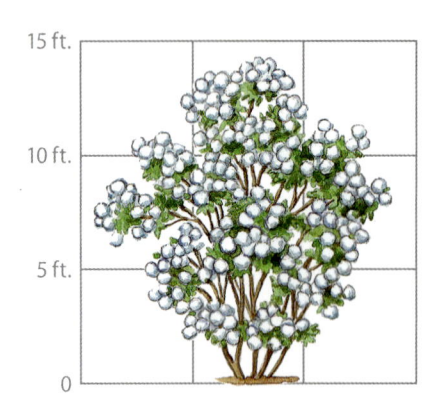

Chinese snowball
Viburnum macrocephalum

Size	10 to 15 ft. tall, 10 to 15 ft. wide
Type	Shrub
Bloom	Green changing to white in spring
Soil	Well-drained, slightly acid
Light	Full sun to part shade
Pests	None serious
Hardiness	Cold: USDA zones 6 to 9 Heat: AHS zones 9 to 1

PHOTO LOCATION: Atlanta Botanical Garden

If you're looking for a shrub that'll have your neighbors stopping by to ask what it is, check out the Chinese snowball in the photo. In early spring the flower clusters start out chartreuse. But they soon change to the crisp white in the inset and last several weeks.

Chinese snowball flowers are sterile, so they don't produce fruit later in the season. That makes it a good choice near your front door or over a patio or sidewalk where you don't want to attract fruit-eating birds.

SHOW IT OFF If you leave branches all the way to the ground, your shrub will have the habit of the plant in the illustration above left. However, the plant in the photo at right has had its lower limbs taken off, and this lets you plant a shade garden directly under it. And who doesn't want more planting space?

Place a Chinese snowball as an accent at the corner of your home. Or grow one as a focal point in a border, anywhere you want to attract attention. In the vignette below, a Chinese snowball ties the pergola to the lower plantings.

KEEP IT HEALTHY Choose a site out of winter wind. The foliage is semievergreen and will look much better if it isn't tattered by storms. If you live north of USDA zone 7 or the winter temperatures become bitterly cold, odds are the leaves will drop off no matter where you plant it. Don't worry; they'll be back in spring, as the flowers open.

Keep the soil moist as Chinese snowball doesn't like to be dry. An organic mulch of wood chips or pine needles is a big help in keeping the moisture level just right.

If you need to tidy up the shape, do your trimming right after the flowers finish so there'll be time for next year's flower buds to form. And, just like a lilac, if your Chinese snowball grows too large and lanky, it can be cut down to rejuvenate. But think carefully before you cut. You'll lose the flowers for at least a year.

Applying too much fertilizer can produce more foliage than flowers. It's better to keep this shrub on a lean diet so you'll get billows of blooms every spring. And your friends and neighbors will all be over to ask you about your striking shrub. □

Corner classic Large shrubs are great for softening the hard angles at a corner. But as you see in this design, they need smaller shade-loving plants underneath to help them fit into the landscape best.

A   **Chinese snowball** *Viburnum macrocephalum*
See information above left

B   **Hosta** *Hosta* 'Blue Angel' Perennial; 18 to 30 in. tall, 36 to 48 in. wide; cold-hardy in USDA zones 3 to 8, heat-tolerant in AHS zones 8 to 1

C   **Oakleaf hydrangea** *Hydrangea quercifolia* Little Honey ('Brihon') Shrub; 3 to 4 ft. tall and wide; cold-hardy in USDA zones 5 to 9, heat-tolerant in AHS zones 9 to 1

D   **Browallia** *Browallia speciosa* Tender perennial; 12 to 24 in. tall, 8 to 12 in. wide; cold-hardy in USDA zones 9 to 10, heat-tolerant in AHS zones 12 to 1

the YEAR IN GARDENING   www.GardenGateMagazine.com

Spring flowers start out bright green, change to white and drop without producing messy fruit.

Mail-order source

Woodlanders, Inc.
www.woodlanders.net
803-648-7522. *Online catalog only*

PLANTS | EDITOR'S CHOICE

'Pretty Bonnets' Columbine

Aquilegia 'Pretty Bonnets'

Size	24 to 30 in. tall, 12 to 14 in. wide
Type	Perennial
Blooms	Large pink, purple, rose and maroon flowers in midspring
Soil	Well-drained
Light	Full sun to part shade
Pests	Occasional leaf miners
Hardiness	Cold: USDA zones 3 to 8 Heat: AHS zones 8 to 1

Have you ever been idly flipping the pages of a seed catalog and come across a photo that immediately made you send in an order? 'Pretty Bonnets' columbine did this for me several years ago.

I could just picture a sweep of these big pink, purple, rose and maroon flowers every spring. But I knew I'd never be able to afford that many plants. So I ordered a packet of seeds and started a flat in January. By late March I could set out my seedlings!

Although they were a bit late, the seedlings did bloom the first year. The flowers weren't as big as I expected that year. But the second year they were full sized — the big, 1½-inch blooms at right.

You can see two distinct stages of blooms in the insets. Most larger columbines have spurs, or long tails, on the backs of the blooms, but 'Pretty Bonnets' has only very short ones, making them even more unusual looking. My planting, in the photo, has mostly shades of pink with white edges. (The shorter columbine in the center is 'Winky', a different cultivar.)

'Pretty Bonnets' is 24 to 30 inches tall in bloom — it's nice at the front of a border or at the back of a low-growing little combo, like the one below. Since columbine is airy, it won't cover anything up behind it.

It blooms in mid-spring, and after you deadhead (I'll tell you how in a minute), the mound of foliage is tidy and attractive, too. So this makes it a great companion for later-blooming plants as it doesn't look ratty.

TAKE CARE Columbine does well in part shade. This border with eastern exposure offers gentle sun in the morning and shade from the harsher late-day light.

Plants don't need staking while in bloom, but once they set seed, they tend to fall over. So cut the flower stems back at the base to clean them up. I usually leave a couple stalks of each color to allow for some self-seeding to keep my patch thick.

By early summer, columbine leaf miners sometimes leave trails in the leaves but usually don't do any lasting damage. When I encounter this, I cut the foliage back after the plants bloom, and usually get a fresh, miner-free mound of foliage within a few weeks.

If I could shake a few seeds of this perennial into your pocket for your garden, I would. But introducing you to it is the next best thing. Enjoy! ☐

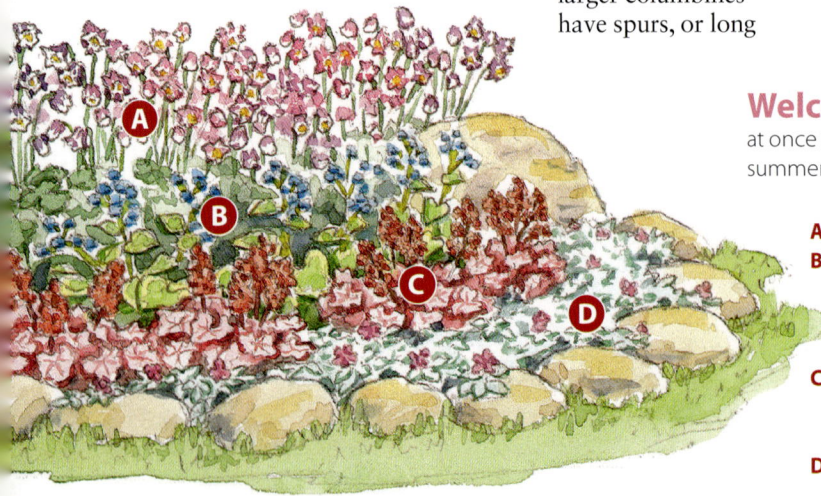

Welcome spring This easy-going combo blooms all at once in spring, then has interesting foliage to carry it through summer and fall. Grow it in part shade.

A **Columbine** *Aquilegia* 'Pretty Bonnets' See information above left

B **Brunnera** *Brunnera macrophylla* 'Hadspen Cream' Perennial; small blue flowers in spring, variegated heart-shaped leaves; part to full shade; 12 to 18 in. tall, 18 to 24 in. wide; cold-hardy in USDA zones 3 to 7, heat-tolerant in AHS zones 7 to 1

C **Coral bells** *Heuchera* 'Milan' Perennial; pink blooms, burgundy-silver leaves; sun to part shade; 14 in. tall, 18 in. wide; cold-hardy in USDA zones 4 to 9, heat-tolerant in AHS zones 9 to 1

D **Spotted deadnettle** *Lamium maculatum* 'Beacon Silver' Perennial ground cover; pink flowers, silver foliage; part to full shade; 4 to 8 in. tall, spreading; cold-hardy in USDA zones 3 to 9, heat-tolerant in AHS zones 9 to 1

Any new plants that have come up have looked like their parents. But I wouldn't be surprised if I started seeing some variation at some point, as columbines cross easily.

'Pretty Bonnets'

'Winky'

'Pretty Bonnets'

Just opening…

…fully open

Mail-order source

Pinetree Garden Seeds
www.superseeds.com
207-926-3400. *Catalog free*

PLANTS | SUMMER PERENNIAL

Gorgeous colors, dramatic shape —
Your Garden Needs Delphiniums!

Side branch

DELPHINIUM
Delphinium elatum and hybrids

Perennial

Flowers in shades of blue, pink and white in early to midsummer

Full sun

Moist, well-drained, neutral to slightly acid soil

Crown rot and slugs are occasional problems

Up to 6 ft. tall, 2 to 3 ft. wide

Cold-hardy in USDA zones 3 to 8

Heat-tolerant in AHS zones 8 to 1

Botanical Names

Daylily
  Hemerocallis hybrids
Hosta *Hosta* hybrids

Mail-order sources

Busse Gardens
www.bussegardens.com
800-544-3192. Catalog $3

Graceful Gardens
www.gracefulgardens.com
607-387-5529.
Catalog online only

I like a challenge, especially a garden challenge. Sure, I like to grow the basics, such as daylilies and hostas. But there's something very satisfying about success with a difficult plant. For many folks, getting tall delphiniums to look like they do in books can be a challenge. Want to be the envy of your gardening friends? I can help!

NOT ALL SPECIES ARE CREATED EQUAL First, if you want those 6-foot flower-packed spikes, you have to be sure to buy the right ones. In general, there are two types: *Grandiflorums* are shorter and billowing, and *elatum*s send up the tall spikes. To identify the tallest ones as you're shopping, look for *elatum* somewhere on the plant tag. New Millennium Hybrids or Pacific Giants are two popular series. The Magic Fountains series gives you that same look but on a slightly smaller scale, with plants growing only 3 to 5 feet tall.

MORE THAN JUST BLUE FLOWERS It's mostly the shapely blue spires that attract gardeners. But delphiniums also come in lots of other colors. Along with the pale blue 'Summer Skies' at right, you'll find three examples of the color range in the small photos below.

Did you notice the little tuft of petals in the center of each flower? It's called a "bee" and may be the same color as the outer petals, or it could be darker or lighter. It adds lots of visual interest to the flower. For example, the white bee in the dark flower will give each floret a glow so it shows better from a distance. Up close a dark bee, such as a black bee in a white flower, keeps the white from looking washed out in bright sunshine.

Flowers open from the bottom of the spike and go up. Some cultivars have spikes that are densely packed with flowers. Others, such as 'Summer Skies' in the large photo at right, have a looser, more casual flower spacing. I think the looser ones stand better in the wind, but both types really need to be staked. Speaking of staking, I bet you barely noticed the stakes in this photo. I'll show you how to use this inconspicuous and sturdy method in "Stake 'em like a pro" at far right. Then turn the page to get more surefire tips for growing beautiful delphiniums every year.

'Astolat'

'Magic Fountains Dark Blue'

'Double Innocence'

the YEAR IN GARDENING   www.GardenGateMagazine.com

'Summer Skies'

If a tall spike breaks off you'll still get to enjoy the shorter side branches.

✱ stake 'em like a pro

Supporting the entire flower head is the only way to ensure your blooms will look as good as the tall blue ones in this photo. You'll need a bamboo stake for each stem and lengths of twine or strips of old stockings to tie the stems to the stake. The figure-8 pattern I'm using here helps the stem stay secure without becoming strangled by the tie.

1 After you push each stake into the soil about a foot, make sure it'll be at least as tall as you think the flower stems will grow.

Just as buds form, tie each stem to a stake about two-thirds of the way up from the ground.

2 When flowers reach their full height, tie just below the flower head.

3 As soon as flowers start to open, tie the flower head in one or two spots.

Snip off the excess stake with your pruners.

PHOTOS: Doug Appleby (Astolat, 'Double Innocence'; stake 'em like a pro)

OUR BEST TIPS FOR SUCCESS

Delphiniums are the prima donnas of the garden world: Make them happy and they reward you with beautiful flowers. So let's take a look at how to grow dramatic delphiniums.

START WITH THE LOCATION Choose a spot in full sun. The exception is if you live where summers are hot and dry. There, delphiniums will perform better if they get some protection from the hot afternoon sun. Well-drained, neutral to slightly acid soil is perfect for delphiniums. Improve the drainage by incorporating lots of compost or humus into the soil. Keep them too wet, especially over winter, and the plants will rot. If your soil is on the dry side, a 2- to 4-inch-thick layer of organic mulch helps keep the ground cool and the moisture level steady.

Late summer is the time to plant delphiniums. This way they'll be completely established by spring and you'll get a bigger flower spike. Planting in spring is fine if it fits your schedule or it's when you find the best selection. However, the flower stems won't grow as tall the first year.

If you like, you can buy plants in spring and propagate them, too. Or if you have established clumps, spring is the time to lift them and take cuttings that you can root. I'll show you how in "More delphiniums for less" below. By late summer your rooted cuttings will be ready to move to the garden so they bloom next spring.

YOUNG CLUMPS = LARGE FLOWERS Delphiniums are like chrysanthemums — plants that are only two or three years old will be the showiest. An old clump will send up lots of stems, but they won't grow as tall and the flowers won't be as big. A few stems on a young plant will give you bigger and sturdier flowers. So, it pays to thin an established plant. Look over the old clump when the stems are 2 to 6 inches tall. Select three to five of the strongest stems and snip, pinch or break off the rest of the crown. That sends all of the energy to the remaining stems so they grow bigger.

HEARTY EATERS Feed delphiniums when the stems are about 18 to 20 inches tall — any earlier, and they'll put the nutrients into leaf and stem production. Pull back the mulch and sprinkle an organic fertilizer. One recommended for roses, such as 6-6-4, is great. You can use chemical fertilizers, but go lightly. Full strength may produce a flush of new growth that tends to be weak and floppy. And dry chemical fertilizers can burn roots and leaves. Don't bother scratching the fertilizer into the soil — some delphinium roots are shallow and could be damaged. Simply cover the fertilizer with mulch. Then feed the plants again about two weeks later to make sure the side branches will flower.

TIMELY PRUNING The main flower stalk of a tall delphinium can have up to 100 individual flowers. Each spike blooms for about two weeks

---

Botanical Names

Chrysanthemum
  Chrysanthemum spp.
Forsythia
  Forsythia spp.
Joe-Pye weed
  Eupatorium maculatum

✱ more delphiniums for less

If you want a lot of plants for little or no money, take cuttings in spring. I'll show you how in the photos at right.

After you take the cuttings and water them in, set the pot outdoors in a cool spot out of direct sun. An east or north exposure is ideal. You should see new leaves and roots after four to six weeks. Then move the starts into individual pots and pinch out the tips to stimulate more leaves. After five more weeks plant the starts in your garden, where they'll bloom next spring.

1 WHEN TO CUT As soon as the spring growth is 2 to 6 in. tall, scrape away enough of the soil to see where the stems join the crown. You can gather cuttings from an old clump you dig from your garden or from a new one you just bought. I cut this one up completely.

2 HOW TO CUT With a sharp hobby knife, cut off a stem, keeping a bit of the woody crown on its base. The top cutting in the inset is perfect. However the bottom one may not root, as it doesn't have any crown with it.

A good cut / Not enough crown

— longer in cool weather. As it fades, cut it, and the stake if you like, off just above a side branch. Those buds will extend the bloom period another two weeks. Once all the flowers finish, cut the entire stem down to within 6 inches of the ground. You may get some later flowers, but the plant will survive the winter better if you don't push it to flower heavily. So don't fertilize it after it blooms if you want to give it a better chance at survival.

OVERWINTERING TIPS Slugs love to munch on delphiniums. If you've had problems, use a mulch of sawdust to help keep them away. And keep slugs from overwintering by getting rid of the dormant foliage rather than leaving it stand.

Crown rot can spell certain death to your delphiniums if you live where winter rains are frequent. Try plugging the hollow stems after you cut them off. Use scraps of foil or wads of fabric to keep water from being funneled into the crown. After the ground is frozen, or as cold as it gets in your zone, cover the crown with mulch. Straw or evergreen boughs let air circulate, preventing the soil from staying too wet. Leave the covering in place until spring when the forsythia blooms.

Now that you have growing tips, check out the design ideas in "Show off your delphiniums" at right. And however you choose to display them, I'm sure you'll enjoy these striking flowers. □

— *Jim Childs*

3 POT IT UP Strip off all but the top few leaves and dip the end of the cutting in rooting hormone. Poke a hole and insert the cutting up to the first leaf. Don't firm the soil around the stem—watering will take care of that. You can fit about six cuttings in a quart-size pot.

Pre-poke the hole so the hormone powder isn't brushed off on the way down.

SHOW OFF YOUR DELPHINIUMS!

Odds are that wherever you plant tall delphiniums they will get noticed. But you probably don't want them to stick out like a sore thumb. Let me share three design techniques you can use with delphiniums no matter what size garden you're working with.

CONTRAST SHAPES Contrasting flower and plant shapes is sure to make any garden more interesting. Since delphiniums have a strong vertical form, you'll want to pair them with round shapes, as well as with plants that have a lower, more horizontal form. Vertical plants will also lead the eye upward. Use tall plants that have a point at the top in small areas to make the garden feel larger. They encourage you to look up at the wide open spaces instead of focusing on the size of the area directly around you.

Strong vertical forms lead your eye up, so a small space often seems larger.

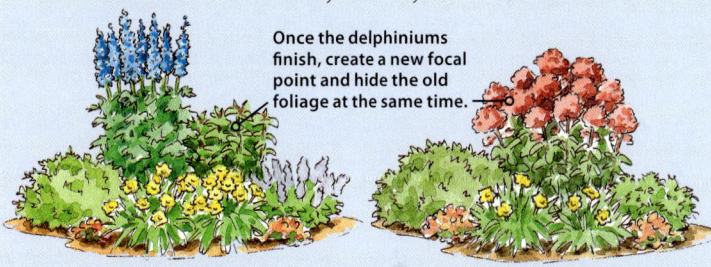

Once the delphiniums finish, create a new focal point and hide the old foliage at the same time.

Early summer   **Late summer**

A CHANGING FOCAL POINT Tall delphiniums make an ideal focal point. Their vertical form always draws attention. The problem arises when you realize that a delphinium focal point only lasts while the clump is in bloom. What can you do? Plant a later-blooming perennial, that's equally as striking, as a neighbor. In this case the fading delphinium is hidden by a Joe-Pye weed that will bloom into fall.

SCATTER THEM AROUND One clump of delphiniums is a focal point, but if you have a long border, go with several. Your eye will be drawn to one, and then quickly on to the next before it focuses on the rest of the garden. Clumps don't have to be the same size or color to visually tie a large garden together and lead your eye down the entire border.

Clumps of delphiniums can be randomly placed or evenly spaced to create repetition.

PLANTS | SUN PERENNIAL

E. charachias wulfenii

Unique Euphorbias

Four fabulous plants fill any garden need!

Euphorbias are intriguing. Whether you're talking about the vibrant colors of the "flowers" and foliage, their interesting habits or how easy they are to grow, they have a lot going for them. But, more than that, they all exude a kind of crazy "other-worldly" quality that's so appealing.

Most euphorbias, or spurges, as they are sometimes called, bloom in spring and early summer. Their long-lasting "blooms" are actually showy bracts at the ends of the stems. These unusual flowers just add to their strange allure. (*E. hypericifolia* is the exception in this story. It sports clouds of tiny white flowers.) And euphorbias don't fade or flop, but keep their great shape all season.

LESS WORK — MORE WOW Euphorbias are tough as nails and incredibly easy to grow. Most prefer full sun to part shade and well-drained soil. With the exception of Griffith's spurge, they rot in clay soil that stays wet in winter. In conditions they like, they tolerate drought and are immune to slugs, aphids and even deer. But most spurges have a milky sap that can irritate your eyes and skin, so wear gloves when you're cutting them back in spring to clean them up.

Though there are tons of great euphorbias, I'll share four of my favorite ones here. You'll learn the best ways to use them in the garden and tips for keeping these eccentric plants looking fabulous! □

— *Deborah Gruca*

PHOTOS: © Jerry Pavia (Mediterranean spurge), © Todd Boland (Griffith's spurge inset)

Bold architectural form
Mediterranean spurge
E. characias wulfenii

This spurge practically shouts, "Hey, look at me!" Just check out the eye-grabbing bright yellow-green flowering stems of *E. characias wulfenii* above! You can use this plant to make a statement in any planting.

The biennial stems wither after the second year's bloom, which is larger and brighter than the first year's. Simply cut the dead growth back to the crown after the plant flowers to keep it looking tidy.

Mediterranean spurge usually lives less than 10 years, but fortunately it reseeds freely.

Size 3 to 5 ft. tall, 3 to 4 ft. wide
Bloom 9-in. yellow-green flower heads in early to late spring
Soil Well-drained to rocky
Light Full sun to part shade
Hardiness
 Cold: USDA zones 7 to 11
 Heat: AHS zones 11 to 1
Source Digging Dog Nursery
 www.diggingdog.com
 707-937-1130

Bright, colorful foliage
Griffith's spurge *E. griffithii*

Have a sunny bed or border that could use fantastic foliage color all season? Griffith's spurge is your plant. In spring, it emerges with red-veined deep-green leaves on dark-red stems. By early summer it produces bright red-orange bracts. And in fall, the leaves also turn bright-red to orange — it's easy to see how 'Fireglow', above, gets its name.

Griffith's spurge is clump-forming, slowly spreading by underground rhizomes. In well-drained soil, the plant can spread more quickly. Single upright stems sprout first. Later in spring, side branches grow to give the plant a bushier habit.

Size 3 ft. tall, 3 ft. wide
Bloom Bright red-orange bracts in early summer
Soil Tolerates clay soil, damp or dry
Light Full sun to part shade (but more colorful in sun)
Hardiness
Cold: USDA zones 5 to 9
Heat: AHS zones 9 to 1
Source Forestfarm
www.forestfarm.com
541-846-7269

Great ground cover
Cypress spurge *E. cyparissias*

Need a ground cover for a rocky or sandy slope where nothing else will grow? Rugged cypress spurge is perfect. You won't see much of its fine blue-green foliage in late spring to early summer when the plant is covered in yellow-green bracts.

Cypress spurge reseeds freely and also spreads by rhizomes. It's not a good choice for a border with other plants: It'll quickly crowd them out. In fact, it can be invasive, so grow it in a spot where its spread is limited. You can hamper reseeding a bit by growing it in some shade and shearing the plant back by half when it's finished flowering. 'Fens Ruby', above, is better-behaved.

Size 9 to 12 in. tall, spreading
Bloom Yellow-green in late spring to midsummer
Soil Well-drained
Light Full sun
Hardiness
Cold: USDA zones 4 to 8
Heat: AHS zones 8 to 1
Source Lazy S's Farm Nursery
www.lazyssfarm.com

First-class container plant
Euphorbia hypericifolia

Clouds of tiny, airy white flowers make this annual spurge stand out from many other euphorbias. Blooming most all summer, they don't need deadheading. The demure Breathless™ Blush ('Balbreblus') in the photo above is just getting started. It quickly grows 8 to 12 in. tall and can really hold its own next to other plants in the garden or a container. In fact, feel free to snip it back if it starts to take over.

Drought- and heat-tolerant, with a handsome mounding habit, it's easy to grow and enjoy. Just don't overwater this plant or it'll sulk.

Size 8 to 18 in. tall, 9 to 12 in. wide
Bloom Tiny white flowers from early to late summer
Soil Moist to dry, well-drained
Light Full sun to part shade
Hardiness
Cold: USDA zones 10 to 12
Heat: AHS zones 12 to 1
Source Local garden centers

PLANTS | AUTUMN PERENNIALS

Flowers of Fall

Late-season gardens don't have to focus only on colorful foliage!

Botanical Names

Aster *Aster* spp.
Fountain grass *Pennisetum alopecuroides*
Mum *Chrysanthemum* hybrids
Sedum *Sedum* spp.

It's easy to have flower-filled borders in spring and summer — there are so many choices. In fall the flower options are more limited, but that doesn't mean you have to settle for just mums and asters. Let me share six fall flowers I think every gardener should try. No matter how much light your garden gets, there's something for you: Allium, perennial sunflower, pineapple sage and plumbago light up a sunny border. Monkshood loves part shade, and nodding ladies' tresses will bloom even in full shade.

After you read about these fantastic fall flowers, you'll want to grow them. Instead of just sticking several of them in here and there, group them in your borders. That's how they look best.

After you read the profiles I'll share five design tips that will help your late-season garden shine. You can use these easy-to-follow ideas whether you plant one of the combinations I've put together for you or you prefer to create your own! □

— *Jim Childs*

'Arendsii' monkshood
Aconitum carmichaelii

Deep violet blue may not be the first color you think of for fall. But blue coordinates well with autumn's traditional rusty oranges and browns.

If you plant monkshood in full sun, be sure to keep the soil moist. When it gets too dry, the stems are stunted and the lower leaves drop off. Since it blooms late, there is no need to deadhead — it won't bloom again until next fall.

Monkshood isn't a fast spreader; it can stay in the same spot for years to form colonies. And 'Arendsii' has sturdy stems that rarely need to be staked unless it's growing in a windy spot. Be sure to wash your hands after handling any part of a monkshood, especially the roots — all monkshoods are poisonous. So, if you have small children or pets, you may want to pass over this perennial.

Type Perennial
Blooms Deep violet blue in midautumn
Light Full sun to part shade
Soil Moist, humusy
Size 36 to 48 in. tall, 12 to 18 in. wide
Hardiness
  Cold: USDA zones 3 to 7
  Heat: AHS zones 7 to 1
Source Fieldstone Gardens
www.fieldstonegardens.com
207-923-3836

'Ozawa' allium
Allium thunbergii

Looking more like a spring flower, this dwarf allium is perfect at the edge of a sunny path. However, make sure it doesn't get shaded out by a floppy neighbor. Grow a few clumps in a rock garden, surrounded by other low plants. Or if you're running out of garden space, tuck a few 'Ozawa' plants under a low ground cover, such as sedum. Let the foliage and the flowers poke up through the mat of leaves.

Even though it's a bulb, this allium is usually sold in a container, like a clump of chives, and is planted in spring. Like the rest of the alliums, 'Ozawa' isn't bothered by deer. And there's no need to deadhead — the flower heads simply disappear over winter.

Type Perennial bulb
Blooms Lavender-violet in midautumn
Light Full sun to part shade
Soil Well-drained
Size 8 to 12 in. tall, 6 to 10 in. wide
Hardiness
Cold: USDA zones 4 to 9
Heat: AHS zones 9 to 1
Source Ambergate Gardens
www.ambergategardens.com
877-211-9769

'Low Down' perennial sunflower
Helianthus salicifolius

You have to pinch most perennial sunflowers or stake them to keep them tidy. And they tend to lean into their neighbors for support. 'Low Down' is a dwarf cultivar perfect for the front of a fall border. Combine several plants with short grasses, such as 'Hameln' fountain grass, for a classic fall combo.

'Low Down' is packed with 2-inch-diameter blooms. In cool fall weather, that color can last up to five weeks. To get a good dense habit and lots of flowers, make sure to plant it in full sun. And once the flowers finish, leave the seedheads to feed birds — there's no worry of it reseeding around your garden.

Type Perennial
Blooms Midautumn
Light Full sun
Soil Moist, well-drained
Size 9 to 12 in. tall, 16 to 20 in. wide
Hardiness
Cold: USDA zones 6 to 9
Heat: AHS zones 9 to 1
Source Plant Delights Nursery, Inc.
www.plantdelights.com
919-772-4794

MORE FALL FLOWERS!

Botanical Names

Amsonia
Amsonia tabernaemontana

Blackberry lily
Belamcanda chinensis

Coral bells
Heuchera spp.

Naked ladies
Lycoris squamigera

Spirea
Spiraea spp.

Nodding ladies' tresses
Spiranthes cernua

This North American native loves moisture. Find a spot near a pond, or even just a low spot in the shade, to keep it growing happily.

Plant the bulbous roots in rich soil that has lots of compost worked in. And get them in the ground no later than mid- to late July so they have time to send out roots. While they often bloom the first year, you'll get better blooms in future years. The first winter or two, it's a good idea to cover the bed with a 2- to 4-inch layer of loose straw or oak leaves to protect the roots. Over time, ladies' tresses will spread to form colonies. Help it spread faster by cutting the spent flower stems down to send more energy into the bulb.

Type Perennial bulb
Blooms White spires from late summer into midautumn
Light Part to full shade
Soil Moist to wet
Size 12 to 24 in. tall, 3 to 12 in. wide
Hardiness
 Cold: USDA zones 4 to 8
 Heat: AHS zones 8 to 1
Source Sunlight Gardens
 www.sunlightgardens.com
 800-272-7396

'Golden Delicious' pineapple sage
Salvia elegans

Plant pineapple sage where you'll brush against it, or every now and then crush a leaf to release the pineapple scent. When the deep-throated red flowers open, the hummingbirds are ready and waiting.

If it isn't cold-hardy for you, dig and pot it up before a frost. Use a large pot and general-purpose potting mix. Water it thoroughly, but don't feed it. Let it go dormant in a dark, frost-free basement, keeping it barely moist. Six weeks before your last frost date, move it into bright sun indoors, cut it back by half and start regular watering and feeding. Move your sage outside when it's safe to plant other annuals and tender plants.

Type Tender perennial
Blooms Bright red from late summer through fall
Light Full sun
Soil Moist, well-drained
Size 3 to 4 ft. tall, 2 to 3 ft. wide
Hardiness
 Cold: USDA zones 8 to 10
 Heat: AHS zones 12 to 1
Source Garden Crossings
 www.gardencrossings.com
 616-875-6355

Plumbago
Ceratostigma plumbaginoides
With this perennial, not only do you get clear deep-blue flowers, but as the weather gets colder, the foliage turns shades of red.

Grow plumbago at the edge of a border where it'll be easy to see. Or plant it as a ground cover over late-season bulbs, such as naked ladies. Their flower stalks will poke through the plumbago and bloom about the same time.

If you've had trouble getting plumbago to survive, always plant it in spring — it needs time to establish strong roots. And even if it's hardy in your zone, toss on a 2- to 4-inch layer of straw as the ground freezes. Be sure to remove the mulch in spring.

Type	Perennial
Blooms	Deep-blue flowers in early autumn
Light	Full sun to part shade
Soil	Moist, well-drained
Size	8 to 12 in. tall, 12 to 18 in. wide
Hardiness	Cold: USDA zones 5 to 9 Heat: AHS zones 9 to 1
Source	Bluestone Perennials www.bluestoneperennials.com 800-852-5243

5 TIPS FOR A FABULOUS FALL

Move your fall flower garden from simply colorful to spectacular with these tips. And go to our Web extra to see the detailed plan for each of these designs.

❶ AVOID ONE-HIT WONDERS Choose plants that look good in more than one season. Perhaps it blooms, then develops fall color or seedheads.

❷ LOOK FOR CONTRAST Contrast textures for drama. In "Tall fall," fine-textured amsonia contrasts with large coral bells foliage.

❸ WORK IN LAYERS Let fall plants like tall perennial sunflowers billow out and cover plants that bloomed earlier in the season.

❹ BREAK TRADITION You might be surprised to see those light blues and pinks in "Classy corner" combined with deep rusty reds and bright gold. But it works, doesn't it? And all colors look richer in fall than they do in summer's sun.

❺ GO FOR IMPACT Instead of dropping a fall bloomer here and there, you'll get a bigger impact if you group them together. Both of these designs combine fall foliage and autumn bloomers for more impact.

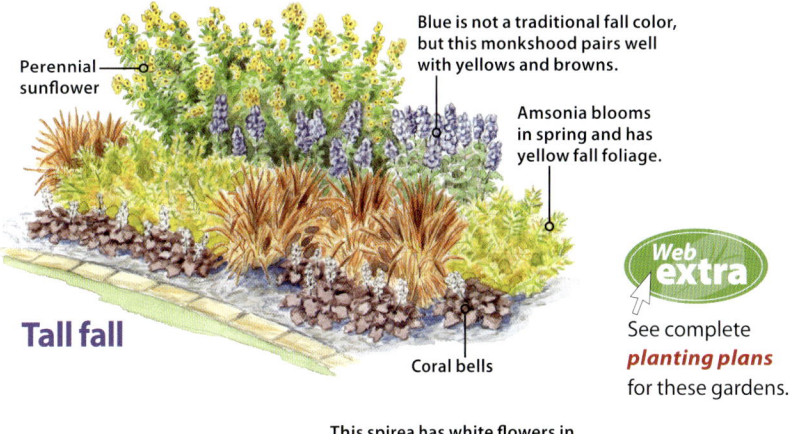

Tall fall
- Perennial sunflower
- Blue is not a traditional fall color, but this monkshood pairs well with yellows and browns.
- Amsonia blooms in spring and has yellow fall foliage.
- Coral bells

Classy corner
- This spirea has white flowers in spring, clean green summer foliage and great red fall color.
- Blackberry lily blooms in summer and produces attractive berries in fall.
- For color earlier in the season, plant spring bulbs under the clumps of plumbago.

Web extra — See complete *planting plans* for these gardens.

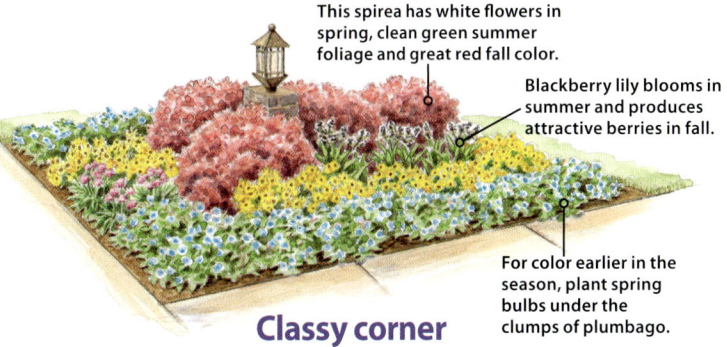

PLANTS | EDITOR'S CHOICE

'Hameln' Fountain Grass

Fountain grass
Pennisetum alopecuroides 'Hameln'

Type	Grass
Blooms	Fuzzy silver white flowers from late summer to fall
Light	Full sun
Soil	Average to well-drained soil
Pests	None serious
Size	24 to 36 in. tall, 24 to 30 in. wide
Hardiness	Cold: USDA zones 5 to 9 Heat: AHS zones 9 to 1

Botanical Names

Aster *Aster* hybrid
Tall sedum *Sedum* hybrids

Colorful flowers may grab the spotlight early in the season. But as summer wanes, ornamental grasses take the stage, especially 'Hameln' fountain grass. It explodes onto the scene with fluffy bottlebrush flowers in summer. Isn't this one from our test garden looking great in the photo at right?

The nice thing about 'Hameln' is its smaller size and earlier bloom time than the species. It's also more well-behaved, only reseeding occasionally. Pull any new 'Hameln' sprouts, though, because the offspring will grow bigger, like the species.

LATE BLOOMER

'Hameln' is a warm-season grass, so it's slow to start in spring. You won't see new growth until the soil has been warm for a week or two. Its green leaves emerge upright, then gradually arch out into a fountainlike display as they lengthen. By late summer, fuzzy 3- to 4-inch-long silver-white flower spikes open and bob in the wind, close to the foliage. They look fantastic backlit by the sun and make great cut flowers for your late-season bouquets.

FALL SHOWOFF

With flowers in tow, 'Hameln' greets fall looking good and it only gets better. As the temperatures cool, its foliage heats up to bronzy orange. Leaves age to beige and hold up for most of winter. But the flowers only last until birds eat the seeds or a hard frost causes them to shatter.

In early spring, before new growth starts, cut back the dead foliage to within 3 or 4 inches of the crown.

Plants need division about every three years or when the center of the plant looks dead. It's simple to do: Just dig the plant from the ground with a spade. Cut off pieces from the outer edge in whatever size you want and discard the dead center. Replant new divisions right away and water.

DIVERSE DESIGN

With its compact size, 'Hameln' is perfect for small gardens or containers. Grow it with other late-blooming perennials, such as tall sedum or asters. In perennial beds be sure to space plants at the recommended spread to show off its arching habit. It's nice having one close enough to a bench so you can touch the soft, fluffy flowers.

Though the days are getting shorter and most plants are winding down for the season, if you have 'Hameln' you'll still have some garden "Wow!" ❑

Path planting Enjoy this late-summer planting along a path that leads to a handsome gate. The rose and Mexican sunflower bloom all season with deadheading. Cut a few fountain grass flowers to add to a colorful bouquet and you can enjoy this garden inside, too!

A **Rose** *Rosa* Carefree Sunshine™ ('Radsun') Shrub; fragrant single yellow flowers; full sun; 3 to 4 ft. tall and wide; cold-hardy in USDA zones 4 to 9, heat-tolerant in AHS zones 9 to 1

B **Mexican sunflower** *Tithonia rotundifolia* 'Fiesta del Sol' Annual; bright orange flowers all summer; full sun; 24 to 36 in. tall, 18 to 24 in. wide; heat-tolerant in AHS zones 12 to 1

C **Fountain grass** *Pennisetum alopecuroides* 'Hameln' See information above left

D **Ground cover sedum** *Sedum spurium* 'Fuldaglut' Perennial; pink flowers in summer; full sun; 3 to 6 in. tall, 12 to 18 in. wide; cold-hardy in USDA zones 4 to 9, heat-tolerant in AHS zones 9 to 1

Mail-order sources

Forestfarm
www.forestfarm.com
541-846-7269. *Catalog free*

Niche Gardens
www.nichegardens.com
919-967-0078. *Catalog free*

PLANTS | SUN PERENNIAL

Gloriosa Daisies

8 ways to flood your garden with color

Rudbeckia hirta

GLORIOSA DAISY
Rudbeckia hirta

Short-lived perennial, can be grown as an annual

Yellow, orange, red, bronze or russet in summer to fall

Full sun

Well-drained soil

Occasionally bothered by powdery mildew

10 to 36 in. tall, 12 to 24 in. wide

Cold-hardiness varies. The hardiest are cold-hardy in USDA zones 3 to 9

Heat-tolerance varies. Most are heat-tolerant in AHS zones 9 to 1

I love (or maybe even need) to have my borders full of lots of beautiful flowers. That's why I grow gloriosa daisy. This sun-garden classic blooms most of the summer (especially if you deadhead the faded flowers regularly). Plus, it attracts birds and clouds of butterflies, but fortunately, not deer. And most will bloom the first year from seed even if you just scatter them in the garden.

There are lots more options in flower colors and habits than there used to be. I've grown many different cultivars, new and old. Let me share eight of my favorites — what I like about them, how big they'll get and how hardy they are. While even the hardy ones tend to live only a few years, I'm willing to deal with that for the long show this plant puts on.

You'll find most of these cultivars at your local garden center. But, just in case, I've included some mail-order sources at right.

1 CHEROKEE SUNSET This award-winning plant blooms in a range of rich colors from yellow and orange to bronze and mahogany. The 3- to 4½-inch flowers can be semi- or fully double and appear the first year from seed. Plants stand about 30 inches tall and hold up better against mildew than other gloriosa daisies in my garden. It's cold-hardy in USDA zones 5 to 8.

2 DOUBLE GOLD Held at the ends of long stems, these 6-inch double blooms work especially well as cut flowers. Cut them just when they're fully open for the longest life. When you sow the seed in the garden, you may see flowers the first year, but these plants will reach their full size the second. The 36-inch-tall plants are cold-hardy in USDA zones 4 to 8.

3 MAYA This dwarf gloriosa daisy produces very double 4- to 5-inch flowers that look a little like gold mums. And on this diminutive plant they really stand out, espe-

32 THE YEAR IN GARDENING   www.GardenGateMagazine.com

cially when planted in a mass at the front of the border. 'Maya' stays a compact 18 inches tall — which also makes it a good container plant choice — and is cold-hardy in USDA zones 3 to 8.

4 CAPPUCCINO Covered with lots of big, 4-inch flowers, 'Cappuccino' is compact and well-branched. Feel free to cut the mahogany and gold flowers that have a coffee-colored tint to the petals — it'll just encourage the plant to set more buds. But be sure to leave a few of the brown cone-shaped seedheads to feed the birds in the winter — they'll appreciate it! 'Cappuccino' is cold-hardy in USDA zones 5 to 8.

5 CHERRY BRANDY You'll get the same number of 3-inch-diameter blooms as with most gloriosa daisies, but with a big difference: mahogany-red flowers. The well-branched plants are drought- and heat-resistant, though they did show some powdery mildew last summer, which was very wet. Leave some seedheads and it will self-seed in your garden (and come true). At 18 to 24 inches tall, it's cold-hardy in USDA zones 5 to 8.

6 DENVER DAISY The eye-catching rust-brown-ringed yellow flowers of 'Denver Daisy' look fantastic in my garden most of the summer. I've noticed it tends to sprout a crazy, odd-shaped petal here and there. But even in a spot that receives just a half day of sun, the 24-inch plant produces bunches of long-lasting 6-inch blooms right up until frost — a bit later in the season than other gloriosa daisies. And this tough plant is cold-hardy in USDA zones 5 to 9.

7 PRAIRIE SUN I love how the petals of 'Prairie Sun's' 4- to 5-inch flowers sport a distinctive orange band around the light green center. By midsummer my plants were so covered in flowers that I cut them for several bouquets and still had plenty left on the plants. The bright, cheery blooms, atop their 36-inch stems, look beautiful in a vase for several days. 'Prairie Sun' is cold-hardy in USDA zones 3 to 8.

8 TIGEREYE GOLD 'TigerEye Gold' has lots of multi-branched stems, packed full of 4- to 6-inch blooms that last for weeks. Because of the tidy, uniform habit, it really shines in mass plantings. Bred to be resistant to powdery mildew, in our test garden, this compact annual had no traces of the fungus on any of the foliage. It's cold-hardy in USDA zones 10 to 12 and reaches 16 to 24 inches tall.

Try a few of these great bloomers in your garden this summer. They'll warm it up for months every year, and you'll enjoy their sunny personalities!

— *Deborah Gruca*

Mail-order sources

Bluestone Perennials
www.bluestoneperennials.com
800-852-5243. *Catalog free*
Plants

Harris Seeds
www.harrisseeds.com
800-544-7938. *Catalog free*
Seeds

Burpee Seeds
www.burpee.com
800-888-1447. *Catalog free*
Seeds

PLANTS | SHADE PERENNIAL

Lenten rose

HELLEBORE
Helleborus spp.

1 to 3 ft. tall,
1 to 3 ft. wide

Flowers of white, pink, yellow, green or burgundy in late winter to early spring

Requires part shade to shade

Prefers well-drained soil, but tolerates dry

Cold hardiness varies by species; the hardiest featured here will survive in USDA zones 5 to 9

Heat-tolerant in AHS zones 9 to 1

Botanical Names

Christmas rose *Helleborus niger*
Corsican hellebore
   Helleborus argutifolius
Crocus *Crocus* spp.
Lenten rose *Helleborus xhybridus*
Snowdrops *Galanthus* spp.
Stinking hellebore
   Helleborus foetidus

Mail-order sources

Big Dipper Farm
www.bigdipperfarm.com
360-886-8133. Online catalog only

Heronswood Nursery
www.heronswood.com
877-674-4714. Catalog free

Pine Knot Farms Perennials
www.pineknotfarms.com
434-252-1990. Online catalog only

These early rising perennials bloom with almost no care!

Hellebores Bring in Spring

Winter in cold-weather areas can be an excruciating time for gardeners. While the garden outside sleeps, we're inside, pacing the floor and waiting for spring. Well, if you have hellebores in your garden, your wait will soon be over. These long-lived perennials emerge and bloom from late winter to early spring — about the same time as crocus and snowdrops.

But unlike spring bulbs, the simple roselike flowers of hellebores last for several months, some right into summer! The blooms come in a variety of colors, from white, pink and burgundy to yellow and chartreuse. Petals may sport solid colors, contrasting edges or patterns like spots or the speckles in photo 1. But even after the flowers finally fade, the leathery foliage stays fresh-looking all year. And if you have mild winters or reliable snow cover, many (especially stinking hellebore) will even be evergreen for you.

A FEW FINE HELLEBORES There are lots of species available, but four of them and their cultivars are the easiest to find and grow: Christmas rose, Lenten rose, Corsican hellebore and stinking hellebore.

Christmas rose — The white Christmas rose at right is the earliest to bloom, though usually not until at least a month after its common name might imply. But, along with the size and shape of its leaves, bloom time can vary so widely among the many cultivars that it's possible to find it blooming in every month somewhere in its range. It stands 12 to 15 inches tall and 18 inches wide with white or cream flowers that sometimes turn pink as they age. Christmas rose is cold-hardy in USDA zones 5 to 9 and heat-tolerant in AHS zones 9 to 1.

Lenten rose — Lenten rose blooms later than Christmas rose, usually starting between January and April. This hellebore hybridizes freely and, as a result, you'll find lots of hybrids, such as red-black 'Mardi Gras Black' and pink and white 'Mardi Gras Picotee Pink' at right. There are also seed strains, such as 'Royal Heritage', which comes in a mix of colors, including white, pink, red, green and occasionally yellow. Lenten rose is easy to grow and after several years, this 18-inch-tall-and-wide plant spreads into large clumps. It's cold-hardy in USDA zones 5 to 8 and heat-tolerant in AHS zones 8 to 1.

Corsican hellebore — Larger than its relatives, Corsican hellebore, at right, reaches 3 feet tall and wide. Its nodding apple-green flowers start opening in late winter. Not as cold-hardy as other hellebores — from USDA zones 6 to 9 — Corsican can nonetheless survive in one zone colder with 2 to 3 inches of a winter mulch of leaves or pine needles or a protective layer of snow. Stinking hellebore, with its unfortunate and undeserved common name, is similar to Corsican except it gets only 32 inches tall and has red-edged blooms. Both are heat-tolerant in AHS zones 9 to 1.

I've provided three good mail-order sources at left where you can find these and other beautiful hellebores. Colorful and long-lasting leaves and flowers are wonderful, but how do you use these plants in the garden? Turn the page and I'll share my favorite ways to design with them.

the YEAR IN GARDENING   www.GardenGateMagazine.com

Lenten rose hybrid

(1) Highlight leathery hellebore leaves with wispy carex foliage.

Christmas rose

'Mardi Gras Black' Lenten rose

'Mardi Gras Picotee Pink' Lenten rose

Corsican hellebore

www.GardenGateMagazine.com *the* YEAR IN GARDENING 35

GROWING GOOD-LOOKING HELLEBORES

Botanical Names

Christmas rose
  Helleborus niger
Corsican hellebore
  Helleborus argutifolius
Lenten rose
  Helleborus orientalis
Maiden grass
  Miscanthus sinensis
Stinking hellebore
  Helleborus foetidus

Hellebores are easy-to-grow perennials that require nearly no care. They have practically bulletproof foliage that's bothered by few pests, except for the rare slug or crown rot. Though the plants prefer moist, well-drained soil, they'll adapt to almost any soil type and established plants are even somewhat drought-tolerant. But with good drainage and consistent moisture, the foliage will look nice until fall and in part shade the leaves are evergreen.

TAKING CARE About the only real care hellebores need is a little cleanup in early spring. It's normal for the plant to look ratty at the end of winter. Wearing gloves to protect against the prickly leaves, simply cut off the dead material with scissors or pruners when you see new growth appear. Even after the flowers open, it's not too late to cut plants back. Just be careful to avoid contact with the irritating sap.

Hellebores are prolific reseeders, which is one way to get more Corsican or stinking hellebores. But the flowers of Christmas rose and Lenten rose seedlings don't often resemble their parents, so it's best to divide these. Early spring is best for Christmas rose, early fall for Lenten rose. I'll show you how I divided my Lenten rose last fall in "Get divisions off to a good start" below.

IN THE GARDEN Because hellebores emerge and bloom so early, they tend to stand out in late winter. Place a few next to an often-used door or path, where you're sure to enjoy the blooms, even when it's too early to get out into the garden.

Hellebores also look right at home situated at the base of winter-interest elements, such as trees and shrubs, fences or stone walls. The subtle blooms of hellebores showcase twisted branches, interesting bark or shrubs with colorful fruit. And later, when the weather warms, the plants will appreciate the shade these structures provide. I have a few Lenten roses planted near some maiden grass that I can see from my kitchen window. The hellebores show nicely against the tawny shades of the grass and even when there's snow on the ground, I can enjoy the flowers from the warmth of my house.

Planted in drifts, hellebores create an elegant tapestry. Try mixing groups of three to five hellebores with burgundy leaves with the same size groups of ones with green leaves. The carpet of color lasts all through the seasons.

My favorite design use for hellebores, though, is in shady woodland settings like the one in photo 2. They look natural mixed in with spring ephemerals and other shade-loving perennials. (I've included the plan and the plant list for this bed at right.)

Bold hellebore foliage provides a nice contrast to small, delicate spring bulbs. Later, it looks right at home surrounded by summer perennials and keeps providing a green backdrop for fall-blooming companions. It's nice that hellebores look good until so late in the season. That means you won't have a long wait before it's time to enjoy them again in the early spring garden. □

— *Deborah Gruca*

GET DIVISIONS OFF TO A GOOD START

PRY IT UP First, tie up the leaves of your hellebore so you can see where to dig. With a garden fork, loosen the soil at least a foot from the crown all around the plant. Carefully pry out the clump so you don't damage the roots.

WASH IT OFF With the clump out of the ground, knock off as much soil as you can with your hands before swishing it around in a tub of water. That way, you can clearly see the tough "plate" below the crowns, the white growing points and the roots.

DIVIDE IT Use a sharp knife to slice through the tough plate and roots, splitting the plant into several pieces, each with at least one growing point. Replant divisions into pre-dug holes right away and water them so they don't dry out.

(2) Hellebores hold their own even when they're surrounded by colorful spring shrubs and perennials.

By summer, the hostas and ferns will take up more space and cover the spring ephemerals' fading foliage.

Scale: 1 square = 1 square ft.

SHADY WOODLAND SETTING

Code	Plant Name	No. to Plant	Blooms	Type	Cold/Heat Zones	Height/Width	Special Features
A	Azalea *Rhododendron* 'Olga Mezitt'	1	Pink; early to midspring	Shrub	4-8/8-1	3-4 ft./3-4 ft.	Glossy evergreen foliage
B	Virginia bluebells *Mertensia virginica*	7	Blue; early spring	Perennial	3-8/8-1	12-18 in./12 in.	Prefers moist soil in part shade; goes dormant in summer; plant around perennials that emerge later to hide gap
C	Spotted geranium *Geranium maculatum*	3	Pink to lilac; spring	Perennial	3-8/8-1	18-24 in./12-18 in.	Naturalizes in moist, humus-rich soil
D	Hosta *Hosta fortunei* 'Albomarginata'	5	Lavender; midsummer	Perennial	3-8/8-1	18 in./36 in.	Deep green leaves edged with cream
E	Christmas rose *Helleborus niger*	1	White; early spring	Perennial	5-9/9-1	12 in./18 in.	Dark, leathery leaves look good all season
F	Lungwort *Pulmonaria saccharata* 'Mrs. Moon'	1	Pink to blue; early spring	Perennial	4-9/9-1	9-18 in./18-24 in.	Narrow leaves with large silver spots
G	Hosta *Hosta* 'Patriot'	1	Lavender; summer	Perennial	3-9/9-1	12-18 in./24-36 in.	Irregular white leaf margins; occasionally bothered by slugs
H	Dutchman's breeches *Dicentra cucullaria*	4	White; early spring	Perennial	3-7/7-1	6-12 in./6-12 in.	Plant goes dormant by midsummer
I	Bloodroot *Sanguinaria canadensis*	1	White; early spring	Perennial	3-9/9-1	6-14 in./6-12 in.	All parts exude red-orange sap; goes dormant in midsummer
J	Lady fern *Athyrium filix-femina*	6	NA	Perennial	4-8/8-1	24-36 in./24-30 in.	Tolerates drier soil than many ferns
K	Coral bells *Heuchera villosa* 'Palace Purple'	1	White; summer	Perennial	2-8/8-1	12-24 in./12-18 in.	Deep purple foliage needs afternoon shade in southern zones; add 2 in. of mulch to prevent winter heaving
L	Lungwort *Pulmonaria* hybrid	1	Pink; early spring	Perennial	3-8/8-1	14 in./18 in.	If flowering declines, divide in early spring or early fall
M	Woodland phlox *Phlox divaricata*	2	Blue; spring	Perennial	3-9/9-1	8-16 in./8-12 in.	Spreads by rooting where stems touch the soil
N	White trillium *Trillium grandiflorum*	1	White; early spring	Perennial	3-9/9-1	12-18 in./12-15 in.	White flowers age to pink; plant goes dormant in summer

PLANTS | SHADE ANNUAL

New Guinea impatiens

New Guinea impatiens

Bedding impatiens

Bedding impatiens

New Guinea impatiens

Dazzler® Pink bedding impatiens

Dazzler® White Improved bedding impatiens

Sonic® Salmon Ice New Guinea impatiens

Infinity® Crimson New Guinea impatiens

(1) Contrasting bright colors, such as chartreuse and pink, make this planting really pop. Because this spot gets several hours of sun each morning, it's possible to combine shade- and sun-lovers.

PHOTOS: Courtesy of Proven Winners (Infinity Crimson); Cameron Sadeghpour (after)

the YEAR IN GARDENING   www.GardenGateMagazine.com

Plant them and stand back... impatiens bloom all summer!

Keep Shade Colorful

Super Elfin® Deep Pink bedding impatiens

Divine™ Orange New Guinea impatiens

Looking for a good investment for your garden? I have one word for you: impatiens! Buy a few plants in spring and you'll have a constant supply of flowers, in almost any color, until first frost. On top of that, impatiens are super easy to grow.

With just one trip to the garden center you can have a vibrant combo like the one at left. It includes the two most common types of impatiens: the bedding types in front and the New Guineas behind them. Both have similar growing needs, but New Guineas have larger flowers and foliage and do best in more sun.

A GREAT START When you're shopping for impatiens, look for compact, healthy plants and make sure the stems aren't broken or mushy. Don't worry if the plants aren't blooming — they will be before long. Although they're not my first choice, leggy bedding impatiens are no problem if that's all I can find. I'll show you how to fix them in "Just a trim" at right.

It's a dilemma when you see impatiens at the greenhouse long before you should plant them. They don't really take off until the soil has warmed and nighttime air temperatures stay above 50 degrees. Plus, planted too early, they rot or get zapped by a late frost. What to do? You can see if the garden center will hold your plants. Or you can set them outside during the day and move them indoors or cover them in a cold frame every night.

Bedding impatiens flower best in part to full shade. Most New Guineas do well with morning sun for about 6 hours, but some cultivars will even take full sun all day long.

I like to put compost on my annual beds in fall to feed the soil. But a balanced slow-release fertilizer in spring will feed yours, too. For container-grown plants, use a potting mix with fertilizer mixed in and a balanced liquid food at quarter strength once a week.

WONDERFUL WATER If there's one maintenance chore you shouldn't skimp on with impatiens, it's watering. Water deeply about once a week to keep plants happy. But don't overwater or they'll rot. Droopy impatiens *may* be too dry, but they might just be too hot. Overheated plants perk up in the evening without water. Plants that get too dry will drop leaves and flowers, even with a soaking.

TROUBLESHOOTING Do your impatiens have mottled-looking leaves that eventually fall off? It could be spider mites. You might notice webbing on the leaves or growing tips, too. A thorough spray with an insecticidal soap usually does the trick.

You've seen how easy it is to grow impatiens. On the next page I'll show you just a few of the many design choices available with this great group of plants.

IMPATIENS
Impatiens hybrids

Flowers in all colors except blue
Part sun to full shade
Moist, well-drained soil
No serious pests
8 to 36 in. tall, 10 to 36 in. wide
Cold-hardy in USDA zones 9 to 11
Heat-tolerant in AHS zones 12 to 1

Before

JUST A TRIM

Can a leggy plant with sparse blooms be rehabilitated? Yes! Just cut it back by a third to a half and give it some time to regrow. In the "before" photo you can see that I'm not even being particularly careful about where I cut. This works for plants that are already in the ground or ones coming out of packs. See how much bushier those same plants are a few weeks later? Another week or so and they'll be flowering better than ever!

After

www.GardenGateMagazine.com

DESIGN WITH IMPATIENS

Before you go shopping for impatiens, take a minute to look over your garden and see where they'll look best. That way you'll be sure which colors and sizes to look for. Let me help you with a few ideas.

BRIGHTEN SHADE Bedding impatiens are the classic shade annual. Drive down any street and you're bound to see a few growing happily under a tree. Planted with other shade-lovers, such as the bleeding heart, ferns and lungwort in photo 2, these Fiesta™ Pink Ruffle impatiens brighten up the darker green foliage around them. Paired with a swath of pale pink annual begonias nearby, they keep this garden from looking gloomy. Impatiens come in so many colors that it's hard to decide which ones to choose. I think pastels look best in the shadiest places under a tree, near a house or next to a privacy fence. The pale colors reflect what little light does get in, creating a dappled effect. Darker reds and oranges show off better in gardens that have morning sun or part shade — it's harder to see them in full shade.

Botanical Names

Bleeding heart
Dicentra formosa
Boston fern
Nephrolepis exaltata
Coleus
Solenostemon hybrid
Coral bells
Heuchera hybrid
English ivy
Hedera helix
Lungwort
Pulmonaria hybrid
Oak *Quercus* spp.

(2) Spots of light color brighten the shade beneath this oak tree and break up the green foliage of perennials that are finished blooming.

GO FOR BIG IMPACT There are some plants that really need to be grown where you can see them up close. Otherwise, you might not get to appreciate their dainty blooms or delicate fragrance. That's not the case with impatiens. I call them "35-miles-per-hour-plants." They have big, bright blooms that just don't quit. And the plants knit together into a ribbon of color so easily that there's no chance you'd miss them, even as you drive by.

Take full advantage of these attributes and do a mass planting. Using a bright color is a great way to attract attention. In photo 3, that little paver path leading to the seating area might go unnoticed without those bright orange flowers. And while the impatiens here are eye-catching, the rust red and chartreuse of the taller 'Henna' coleus behind them makes the impatiens seem even more vibrant.

When impatiens grow together in a mass, it's true that the individual plants can get leggy and aren't that handsome on their own. But since they're packed so closely together, it doesn't really matter. The overall effect is high impact. However, if yours ever get too stretchy and lean, you can simply cut them back to the height you want and they'll branch better and start blooming again in a week or two.

GET SHOPPING Here's a shopping tip to make sure your mass planting looks good: Double check your plant tags to make sure they're all from the same series. The advantage to this is that plants will grow to the same height and form a nice, even clump. You won't have a group of stray plants sticking up above the others or a few growing too short and creating a hole. Another advantage to sticking with one series is that most of the time the colors will look fine together even if they're mixed.

To get the knit-together look of the ones at right, space your plants half the distance of the width range on the tag — usually about 4 to 6 inches apart. Also, when you plant, lay your impatiens out in staggered rows to get the best coverage.

It took three to four weeks for the big grouping of Super Elfin™ Bright Orange in photo 3 to fill in and it looked good for the rest of the season. Believe it or not, this photo was taken in September.

CONTAINER COMBO Not only are impatiens easy to work into garden beds, they're great additions to containers, too. Tuck bedding types into a pot with some shade-loving perennials, such as coral bells or ferns. Impatiens will give you that splash of long-blooming color without a lot of hassle on your

(3) Imagine this scene with dark red impatiens. It would still be pretty, but much more conventional. This salmon-and-rust combo nearly vibrates.

part. Looking for a taste of the tropics in your cold-winter zone? Try New Guineas. With bigger foliage and flowers in a range of intense pinks and oranges, they're perfect for creating that warm, exotic feel for your patio.

There just aren't that many annuals that can give you the bright colors and long-lasting blooms that impatiens can. Even one plant amongst a bunch of foliage can punch things up. For example, the container in photo 4 has a couple of Sunpatiens® Compact Magenta New Guineas in the starring role. Not only do the impatiens add color, but the broader texture from the big impatiens leaves provides good contrast and a place for your eye to rest. I grew this container in part sun but it could easily be moved to a spot with more shade, if needed. One thing to keep in mind with New Guineas, like this one, is that in too much shade, they tend to stretch toward the light. So if you see this happening, try moving the plants into an hour or two more of sun each day.

Now that you've seen a few ways you could work impatiens into your garden, turn the page. There you'll meet some of the more unusual cultivars and see which ones might fit your beds best.

(4) Bring your house plants outside and plant them up with a few impatiens. All three plants enjoy the same part-sun situation, and the colorful New Guinea impatiens add some punch.

CHOOSE YOUR IMPATIENS

Mail-order sources

Annie's Annuals & Perennials
www.anniesannuals.com
888-266-4370
Catalog free
Rare and unusual plants

Park Seed
www.parkseed.com
800-213-0076
Catalog free
A wide variety of seeds and plants

I never used to grow impatiens. I'd walk into garden centers and there would be flat after flat of bright pinks, reds, whites, oranges — shades of every color except blue — and I'd pass them by. You see impatiens at even the smallest garden stand so it's easy to think of them as boring. But try a few six-packs under a tree, and I think you'll see just how amazing these plants really are. You'll have flowers all season long with minimal effort and wonder why you didn't grow them sooner! Impatiens are common, yes, but they are uncommonly great to have in the garden.

If you're still unconvinced that these flower powerhouses are worth the investment, take a look at the amazing variety of colors, shapes and sizes in the gallery below. There's something for every garden style and situation. New on the horizon are bicolors, mostly in stripes, but there are a few cultivars with stars or splatters. Besides that, many plant breeders have been busy expanding the color palette. Now you'll find flowers in yellow, peach and salmon when you go shopping. Let me show you some of the best examples of these, plus some plants with interesting burgundy and variegated foliage, charming miniatures, beautiful doubles and even those that tolerate more sun. But the gallery of impatiens below is just the tip of the iceberg when it comes to what's available in this huge family of plants. Check out "The rare & unusual" at right to see what you might be missing at your local garden center.

Once you've chosen a few of these cultivars to bring home, I think you'll agree that impatiens are the best garden investment you've ever made. □
— *Sherri Ribbey*

Dazzler® Red Star

FANTASTIC FLOWERS Get two colors for the price of one with these flowers with white stripes, stars or splatters.

Accent™ Star series Bedding; orange, red, rose and violet flowers with a white star; 10 to 12 in. tall and wide

Celebrette Purple Stripe New Guinea; purple-and-white-striped flowers; 8 to 10 in. tall, 10 to 12 in. wide

Dazzler® Star series Bedding; red, violet and coral flowers with white center stripe; 9 to 11 in. tall, 13 to 15 in. wide

Fiesta™ Ole Purple Stripe Bedding; double white flowers with irregular purple stripes; 10 to 12 in. tall and wide

Sunpatiens® Variegated Spreading Salmon

FANCY FOLIAGE Add good-looking foliage to flower power for some great-looking impatiens. There's yellow, cream and white to choose from.

Fiesta™ Pink Frost Bedding; double pink flowers, green leaf with a creamy white edge; 10 to 16 in. tall, 10 to 12 in. wide

Painted Paradise™ Lilac New Guinea; single lavender flowers, green leaf with a pale yellow center; 12 to 18 in. tall, 6 to 9 in. wide

Summer Ice series Bedding; double flowers in red, pink and purple, green leaf with a white edge; 6 to 12 in. tall, 6 to 9 in. wide

Sunpatiens® Variegated Spreading New Guinea; salmon or white flowers, green foliage with a yellow center; 24 to 36 in. tall and wide

Firefly™ Pink

MIGHTY MINIS The plants and flowers of minis grow about half as big as other bedding impatiens but they're just as covered with flowers as their bigger cousins.

Butterfly™ series Bedding; single flowers in pink, purple and orange, trailing habit; 8 to 12 in. tall, 12 to 16 in. wide

Firefly™ series Bedding; single flowers in pink, purple, red, orange, salmon and white, can take more sun than other bedding types; 8 to 12 in. tall and wide

Mini-Hawaiian series Bedding; purple or white blooms; 4 in. tall, 4 to 6 in. wide

PHOTO: Brent Isenberger (Sunpatiens Variegated Spreading Salmon)

THE RARE & UNUSUAL

If you're an adventurous gardener, you might want to try growing some of the more exotic members of this huge family of plants. Some have larger flowers or are just larger plants. There's even one that's true blue! Here are four easy-to-grow cousins of your garden center favorites that are well worth a spot in your garden.

A **Policeman's helmet** *Impatiens glandulifera* 'Wine Red' Annual; large deep rose flowers; reseeds easily — the species is considered a weed in some states; part shade; 36 to 48 in. tall, 18 to 24 in. wide; heat-tolerant in AHS zones 12 to 1

B *Impatiens arguta* Tender perennial; blue flowers in cool weather, purple in hot; grows well in dry soil; part sun to full shade; 2 ft. tall, 3 to 4 ft. wide; cold-hardy in USDA zones 6 to 10, heat-tolerant in AHS zones 12 to 1

C **Poor man's rhododendron** *Impatiens sodenii* 'Flash' Tender perennial; big 3-in. flowers, well-branched; part sun; 4 to 5 ft. tall, 3 ft. wide; cold-hardy in USDA zones 10 to 11, heat-tolerant in AHS zones 12 to 1

D **Sapphire jewelweed** *Impatiens namchabarwensis* 'Blue Diamond' Tender perennial; true blue flowers; reseeds; part sun to full shade; 1 to 3 ft. tall and wide; cold-hardy in USDA zones 10 to 11, heat-tolerant in AHS zones 12 to 1

PHOTOS: Courtesy of Annie's Annuals & Perennials

Tioga™ Light Pink Improved

DOUBLE DUTY How about a miniature rose look-alike? Double impatiens have you covered in a wide variety of colors.

Fanciful™ series Bedding; semidouble flowers in orange, pink and white; 10 to 12 in. tall, 12 to 16 in. wide

Fiesta™ series Bedding; double flowers in pink, orange, purple, red and white; 10 to 16 in. tall, 10 to 12 in. wide

Rockapulco™ series Bedding; double flowers in pink, orange, red and white; 10 to 20 in. tall, 10 to 12 in. wide

Tioga™ series Bedding; semidouble flowers in pink, red, purple, orange and white; 24 in. tall and wide

'Jungle Gold'

COLOR EXPLOSION Expand your color palette for the garden with these exciting colors and markings. And more new shades are sure to come.

Envoy series Bedding; peach, pink and violet flowers; 12 to 14 in. tall, 9 to 12 in. wide

'Jungle Gold' Bedding hybrid; yellow flowers, takes drier conditions than other impatiens; 15 to 18 in. tall, 12 to 14 in. wide

Mosaic™ series Bedding; purple, orange, pink and red flowers speckled with white; 12 to 14 in. tall and wide

Stardust series Bedding; white center star with a dusting of pink or purple along the petal edge; 8 to 10 in. tall, 10 to 12 in. wide

Sunpatiens® Vigorous Red

SUN-LOVERS Don't have any shade in your yard? No problem. Try these cultivars that will do just fine in 6 to 8 hours of sun.

Fanfare® series Bedding; white, pink, purple and orange flowers, spreading habit; 16 to 20 in. tall, 18 to 24 in. wide

Sunny Lady series Bedding; white, pink, orange, purple and red flowers; needs afternoon shade in Southern gardens; 8 to 10 in. tall and wide

Sunpatiens® Vigorous series New Guinea; pink, purple, orange and white flowers; 24 to 36 in. tall and wide

Tango New Guinea; tangerine orange flowers; 12 to 18 in. tall, 6 to 9 in. wide

PLANTS | SUN PERENNIAL

An Iris for Everyone

Tough situation? No worries! There's an iris that will thrive in your yard.

If you love irises but just never thought you had the right spot for them, you're in for a treat. I want to show you five not-so-well-known irises that'll shine in all sorts of conditions. Need one that'll work into your flower border without forcing you to wage a battle with iris borers and rot? Got it. And if you have a spot that's always been too shady for bearded irises, I have one for that, too. Plus, meet irises that'll bloom super early and with flowers of that hard-to-find iris color, red. Among these irises, you'll find a wide range of colors and sizes from 3 inches to 5 feet tall — truly something for every gardener.

See how well the blue-flowering 'Caesar's Brother' Siberian irises contrast with the mound-forming peonies around them? You'll find that upright habit and strappy foliage in all the irises you'll meet here. So combine them with other plants for plenty of contrast in plant habit and texture. And when you mix them into a border, don't worry about them getting squeezed out by their companions. They're all vigorous growers that can hold their own in a crowd.

Speaking of vigorous growth, once in a while you'll have to divide these irises. The first four irises I'll show you have rhizomes — just dig up the clump, discard the dead centers and split the new growth into chunks before replanting. Easy! (And we'll share tips for dividing reticulated iris, which is a true bulb, as well.)

So whether you're looking for a substitute for bearded irises or you just want to spice up your spring flower lineup, you'll find something here for your garden, no matter what the conditions. ☐

— *Amanda M.W. Glazebrook*

Size	24 to 48 in. tall, 18 to 24 in. wide
Bloom	Late spring to early summer
Color	Blue, purple, burgundy, white, yellow or pink
Soil	Moist and well-drained to wet
Light	Full sun to part shade
Hardiness	Cold: USDA zones 3 to 9 Heat: AHS zones 9 to 1
Source	Schreiner's Iris Gardens www.schreinersgardens.com 800-525-2367

The iris for any situation
Siberian iris *Iris sibirica*

If you can plant only one iris, this is it! Siberians take full sun or part shade, moist soil or well-drained soil, and they're more resistant to iris borers than other iris species.

The photos at right show you just some of the variety in flower color and petal markings. Check out the pale blue of 'Steve Varner', bicolor 'Butter and Sugar' and the noticeable yellow "signal" (the marking on the falls, or lower petals) of 'White Swirl'. Siberian irises look great mixed into a perennial border or along the edge of a pond. You'll know it's time to divide when there's a dead area in the center of the clump. Divide in spring as soon as they finish blooming, or in late summer.

PHOTO: © Joan de Grey ('Butter and Sugar'); © Donna and Tom Krischan ('White Swirl')

44   *the* YEAR IN GARDENING   www.GardenGateMagazine.com

'Steve Varner'

'Butter and Sugar'

'White Swirl'

'Caesar's Brother'

MORE UNUSUAL IRISES

The elusive red
Louisiana iris *Iris* **hybrids**

Burgundy and maroon are the closest shades an iris gets to red, right? Wrong! 'Cherry Cup' and 'Red Dazzler', here, are as red as an iris can get. (With Louisianas, you'll find plenty of other colors, too!)

Louisiana irises thrive in the heat of the South, but can stand the cold to zone 4. In zone 7 and warmer, the foliage is evergreen. These irises can adapt to almost any soil type, as long as they have lots of moisture. They're especially happy in boggy soil, but you can grow them in ordinary garden soil as long as you water frequently. Plant rhizomes ½ in. below the soil's surface, and cover them with 1 to 2 in. of mulch to keep the soil moist. Space rhizomes 2 ft. apart (they spread quickly), and expect to divide them every two or three years in late summer.

'Cherry Cup'

Size	2 to 4 ft. tall, 2 to 3 ft. wide
Bloom	Midspring
Color	Red, burgundy, pink, cream, white, orange, yellow, blue, purple
Soil	Moist, acid
Light	Full to part sun
Hardiness	Cold: USDA zones 4 to 10 Heat: AHS zones 10 to 1
Source	Louisiana Iris Farms www.louisianairis.com 337-277-9930

'Red Dazzler'

PHOTO: © Joseph G. Strauch, Jr. ('Red Dazzler')

The shade lover
Roof iris *Iris tectorum*

Do you have a shade garden, but long to grow irises? Then roof iris (which has sometimes been grown on thatched roofs of homes) is for you! It does best in full sun to part shade.

Roof iris needs loose, well-drained soil, like the humusy soil of a woodland garden. It spreads rapidly — plant divisions 2 ft. apart and you'll have a lush cover in just 2 years. Make sure rhizomes aren't planted too deeply, only about ½ in. below the soil's surface. Divide roof iris in late spring, after it blooms, or in early fall, so new divisions have time to get established. Too much fertilizer leads to lush foliage and few flowers, so topdress your irises with compost in fall, and don't feed the rest of the year.

Size	12 to 18 in. tall and wide
Bloom	Early to midspring
Color	Lavender or white
Soil	Well-drained
Light	Full sun to part shade
Hardiness	Cold: USDA zones 4 to 9 Heat: AHS zones 9 to 1
Source	Nicholls Gardens www.nichollsgardens.com 703-754-9623

The water lover
Yellow flag iris *Iris pseudacorus*

Yellow flag irises are beautiful near — or even in — a garden water feature. These tall plants thrive in wet soil, and the upright foliage is as attractive as the yellow- or cream-colored blooms.

Yellow flag likes full sun to part shade. It'll self-seed in ideal conditions, and can spread rapidly. (In some areas, it can even be invasive, so remove seed pods, pull volunteer plants and don't plant them along the edge of a naturally occurring pond or stream.) You can also plant this iris in flower borders or even containers if you water it regularly. Your plant will stay smaller and flower less than its underwater counterparts, but it won't get out of control so easily. Divide yellow flag iris in fall.

Size 3 to 5 ft. tall, 2 to 3 ft. wide
Bloom Midspring
Color Yellow or cream
Soil Moist to wet
Light Full sun to part shade
Hardiness
  Cold: USDA zones 5 to 9
  Heat: AHS zones 9 to 1
Source Iris City Gardens
  www.iriscitygardens.com
  800-934-4747

The early bloomer
Reticulated iris *Iris reticulata*

Most irises are mid- to late spring bloomers. But reticulated iris is an exception. This fragrant miniature iris, reaching just 3 to 6 in. tall, pops up in very early spring, at about the same time as snowdrops and crocuses. Straplike foliage appears as the blooms are finishing and can stretch up to 16 in. tall.

Unlike other irises, which grow from rhizomes, reticulated irises are true bulbs. They like well-drained soil that stays dry in the summer. (Too much summer moisture can cause them to rot.) In fall, plant bulbs deeper than you'd think for the size of the bulb — at least 3 to 4 in. deep. This will keep them from multiplying so quickly that their flowering lessens from year to year.

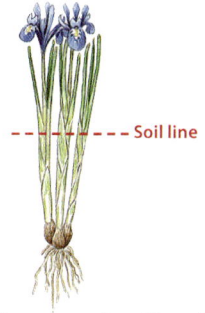

Size Flowers are 3 to 6 in. tall, foliage up to 16 in. tall, 3 in. wide
Bloom Early spring
Color Blue, purple or white
Soil Well-drained
Light Full sun to part shade
Hardiness
  Cold: USDA zones 5 to 9
  Heat: AHS zones 9 to 1
Source John Scheepers, Inc.
  www.johnscheepers.com
  860-567-0838

PLANTS | EDITOR'S CHOICE

'Red Rocks' Penstemon

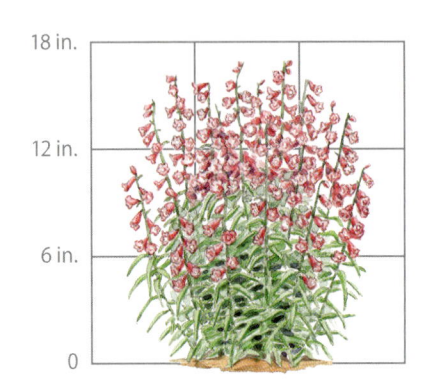

Penstemon 'Red Rocks'

Type	Short-lived perennial
Bloom	Rose-pink flowers late spring to summer
Soil	Lean, sharply drained
Light	Full sun
Pests	None serious
Size	12 to 18 in. tall, 12 to 15 in. wide
Hardiness	Cold: USDA zones 5 to 8 Heat: AHS zones 8 to 1

Have a hot, dry spot in your garden? Don't despair. These are exactly the conditions in which 'Red Rocks' penstemon thrives.

As long-lasting as they are beautiful, the flowers on this drought-tolerant perennial make an instant impact. And the blooms attract hummingbirds and other winged visitors like a rose-pink magnet (but fortunately, they're not appealing to deer).

EASY DOES IT
Penstemons have a reputation for being tricky to grow. That can be true, but only if you don't give them the heat and sharp drainage they need.

Don't bother planting 'Red Rocks' in soil with clay in it — that spells certain death for the plant. And soil with lots of compost mixed into it will result in floppy stems. So work some gravel or coarse sand into the planting hole. The soil should stay loose and crumbly when you squeeze a handful of it into a ball. Or place the plant so the top of the root ball is just above the surface of the soil. If you want to mulch, use a ½- to 1-inch layer of crushed gravel or chicken grit to prevent crown rot. It contrasts nicely with the dark foliage, too. Don't overfertilize 'Red Rocks' — too much nitrogen (like lots of compost) will make the stems floppy. A single fall feeding of an organic, low-nitrogen food, such as Neptune's Harvest, is fine.

Though it's perfect massed in dry, sunny spots like rock gardens, in general, this penstemon can also tolerate more moist, humid conditions than other penstemons can. So go ahead and combine it with other perennials in mixed borders or try a few in container plantings.

'Red Rocks' does appreciate a little moisture as the new plants get growing. Once established, water the plant deeply, but infrequently, so it'll grow deep roots.

To get a rebloom (albeit much smaller than the first one), deadhead by cutting the flower stems off at the base. Penstemons usually live just two or three years; doing this may help the plant live longer by directing more energy into the roots. But, at any rate, deadheading tidies the plants.

Follow these simple steps and both you and the hummingbirds will be enjoying these fascinating flowers! □

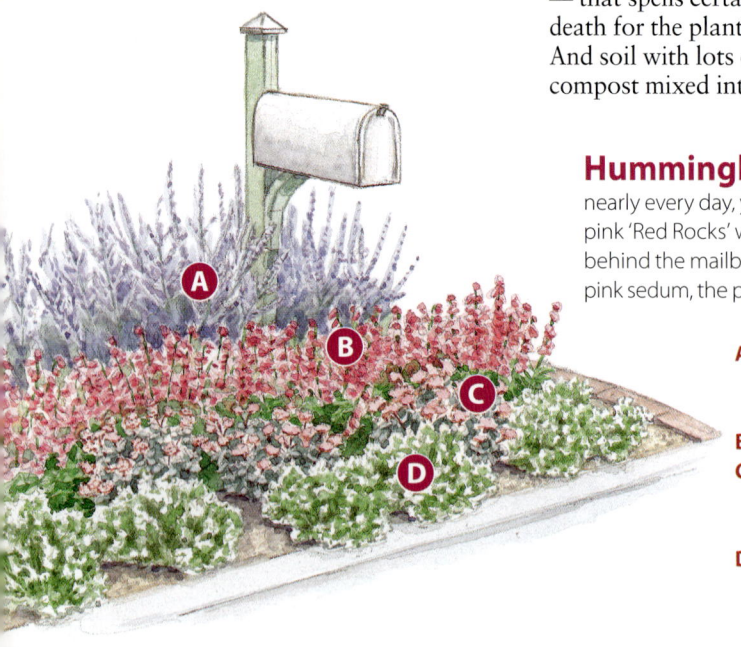

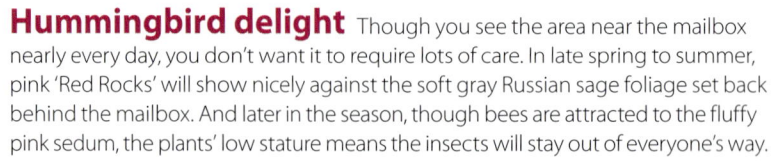

Hummingbird delight Though you see the area near the mailbox nearly every day, you don't want it to require lots of care. In late spring to summer, pink 'Red Rocks' will show nicely against the soft gray Russian sage foliage set back behind the mailbox. And later in the season, though bees are attracted to the fluffy pink sedum, the plants' low stature means the insects will stay out of everyone's way.

A **Russian sage** *Perovskia* 'Blue Spire' Perennial; lavender-blue flowers in late summer to fall; full sun; 3 to 4 ft. tall, 2 to 3 ft. wide; cold-hardy in USDA zones 5 to 9, heat-tolerant in AHS zones 9 to 1

B **Penstemon** *Penstemon* 'Red Rocks' See information above left

C **Sedum** *Sedum* 'Vera Jameson' Perennial; pink late-summer flowers on burgundy foliage; full sun; 8 to 12 in. tall, 15 to 18 in. wide; cold-hardy in USDA zones 4 to 9, heat-tolerant in AHS zones 9 to 1

D **Creeping baby's breath** *Gypsophila repens* Perennial; tiny white flowers in early summer; full sun; 4 to 6 in. tall, 12 to 18 in. wide; cold-hardy in USDA zones 3 to 9, heat-tolerant in AHS zones 9 to 1

Mail-order sources

High Country Gardens
www.highcountrygardens.com
800-925-9387. *Catalog free*

Bluestone Perennials
www.bluestoneperennials.com
800-852-5243. *Catalog free*

PLANTS | SPRING PERENNIAL

Peonies: Better Than Ever!

Fill your spring with blooms.

Those luscious pink, white or deep red peonies that Grandma grew were a welcome sight in spring and had a wonderful fragrance. The only problem was that they didn't last long, and quite often the heavy flowers ended up on the ground following a spring rain. Well, things have changed over the years. You won't have to pick the new ones up out of the mud: Stronger stems and compact habits keep them standing up. And you can also add yellow, peach and salmon peonies to your border — colors Grandma never would have expected in her peonies.

There are a lot of peony species, but most of what's grown in gardens comes from the three groups you see in the illustrations below: Traditional, rock garden and intersectionals. All of these types of peonies die down to the ground in the fall.

You have seen *traditional peonies* growing in gardens for years. They're cold-hardy, drought-resistant, low-maintenance and long-lived. Their luscious flowers send gardeners for their checkbooks.

Rock garden peonies have a tidy mounded habit, and their foliage is often more deeply lobed than other types. Because of their small size, they work well in rock gardens or any tight garden space. But don't let the name stop you: These versatile plants require the same care as other peonies and are happy in perennial borders, too.

The latest and greatest generation of peonies are *intersectionals*. They have sturdy stems, nicely shaped foliage and more flower color options than the traditional types; and they're nearly as hardy.

NEW COLORS Yellow, peach and coral have joined the ranks of colors that you will find in peony catalogs these days. And intersectional peonies are a big part of that color revolution. 'Hillary', at right, starts out with rosy pink buds that change to the peach-pink shown here. As the flower ages, the outer petals fade to cream while the center stays dark. Yellow used to be a color that just couldn't be found. Then 'Bartzella' burst onto the scene about 20 years ago. There have been other yellow peonies introduced since then, but this is still one of the best yellows. Not all the new colors come from intersectional introductions, though. Check out the coral-pink blooms of traditional 'Coral Charm'. Other traditional peonies in out-of-the-ordinary colors include 'Coral Sunset', red-and-white-striped 'Circus, Circus' and deep red 'Chocolate Soldier'.

SHAPELY FLOWERS A variety of different flower shapes is a must for any good-looking garden. Fortunately, peonies have several to choose from. You'll still find many of the traditional-looking doubles along with bomb flower types. Bombs have a single row of lower petals topped off by a big fluffy pompon center. There

'Coral Charm'

TRADITIONAL PEONY
Paeonia hybrid

1½ to 3 ft. tall and wide
Flowers in shades of pink, white, red and yellow
Cold-hardy in
　USDA zones 3 to 8
Heat-tolerant in
　AHS zones 8 to 1

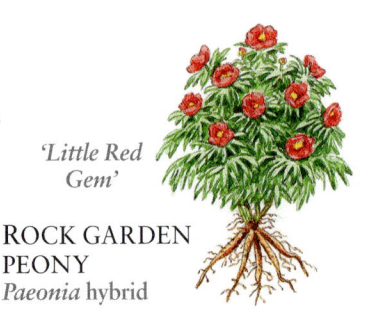

'Little Red Gem'

ROCK GARDEN PEONY
Paeonia hybrid

15 to 24 in. tall and wide
Red, pink or white flowers and finely cut foliage
Cold-hardy in
　USDA zones 3 to 8
Heat-tolerant in
　AHS zones 8 to 1

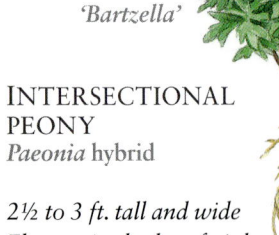

'Bartzella'

INTERSECTIONAL PEONY
Paeonia hybrid

2½ to 3 ft. tall and wide
Flowers in shades of pink, white, red and yellow
Cold-hardy in
　USDA zones 4 to 8
Heat-tolerant in
　AHS zones 8 to 1

Color

'Hillary' intersectional

'Bartzella' intersectional

'Coral Charm' traditional

Shape

'Garden Peace' traditional

'Pink Dogwood Whisper' traditional

'Green Lotus' traditional

Foliage

'Golden Frolic' traditional

'Little Red Gem' rock garden

---

are a lot more single, semi-double and anemone shapes now, too. Anemone shapes, also called Japanese, have a single row of petals and a smaller fuzzy center. Even single flower forms can look quite different these days. Compare the cup-shaped waxy white flowers of 'Garden Peace' to the open and serrated petals of 'Pink Dogwood Whisper'. There are even some cultivars, like spidery 'Green Lotus', that seem to defy classification.

FOLIAGE COUNTS Those beautiful flowers are definitely the best reason to grow peonies. But let's face it: You have to live with that plant the rest of the season, and you want it to look good, too. Most peony foliage is plain old green — some deeper and some lighter in hue. To add punch to your spring border, try traditional 'Golden Frolic'. It has gold foliage in spring that matures to chartreuse by summer. You can rely on most intersectionals to have attractive deeply cut blue-green leaves. These plants have a stately, almost elegant look in the landscape, even without flowers. For some out-of-the-ordinary-looking foliage, check out 'Little Red Gem'. Many rock garden peonies have very deeply cut leaves, but this one looks almost lacy.

The peonies in these photos are just the tip of the iceberg when it comes to what's available. I've included some mail-order sources at right to get you going. But before you start your spending spree, turn the page for ideas on how to work these beauties into your garden. You'll also find a few tips on how to keep them looking their best.

Mail-order sources

Adelman Peony Gardens
www.peonyparadise.com
503-393-6185. *Catalog free*

Klehm's Song Sparrow Farm and Nursery
www.songsparrownursery.com
800-553-3715. *Catalog free*

Swenson Gardens
www.swensongardens.com
763-350-2051. *Online catalog only*

PHOTOS: Courtesy of Swenson Gardens ('Hillary' and 'Coral Charm'); courtesy of Klehm's Song Sparrow Farm and Nursery ('Garden Peace', 'Pink Dogwood Whisper', 'Green Lotus', 'Golden Frolic' and 'Little Red Gem')

GROW **GREAT PEONIES**

Botanical Names

Coneflower
Echinacea purpurea
Daffodil
Narcissus hybrid
Phlox
Phlox paniculata
Salvia
Salvia hybrid
Sedum
Sedum cauticola
Siberian iris
Iris sibirica
Tulip
Tulipa hybrid

Show off your peonies

Such beautiful flowers are meant to be enjoyed. So make sure to place your peonies where you can see them every day when they're in bloom. That's what I did in the back entry planting below. "Peony welcome" includes several cultivars so you can prolong the flower show, along with some other plants that will take over once the peonies are done. For the complete planting plan, check out our Web extra.

Intersectionals' attractive blue-green leaves make a great backdrop for later-blooming perennials, such as the coneflowers and salvia below. Small rock garden peonies work well at the front of the border. And their foliage is attractive the rest of the season, too. If there's one thing peonies don't like, it's competition from larger plants. So as you look for places to plant, keep peonies 3 to 4 feet away from the base of trees and shrubs.

Keep them happy

It would be hard to find an easier plant to grow than peonies. Some plants have been known to live for 50 years or more with little care. Even so, if you're going to invest in special plants like these, you want to get the best performance they can give. After all, some cultivars come with a hefty price tag. Here are some tips for growing good-looking plants:

SHOP SMARTER In spring you may see potted peonies in garden centers. But the selection is usually pretty limited. Mail-order nurseries have enough cultivars to make your head spin, and most of them come bare-root in the fall. Before you order, ask how many eyes the plants have (eyes are the pink buds sprouting on the roots). Three to five eyes is the optimum size for a peony to adapt to new situations. Plants may flower the first spring but those blooms are usually small. They'll become full sized in about three years.

COVER THE BASICS Peonies do best with full sun and well-drained soil. Planting depth is key. Where winter temperatures dip below zero, the base of the eyes should be about 2 inches deep; in warmer areas, a little higher. In fact, in zones 7 and warmer, you might want to plant them just ½ inch below the soil. This lets roots stay cooler in winter and starts them blooming sooner in spring before the weather gets hot.

Though peonies are cold-hardy, you can help your new plants along with 3 to 4 inches of organic mulch in late fall. In spring, pull the material away for the new growth. You shouldn't have to mulch again.

You don't need to fertilize peonies much. A low-nitrogen formula, such as 10-15-10, every other year in spring, or an annual application of compost is sufficient.

PEONY WELCOME

How would you like beautiful peony blooms framing your entry for weeks? Use cultivars that flower at different times so you can enjoy them all spring. Additional plants keep the garden looking good for the rest of the season. In each illustration here, there's a peony in peak bloom along with its companions. For other peony colors and flower shapes that bloom at the same time, check out the list below each illustration.

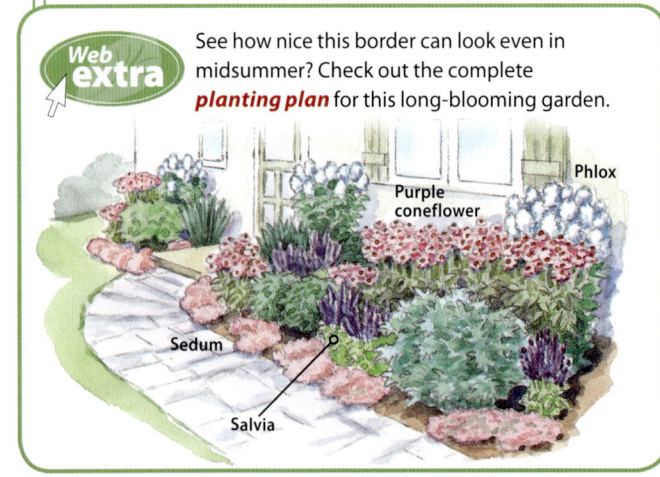

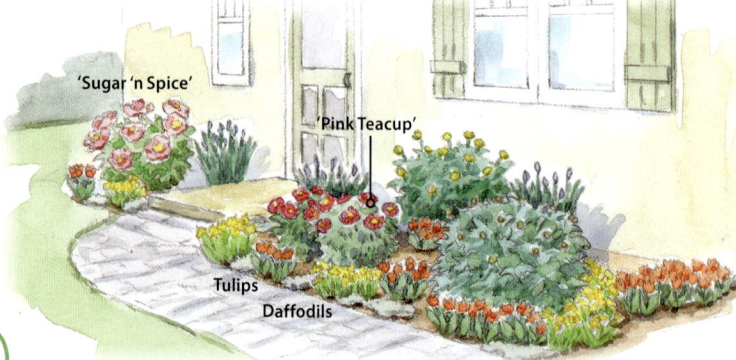

Web extra See how nice this border can look even in midsummer? Check out the complete *planting plan* for this long-blooming garden.

Early spring peonies
These cultivars are some of the first to open in spring. Look for them when the first tulips and daffodils are blooming.

'Sugar 'n Spice' (above) Single salmon-orange flowers; traditional; 24 to 36 in. tall and wide

'Pink Teacup' (above) Single deep-pink flowers with yellow centers; finely cut foliage; rock garden; 18 to 20 in. tall and wide

'Red Charm' Fragrant deep-red bomb; traditional; 24 to 36 in. tall and wide

'Goldilocks' Soft yellow bomb with occasional red edging to the petals; traditional; 24 to 36 in. tall and wide

'Tinkerbell' Single fragrant rose pink with yellow center; rock garden; 18 in. tall and wide

Peonies are pest- and disease-resistant but, like most plants, they occasionally need help. Check out "Four problems and how to fix them" at right for solutions.

SOUTHERN TIPS FOR PEONIES Gardeners in USDA zones 7 and warmer have always struggled to grow these beauties because the roots need a cold period in winter and the flowers don't do well in heat and humidity. I've already told you how shallow planting can help with this. Here are three more tips: First, choose early blooming cultivars so the flowers open before the heat really gets going. Second, choose single or anemone flower forms because they have fewer fungal problems. Third, give your plants some afternoon shade to keep them cool.

These new peonies are classics in the making. Grandma would most definitely approve. □

— *Sherri Ribbey*

FOUR PROBLEMS AND HOW TO FIX THEM

❶ No buds
- ☐ Is it recently planted, moved or divided? Give it a year or two.
- ☐ It could be planted too deeply. Make sure the tips of the growth buds are no more than 2 in. below the soil's surface. If a plant has been there for years, make sure accumulated mulch or debris isn't the problem.
- ☐ There may not be enough sun. Peonies need at least six hours each day.
- ☐ A late frost may have zapped the buds. Better luck next year.
- ☐ Peonies hate being overcrowded. Minimize root competition from larger plants — keep them 3 to 4 ft. from the base of trees and shrubs.
- ☐ Too much nitrogen encourages foliage but not flowers. Stop feeding them and don't put down lawn fertilizer nearby it could wash into the bed.

❷ Black buds
- ☐ Did you get a late frost? Wait for next year or, if this happens every year, replace cultivars you have with later-blooming ones.

❸ Buds open partially but petals turn brown and fall off
- ☐ Thrips could be eating them. Treat plants with an insecticide according to package directions.

❹ Big ugly spots on leaves, stems or flowers
- ☐ Botrytis blight or leaf blotch sometimes take hold. Remove infected parts as they develop and get rid of all the dead stems and foliage in fall. If plants become infected every year, spray a fungicide in early spring according to package directions.

Midspring peonies
As the tulips finish up and the Siberian iris get going, you'll see the midspring cultivars take off.

'Bartzella' (above) Semi-double yellow flowers with a light fragrance; intersectional; 36 in. tall, 24 to 36 in. wide

'Do Tell' Shell-pink anemone flowers; traditional; 30 to 36 in. tall and wide

'Cora Louise' Semi-double white with purple center; intersectional; 24 in. tall and wide

'Eskimo Pie' Double white flowers; traditional; 20 in. tall and wide

'Julia Rose' Single to semi-double cherry red flowers that fade to yellow; intersectional; 28 to 34 in. tall and wide

'Raspberry Charm' Semi-double raspberry red with a yellow center; traditional; 24 to 36 in. tall and wide

Late spring peonies
With annuals just beginning to bloom and summer perennials getting started, you'll see these late cultivars in flower.

'Ursa Minor' (above) Fragrant raspberry pink bomb; traditional; 30 in. tall and wide

'Denise' Double white with a pink blush and red marks on the center petals; light fragrance; traditional; 30 in. tall and wide

'Nippon Beauty' Deep-red anemone flowers with a light fragrance; traditional; 24 to 36 in. tall and wide

'Garden Treasure' Fragrant semi-double yellow flowers; intersectional; 30 in. tall and wide

'Elsa Sass' Double white fragrant flowers; traditional; 28 in. tall and wide

PLANTS | SPRING PERENNIAL

Yes, you *can* grow these charming spring perennials! Our 3 top picks.

Easy Primroses

Botanical Names

Crocus *Muscari armeniacum*
Daffodil *Narcissus* spp.
Hyacinth *Hyacinthus* spp.
Primrose *Primula* spp.
Squill *Scilla siberica*
Tulip *Tulipa* spp.

Everybody has tulips, crocus or daffodils blooming in spring, maybe even hyacinth or squill. Not everyone grows primroses — but they should! Primroses are super cold-hardy and pest- and disease-resistant. And they have colorful, charming flowers for up to three weeks! With a range of bloom times, you can have flowers from the time temperatures warm in spring until summer flowers are ready to pop.

If you've had disappointing results with primroses in the past, don't give up. Some are tricky to grow. But I'll show you three of the most easy-going types and how to grow them at righ. Then I'll give you a plan in "Pretty primroses" below.

GROWING TIPS Where summers get hot and humid, plant your primroses under deciduous trees. There they'll get the sun they need to flower in spring. And when the trees leaf out in summer, they'll be protected from the worst of the heat. Use a couple inches of organic mulch to help keep soil moisture even — letting it dry out is hard on the plants. Even so, don't be surprised if your plants disappear in the heat of summer. It's not unusual for primroses to go dormant and return again in spring. Winter snow cover is often unreliable so provide some protection. Use straw or evergreen boughs rather than leaves, which can mat down and smother plants.

Give primroses a shady, moist place to grow and you'll find they even spread. One small plant can turn into a dozen in a few years. So you see, primroses aren't that hard to grow. You just need the right type and a few helpful hints. □

—*Sherri Ribbey*

PRETTY PRIMROSES

Get your garden going early with this plan. Any of the primroses I'm showing you at right will work in this situation.

These plants are near a concrete sidewalk, which radiates heat, so keep an eye on the soil. Depending on the weather, it may dry out quickly, and you'll need to water often. A 2- to 3-in. layer of mulch will help conserve moisture.

When the primroses are done blooming, the foliage stretches and looks a little gangly — kind of like bulb foliage. But fortunately, the other plants in this plan can help. Broad hosta leaves and variegated heart-shaped brunnera foliage will draw attention and cover the fading primroses.

That's not the end of this garden bed. Late summer highlights ligularia and astilbe flowers so your season goes out with a bang.

Plain green yew foliage is a great backdrop for colorful flowers and variegated foliage.

Grow primroses near plants that will grow large enough to cover the fading foliage in summer. These 12 primroses will hide beneath hostas and brunnera.

THE GARDEN'S PALETTE

Code	Plant Name	No. to Plant	Type	Blooms	Height/Width	Cold/Heat Zones
A	Ostrich fern *Matteuccia struthiopteris*	3	Perennial	NA	36-60 in./18-24 in.	3-7/7-1
B	Ligularia *Ligularia* 'Britt Marie Crawford'	1	Perennial	Yellow	3-4 ft./2-3 ft.	3-9/9-1
C	Astilbe *Astilbe* 'August Light' ('Augustleuchten')	11	Perennial	Red	24-28 in./15-24 in.	4-9/9-1
D	Hosta *Hosta* 'Halcyon'	4	Perennial	Lilac	18-24 in./30-36 in.	3-9/9-1
E	Brunnera *Brunnera macrophylla* 'Looking Glass'	2	Perennial	Blue	12-18 in./12-18 in.	4-9/9-1
F	Old-fashioned bleeding heart *Lamprocapnos spectabilis*	1	Perennial	Pink and white	24-36 in./18-30 in.	3-8/8-1

Himalayan primrose
Primula denticulata

Color arrives early in your garden with Himalayan, or drumstick, primrose. Ball-shaped flowers of purple, white or red open when the azaleas and peonies bloom, and they last up to three weeks! Cut a few to bring inside — they make a great addition to spring bouquets. But let some go to seed and in a few years you'll have a nice little patch.

Flowers open near the ground and often show up even before the foliage does. As the stems grow up, the leaves stretch out, too. So much so, that they can often reach up to 12 in. long by the end of the season.

Blooms Purple, white or red
Light Part shade
Soil Moist, humus-rich, well-drained
Size 12 to 18 in. tall, 15 to 18 in. wide
Hardiness
  Cold: USDA zones 3 to 8
  Heat: AHS zones 8 to 1
Source Fritz Creek Gardens
  www.alaskahardy.com
  907-235-4969

Asiatic primrose
Primula sieboldii

Would you believe that some of the prettiest primrose flowers are the easiest plants to grow? It's true. Asiatic primrose flowers are quite variable and there are dozens of cultivars from which to choose. Lacy pink and white 'Pink Snowflakes', above, has all you could want in a primrose flower. Petal backs are a darker pink than the front, and the edges are as frilly as they get.

This primrose typically goes dormant in the summer, so don't worry if it disappears after it's done blooming. It'll show up again the following spring. Just be sure to keep watering the area where it's growing.

Blooms Pink, red, lilac or white
Light Part shade
Soil Well-drained
Size 8 to 16 in. tall, 15 to 18 in. wide
Hardiness
  Cold: USDA zones 3 to 8
  Heat: AHS zones 8 to 1
Source Lazy S's Farm Nursery
  www.lazyssfarm.com
  (online catalog only)

Cowslip
Primula veris

Are your summers hot and humid? Then grow cowslip. This once-common British wildflower has adapted well to North American gardens. It's more tolerant of a range of growing conditions than other species, though it does still need consistent moisture. So if your soil isn't quite perfect or the snow cover isn't reliable in winter, this primrose is for you.

Nodding yellow flowers are fragrant and appear early to midspring. Plant some near a seating area where you can appreciate the scent. With a low-growing habit, cowslip is nice along a path with other shade perennials.

Blooms Yellow
Light Part shade
Soil Moist, well-drained
Size 6 to 12 in. tall, 12 to 16 in. wide
Hardiness
  Cold: USDA zones 3 to 8
  Heat: AHS zones 8 to 1
Source Evermay Nursery
  www.evermaynursery.com
  207-827-0522

PLANTS | SHRUB

The Easiest Roses You'll Ever Grow!

They're beautiful *and* low-maintenance.

Knock Out

SHRUB ROSES
Rosa hybrids

2 to 5 ft. tall and wide

Flowers in all colors except blue

Full sun

Black spot and Japanese beetles are occasional problems

Cold-hardiness varies; of the varieties featured here, Flower Carpet Amber is cold-hardy in USDA zones 4 to 9; the others, 5 to 9.

Heat-tolerant in AHS zones 9 to 1

Mail-order sources

You'll find most of these plants at your local garden center. If you can't find Sunny Knock Out, White Out or Carefree Celebration try:

Edmunds' Roses
www.edmundsroses.com
888-481-7673 *Catalog free*

Regan Nursery
www.regannursery.com
800-249-4680
Online catalog only

How would you like roses that are so easy to grow they're practically care-free? Give shrub roses a try. The plants in this growing group have fewer pest problems and survive winters better than some other groups of roses, such as hybrid teas. Plus, they're real flower machines — once they start blooming in late spring, they usually keep coming in waves through fall. And that's why everyone likes them so much! Speaking of popularity, you've probably seen or even grown the well-known shrub rose Knock Out®. It's the first in the popular series of roses with the same name. In fact, a lot of newer roses are part of a series like this, with a shared name and some common characteristics. Let's take a look at a few of my favorite shrub roses.

1 OSO EASY™ PAPRIKA ('ChewMayTime') Looking for a series of roses for your small garden space? Try the Oso Easy line. My favorite is Paprika. I moved this tough little rose one hot summer day and it didn't miss a beat. It just needed a little extra watering after the move but it never even stopped blooming. Paprika grows 1 to 2 feet tall and wide.

2 SUNNY KNOCK OUT® ('Radsunny') New to the Knock Out line, Sunny has a light fragrance and semi-double yellow flowers that fade to cream. This one's just as vigorous as the others in this line but with more of an upright habit. Growing 3 to 5 feet tall and 3 to 4 feet wide, this new introduction will bloom all season just like its predecessors.

3 CRIMSON MEIDILAND® ('Meizerbil') With clusters of bright red flowers and a low, arching habit this rose is a beauty along the retaining wall in our test garden. And when temperatures start to cool in fall, the leaves turn deep burgundy. Crimson Meidiland is 2 feet tall and 4 feet wide.

4 EASY ELEGANCE® MACY'S PRIDE ('Baicream') Easy Elegance roses are named for their ease of care. And Macy's Pride is one of the prettiest. It has pointed buds like a hybrid tea and they start out lemon yellow and open to creamy white with a hint of pink. Plants grow 2 to 3 feet tall and wide.

5 CAREFREE CELEBRATION™ ('Radral') The name says it all with this series of roses. It has excellent disease resistance. The flowers have a light fragrance and the peach-orange color gets more intense in hot, humid climates. Carefree Celebration grows 4 feet tall and wide.

6 WHITE OUT™ ('Radwhite') It's hard to find a cold-hardy, disease-resistant white rose. But White Out does the trick. Though not quite as blackspot-resistant as the others here, this white shrub rose won't be overwhelmed by it. White Out grows 3 to 4 feet tall and wide.

7 FLOWER CARPET® AMBER ('NOA-97400A') Flower Carpet roses have been around for a while, but the breeders have come up with some pretty new colors. The newest, Amber, is the *Garden Gate* staff's favorite color. It grows 2 to 3 feet tall and 3 feet wide and is the most cold-hardy of this bunch, tolerating USDA zones 4 to 9.

Not only are shrub roses easier to grow, they're easier to design with, too. Turn the page for some ideas.

PHOTO: Brent Isenberger (1)

56   the YEAR IN GARDENING   www.GardenGateMagazine.com

www.GardenGateMagazine.com *the* YEAR IN GARDENING 57

SHOW OFF
YOUR SHRUB ROSES!

It used to be that everyone grew roses in a special garden with plenty of space around them to prevent disease. Not anymore! You can work disease-resistant shrub roses into any border with ease.

COLORFUL HEDGES Massed together along the back of a border, the Knock Out roses in photo 1 make a hedge with eye-popping color from spring to fall. Have you ever noticed that some types of roses, especially hybrid teas, can look bare and leggy by the end of the season? Shrub roses don't have this problem. But one way to ensure your plants have plenty of branches is with Epsom salts. In spring, lightly scratch ½ cup into the soil around each plant. This encourages more branches to sprout from the base for a fuller, flower-filled shrub.

Once those colorful flowers fade, you can deadhead, but it isn't required. The rose will put out new growth anyway. Snipping spent flowers will encourage a faster rebloom, though. Wait for the whole spray or cluster of blooms to fade, then snip it off.

It's nice to know that planting depth isn't a big deal with these roses. Since shrub roses aren't grafted, you don't have to worry about planting it several inches below the soil to protect a graft union from freezing temperatures. Shrub roses are better at surviving cold than other roses, and that comes in handy with a hedge — nobody wants to lose a plant right in the middle.

(2) Shrub roses add season-long color to whatever mix of plants suits your area. Yellow Graham Thomas fits right in with these shrubs, perennials *and* succulents.

SUNNY MIX Shrub roses aren't limited to flowery perennial borders or cottage gardens, either. Take a look at the yellow Graham Thomas® in photo 2 above. You don't normally think of roses growing happily along with succulents in a garden bed. But all roses flower best in full sun — at least 6 hours a day — so even though it's an unusual combination, these plants are a natural fit. In hot-summer areas, such as USDA zones 8 to 9, flowers will last longer and hold their color better if you give them some late afternoon shade.

(1) Create a colorful hedge that provides privacy or screens a view with taller varieties, such as the 3- to 4-ft. Knock Outs here.

(3) A buffer plant between the rose and sidewalk, such as this catmint, ensures thorny rose canes can't reach out and grab you as you walk by.

No matter where you live, roses need some extra water to get them through dry summers. One deep soaking a week, instead of several shallow ones, encourages roots to grow deeper. A 2- to 3-inch layer of organic mulch also helps retain moisture, keeps roots at an even temperature and deters weeds.

FANTASTIC FRONT ENTRY Since most shrub roses flower from spring to fall, they make high-impact entry plantings. Pale pink Flower Carpet Appleblossom and bright Pink Supreme in photo 3 sure made me slow down for a closer look. Those big swathes of color move your eye along the sidewalk to the front door. The other nice thing about growing shrub roses in a front yard is there's no need for any complicated (or potentially unsightly) winter protection. Just mound a few inches of soil or mulch over the crown after a hard freeze in fall. Then in spring, carefully pull the cover away so the new growth can take off.

Shrub roses do have thorns, so don't plant them right next to a walkway or seating area as they may snag people or clothing. If a branch is in the way, go ahead and cut it off; the rose won't mind a bit. Speaking of cutting, pruning shrub roses is a cinch. In spring, when you're cleaning the perennial bed, just take off any rose canes that didn't survive winter.

Even though shrub roses are tough, occasionally they have problems. Blackspot and Japanese beetles sometimes show up, so check out "Pest problems?" at right to see how to deal with them.

So let go of that reluctance to grow roses and try a few worry-free shrub roses! □

— *Sherri Ribbey*

PEST PROBLEMS?

Shrub roses are pest- and disease-resistant, but they're not immune. Here are solutions for two common problems, whether they're just a minor nuisance or are making your plants look really bad.

Blackspot

Blackspot spores hang out in the soil and are spread by splashing from rainwater or overhead watering. Black spots show up on foliage that eventually turns yellow and falls off. It usually won't kill the roses, but it weakens them, and they sure look ugly.

DON'T WORRY If just a few leaves have spots, cut them off. Then clean up any infected ones from the ground and send them all away in the trash (if your local waste authority allows) or bury them.

HOW TO PREVENT Had problems in the past? Avoid overhead watering. Then prevent blackspot by mixing 1 tsp. of baking soda and ½ tsp. of dish soap, such as Ivory®, with 1 quart of water. Put it in a spray bottle and coat leaves once a week starting in early summer or when it starts getting hot. Spray on cloudy days or in the evening to avoid burning foliage.

LAST RESORT When blackspot gets out of hand and covers most of the foliage, spray the leaves thoroughly with a fungicide.

Japanese beetles

They're gregarious little beetles, so if you see one, keep looking because there are probably more.

DON'T WORRY If just a few beetles are devouring plants, hand pick them and drop them in a bucket of soapy water or squish them.

HOW TO PREVENT Beetles keep showing up? Go after the grubs. Try milky spore, the soil-dwelling bacteria *Bacillus popilliae*. You can water it into your lawn to kill grubs in areas where winter temperatures stay above zero. Research continues on *Steinernema glaseri*, a nematode that hunts grubs and survives in colder climates.

LAST RESORT For an infestation that covers your plants, spray the insecticides Merit™ (containing imidacloprid) or Cyper WP (containing cypermethin) on plants in early summer.

PLANTS | EDITOR'S CHOICE

Brilliance Lemon Strawflower

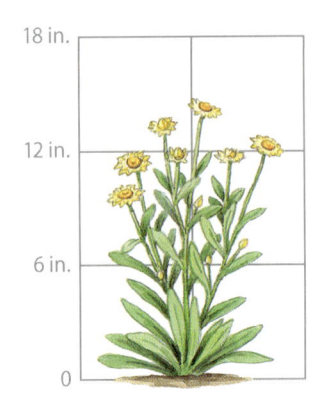

Xerochrysum bracteata
Brilliance Lemon
(Formerly known as *Brachteantha* and *Helichrysum*)

Size	8 to 14 in. tall, 8 to 10 in. wide
Type	Perennial
Bloom	Bright yellow flowers from summer through fall
Soil	Tolerates drought but blooms best in moist, well-drained soil
Light	Full sun
Pests	Occasional powdery mildew
Hardiness	Cold: USDA zones 9 to 12 Heat: AHS zones 12 to 1

Strawflowers provide nonstop color all summer, and Brilliance™ Lemon is no exception. And if that's not enough, this tender perennial is popular with butterflies, too. It's even deer resistant. About the only thing missing is fragrance.

The flowers open in full sun, but close at night and when it rains. This defense mechanism keeps the papery flowers dry so they don't rot.

FIND THE BEST SPOT
Pick up Brilliance Lemon strawflowers at your local garden center and tuck them into your flower beds. Their colorful, long-lasting flowers make them great in containers, like this 10-by-16-inch ceramic one. You'll find a plant list for this summer combo below.

These daisy-shaped flowers contrast nicely with spikes of salvia or lavender. And pairing strawflowers with angelonia, calibrachoa or other long-blooming annuals will give you lots of summer color. Grasses and succulents, such as sedum, make good companions too, because they like the same growing conditions. But don't plant strawflowers next to a fountain. The splashing water might keep the flowers closed.

CARE AND FEEDING
Strawflowers are quite drought-tolerant. But you'll find there will be more, and larger, flowers if you keep the soil moist and the plant well-fed. Use a water-soluble, balanced fertilizer, such as a 30-30-30, every couple of weeks when you water.

Try to water in the morning and keep the leaves dry. Wet foliage, especially late in the day, leads to powdery mildew. While it's not fatal, it does weaken the plant so you won't get as many flowers. And if this annual stays healthy, the flowers keep coming until the temperature drops to 30 degrees.

Be sure to pick a few flowers for fresh bouquets. They'll last up to two weeks in a vase. Or pick them when there are just two to four rows of petals open, like the ones in the lower part of this photo. Fasten a few stems together and hang them to dry for several weeks. Arrange them in bouquets and you can enjoy this easy-to-grow annual even on drab winter days. ☐

Sunny morning This combo would be great on a sunny patio or retaining wall. Or, instead of a heavy glazed container, plant everything in a windowbox. Position it outside your kitchen and let the morning sun shine through it as you enjoy your first cup of coffee.

A **Strawflower** *Xerochrysum bracteata* **Brilliance Lemon** See information above left

B **Leatherleaf sedge** *Carex* **'Red Rooster'** Perennial; feathery red-brown foliage; full sun to part shade; 16 to 24 in. tall, 18 to 24 in. wide; cold-hardy in USDA zones 7 to 9, heat-tolerant in AHS zones 9 to 1

C **Calibrachoa** *Calibrachoa* **Minifamous™ Double Yellow** Tender perennial; small double yellow flowers; full sun to part shade; 4 in. tall, 12 to 20 in. wide; cold-hardy in USDA zones 9 to 11, heat-tolerant in AHS zones 12 to 1

D **Lysimachia** *Lysimachia congestiflora* **Walkabout Sunset®** Perennial; variegated foliage and golden orange flowers; full sun to part shade; 8 to 12 in. tall, 10 to 15 in. wide; cold-hardy in USDA zones 7 to 9, heat-tolerant in AHS zones 12 to 1

Pick the flowers at this stage, hang them upside down to dry and they'll open the rest of the way.

did you know...

The great divide
Chris Strasser, Texas

Q *I've had a Boston fern (Nephrolepis exaltata) in the same pot for years. What's the best way to divide it?*
A When your fern starts to look like the one in photo 1, it's time to divide.

Lift the fern out of the pot and lay it on its side. Then use a small pruning saw to cut through the tough roots. Cut the fern into two or more sections, depending on how many new plants you want. Just make sure each division has some leaves and roots like the ones in photo 2.

In photo 3 one of the divisions has been set in a pot that's at least 2 inches larger in diameter than the root mass. Don't bother teasing the roots apart — they've been through enough. New growth will sprout from the edges, so set the crown an inch or two higher than the potting mix. Next, trim off any brown or broken fronds and set the container in a saucer of water. Let the soil absorb as much water as it can hold before you move the fern to a shaded spot.

Keep the soil very moist until you see new top growth. Then resume normal watering and fertilizing.

Keep them in the dark
David Holland, New York

Q *Do street lights affect my plants?*
A A small amount of light at night probably won't bother most of your plants much. But too much light will disrupt the darkness needed for the plants to regenerate *phytochrome*. This pigment lets a plant know when it's time for a seed to germinate, when to set flower buds and when to drop its leaves.

Ever wonder why chrysanthemums only bloom in fall? The ratio of daylight to darkness triggers production of phytochrome to tell the plant it's time to bloom.

Elms, sycamores and zelkovas are common street trees affected by extra night light. Instead of sending the nutrients they've built up over summer down to the roots for winter storage, those nutrients stay in the foliage. That's OK until the green leaves are killed by frost and drop off. Most of the food the tree has made will have been wasted. While this probably won't kill the plant, it can severely retard its growth, or make it susceptible to disease or pests.

It's time for a fresh start
Joe Becks, Virginia

Q *I've kept a parsley plant in my kitchen window all winter. Can I move it outside when the weather warms up?*
A You can, but your overwintered plant will probably bolt, which means it will flower and set seed. Parsley's a biennial — it makes vegetative growth the first year. The second year it puts most of its energy into blooms, then sets seeds and dies.

Start a new crop each spring by pouring

1 You know it's time to divide your fern when you see lots of brown stems at the base.

2 A small pruning saw makes it easy to cut through the tough roots of a Boston fern.

3 After the division is repotted, trim off any damaged fronds and water the pot thoroughly.

There's a hungry worm hiding inside this tightly rolled canna leaf.

in the news

Monarch troubles
Are you noticing fewer monarch butterflies (*Danaus plexippus*) in your garden this year? Record rainfall in January and February caused major landslides and flooding in Mexico where these butterflies overwinter, and the results have been devastating. Initial reports show that about 50 percent of the monarch population there died. In some areas the mortality rate was as high as 70 percent.

Great sunflower project
Here's a program that's right up every gardener's alley. The Great Sunflower Project is looking for people willing to grow the annual sunflower 'Lemon Queen' (*Helianthus* hybrid). Once the sunflowers are blooming, time how long it takes for five bees total of either type — honey or bumble — to stop by for a visit. The data will be used by scientists to monitor bee populations in different areas of the country. By sticking with one variety of sunflower, everyone's comparing the same information. You can find more information about the project and sign up online at www.greatsunflower.org. There are also tips for collecting data, identifying bees and other information. If you can't find this sunflower locally, visit Baker Creek Heirloom Seeds at www.rareseeds.com or call 417-924-8917.

Indoor plant update
Researchers at the University of Georgia and Konkuk University and the National Horticultural Research Institute in South Korea now have an expanded and refined list of indoor plants that filter volatile organic compounds (VOCs). Here are the five best:
- Purple waffle plant (*Hemigraphis alternata*)
- English ivy (*Hedera helix*)
- Variegated wax plant (*Hoya carnosa*)
- Asparagus fern (*Asparagus densiflorus*)
- Purple heart (*Tradescantia pallida*)

110-degree water over fresh seeds. Soak them overnight, drain the water and press the seeds into a container of potting mix. Cover it loosely with plastic and set the pot in a warm, dark spot. Keep the mix moist and when you see new growth starting, in about four weeks, move the seedlings into light.

Canna rollers
Susan A. Whittaker, Georgia

Q *The leaves on my cannas are rolled and stuck together. What's going on?*

A Your plants are infested with canna leaf rollers. There are two different types, but the symptoms and treatments are the same.

The adult insects lay eggs on new leaves. In the caterpillar stage they "stitch" the edges of young canna leaves together with a silken thread so they won't unfurl. That provides the perfect hiding place as the caterpillar eats the leaf it's rolled in.

If you just have a few damaged leaves, pull the edges apart and squish the worm inside. Or if lots of leaves are already badly chewed up, snip them off and step on them. Then, in case there are any eggs on the leaves, don't toss them on the compost pile. Send them away in the trash or bury them at least 3 feet deep in the soil. B_t (*Bacillus thuringiensis*) mixed with water and sprinkled over the leaves is a good control if you find too many worms to deal with manually.

---

product pick

What's Wrong With My Plant? (And How Do I Fix It?)

Do you have a shrub with wilting leaves or a perennial that isn't blooming? Check out this book by David Deardorff and Kathryn Wadsworth for the answer. Organized into three sections, the first is a flow chart that tackles diagnosing what ails your plant. Section two is filled with organic solutions for your garden problems. And the third and final section has a photo gallery of common problems to further help determine what's troubling your plant.

Bottom line It's a handy reference book for figuring out how to help your plants stay healthy.
Source Local and online bookstores and www.GardenGateStore.com
Price $24.95; softcover; 456 pages

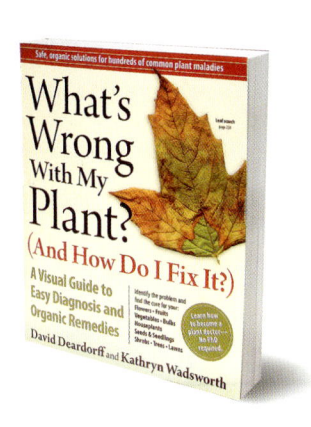

did you know... (CONTINUED)

A section of heavy-duty PVC pipe will keep mint from taking over your garden.

Keep mint contained
Stephanie Batson, Pennsylvania

Mint is a great herb to have around. But give this hardy perennial an inch, and it will take a mile. Fortunately, Stephanie found a way to grow mint for her culinary endeavors *and* keep it from taking over her garden. First, she cut a 12-inch piece from a 12-inch-diameter PVC pipe. Then she dug a hole and placed the pipe in the ground. There's about 4 inches of the PVC above the soil in the photo above, and that's enough to keep the mint in bounds. With the pipe in the ground she refilled the hole, planted the mint and watered it in. Now her mint stays put.

Standing tall
Carol Gill, Ohio

As the gardening season starts to wind down Carol likes to harvest and dry flowers for long-lasting bouquets. Hydrangea, love-lies-bleeding and cockscomb celosia are some of her favorites. But sometimes a stem breaks off or is just too short for the vase. Instead of pitching it, she attaches a chopstick to the flower stem. By extending the stem, the flowers are tall enough to be placed in the arrangement and have plenty of support.

Use transparent tape to attach the chopstick to the flower stem.

Roll the chicken wire under to form a handle.

Pull glads with ease
Lance Nilson, Wyoming

Lance invented an easy way to get his favorite gladiolus corms out of the ground in fall before they're zapped by cold temperatures. In spring, after he digs a planting trench for his glads, he cuts a piece of chicken wire big enough to line it like the illustration above shows, leaving 5 or 6 inches above the soil on each side. Lance then places the glads on the wire and fills the hole with soil. Then he rolls up the ends of the wire that are still above ground, creating handles. In fall, when the glads' foliage has died back, Lance cuts off the brown leaves, tugs on the rolled handles and a "tray" full of glad corms emerges. After shaking off the extra soil, Lance stores the glads and the chicken wire until it's warm enough to plant again next spring.

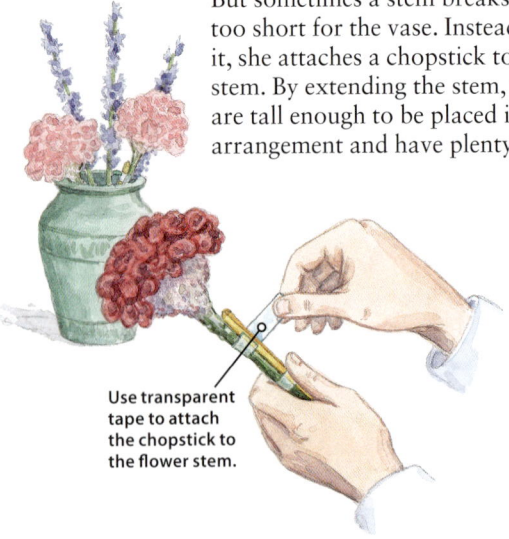

For the birds
Lucille Prehoda, Virginia

Q *What perennials can I plant that have seeds that will help feed the birds in my garden?*

A There are many perennials that provide seeds. Here are six easy-to-grow bird favorites:

Anise hyssop *Agastache foeniculum* Purple flowers from mid-summer to early fall, seeds in winter; full sun to part shade; 24 to 36 in. tall, 18 to 24 in. wide; cold-hardy in USDA zones 5 to 9, heat-tolerant in AHS zones 9 to 1

Aster *Aster xfrikartii* Purple flowers in summer to early fall, seeds in late summer to fall; full sun to part shade; 18 to 36 in. tall, 18 to 24 in. wide; cold-hardy in USDA zones 5 to 8, heat-tolerant in AHS zones 8 to 1

Brown-eyed Susan *Rudbeckia triloba* Yellow flowers with brown centers summer to fall, seeds in summer to fall; full sun to part shade; 24 to 36 in. tall, 12 to 18 in. wide; cold-hardy in USDA zones 4 to 8, heat-tolerant in AHS zones 8 to 1

California poppy *Eschscholzia californica* Yellow-orange flowers in late spring to early fall, seeds in summer to fall; full sun; 12 to 18 in. tall, 6 in. wide; cold-hardy in USDA zones 6 to 11, heat-tolerant in AHS zones 12 to 1

Purple coneflower *Echinacea purpurea* Purple-pink flowers in summer, seeds in winter; full sun to part shade; 2 to 3 ft. tall, 2 ft. wide; cold-hardy in USDA zones 3 to 9, heat-tolerant in AHS zones 9 to 1

Hot hostas
Dee Troxell, Arizona

Q *Are there any hostas that I can grow in the Southwest, USDA zone 8?*

A Yes, there are a few. August lily (*Hosta plantaginea*), shown in the photo at right, is one of the most heat-tolerant types. And there are several cultivars listed below that have this hosta in their ancestry, so they're worth a try, too. You can tell cultivars that have been bred from this species because they usually have fragrant flowers.

However, even these hostas may not perform as well, or grow as large, as they do in colder regions. It's not the summer heat that causes the problem, it's the lack of a cold dormancy. Unlike tropical plants, such as palms or philodendrons, hostas need a winter chill. Without it, the plants lose their vigor and slowly decline.

Some folks in regions with mild winters find that growing hostas in containers is more successful than growing them in the ground. The thought is that the roots get colder in winter if you keep them above ground in a pot. That helps plants die back earlier so they get a better rest. You'll want to keep the soil moist, but growing hostas in pots also allows you to move them into a shaded area. Odds are the temperature around the roots will stay colder longer there.

in the news

Flowers that last longer!
Researchers with the Agricultural Research Service (ARS) and the University of California-Davis have found a way to make plants last longer. By spraying low concentrations of thidiazuron (TDZ) on flowering plants, they've been able to make both flowers and foliage last much longer. TDZ is a synthetic version of the natural compound cytokinin, a plant hormone that's safe for use around humans and the environment. Though research is still going on, you may see a spray sometime in the future that helps your plants stay in bloom longer!

Which coneflower is best?
With so many coneflower (*Echinacea* spp.) introductions in the past few years, it's hard to know which one to buy. Plant evaluation results from the Mt. Cuba Research Center in Delaware can help. This three-year project looked at five species and 43 cultivars of coneflower. Under normal sunny garden conditions with occasional watering and mulch, the top two performers were 'Pica Bella' and 'Elton Knight'. Others with high scores include 'Fatal Attraction', 'Tiki Torch' and 'Sunrise'. Visit www.mtcubacenter.org/research/plant_evaluations.html for complete results and a second evaluation on asters. Future studies on coral bells, tickseed, phlox and other plants are in the works, so stay tuned!

Geranium confusion?
If you've ever thought that Rozanne (*Geranium* 'Gerwat') and 'Jolly Bee' hardy geranium looked the same, you were right. Recent genetic testing found that there's virtually no difference between these two cultivars. So the name 'Jolly Bee' was discontinued in 2010. From now on, you'll see Rozanne when you go shopping.

WARM-WINTER HOSTAS
- 'Aphrodite'
- 'Fragrant Bouquet'
- 'Invincible'
- 'Royal Standard'
- 'So Sweet'

August lily

did you know... (CONTINUED)

A tightly sheared boxwood may be so dense that it has only bare twigs in the center.

Plucking out one twig at a time is a good way to open up the middle of the shrub.

Easy plucking
Wendy Carlyle, Missouri

Q For years I've sheared boxwood, but I want a more natural look. Any tips?

A Plucking, or snapping small branches out of a shrub with your fingers, is a technique that's been used on boxwoods for centuries. It controls the size and opens up the structure so more air and light get into the shrub. Your boxwood will have healthier leaves and twigs, and it'll still have a tidy habit.

In the top left photo you can see how dense the growth is. A boxwood in full sun, like this one, will need more plucking because it will be denser than one growing in shade. And a boxwood that has been sheared for several years may only have bare twigs in the center.

Reach into the shrub and grasp a single twig as you see in the second photo. Using your fingers and thumb, snap it off. Keep moving over the plant, plucking off small pieces. Take out enough so at least some sunlight can reach deep into the plant.

To figure out what size branches you can pluck, use the height of the shrub as a guide. If your boxwoods are around a foot tall, only pluck out twigs 2 to 4 inches long. Shrubs 1 to 2 feet tall can have up to 6-inch-long stems taken out. The shrub in these photos is more than 2 feet tall, so the pluckings can be up to 8 inches long.

Plucking will be an ongoing process. Take out a few branches whenever you have time. Or if you notice a part of the boxwood has grown too large or too dense, just snap off a few twigs.

You can pluck any time of year, but late winter or early spring is best. That way if you remove too much or are unhappy with the look, new growth will quickly fill in to even out the shrub's appearance.

It may take a couple of years of plucking to bring an overgrown boxwood down to the size you want. But after that you'll be able to maintain a natural form without drastic pruning or shearing.

Butterfly bush-whacking
JoAnne Hawrysz, Iowa

Q I left my butterfly bushes standing over winter. What do I need to do this year?

A Simply cut your butterfly bush (*Buddleja davidii*) back hard in spring.

Though it's a shrub (some cultivars can get 10 ft. tall), treat it like a perennial and cut it down to 2 to 3 inches above the ground.

Butterfly bush is cold-hardy in USDA zones 5 to 9, but in winter it usually dies to the ground in zone 5. However, you should cut the plant back hard even if you garden in warmer zones. It encourages a neater, more compact habit and bigger flowers.

Then be patient — butterfly bush doesn't emerge until very late in spring or early summer. Once it starts growing, the plant quickly reaches full size and blooms on the new growth in late summer.

On the up and up
Tony Webster, Pennsylvania

Q Can I train a young weeping Norway spruce into a tree form?

A Without your help, this tree would be a ground cover — the young stems can't grow upright on their own. However, with a little staking, you can train this evergreen into an upstanding citizen of your garden.

When you buy one at the garden center, odds are the main stem, or leader, is tied to a stake. As this stem grows, it'll become rigid and able to stand on its own. But, once the leader reaches the top of the stake, it'll bend over and weep from that point. So if you want a taller tree, you'll need a taller stake.

In the illustration below you'll notice a 12-inch-long piece of PVC pipe sunk into the ground next to the trunk. It's a bit larger in diameter than the stake the trunk is tied to. This way, you'll be able to insert a new stake as the trunk grows taller without damaging the tree's roots. And be sure to change the fabric ties each year so they don't strangle the stem as it grows thicker. Once the spruce is as tall as you'd like it, leave the stake in place until the trunk is rigid and can stand on its own. Then remove the stake, pull the pipe out of the ground and let the branches weep.

Use soft ties, such as old stockings, so they don't cut into the trunk.

A 12-in. sleeve of PVC pipe holds the tall stake.

Redbud seeds that fall to the ground may remain dormant for years.

Seed to tree
May Schulz, South Dakota

Q Can you propagate redbuds from the seeds in the seedpods?

A Yes, with a little effort. After the early spring flowers of redbuds (*Cercis* spp.) have dropped, the tree forms 2- to 4-inch-long brown seedpods. Each pod contains 4 to 10 hard brown seeds. By fall, the pods begin to split open and release the ripe seeds, but often pods remain on the tree into winter. Seeds that fall to the ground may sometimes lie dormant for several years.

To get yours started, collect the ripe brown or black seedpods in late summer or fall. Remove the seeds and store them in sealed containers in the refrigerator until about the middle of February. Then rub the seeds briefly between two pieces of sandpaper to roughen the hard seed coats. This will help them absorb water and sprout. Boil a pan of water and remove it from heat. Put the seeds in the water and leave them soaking for a few days. Plant the seeds ¼ inch deep in pots of moist sand or potting mix and store them in the refrigerator or where they'll stay at 40 degrees for five to eight weeks. Place them, in their pots, out in the garden in spring. As the weather warms, the seeds will germinate.

Fast shade
Lucille Prehoda Logan, Virginia

Q I lost the shade in my garden this year when several trees were taken down. Can you recommend a few fast-growing shade trees?

A Here are three good shade trees that will grow 2 to 3 feet per year:
Bald cypress *Taxodium distichum* Pyramidal deciduous conifer; 40 to 70 ft. tall, 20 to 45 ft. wide; cold-hardy in USDA zones 4 to 10, heat-tolerant in AHS zones 10 to 1
Linden *Tilia* spp. Pyramidal form with fragrant summer flowers; 50 to 80 ft. tall, 25 to 50 ft. wide; cold-hardy in USDA zones 2 to 9, heat-tolerant in AHS zones 9 to 1
Japanese zelkova *Zelkova serrata* Leaves turn yellow in fall; 50 to 70 ft. tall, 25 to 45 ft. wide; cold-hardy in USDA zones 5 to 8, heat-tolerant in AHS zones 8 to 1

in the news

Look out, kudzu!
Kudzu (*Pueraria montana lobularia*) is sometimes called "the weed that ate the South" because it grows up to 1 foot per day. Scientists at the Agriculture Research Service may have found something that can keep up, though: the fungus *Myrothecium verrucaria*, which is commonly found in the soil. This fungus infects kudzu so quickly that plants sprayed in the morning show signs of damage by midafternoon. In addition, it's been found to be effective as a pre-emergent against purslane and spurge. It doesn't damage nearby plants, either. Researchers have applied for patents and are hoping to find a company willing to develop this new herbicide for public use.

Black walnut tree decline
There's a new problem for black walnut trees (*Juglans nigra*): Black walnut decline is killing them off in the western United States and Mexico.

The most obvious symptoms are branches that fail to leaf out in spring, or die sometime during the summer. Dieback starts in the upper crown and moves downward. A tree dies within two to five years. There's no known cure for this disease (also known as thousand canker disease), and the cause was unknown until recently. It's believed to be caused by the fungus *Geosmithia morbida*, which is introduced into the tree by the walnut twig beetle (*Pityophthorus juglandis*). The cankers that form eventually starve the tree of nutrients. Research is being done to find ways to prevent and treat this disease.

News from you!
Do you automatically turn into any parking lot that has a greenhouse? Are the top three most recent locations on your GPS garden centers? If your answer is yes to either of these, you're not alone! In an online survey last spring, we asked our readers just how much you spent last year on plants and if you're brave enough to admit it. Here's what you said:

How much did you spend on plants and seeds last year?
- $0-$50
- $51-$100
- $101-$300
- More than $300

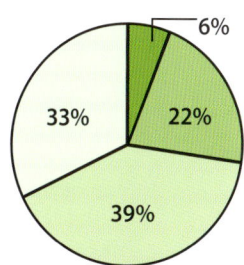

6%
22%
33%
39%

Do you admit how much you've spent to your significant other?
- Yes, for the most part
- No way, he/she'd never let me go to the garden center again!
- I don't have a significant other — I can spend what I want!

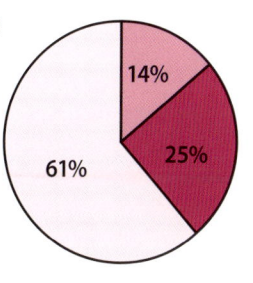

14%
25%
61%

did you know... (CONTINUED)

Hydrangea shelter
Jim Brown, Iowa

Those first few days after putting new transplants in the garden are critical. Sun and wind can cause a lot of damage, setting plants back or even killing them. While planting some small mum cuttings, Jim found a way to give his transplants a little extra protection as they adjusted to life outside.

First, he grabbed a few dried mophead hydrangea flowers left over from an early spring pruning. Then he stuck them in the ground as close to the mums as possible so the flowers provided shade. Placed on the sunny side (south or southwest) of the plant, they made great "umbrellas." Because the flowers are dense, they provide a little shelter from the wind, too. The dried flowers don't hold up forever. After a month or so they deteriorate and the mum grows large enough to cover the leftover pieces.

Push the hydrangea into the soil so it shades the new plant.

Easy dahlia planting
Angela Tape, New Jersey

Angela has to dig her dahlias in the fall because they won't survive the winter in her zone 6 garden. But there's clay soil in that part of the garden and digging in it is a real chore. So she found a way to keep that back-breaking work to a minimum. In the fall, when it's time to dig the tubers Angela gets a heavy plastic 1-gallon nursery pot (any size will do.) After she has the tubers out of the ground she fills the container with nice, loamy soil from her vegetable garden or a nearby perennial bed. After that, the soil-filled container goes into the ground with the rim roughly at soil level. It serves as a place holder until next spring.

In spring, when all danger of frost is past, Angela pulls the container back out of the ground and plants the dahlia tubers in the hole, dumping the soil in over it.

Peony basket
Sue Heath, California

Sue was about to toss a rusty old metal hanging basket when she got an idea: Why not use it to prop up her peonies?

She set the 16-in.-diameter basket in the top of the 15-in. hoop that she used in previous years. The crossing wires of a basket like the one in the illustration add extra support for the peonies, which used to lean toward the outer edge of the hoop. Now the blooms are more evenly spaced. The big leaves cover the cage and the basket once the plants are in full bloom. For taller peonies, flip the basket upside down and attach it to the hoop with twist ties.

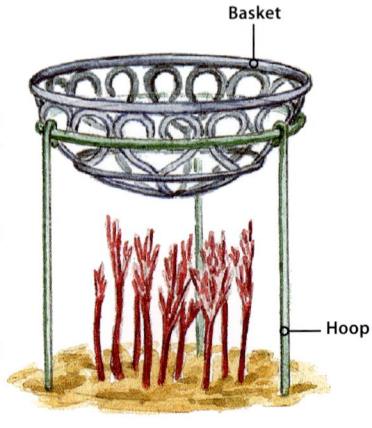

Basket
Hoop

High on gardening
Tonya Reynolds, Colorado

Q I live at an altitude of about 8,000 ft. What perennials can I grow?

A Perennials for high altitudes have to be tough. The sun is more intense, it can be very windy and the soil is often shallow with little humus to hold moisture. Look for plants that stay low to the ground, have small or thick leaves and do best in quickly draining soils. Here's a list of five to try.

Catmint *Nepeta* spp. Perennial; long-blooming purple to blue flowers; drought-tolerant; 6 to 48 in. tall, 18 to 48 in. wide; cold-hardy in USDA zones 3 to 9, heat-tolerant in AHS zones 9 to 1

Lavender cotton *Santolina chamaecyparissus* Perennial; gray foliage with small yellow flowers in summer; drought- and wind-tolerant; 12 to 18 in. tall, 24 to 36 in. wide; cold-hardy in USDA zones 5 to 9, heat-tolerant in AHS zones 9 to 1

Red hot poker *Kniphofia uvaria* Perennial; red, yellow and orange blooms in late spring or summer; tolerates hot sun, wind and drought; 2 to 4 ft. tall, 18 to 24 in. wide; cold-hardy in USDA zones 5 to 9, heat-tolerant in AHS zones 9 to 1

Sea thrift *Armeria maritima* Perennial; low-growing pink flowers in early summer; tolerates wind, hot sun and dry soil; 8 to 10 in. tall, 6 to 12 in. wide; cold-hardy in USDA zones 4 to 9, heat-tolerant in AHS zones 9 to 1

Yellow ice plant *Delosperma nubigenum* Perennial; yellow daisy flowers in spring; succulent leaves withstand hot sun and dry conditions; 2 in. tall, spreading; cold-hardy in USDA zones 4 to 9, heat-tolerant in AHS zones 9 to 1

Snow insulation
Carl Warrick, Wisconsin

Q *We've had an unusually cold and snowy winter. Will my perennials be OK?*

A Yes, snow is Mother Nature's best garden insulation — and it's free. Depending on the moisture content of the snow, it is estimated that 10 inches of snow has an insulating factor of R-18. That's the same as 6-inch-thick fiberglass batting.

Snow that has gently settled on the ground is 90 to 95 percent air. That air traps heat from the ground that has built up on sunny days. Ordinarily it's released into the atmosphere, but the layer of snow holds it in close to the ground, keeping plants a few degrees warmer.

Packed snow that's been shoveled or run through a snow blower has *some* insulating capabilities and won't harm perennials. But heavy snow can break branches on shrubs.

Anemic geraniums
Laura Aldrich, Tennessee

Q *The ivy geraniums in my hanging baskets are growing, but the new leaves are yellow. Why?*

A These cascading geraniums are sometimes prone to heat-induced iron deficiency. It seems the plants can't absorb iron from the soil quickly enough when temperatures go above 80 degrees Fahrenheit. But extra doses of an easily absorbed iron can fix the problem.

Pick up chelated iron at your local garden center. The liquid form will give you the quickest results, but powdered or granulated will work, too. Mix the iron with water and drench the plants and the soil around them every few weeks during the summer. Don't let the iron mix dribble onto hard surfaces, such as brick or concrete, or it'll leave a stain that's hard to remove.

Bloomin' begonias
Marjorie Potirala, Illinois

Q *I noticed that my tuberous begonia plant has both single and double flowers. What causes this?*

A Tuberous begonias are *monoecious*, meaning they have both male and female flowers on the same plant. Usually, the buds that develop at the end of the stems open as double flowers, which are male flowers. Other buds next to the male flower may develop into other male flowers or smaller, single female flowers. You can leave these adjacent buds alone, but sometimes the smaller flowers will crowd and slightly deform the petals of the main male flower.

Pinch out the buds on either side of the center bud when they're about pea-sized, and the plant will direct its energy toward forming larger, showier male flowers. This will extend your begonia's bloom time, as it won't waste energy producing seeds.

What is it?
Janice Wright, Michigan

Q *I picked up seedlings at a plant swap, but forgot to write down the name. Can you identify this flower for me?*

A It's blue woodruff (*Asperula orientalis*). While the sweetly scented lavender-blue flowers are enough to recommend it, this annual is also popular with butterflies. It grows 12 inches tall but only about 3 or 4 inches wide. Give it a spot in part shade where the soil stays moist. You may want to deadhead at least some of the spent flowers — this annual can be an aggressive reseeder.

Diane's Flower Seeds, at www.dianeseeds.com, sells blue woodruff seeds. Direct sow in late winter or early spring for summer blooms.

Deadhead at least some of the flowers when they're spent — blue woodruff can reseed aggressively.

The Big Kiss series of gazanias gladly accepts hot and dry conditions. Meet more great new plants for your garden on page 72.

top picks

our favorite new plants, plus bold bloomers and multi-season standouts.

LOOKING FOR SOMETHING A BIT DIFFERENT? Have we got ideas for you! From unique tulips to the newest introductions on the market, these plants are practically guaranteed to grab attention. And with marathon bloomers and multiseason showoffs to boot, there's plenty of time to turn heads.

New Plants for 2010............................ **72**
Out-of-the-Ordinary Tulips **80**
Big, Beautiful Blooms **86**
Readers' Favorite Cut Flowers **92**
Long-Blooming Perennials **98**
Multiseason Showoffs........................ **104**

top new annuals

new plants 2010

New plants are a favorite topic here at *Garden Gate*, as well as with our readers. And for good reason! Every year, breeders come up with new and exciting flower or foliage colors and smaller or taller versions of favorite plants. Some varieties are even more cold-hardy or heat-tolerant. This year is no exception. We found some new twists on old favorites like the petunia and zinnia at right. Or check out some of the improved cultivars, like the river birch with whiter bark than other varieties or the hydrangea with huge pink and white blooms on page 78. There are plenty of other tough new varieties you may want to try, too. Keep reading to learn more about why we like them.

Don't get discouraged if you can't find your favorites right away, though. New plants, especially the woody plants on this list, will be hard to find (and more expensive) for a year or two. It takes time for nurseries to grow enough stock for everyone who wants one.

Can't get enough new plants? No problem. Visit our Web extra to check out 10 more of this year's exciting new introductions. Now let's take a look at some new plants! □

— *Sherri Ribbey*

Web extra Check out our **slide show** of 10 more exciting new plants!

PHOTO: Brent Isenberger (gazania)

Big Kiss White Flame gazania
Gazania splendens

Bring on the heat! Gazanias don't mind. The new Big Kiss™ series of gazanias is the perfect solution to those hot, dry areas where other annuals shrivel up and die. Sturdy stems support 4½-inch-wide flowers that are larger than other varieties. Like most gazanias, the flowers of this new variety close at night and on cloudy days. Big Kiss comes in two colors: White Flame, above, and Yellow Flame.

Group a few Big Kiss gazanias along the edge of a hot, sunny sidewalk or grow some in a container on your deck.

Type Tender perennial
Size 8 to 10 in. tall and wide
Bloom Spring to fall
Soil Well-drained
Light Full sun
Hardiness
　　Cold: USDA zones 10 to 11
　　Heat: AHS zones 12 to 1
Introducer Goldsmith Seeds
Source Local garden centers
What's new? Bigger flowers!

the YEAR IN GARDENING　　www.GardenGateMagazine.com

Pretty Much Picasso petunia
Petunia hybrid

Practically everyone has grown petunias — but not like this one! Pretty Much Picasso™ has a unique color combo. These chartreuse and purple flowers were a big favorite among our garden visitors. Though this trailing petunia gets a bit leggy by midsummer, we found that cutting it back made it more compact and full of flowers. It's easy to do: Just trim the stems back by as much as half when they get too long. Then feed the plant with an all-purpose, water-soluble fertilizer. You'll see blooms again in a week or so.

Type Annual
Size 8 to 12 in. tall, 24 to 36 in. wide
Bloom Spring to fall
Soil Well-drained
Light Full sun
Hardiness
　Cold: Annual
　Heat: AHS zones 12 to 1
Introducer Proven Winners®
Source Local garden centers
What's new? The wildest color combination to come along in years

Zahara Starlight Rose zinnia
Zinnia marylandica

Zahara® zinnias are a relatively new series of tough little plants that can tolerate hot, dry conditions and resist powdery mildew. They come in a nice range of colors, too. There's white, red, yellow, coral and more. The newest addition to this group is a real standout, though — pink-striped Zahara Starlight Rose. You'll get the most intense pink stripe with full sun, cool nights and a liquid fertilizer every seven days.

Even though our plants were grouped tightly together with salvia and petunias in containers, they didn't show any signs of powdery mildew.

Type Annual
Size 12 to 18 in. tall and wide
Bloom Spring to fall
Soil Well-drained
Light Full sun
Hardiness
　Cold: Annual
　Heat: AHS zones 12 to 1
Introducer Simply Beautiful®
Source Local garden centers
What's new? Pretty color pattern

top new perennials

Jumping Jack viola
Viola 'Balvijac'

Cool spring weather is prime garden time for violas. But once it starts getting hot, these pretty little plants tend to give up. Not Jumping Jack — this new viola has staying power. While it peaks in spring, this viola keeps producing colorful blooms even through the heat of summer. Water Jumping Jack regularly the first year you grow it. But the following year it will get along with occasional watering like other perennials. Just give it a drink during dry spells. If you do notice that the plants have stalled a little in the heat, cut them back by about half to encourage more blooms. You don't have to worry about reseeding, either. Jumping Jack stays in a nice tidy clump.

Type Perennial
Size 6 to 8 in. tall, 6 to 10 in. wide
Bloom Spring to fall
Soil Well-drained
Light Full sun to part shade
Hardiness
 Cold: USDA zones 5 to 10
 Heat: AHS zones 10 to 1
Introducer Ball Horticultural Co.
Source Local garden centers
What's new?
 A heat-tolerant viola!

Younique Lilac astilbe
Astilbe 'Verslilac'

It's no wonder so many people like astilbe. It's one of the few showy flowers that does well in shade. Younique Lilac™ is no exception. You can jazz up your shade garden with its big feathery lilac pink flowers. Younique Lilac has more flower scapes, or stems, per plant than other varieties so you'll have plenty of those colorful flowers to enjoy. And if this color doesn't strike your fancy, try one of the others in the series: deep pink, pale pink or white. In addition to the pretty flowers, the foliage stays in a tidy mound.

Type Perennial
Size 16 to 20 in. tall and wide
Bloom Early to midsummer
Soil Moist, well-drained
Light Full sun to full shade
Hardiness
 Cold: USDA zones 4 to 9
 Heat: AHS zones 9 to 1
Introducer Walters Gardens
Source Local garden centers or www.PerennialResource.com to find a retailer near you
What's new?
 Even showier than most astilbes

PHOTOS: Courtesy of Ball Horticultural Company (viola); courtesy of Walters Gardens, Inc. (astilbe)

'Tequila Sunrise' geum
Geum hybrid

This new geum picks up the slack when tulips and daffodils start to fade in late spring. Single to semi-double yellow flowers brushed with red top off 18- to 24-inch dark red stems. Deadhead spent blooms to encourage side branches to develop more quickly and you'll have flowers for up to four weeks. 'Tequila Sunrise' is a sterile hybrid so it won't reseed like some geums do. The flowers are small, 1 to 1½ inches in diameter, so group three or more plants together for the best show.

Flowers aren't the only good thing about this geum. The attractive mound of round, puckered leaves looks good even when it isn't flowering.

Type Perennial
Size 8 to 10 in. tall (foliage), 10 to 12 in. wide
Bloom Spring
Soil Moist, well-drained
Light Full sun
Hardiness
Cold: USDA zones 5 to 10
Heat: AHS zones 10 to 1
Introducer Intrinsic Perennial Gardens
Source Klehm's Song Sparrow Farm and Nursery
www.songsparrow.com
800-553-3715

What's new?
Good-looking flowers that last for 4 weeks

'Purple Rooster' bee balm
Monarda didyma

Bee balm is a great native plant for attracting butterflies and hummingbirds, and it's deer-resistant, too. The big problem is that a lot of varieties have a real problem with powdery mildew. This dusty white fungus usually shows up around midsummer and makes plants look ratty. 'Purple Rooster' is so resistant you can plant this taller bee balm in the middle of the border without any worry. The foliage stays clean and green all season long. Topped off with large, deep-purple flowers, 'Purple Rooster' will make a big impact in your garden.

Type Perennial
Size 36 in. tall, 26 in. wide
Bloom Summer
Soil Moist, well-drained
Light Full sun
Hardiness
Cold: USDA zones 4 to 9
Heat: AHS zones 9 to 1
Introducer Walters Gardens
Source Local garden centers or www.PerennialResource.com to find a retailer near you

What's new?
Great mildew resistance and deep purple flowers

PHOTOS: Courtesy of Intrinsic Perennial Gardens (geum); courtesy of Walters Gardens, Inc. (bee balm)

top new perennials *continued*

'Crystal Pink' tall sedum
Sedum spectabile

Sedums are some of the most low-maintenance plants you can grow, so make sure you try this new variety. A lot of other tall sedums tend to sprawl outward as summer progresses, but 'Crystal Pink' stays standing tall. There's no need for pinching or staking. Those sturdy stems are topped off with clear pink flowers that are magnets for butterflies and other insect pollinators. Leave the flowers standing for added winter interest.

Grow 'Crystal Pink' along with other butterfly-attracting beauties, such as coreopsis, yarrow and purple coneflower.

Type Perennial
Size 16 in. tall and wide
Bloom Summer to fall
Soil Poor, well-drained
Light Full sun
Hardiness
  Cold: USDA zones 4 to 9
  Heat: AHS zones 9 to 1
Introducer Terra Nova Nurseries
Source Local garden centers
What's new? Clear pink flowers on stems that don't flop

'Susquehanna' foamflower
Tiarella cordifolia

Got shade? No problem for this new foamflower. It's the smallest of several new varieties of native foamflower. This species spreads by runners instead of forming clumps, as other types do. Whether your garden's soil is dry or moist, 'Susquehanna' can spread up to 24 inches in a single season, making it an excellent ground cover. Those dainty white flowers emerge in late spring on 6- to 8-inch stems and float above the foliage. The photo above shows its spring foliage look, which is a little lighter. As the summer progresses, the markings get larger and darker.

Type Perennial
Size 2 to 4 in. tall (foliage), 24 to 36 in. wide
Bloom Late spring to summer
Soil Average to moist, well-drained
Light Full to part shade
Hardiness
  Cold: USDA zones 4 to 9
  Heat: AHS zones 9 to 1
Introducer Dunvegan Nursery
Source Lazy S's Farm and Nursery
  www.lazyssfarm.com
What's new? Fast-growing flowering ground cover for shade

PHOTOS: Courtesy of Terra Nova Nurseries, Inc. (tall sedum); courtesy of Sinclair A. Adam, Jr. (foamflower)

76 *the* YEAR IN GARDENING   www.GardenGateMagazine.com

top new bulb

Bijou clematis
Clematis 'EVIPO030'

If you think every clematis needs a trellis to climb, think again. This new variety only grows a foot or two tall. You can grow it up a small obelisk if you'd like, but it also makes a nice ground cover. It forms a mound, loaded with big 3- to 4-inch purple flowers. Bijou also looks good in a hanging basket — you'll have friends asking what that new trailing flower is. But don't toss it out with the annuals — this clematis is plenty cold-hardy. Just plant it in the ground before a hard frost. Bijou is part of pruning group B, which means you remove only dead or damaged stems in early spring.

Type Perennial vine
Size 12 to 24 in. tall, 12 in. wide
Bloom Midspring to fall
Soil Moist, well-drained
Light Full sun to part shade
Hardiness
   Cold: USDA zones 4 to 9
   Heat: AHS zones 9 to 1
Introducer Raymond Evison Clematis
Source Klehm's Song Sparrow Farm and Nursery
   www.songsparrow.com
   800-553-3715
What's new?
   A tiny vine covered in big flowers

'Lucky Star' gladiolus
Gladiolus hybrid

There has always been one thing lacking that would make glads the perfect cut flower — fragrance. 'Lucky Star', a cross between good old-fashioned floral types and Abyssinian glads (*Gladiolus callianthus*), solves that dilemma. The name may sound familiar, because it was originally introduced in 1966 but was lost to the retail market. Now it's been rediscovered and is available for sale again. The light, sweet fragrance of 'Lucky Star' is most noticeable on hot, humid evenings. You might even see night-pollinating moths hovering nearby ready for a sip of nectar.

Type Bulb
Size 48 in. tall, 3 to 6 in. wide
Bloom Late summer
Soil Well-drained
Light Full sun
Hardiness
   Cold: USDA zones 8 to 10
   Heat: AHS zones 12 to 1
Introducer Old House Gardens
Source Old House Gardens
   www.oldhousegardens.com
   734-995-1486
What's new?
   Fragrance from a gladiolus!

PHOTOS: Courtesy of Raymond J. Evison (clematis); courtesy of Old House Gardens (gladiolus)

top new tree and shrub

City Slicker river birch
***Betula nigra* 'Whit XXV'**
River birches are sought after for their beautiful peeling bark, and City Slicker® won't disappoint. The bark is some of the lightest of any variety. And you don't have to wait long to see it, either: The bark starts peeling on branches as small as 1 inch in diameter. Our tree was small when we got it but it's grown steadily through four years of hot, humid summers and cold, snowy winters. Glossy dark green leaves are a welcome change from the usual pale green seen on other varieties. In fall they turn yellow-gold. This tree will be available in limited numbers in 2010, with an increasing supply in following years.

Type Tree
Size 35 ft. tall, 35 ft. wide (single stem — wider for multistem)
Bloom NA
Soil Well-drained
Light Full sun
Hardiness
  Cold: USDA zones 5 to 9
  Heat: AHS zones 9 to 1
Introducer Lacebark Inc.
Source Sooner Plant Farm
  www.soonerplantfarm.com
  918-453-0771
What's new?
  Lighter bark and glossy dark green leaves

Vanilla Strawberry hydrangea
***Hydrangea paniculata* 'Renhy'**
This new hydrangea will knock your socks off! Vanilla Strawberry™ sports big 12-inch flowers that start out creamy vanilla white and gradually change to soft pink, then deep strawberry pink. Its unique color combination isn't just a flash in the pan, either. These beautiful flowers remain looking good for up to four weeks, and strong red stems keep them upright where you can see them. New blooms provide a multicolored show from summer to fall. Pruning is easy; in late winter to early spring, cut off any damaged stems.

Type Shrub
Size 6 to 7 ft. tall, 4 to 5 ft. wide
Bloom Summer to fall
Soil Well-drained
Light Full sun to part shade
Hardiness
  Cold: USDA zones 4 to 8
  Heat: AHS zones 8 to 1
Introducer Bailey Nurseries
Source Local garden centers
What's new?
  Great big flowers that change color

6 bonus new plants

Lucky™ Pure Gold lantana *Lantana camara*

TYPE Tender perennial

WHAT IT LOOKS LIKE Solid yellow flowers; good branching produces a compact habit; 12 to 16 in. tall, 12 to 14 in. wide

HOW TO GROW IT Full sun; well-drained soil; cold-hardy in USDA zones 9 to 11, heat-tolerant in AHS zones 12 to 1

INTRODUCER Ball Horticultural

SOURCE Local garden centers

Illusion™ Emerald Lace sweet potato vine *Ipomoea batatas*

TYPE Tender perennial

WHAT IT LOOKS LIKE More compact than other varieties; 8 to 10 in. tall, 24 to 36 in. wide

HOW TO GROW IT Full sun; well-drained soil; cold-hardy in USDA zones 8 to 11; heat-tolerant in AHS zones 12 to 1

INTRODUCER Proven Winners®

SOURCE Garden Crossings www.gardencrossings.com, 616-875-6355

'Eternal' snapdragon *Antirrhinum* hybrid

TYPE Tender perennial

WHAT IT LOOKS LIKE Variegated leaves; pink flowers in spring with a repeat in fall; 12 in. tall, 10 in. wide

HOW TO GROW IT Full sun; moist, well-drained soil; cold-hardy in USDA zones 7 to 9, heat-tolerant in AHS zones 12 to 1

INTRODUCER Skagit Nursery

SOURCE Local garden centers

'Route 66' coreopsis *Coreopsis verticillata*

TYPE Perennial

WHAT IT LOOKS LIKE Red and yellow flowers summer to fall; more red in fall (in photo); 24 to 28 in. tall, 20 to 24 in. wide

HOW TO GROW IT Full sun; well-drained soil; cold-hardy in USDA zones 5 to 9, heat-tolerant in AHS zones 9 to 1

INTRODUCER ItSaul Plants

SOURCE Great Garden Plants www.greatgardenplants.com, 877-447-4769

'Pink Lemonade' blueberry *Vaccinium* hybrid

TYPE Shrub

WHAT IT LOOKS LIKE Pink berries that are good to eat; need two plants for pollination; red fall foliage; 5 ft. tall and wide

HOW TO GROW IT Full sun; moist, well-drained acid soil; cold-hardy in USDA zones 4 to 7, heat-tolerant in AHS zones 7 to 1

INTRODUCER Briggs Nursery

SOURCE Local garden centers; very limited release this year so it may be hard to find

Pumpkin Patch™ rose *Rosa* 'Wekmongros'

TYPE Shrub; floribunda type

WHAT IT LOOKS LIKE Caramel-orange flowers spring to fall; fragrant; 5 ft. tall, 2 to 3 ft. wide

HOW TO GROW IT Full sun; moist, well-drained soil; cold-hardy in USDA zones 5 to 8, heat-tolerant in AHS zones 8 to 1

INTRODUCER Weeks Roses

SOURCE Regan Nursery www.regannursery.com, 800-249-4680

Out-of-the-Ordinary Tulips

Tulips are the quintessential spring flower. Now, I don't have anything against the colorful modern hybrids that you see everywhere, but, to me, the most interesting tulips are the weird and wonderful ones with crazy flowers or foliage. Out-of-the-ordinary shapes, patterns and textures, or variegated leaves really pump up the excitement in spring gardens. And what garden can't use more fascinating flowers?

I'll cover nine of the most uncommon tulips in this story. Some, like the green or black ones, stand out because of their unusual colors. Others have very untuliplike shapes, such as the horned, peony-flowered and lily-flowered ones, or eye-catching textures, fringes or even multiple flowers on each plant. Size varies among plants, so I'll list the ranges with each one I mention, along with its hardiness zones and whether it blooms in early, mid- or late spring. On p. 85, I'll let you know some tips for growing healthy tulips — whether they're unusual or not. And below, I've included three good mail-order sources so you can get some of these "out-of-the-ordinaries" into your own garden!

— *Deborah Gruca*

Mail-order sources

Brent and Becky's Bulbs
www.brentandbeckysbulbs.com, 804-693-3966. *Catalog free*

John Scheepers, Inc.
www.johnscheepers.com, 860-567-0838. *Catalog free*

Blooming Bulb
www.bloomingbulb.com, 800-648-2852. *Online catalog*

Fringed petals

Tulips in this group all have petals edged with fancy fringes. The degree of "fringiness" can vary wildly. Some are so intricate that you have to look at them up close to see the fine crystallike petal edges. To me they look like they've been touched with frost, though most bloom late enough in spring that this doesn't usually happen. (And, luckily, most tulips can handle frost easily, without skipping a beat.) Others, like the one above, have such extreme fringes that they look like someone went crazy with a pair of scissors!

Several types of tulips can be affected by this mutation, so you'll find fringed tulips in a range of sizes that bloom from mid- to late spring. And though there are a few double tulips that are fringed, most are single-flowered. All make a nice impact in the garden and are even easier to appreciate up close as cut flowers in arrangements.

try **these**

Delicate pink frills 'Fancy Frills' (in photo); single flowers have ivory base blending to rose-pink above, with light pink fringes in mid- to late spring; 16 to 18 in. tall; cold zones 3 to 8, heat zones 8 to 1

Double red-orange with orange fringes 'Sensual Touch'; tightly packed petals open in mid- to late spring; 14 to 17 in. tall; cold zones 3 to 8, heat zones 8 to 1

White and lacy 'Honeymoon'; single snow-white flowers in mid- to late spring; 12 to 16 in. tall; cold zones 3 to 8, heat zones 8 to 1

Horned tulip

An heirloom, horned tulip (*Tulipa acuminata*) has been around since at least the early 1800s. It can be tough to find — check the three sources at left. It's well worth the effort — just look at the photo above! Unusual long, twisted and pointed red and yellow petals are sure to grab the attention of garden visitors who happen upon it.

Like the flowers, the 12- to 18-inch-tall stems are very slender, so plant the bulbs where they'll have some protection from strong winds. And give the delicate flowers a good background so they'll show up better. Pair them with other similar-but-lighter-colored tulips or plants with bold foliage, such as the ones in "Looks good with" below.

Grow this species tulip in compost-rich, well-drained soil and it will spread into a nice mass in a few years. In spring, top dress with compost and, if the weather's dry, water the plants when you see the new growth emerge so you'll get the largest flowers.

looks good with

Pretty partner 'Apricot Beauty' tulip; fragrant, single apricot flowers in early to midspring; 12 to 14 in. tall; cold zones 3 to 8, heat zones 8 to 1

Dark background Bergenia *Bergenia cordifolia* 'Redstart'; perennial; deep-green leaves with red blooms in spring; 18 to 24 in. tall, 10 to 12 in. wide; cold zones 3 to 8, heat zones 8 to 1

Parrot-flowered

Of all the tulips on these pages, the parrots are my all-time favorites. Brightly colored, twisted, crimped and ruffled petals remind me of the exotic creatures for which they're named. At 18 to 24 inches tall, 'Salmon Parrot', above, is an exceptional example of those large, wonderfully textured flowers.

These late-spring beauties tend to steal the show wherever they're growing. Combine them with single-flowered tulips or other spring bloomers of subtler colors, to make them show well without making the planting look too busy.

The heights of the plants in this group vary but most have the sturdy stems necessary to hold up the large flowers. Even then, it's a good idea to site these plants in a spot sheltered from strong winds. Better yet, plant them in containers where you can relish their beauty up close.

try these

Salmon, green and yellow 'Salmon Parrot' (in photo); scalloped-edged flowers open in mid- to late spring; 18 to 24 in. tall; cold zones 4 to 7, heat zones 7 to 1

Red-edged gold 'Texas Gold'; rich gold flowers with a thin red margin in late spring; 16 to 18 in. tall; cold zones 3 to 9, heat zones 9 to 1

Red-streaked yellow 'Flaming Parrot'; deep gold blooms with scarlet flames open mid- to late spring; 25 to 27 in. tall; cold zones 3 to 8, heat zones 8 to 1

top unusual tulips *continued*

Petal-packed
Peony or double-flowered tulips stand out from the rest of the crowd because the blooms that resemble peonies are so packed with petals. Cultivars span the tulip-blooming seasons, with the early spring ones usually opening on shorter stems than their late-spring cousins. But all have at least twice the number of petals on each beefy bloom!

In times past, because these blooms were so heavy, the stems would often bend or break, especially in hard rain or winds. The stems of modern cultivars are bred to be much sturdier, but like the parrots and the horned tulip, don't plant them in breezy spots, just to be on the safe side. And if a few of these hefty blooms do happen to hit the ground, look at it as an excuse to cut them and use them in a vase. They make dramatic focal point flowers in cut arrangements and many of them are fragrant, as well.

try these

Fragrant white 'Mount Tacoma' (in photo); white petals with a light fragrance in late spring; 14 to 16 in. tall; cold zones 3 to 7, heat zones 7 to 1

Compact yellow 'Yellow Baby'; fully double buttery yellow in early spring; 8 to 10 in. tall; cold zones 3 to 8, heat zones 8 to 1

Deep violet-purple 'Blue Spectacle'; deep violet-purple in late spring; 12 to 16 in. tall; cold zones 3 to 8, heat zones 8 to 1

Bountiful blooms
If you cherish tulips, bouquet-flowered ones give you even more to love. With their multiple blooms, they add tons of color to any spring border. Look closely at the photo and you'll see that there are actually several flowers on each plant, rather than the one bloom per bulb of most tulips. Not only do they make an impact in the garden, but they also make great cut flowers. And, as the name "bouquet-flowered" implies, it takes just a few stems to fill even the largest vase.

There are some types of tulips that will produce multiple blooms like this when the bulb size is very large, but it's impossible to tell just by looking at the bulb. On the other hand, there are tulips like 'Color Spectacle', in the photo, and the others in the list below, that naturally and consistently form several flowers on each stem. In addition, you'll find some that have names that reflect that trait, such as 'Red Bouquet' and 'White Bouquet'.

try these

Brilliant red and gold 'Color Spectacle' (in photo); yellow flowers with bright red flames in late spring; 18 to 20 in. tall; cold zones 3 to 9, heat zones 9 to 1

Color change 'Antoinette'; flowers start pale yellow and age to deep salmon-orange in late spring; 14 to 16 in. tall; cold zones 3 to 8, heat zones 8 to 1

Pink-edged ivory 'Candy Club'; white with pink streaks and edges in late spring; 16 to 18 in. tall; cold zones 3 to 8, heat zones 8 to 1

Lily-flowered

If a tulip can be called "elegant," lily-flowered ones certainly are. With their slender flowers and long, tapered petals that curve gracefully outward at the pointed tips, they bring a quiet sophistication to the spring garden. The curve of the petals is emphasized even more as the blooms gradually open wide into starlike shapes.

Lily-flowered tulips come in nearly every color, including a few bicolors, and a range of sizes. Most have a bloom time that bridges that gap between mid- and late-spring tulips, which makes them handy for planning long-blooming borders. Lily-flowered tulips are some of the longest-lived tulips you can find, so once you plant them, you can expect to enjoy them for many years.

try these

Deep salmon-rose 'Mariette' (in photo); tapered deep salmon-rose blooms in mid- to late spring; 18 to 20 in. tall; cold zones 3 to 8, heat zones 8 to 1

Fragrant, primrose yellow 'West Point'; yellow blooms in mid- to late spring; 18 to 22 in. tall; cold zones 3 to 7, heat zones 7 to 1

Very fragrant 'Ballerina'; yellow-orange with bright red flames in mid- to late spring; 18 to 24 in. tall; cold zones 3 to 7, heat zones 7 to 1

Green tulips

Even though green, or viridiflora, tulips are demure in size, they bring no less color to the spring garden than any of the other tulips in this story. These late-spring bloomers come in a range of colors, but all sport a prominent splash or "flame" of green on the outside of the petals. This unusual coloring makes them easy to coordinate with the green leaves of just about every plant you can pair them with.

The tallest green cultivars top out at no more than 22 inches, making them a perfect fit at the front of the border or in containers. They'll make more of an impact if you plant them in groupings of at least five. Their single flowers, which last up to three weeks in the garden, are relatively large for the size of the plants. That makes them show up well wherever you grow them.

try these

Green-streaked cream 'Spring Green' (in photo); blooms in late spring; 16 to 18 in. tall; cold zones 3 to 8, heat zones 8 to 1

Yellow flushed with pink 'Golden Artist'; flowers with somewhat ruffled petals open in late spring; 12 to 16 in. tall; cold zones 3 to 7, heat zones 7 to 1

Green-feathered, deep salmon-pink 'Palestrina'; parrot-flowered blooms open in late spring; 14 to 16 in. tall; cold zones 3 to 7, heat zones 7 to 1

PHOTO: © Jerry Pavia (green tulips)

top unusual tulips *continued*

Black flowers

OK, I'll be the first to admit that there are no "true black" flowers in nature. But that doesn't seem to stop breeders from trying to develop them or gardeners from growing them! Though they're considered to be "black," the descriptions for these plants usually use words like "darkest," "velvety maroon" or "has a purple or brown sheen."

However, even as growers all claim to have the blackest cultivar, you must admit that these tulips can make an impact. It's fun to have such an unusual color in the garden, but on top of that, black tulips are great for contrasting with white or cream-colored flowers for an eye-catching combo. Or mass them to create a pool of "shade" in full sun or a meandering river of dark petals through a planting of other brightly colored tulips.

try these

Black peony 'Black Hero' (in photo); black peony-flowered with maroon sheen in late spring; 16 to 20 in. tall; cold zones 3 to 7, heat zones 7 to 1

Velvety black 'Queen of Night'; lustrous, single deep maroon-purple flowers on tall stems in late spring; 20 to 24 in. tall; cold zones 3 to 7, heat zones 7 to 1

Crinkle-petalled 'Black Parrot'; heavily frilled, featherlike deep purple blooms in midspring; 18 to 20 in. tall; cold zones 3 to 8, heat zones 8 to 1

Fancy foliage

With all the unusual and wonderful tulip flowers to swoon over, don't forget that the blooms are just part of the pretty package. Looking for mottled or striped leaves? Or ones snappily edged in a contrasting color? You'll find all of these and more!

Though they don't have their own separate tulip group, there are plenty of tulips with mottled or variegated foliage. (Interestingly, many variegated leaf tulips are bouquet-flowered, as well, with multiple flowers per stem.) And fancy foliage adds another dimension of interest to these great plants. After all, as pretty as they are, the flowers may last just a few weeks. You'll be looking at the foliage for a much longer stretch in your spring garden.

try these

Pink-and-white-leafed 'New Design' (in photo); pale pink flowers in midspring; pink-tinted white leaf margins look like miniature hosta leaves as they emerge; 14 to 16 in. tall; cold zones 3 to 8, heat zones 8 to 1

Purple leaf mottling 'Juan'; single bright orange and yellow flowers in early spring (often produces multiple flowers per stem); 14 to 16 in. tall; cold zones 3 to 8, heat zones 8 to 1

White margins 'China Town'; green flowers edged with pink flare outward at tips in mid- to late spring; 10 to 14 in. tall; cold zones 3 to 8, heat zones 8 to 1

TIPS FOR GROWING TERRIFIC TULIPS

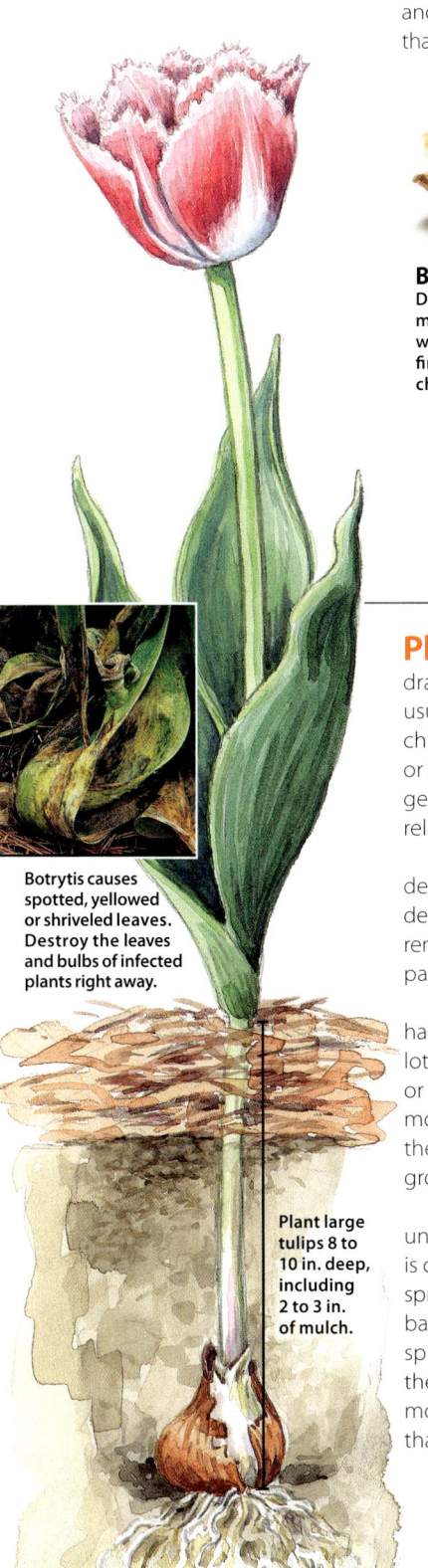

Purchasing When you're looking for bulbs in fall, choose unblemished ones that feel heavy. I've had really good experiences with the mail-order companies I shared on p. 80. If you mail-order bulbs that don't live up to your expectations, check into the return and refund policy. Store bulbs until planting time in a dry area that's cool (50 to 70 degrees F). Keep them away from fruits and vegetables, which give off ethylene gas that can cause the bulbs to not flower.

✱ BUY Healthy bulbs look smooth and feel firm. It's OK if they're missing their papery tunics.

BEWARE Do you see a blue-gray mold on the surface? Try wiping it off. If you can, it's fine to plant. If not, don't choose it.

PASS Round or irregular-shaped discolored spots could be fusarium, a fungal disease. Leave this bulb behind.

Planting Plant bulbs in fall in well-drained soil that's rich in organic matter, usually just after your first frost. (Plant pre-chilled bulbs in zones 8 and 9 in November or December.) Site them where they'll get full sun in spring, and the soil will be relatively dry in summer.

PLANTING DEPTH Dig holes 4 to 6 in. deep and apart for small tulips, 8 to 10 in. deep and apart for large tulips. (If you mulch, remember that you can count the mulch as part of the bulb's planting depth.)

To plant just a few bulbs, a trowel or hand-held bulb planter is fine. If you have lots to plant, a long-handled bulb planter or bulb auger will make the work go more quickly. Water immediately and, if the weather is dry, water weekly until the ground freezes.

MULCHING Wait to mulch your bulbs until after the ground freezes (or weather is consistently cold in the South), then spread 2 to 3 in. of pine needles or chopped bark. If you have voles, wait until very early spring before you mulch to discourage them from nesting. It will help conserve moisture in the soil and discourage weeds that will compete with the bulbs.

Botrytis causes spotted, yellowed or shriveled leaves. Destroy the leaves and bulbs of infected plants right away.

Plant large tulips 8 to 10 in. deep, including 2 to 3 in. of mulch.

Place bulbs in cage and refill hole with soil.

Secure the top of the cage with twist ties or wire.

Protecting To hungry critters, all parts of tulips are tasty. Here are some tips to discourage pests from chipmunks to deer.

FALL To keep your bulbs safe from digging pests, such as chipmunks and voles, make round cages from ½-in. hardware cloth. The diameter depends on how many bulbs you want to plant. One that's a foot across will hold five medium-sized bulbs. Dig the hole, put in the cage and arrange the bulbs in it. Refill with soil. Cover the top of the cage with a hardware cloth lid, securing it with wire or zip ties and refill the rest of the way with soil.

Another way to thwart diggers like squirrels and chipmunks is to lay a piece of chicken wire over the soil after you plant.

Or, an even easier tip is to spray the bulbs with a rabbit or deer repellent, such as Liquid Fence® or RO-PEL®, before you plant them. Doing this gives the bulbs a nasty smell and taste to marauding critters.

SPRING To protect the new foliage from nibblers like rabbits and deer, give the leaves a bitter taste by spraying them with the same repellent you used on the bulbs. The spray washes off, so repeat after each rain. You may need to switch to other repellents (like the homemade one at right) every few weeks, as the critters grow used to the taste.

✱ Homemade pest repellent
- 1 tsp. cayenne pepper
- ½ tsp. Ivory® or other mild dish soap
- 1 qt. warm water

Provide nutrients Scratch a bulb fertilizer with an analysis of 9-9-6 or 5-10-12 into the top few inches of soil after planting. In spring, topdress with compost or sprinkle on a little granular 10-10-10 just as perennials start to emerge.

After the flowers finish, leave the foliage on the plant until it starts to turn yellow, to help the bulb make its own food for next year.

PHOTOS: © Betty Strauch (botrytis); Doug Appleby (purchasing and protecting)

www.GardenGateMagazine.com *the* YEAR IN GARDENING 85

Big, Beautiful Blooms

So you say you love color? I know I do! Want to know an easy way to add a big punch of color to your garden? Grow plants with huge flowers!

It's fun to grow plants with big blooms; you get to enjoy the flowers even from across the yard. Whether they're shaped like trumpets, globes or spikes, they really grab the spotlight in the border. And large flowers come on plants of all sizes. So, even in a small bed, it's easy to find space for at least a few!

Big blooms naturally grab your attention as they add a real splash of color and excitement to your border — as long as you don't overdo them.

On the next pages, I'll share nine of my favorite bulbs, annuals, perennials and shrubs with large, lovely flowers that are at least 8 inches in size. And I'll tell you how to grow them to their fullest potential, as well as let you know which varieties have the biggest blooms.

On the last page, you'll find tips on how to design with these plants so they look like they belong in any size garden. Plus, I've added a plan for a flower bed that includes a few big-flowered beauties. ☐

— *Deborah Gruca*

Dinnerplate dahlia
Dahlia hybrids

You can tell from the name that the blooms of these dahlia varieties are big — some grow up to 12 inches across! Flowers this size, like 'Normandy Bright Day', above, take a little longer to form, so most don't start to open until midsummer.

Place a stake next to the tuber when planting to give these plants some extra support in the wind. And if you want the really giant blooms, when the flower buds are pea-sized, remove the smaller side buds, leaving just the one at the tip of the stem. Also, give the plant plenty of water while the flower is forming. Doing both these things will encourage the top bud to grow as large as possible.

Type Tuber
Size 42 to 60 in. tall, 18 to 30 in. wide
Blooms 8- to 12-in.-diameter pink, white, red, orange, purple or yellow midsummer to frost
Light Sun
Hardiness
Cold: USDA 8 to 11
Heat: AHS 12 to 1
Source B&D Dahlias
www.bddahlias.com
206-824-6281

try these
Pink 'Normandy Bright Day' (in photo)
Bright orange 'Bodacious'
White-splashed purple 'Ryn Fou'

Angel's trumpet
***Brugmansia* spp.**

Angel's trumpet is a fast-growing tender perennial with woody stems and dramatic trumpet-shaped flowers. The fragrant blooms attract moths, butterflies and hummingbirds. If you grow this big plant in a container, be sure it's at least 14 inches in diameter. (That's 'Dr. Seuss' in the pot above.)

Keep the soil moist and feed the plant with a general-purpose fertilizer every two weeks while it's actively growing. In zones 7 and colder, bring plants inside before the first frost. Store in a cool (40 to 50 degrees), dark place and water just enough to keep the soil from drying out. In spring, move outdoors and resume normal watering and feeding.

Type Tender perennial
Size 5 to 15 ft. tall, 5 to 8 ft. wide
Blooms 12-in. white, yellow or pink, summer to fall
Light Sun to part shade
Hardiness
Cold: USDA 8 to 11
Heat: AHS 12 to 1
Source Logee's Tropical Plants
www.logees.com
888-330-8038

try these
Yellow-flowered 'Dr. Seuss' (in photo)
Ruffled-edge, deep pink 'Ecuador Pink'
White 'Super Nova'

Blood lily
Scadoxus multiflorus

Each bulb of this unusual plant produces one fluffy red flower (which is really a single umbel made up of hundreds of flowers) that lasts for about two weeks in summer. Sometimes two or three leaves unfurl from the base of the flower stem as the buds open. But more often the foliage appears later.

Because blood lily flowers best when it's rootbound, it's usually grown in containers. For one bulb, use a 6- to 8-inch-diameter pot; for three bulbs, a 12-inch pot.

Where it's not hardy, cut back the foliage in late fall, store the pot in a cool, dark place and do not water. In spring, put it in a sunny spot and resume watering.

Type Bulb
Size 12 to 18 in. tall, 9 to 15 in. wide
Blooms 6- to 8-in.-diameter red umbel in summer
Light Sun to part shade
Hardiness
Cold: USDA 8 to 11
Heat: AHS 11 to 1
Source McClure & Zimmerman
www.mzbulbspring.com
800-546-4053

handy tip
Wear gloves when planting or cutting back blood lily, as the sap can irritate your skin.

top big blooms *continued*

Hardy hibiscus
Hibiscus moscheutos

If you're looking for an easy-to-grow plant with huge flowers, look at hardy hibiscus. There are dozens of hybrids that range in size from 2 to 12 feet tall.

Most of them produce gigantic colorful blooms in mid- to late summer, with more sporadic flowers until frost. Though each bloom lasts just one day, plants are covered with so many buds that there are always flowers. At 3 to 4 feet tall, 'Strawberry Swirl', above, is a shorter one with 10-inch-diameter pink and white flowers.

Hardy hibiscus doesn't need any special care or have many pest problems. Even the tall ones don't require staking.

Type Perennial
Size 2 to 12 ft. tall, 2 to 4 ft. wide
Blooms 8- to 12-in.-diameter white, pink, red or purple midsummer to frost
Light Full sun to part shade
Hardiness
 Cold: USDA 4 to 10
 Heat: AHS 10 to 1
Source Local garden centers

try these
Pink and white-flowered
 'Strawberry Swirl' (in photo) (also sold as 'Strawberries and Cream')
Fiery red 'Fireball'
White 'Blue River II'

Volcano® Pink with Red Eye garden phlox
Phlox 'Barthirtyfour'

Not all phlox are giants, but this one has unusually huge, dome-shaped panicles of flowers. With its compact, bushy habit, it provides loads of color in the garden. Fragrant, butterfly-attracting blooms open from midsummer to early fall — deadhead the faded flowers for the maximum bloom period. Simply cut the entire plant back by one-third after the first flush of blooms. That will encourage fresh growth and more flowers, though the blooms will be smaller later in the season.

This cultivar is very resistant to powdery mildew, which plagues most garden phlox.

Type Perennial
Size 20 to 30 in. tall, 24 to 30 in. wide
Blooms 6- to 8-in.-diameter pink with red eye midsummer to early fall
Light Sun to part shade
Hardiness
 Cold: USDA 4 to 9
 Heat: AHS 9 to 1
Source Local garden centers

bigger blooms
Give the plant consistently moist to wet soil and dig and divide it every two to three years in early spring.

Pacific Hybrids delphinium
Delphinium hybrids

If the sight of stately spikes appeals to you, take a look at delphiniums. They always call attention to themselves and add vertical accents to any border.

Lots of species and hybrids of delphinium are available, but the biggest and showiest are the Pacific Hybrids in the photo above. Masses of 3-inch flowers crowd the long spires. Flower colors range from blue to pink and purple to white.

Delphiniums can stand a little shade during the hottest part of the day, and even appreciate it in zone 7. But full sun will give you bigger blooms. It's best to stake the plant to keep it upright in wind and heavy rain.

Type Perennial
Size 24 to 60 in. tall, 14 to 18 in. wide
Blooms 12- to 18-in. spikes of blue, pink, purple, lavender or white in early summer
Light Sun to part shade
Hardiness
 Cold: USDA 3 to 7
 Heat: AHS 7 to 1
Source Bluestone Perennials
 www.bluestoneperennials.com
 800-852-5243

bigger blooms
Mix organic matter into the soil before you plant and topdress with 2 in. of compost each spring.

Foxtail lily
Eremurus spp.

"Fuzzy exclamation point" is an apt description for this towering perennial. In late spring to early summer, a tall, leafless flower stem emerges from a clump of grasslike foliage. 'Orange Marmalade', above, has 2- to 3-foot flower spikes!

Starting at the base of the stalk and working up, tiny starlike flowers open over the course of a few weeks. Older flowers at the base of the cluster fade even as the higher ones open. Brush away the faded flowers for a tidier look. After all the flowers finish, the leaves die back to the crown.

Foxtail lily flowers look great and last a long time in bouquets, if you can bear to cut them (or even find a big enough vase!).

Type Perennial
Size 2 to 10 ft. tall, 18 to 24 in. wide
Blooms 18- to 48-in. spikes of yellow, orange, pink or white late spring to early summer
Light Part sun
Hardiness
 Cold: USDA 5 to 8
 Heat: AHS 8 to 1
Source Brent and Becky's Bulbs
 www.brentandbeckysbulbs.com
 877-661-2852

try these
Orange-flowered
 'Orange Marmalade' (in photo)
White-flowered *Eremurus himalaicus*

top big blooms continued

Panicle hydrangea
Hydrangea paniculata

It's good that hydrangeas are sturdy shrubs. They need to hold up all of the large fluffy blooms. Those conical white or chartreuse summer flowers (which make great cut flowers) take on a pink tint in fall. Eventually, they turn a papery brown.

At 6 to 8 feet tall, 'Limelight', above, is more compact than many panicle hydrangeas. But if you want to keep it even smaller, prune it back in late winter or early spring This results in bigger flowers in summer, as well! It blooms on the current season's growth, so you don't have to worry about cutting off the flowers or losing blooms due to a late-spring freeze.

PHOTO: Eric Flynn (Hydrangea and inset)

Type Shrub
Size 3 to 25 ft. tall, 8 to 16 ft. wide
Blooms 6- to 12-in. panicles of white in summer
Light Sun to part shade
Hardiness
  Cold: USDA 3 to 9
  Heat: AHS 9 to 1
Source Klehm's Song Sparrow Farm and Nursery
  www.songsparrow.com
  800-553-3715

try these
6 to 8 ft. 'Limelight' (in photo)
Dwarf, 3 to 4 ft. 'Pee Wee'
Up to 25 ft. tall 'Grandiflora'

Annual sunflower
Helianthus annuus

Nothing says "summer" like a cheery sunflower! And, thanks to lots of cultivars, you can get those big blooms on plants in a range of sizes. Back-of-the-border beauty 'Russian Giant', with 12-inch-diameter flowers, grows to an impressive 10 feet tall. 'Sunspot', in the photo above, has flowers that are 10 inches across, but stays a compact 2 feet tall.

Sunflowers are easy to grow from seed in the garden, and will bloom in 60 to 90 days. The flowers last for weeks, and of course, the resulting seeds will be a tasty treat for birds visiting your garden.

Type Annual
Size 1 to 15 ft. tall, 2 ft. wide
Blooms 6- to 12-in.-diameter golden yellow to coppery red in summer
Light Full sun to part shade
Hardiness
  Cold: Annual
  Heat: AHS 12 to 1
Source Thompson & Morgan
  www.tmseeds.com
  800-274-7333

try these
Single, 2-ft.-tall 'Sunspot' (in photo)
Towering, 10-ft.-tall 'Russian Giant'
Orange and red 'Harlequin'

DESIGNING WITH BIG FLOWERS

You might think that large flowers and plants should only be used in big gardens. But actually, gardens of all sizes need the size contrasts and vertical interest big flowers and plants offer. Here are a few tips for working big flowers into any garden space. See how I've applied them to the 9-by-12-foot corner bed below.

SELECT YOUR SHAPES Large flowers automatically stand out, but are accentuated even more when you surround them with small, finer-textured plants and flowers. The different textures of the plants help each one to stand out, rather than blend together.

Does your garden look dull with too many daisy-shaped blooms? Jazz it up by adding globe-shaped flowers, like the blood lily, or spikes, such as the delphinium flowers. The larger the globes or spikes, the greater the impact they'll make.

COLOR EFFECTS Maximize the impact of large flowers by choosing hot colors like red or orange that really show up in the landscape. If your garden is bigger than 10 or 12 ft. long, plant a group of three or five of them. On the other hand, if you want your large flowers to blend into the background more, choose ones in the blue or purple color range, such as the clematis growing on the fence.

Place plants with big flowers that bloom at different times of the season around the garden. During the year the focal point will "move" from one spot to another. These delphiniums were the focus of the garden in early summer.

Not all large flowers come on large plants. A compact grower in a pot won't get lost when you place it in your border.

THE GARDEN'S PALETTE

Code	Plant Name	No. to Plant	Blooms	Type	Cold/Heat Zones	Height/Width	Special Features
A	Hardy hibiscus *Hibiscus moscheutos* 'Fireball'	1	Red; midsummer	Perennial	4-9/9-1	4-5 ft./ 2-3 ft.	Deeply cut foliage; plant may die to the ground in winter; cut old canes to the ground in early spring
B	Clematis *Clematis* 'Louise Rowe'	1	Pale blue; early to midsummer	Perennial vine	4-9/9-1	6-8 ft.	Blooms on both old and new wood, with single, semi-double and double flowers on plant at the same time
C	Delphinium *Delphinium* 'Blue Bird'	3	Blue; early summer	Perennial	3-7/7-1	3-4 ft./ 14-18 in.	Blue flower with white "bee" or center; very mildew resistant; stake flowers to protect from wind
D	Blanket flower *Gaillardia xgrandiflora* 'Dazzler'	3	Orange; summer to fall	Perennial	3-9/9-1	24-30 in./ 18 in.	Orange and yellow blooms make good cut flowers; heat- and drought-tolerant; deadhead to prolong bloom
E	Geranium *Geranium* 'Rozanne' ('Gerwat')	6	Blue; early summer	Perennial	4-8/8-1	12-18 in./ 12-18 in.	Blue flowers with white center dot attract butterflies; shear back by half in summer to rejuvenate plant
F	Blood lily (in container) *Scadoxus multiflorus*	2	Red; summer	Bulb	8-11/11-1	12-18 in./ 9-15 in.	Looks best in groups of at least two or three; all parts are toxic if eaten
G	Coneflower *Echinacea purpurea* 'White Swan'	5	White; summer	Perennial	3-9/9-1	24-36 in./ 18-24 in.	White blooms have copper-orange center; heat- and drought-tolerant; leave seedheads to feed birds in winter
H	Black-eyed Susan *Rudbeckia hirta* 'Prairie Sun'	4	Orange/yellow; summer to fall	Perennial	3-8/8-1	30-36 in./ 18-24 in.	Flowers have orange petals with yellow tips and green centers; leaves and stems covered with short bristles

Readers' Favorite Cut Flowers

Growing cut flower gardens

- Put the bed in a sunny spot and amend the soil before you plant.
- For easy care and harvesting, plant in rows that are 3 to 4 ft. apart.
- Grow taller plants to the north of shorter ones, so they don't shade them out.
- Group plants according to their bloom time to simplify harvesting. This also makes it easier to tear out early blooming annual plants and replace them with summer bloomers.

I've always loved cut flowers. To me, cutting the freshest and most perfect blooms from the garden and arranging them in a vase ranks right up there with seeing a border in full bloom. And from the looks of it, our readers feel the same way. When we asked you for your favorite cut flowers, you responded with a wide assortment of plants, and several rose to the top.

Some of you also told us that, while you like cut flower arrangements, you hesitate to cut the blooms in your own garden. Maybe you're afraid to sacrifice them or you just don't think you have the right type of flowers. But there are lots of good reasons to cut the flowers in your garden.

BARGAIN BOUQUETS If you're…ahem… "thrifty" like me, the cost of big arrangements from the florist shop is more than you want to pay, except for special occasions. On the other hand, cutting flowers from your own garden is "dirt cheap," and definitely won't break your budget. And don't be afraid that you won't have any flowers left outside. Just cut a few choice blooms from different beds and fill in with annuals or foliage and twigs. It's a great opportunity to include things that the local flower shop doesn't carry.

LONGER FLOWER LIFE In the garden your flowers are baked by the sun and buffeted by wind and rain. Have you ever waited patiently for your prized peonies to open, only to have them land in the mud after a sudden downpour? Even in perfect weather, winged critters are always visiting. And once flowers are pollinated, their job is done and they quickly fade. Blooms cut and living safely in your house sometimes last even longer than they do in garden conditions.

GOOD FOR THE PLANTS Are you afraid you'll hurt your plants if you cut off the flowers? Don't worry. Most plants bloom *more* if you cut the flowers because they use the energy they would have used for producing seeds for making and opening more buds. Plus, getting up close to your plants is a good way to keep an eye out for pest or disease problems. That way, you can take care of them before they get out of hand.

When I want to create a bouquet, I usually just go out in the garden and cut whatever is looking good right then. But you can also plant special beds with flowers just for cutting to ensure a large and constant supply of flowers. Check out "Growing cut flower gardens" at left for tips on growing flowers in dedicated cutting gardens.

FLOWERING FAVORITES Unfortunately, I couldn't fit all of our readers' favorite flowers into this story. But on the next pages, I'll share eight of them, in order of their bloom time. And later, I'll talk about how to harvest flowers and the special treatment that some plants need for the longest vase life, along with other tips for creating beautiful bouquets. □

— *Deborah Gruca*

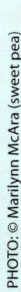

Daffodil
***Narcissus* hybrids**

Daffodils make great cut flowers, but the large cup, small cup and double types last longest in a vase. 'Pink Charm', above, is a large cup midspring bloomer that stands 14 to 16 inches tall.

Cut daffodils just as the buds start to show color. (They don't rebloom after they're cut — so plant plenty.) To stiffen the stems, recut at least ¼ inch off the ends, wrap them up to the buds in newspaper secured with a rubber band and place them in warm water for two hours. The cut stems bleed a sap that's toxic to other flowers, so keep daffodils in a vase by themselves or wait at least 24 hours before adding them to a mixed bouquet.

Type Bulb
Size 4 to 24 in. tall, 4 to 12 in. wide
Bloom White, yellow, salmon, orange or bicolored in spring
Soil Moist, humus-rich, well-drained
Light Full sun
Hardiness
  Cold: USDA zones 3 to 9
  Heat: AHS zones 9 to 1
Scent Slight to very sweet
Vase life 4 to 8 days
Source
  Brent and Becky's Bulbs
  www.brentandbeckys bulbs.com
  877-661-2852 (bulbs)

Sweet pea
Lathyrus odoratus

The sweet-scented flowers of this climbing annual come in a range of colors. Soak the seeds overnight and plant them in full sun in soil with plenty of compost mixed in. Grow them on a support, such as a bamboo trellis.

Sweet peas do best in cool weather. Where the ground doesn't freeze in winter and the summers are hot, plant the seeds in fall. In gardens with moderate to cold winters and hot, sometimes early summers, plant as early in spring as the soil can be easily worked.

Cut the flowers anywhere along the stem when half the florets are open. The floppy stems make great filler flowers in cut arrangements.

Type Annual
Size 3 to 8 ft. tall, 2 to 3 ft. wide
Bloom White, cream, pink, purple, red or orange in spring to summer
Soil Moist, well-drained, humusy
Light Full sun to light shade
Hardiness
  Cold: Annual
  Heat: AHS zones 8 to 1
Scent Sweet
Vase life 3 to 7 days
Source
  Renee's Garden
  www.reneesgarden.com
  888-880-7228 (seeds)

top cut flowers *continued*

Shrub rose
Rosa hybrids

It's not hard to see why the all-time reader favorite cut flowers are roses. Shrub roses look (and smell!) beautiful in vases. They bloom on and off all summer and don't need special pruning, making them easy to grow. A little slow-release fertilizer in spring and biweekly feedings of liquid fertilizer until midsummer keep the flowers coming. 'Bonica', above, is covered with clusters of 3-inch double pink flowers that have a light apple scent. And branching flowers like this help hold the other stems in place in an arrangement. Cut stems when the outer petals start to open, and snip off the thorns to make it easier to arrange the flowers.

Type Shrub
Size 2 to 5 ft. tall and wide
Bloom All colors but blue and purple in early summer to fall
Soil Moist, well-drained
Light Full sun
Hardiness
Cold: USDA zones 3 to 9
Heat: AHS zones 9 to 1
Scent Many are fragrant to very fragrant
Vase life
3 to 7 days
Source
Regan Nursery
www.regannursery.com
800-249-4680
(bare-root plants)

Peruvian lily
Alstroemeria hybrids

Peruvian lilies are a popular cut flower because they easily last for two weeks in a vase. Also, they come in a wide array of beautiful colors and patterns. That's Peachy Orange from the Pacific Sunset™ series above.

Most Peruvian lilies are cold-hardy to zone 8, but yellow Peruvian lily (*A. aurea*) is reliably hardy to zone 7, and 'Sweet Laura' to zone 5. If it isn't hardy for you, simply treat the plant as an annual.

Cutting Peruvian lily at the base of the stems just as the buds begin to open encourages the plant to bloom more.

Type Bulb
Size 12 to 48 in. tall, 18 to 36 in. wide
Bloom Yellow, orange, pink, red, mauve, lavender or cream in summer
Soil Rich, well-drained
Light Sun to part shade
Hardiness
Cold: USDA zones 5 to 10
Heat: AHS zones 12 to 1
Scent A few are sweet
Vase life
7 to 14 days
Source
Edelweiss Perennials
www.edelweiss
perennials.com
503-263-4680 (4-in. pots and bare-root plants)

PHOTO: © Missouri Botanical Garden, John Smelser (shrub rose)

Lisianthus
Eustoma grandiflorum

Lisianthus buds and flowers resemble roses, but last longer in the vase. Buds form in clusters, with the lower ones opening first. The bloom time for a single stalk, from the first to the last bud, can last up to four weeks! Eight- to 10-inch-tall 'Florida Blue Sky', above, produces double blue flowers.

Whether they're single or double, lisianthus flowers make great accents in arrangements. Cut the stems above the basal foliage when the first buds are open (the plant won't produce more flowering stems). Also, for the longest vase life, add ¼ cup of sugar to each quart of water along with the preservative.

Type Tender perennial (can be grown as an annual)
Size 6 to 36 in. tall, 6 to 8 in. wide
Bloom Pink, blue, purple, white, yellow and bicolors in summer to fall
Soil Well-drained, neutral to alkaline
Light Full sun to part shade
Hardiness
　Cold: USDA zones 8 to 10
　Heat: AHS zones 12 to 1
Scent None
Vase life 2 to 4 weeks
Source Buy started plants at local garden centers

Dahlia
Dahlia hybrids

Dahlias are colorful additions to any bouquet. That's 4- to 5-inch pink 'Rembrandt' and orange 'Art Deco' above. Both stay 12 to 20 inches tall.

Plant tubers in spring horizontally in the soil 4 to 6 inches deep and 18 to 24 inches apart. Don't water until you see growth emerge from the soil, as the tubers are prone to rot with too much moisture.

Pinch the tallest stems back when the plants are 8 inches tall for shorter, stronger stems. Stake dahlias that grow more than 3 feet tall. Feed with a low-nitrogen fertilizer, such as 5-10-10.

Grow dahlias as annuals or dig and store the tubers in fall.

Type Tuber
Size 12 to 72 in. tall, 12 to 36 in. wide
Bloom All colors but blue in midsummer to fall
Soil Moist, well-drained
Light Full sun to part shade
Hardiness
　Cold: USDA zones 7 to 11
　Heat: AHS zones 12 to 1
Scent None
Vase life 5 to 7 days
Source J. W. Jung Seed
www.jungseed.com
800-297-3123 (tubers)

DESIGN: Tom Bolkowski & Adam Levine (dahlia)

top cut flowers *continued*

Spanish lavender
Lavandula stoechas

Like most lavenders, Spanish lavender prefers full sun and regular moisture, but it absolutely requires well-drained soil. Damp soil or clay causes the roots to rot. In fact, don't even use organic mulch, just top the soil with grit or oyster shells around the crown. In zones 7 and colder, grow lavender in containers or treat them as annuals.

Both the foliage and the flowers are fragrant, and can be used for fresh or dried arrangements. For longest vase life, cut at the base of the stem right after the flower spikes start to open and split the lowest ¼ inch. To dry, cut as they start to bloom and hang them in a cool, dark room for two weeks.

Type	Perennial
Size	1 to 4 ft. tall, 1 to 5 ft. wide
Bloom	Purple or white in summer
Soil	Extremely well-drained
Light	Full sun
Hardiness	Cold: USDA zones 8 to 11 Heat: AHS zones 12 to 1
Scent	Fragrant flowers and leaves
Vase life	7 to 14 days
Source	You can buy potted plants at local garden centers

Japanese anemone
Anemone hybrids

This easy-to-grow perennial prefers full sun in areas with cool summers, with a little shade during the heat of the day in hot-summer areas. The plant has nearly no disease or pest problems, but must stay relatively dry during winter, so the rhizomes don't rot. (Check before planting; it can be invasive in some areas.)

'Honorine Jobert', above, grows 3 to 4 feet tall and rarely needs staking. Fat buds open to single white blooms on graceful stems.

Just before the buds open, cut the stems above a set of leaves — cutting encourages more flowers on the stem to open. Tuck them into a bouquet for pink or white accents.

Type	Perennial
Size	2 to 5 ft. tall, 1 to 3 ft. wide
Bloom	White or pink in fall
Soil	Moist, well-drained
Light	Full sun to part shade
Hardiness	Cold: USDA zones 4 to 8 Heat: AHS zones 8 to 1
Scent	None
Vase life	4 to 7 days
Source	You can buy potted plants at local garden centers

MAKING ARRANGEMENTS

How to make a bouquet last

- Harvest flowers when it's cool — in early morning, after the dew has dried.
- As the buds open, cut the stems at an angle for the largest surface area and remove the foliage that will be under water so it won't rot.
- Place the stems in a clean container of water and keep them out of direct sun.
- Inside, recut an inch off the stems under water (to keep air bubbles from blocking the stems). Place stems in 100- to 110-degree water (you can easily hold your finger in water this temperature for several seconds) with floral preservative powder (or the homemade recipe below) mixed in.
- Let flowers stand at room temperature for one to two hours to absorb water before arranging.
- Every few days, replace the vase water and preservative and recut the stems under water.
- Some stems absorb water better with special treatment: sear the ends of sap-oozing stems with a flame; smash the ends of woody stems, and fill hollow stems with water, holding it in until you plunge it into the vase.

1 Foliage
2 Spikes
3 Structure
4 Nontraditional flowers

Don't forget to cut

When it comes to cutting, almost anything goes. Here are a few you may not have thought of:

1. **Hosta** *Hosta* 'Paul's Glory' Perennial; part to full shade; 18 in. tall, 24 in. wide; cold-hardy in USDA zones 3 to 9, heat-tolerant in AHS zones 9 to 1
   Tuck stems around other flowers to help soften the vase edge.

2. **Maiden grass** *Miscanthus sinensis* 'Morning Light' Perennial; full sun to part shade; 4 to 6 ft. tall, 3 to 5 ft. wide; cold-hardy in USDA zones 5 to 9, heat-tolerant in AHS zones 9 to 1
   Cut the stem after the flower has opened; can be used fresh or dried.

3. **Curly willow** *Salix avellana* 'Contorta' Shrub; full sun to part shade; 8 to 10 ft. tall, 6 to 10 ft. wide; cold-hardy in USDA zones 4 to 8, heat-tolerant in AHS zones 8 to 1
   Remove the leaves to reveal the interesting twisted stems.

4. **Flowering kale** *Brassica oleracea* Tender perennial; full sun; 12 to 18 in. tall, 12 to 18 in. wide; cold-hardy in USDA zones 7 to 11, heat-tolerant in AHS zones 12 to 1
   Cut at the base of the stem and choose a heavy vase.

Vase basics

Design a flower arrangement like a pro — here's how!

1 Build a framework Use four or five sturdy stems in the vase to build a "framework" to help hold up the other stems and to create the main shape of the arrangement.

Good choices
- Purple coneflower
- Daisy
- Gladiolus
- Zinnia

2 Place a few focal points Cut the stems of large or showy flowers so the blooms sit lower in the arrangement, evenly spaced. You want these blooms to draw your eye toward the center of the bouquet.

Good choices
- Dahlia
- Lily
- Sunflower

3 Add several accent flowers Tuck them in among the other flowers, setting some back into the arrangement slightly to give it more interest and depth.

Good choices
- Alstroemeria
- Lisianthus
- Cosmos
- Lavender

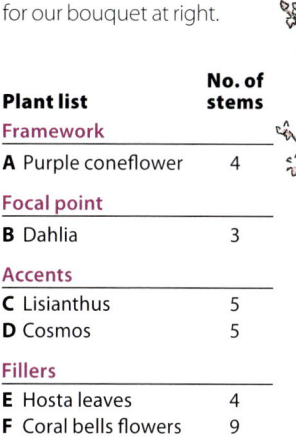

4 Finish with fillers Use foliage, airy flowers or other materials. We used coral bell flowers, hosta leaves and cinnamon ferns for our bouquet at right.

Plant list	No. of stems
Framework	
A Purple coneflower	4
Focal point	
B Dahlia	3
Accents	
C Lisianthus	5
D Cosmos	5
Fillers	
E Hosta leaves	4
F Coral bells flowers	9
G Cinnamon fern	3

Web extra See 3 more great *bouquet recipes.*

Do preservatives really work?

Yes! They can help cut flowers last several days longer than they would in plain water. Commercially made powders deter bacterial and mold growth, provide sucrose to feed the flowers, and acidify the water (which helps stems take up more water). You can buy the powder in packets from most florist shops or in jars from floral supply Web sites. For an occasional bouquet, mix up your own preservative:

Recipe
- 2 Tbsp. fresh lemon juice
- 1 Tbsp. sugar
- ½ tsp. household chlorine bleach
- 1 qt. warm water

Long-Blooming Perennials

We all want that dream perennial that starts to bloom in spring and carries on all summer. It should look good at least until it gets knocked out by cold weather, right? OK, I know for most of us there just isn't such a perennial. But there are lots of them that bloom for a month or more. Let me introduce you to 11 of them.

CHOOSE THE BEST PLANTS Many of the plants you'll see here are named cultivars of long-blooming species. I've chosen them because I like one of their special traits, such as a unique color or a compact habit. I'll also introduce you to other long-blooming members in the same family in "Try these" at the end of some of the profiles.

Most of these long-blooming perennials will bloom best if you pick off the spent flowers. I'll tell you the best way to do this and share more tips, too.

CHANGE IS GOOD A flower bed that evolves with the seasons is more interesting than one that looks the same from spring through fall or year after year. Combining long-blooming perennials with other flowers that drift in and out of bloom means you'll have a different view to enjoy every week. That's why with many of the descriptions here I'll include a few other plants that make good companions. You'll find them listed in "Looks great with" at the bottom of the profile. So let's start in spring with a bleeding heart, and progress through the seasons. ◻

— *Jim Childs*

Bloom time bar In each profile you'll find a key to help you determine when and how long each plant blooms. Where the color bar's white, there are no blooms. The darker the bar, the more blooms, gradually decreasing back to no flowers.

Fernleaf bleeding heart
Dicentra eximia **and hybrids**

Most fernleaf cultivars bloom all summer with some shade and plenty of moisture. 'King of Hearts' in the photo above is one of the most heat-tolerant cultivars. But it'll still perform best in moist soil and shade. Let any of the cultivars get too dry, and they'll go dormant. To keep fernleaf bleeding hearts blooming their best, remove stems as the spent flowers begin to fade. Use a pair of scissors and snip the entire stem off even with the foliage. This may seem tedious, but you don't need to do it very often, just every couple of weeks.

Blooms Pink or white hearts
Light Part shade to shade
Size 12 to 24 in. tall and wide
Hardiness
  Cold: USDA zones 3 to 9
  Heat: AHS zones 9 to 1
Source Great Garden Plants
  www.greatgarden
  plants.com
  877-447-4769

looks **great with**

Create texture contrast with these bolder-foliaged perennials.
Hosta *Hosta* spp.
Lungwort *Pulmonaria* spp.

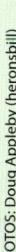

Heronsbill
Erodium pelargoniiflorum

Also known as "stork's bill," heronsbill is a long-blooming perennial. And even cultivars, such as 'Sweetheart' in the photo above, are easy to grow from seed, often blooming the first year. Seeds started indoors in fall will bloom the following spring and again in fall. Or start seeds in late winter and they'll bloom by autumn.

Pick off the dead flowers to keep this plant blooming its longest. Bend the spent stalks back to break them off as you would an annual geranium flower.

Grow heronsbill as a ground cover in a small area. Even when it's not in bloom the fuzzy foliage looks great. And deer won't eat it, either.

Blooms White with plum-purple splashes
Light Full sun to part shade
Size 10 to 12 in. tall, 18 to 24 in. wide
Hardiness
Cold: USDA zones 7 to 9
Heat: AHS zones 12 to 1
Source Park Seed
www.parkseed.com
800-213-0076

looks great with
These plants are drought-tolerant and also grow best in full sun.
Lamb's ear *Stachys byzantina*
Moss rose *Portulaca grandiflora*
Sedum *Sedum* spp.

Perennial geranium
***Geranium* Rozanne ('Gerwat')**

There are lots of perennial geraniums, but once Rozanne's 2½-inch-diameter flowers start blooming in late spring, they won't stop until fall. And this hybrid holds up better in the heat than many of its relatives. Even so, if it gets too dry or the mound of foliage looks ragged, shear all of the stems back to 3 inches. It'll quickly regrow and start blooming again in just a few weeks. As cool fall temperatures arrive, the foliage turns red-brown until it goes dormant for winter.

Grow Rozanne near the middle of the border. And because of the long bloom period, it's even great in containers, too.

Blooms Violet-blue with white centers
Light Full sun to part shade
Size 18 to 20 in. tall, 18 to 36 in. wide
Hardiness
Cold: USDA zones 4 to 8
Heat: AHS zones 8 to 1
Source W. Atlee Burpee & Co.
www.burpee.com
800-333-5808

try these
Pale-pink flowers *G. sanguineum striatum*
Rosy-pink flowers *G.* 'Orkney Cherry'
Deep-violet flowers *G.* 'Nimbus'

top long-blooming perennials *continued*

Spiderwort
***Tradescantia* hybrids**

Each flower lasts just one day, but there are loads of buds clustered at the top of each spiderwort stalk. Once a cluster is finished, cut it off to prolong the season of bloom. And since spiderwort can reseed, deadheading helps prevent it coming up in spots where you don't want it. You can cut off just the spent head if you like. Or follow the stem into the foliage and cut it near the base. New stems may bloom again, but don't expect the same quantities of flowers that you get in late spring and summer.

'Sweet Kate' spiderwort in this photo gives you lots of flowers *and* colorful gold foliage. At only 12 to 15 inches, it's also shorter than many cultivars.

Blooms Shades of purple, pink or white flowers
Light Part shade
Size 12 to 24 in. tall, 12 to 18 in. wide
Hardiness
　Cold: USDA zones 4 to 9
　Heat: AHS zones 9 to 1
Source Brent and Becky's Bulbs
　www.brentandbeckys bulbs.com
　877-661-2852

try these
White flowers 'Innocence'
Dwarf — only 8 in. tall 'Little Doll'

Little winecups
Callirhoe involucrata

Got a difficult sunny spot where nothing really thrives? Little winecups loves the heat and, once established, tolerates dry soil, too. Let its loose mat of leaves and flowers sprawl across the ground, in a rock garden or on a slope, or even cascade over a sunny wall.

Little winecups will reseed — not aggressively, but it will spread. Unlike some spreading plants, roots won't form where the stem touches the ground. All of the stems originate in the center of the plant, joined to a large taproot. But that root system makes it difficult to move or divide an old plant. So if you want to move a few plants, look for some of the seedlings.

Blooms 1- to 2-in.-wide wine-red to magenta flowers with a white eye
Light Full sun
Size 6 to 12 in. tall, 24 to 30 in. wide
Hardiness
　Cold: USDA zones 4 to 9
　Heat: AHS zones 9 to 1
Source High Country Gardens
　www.highcountry gardens.com
　800-925-9387

looks great with
Pair them with other perennials that tolerate hot, dry conditions.

Blue fescue *Festuca glauca* 'Elijah Blue'

Silvermound artemisia *Artemisia schmidtiana*

PHOTOS: Steven Nordmeyer (spiderwort); © Charles Mann (little winecups)

100　*the* YEAR IN GARDENING　　www.GardenGateMagazine.com

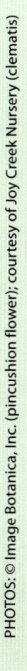

Pincushion flower
Scabiosa columbaria

Want to attract butterflies and hummingbirds? Plant pincushion flowers in your flower beds. Or try a few in your mixed containers. 'Harlequin Blue', in the photo above, is more compact and has foliage that is more finely divided than many cultivars. And the flowers stand up better, too.

Keep pincushion flowers deadheaded to make sure the blooms don't stop. Snip the stems back into the mound of foliage if you can.

As you're planting this perennial, no matter what the catalog or tag tells you, crowd the plants. The flowers will show best if you set several plants in a tight grouping, 8 to 10 inches apart.

spring summer fall

Blooms Lavender, pink or yellow pincushions
Light Full sun
Size 12 to 24 in. tall, 12 to 18 in. wide
Hardiness
Cold: USDA zones 3 to 8
Heat: AHS zones 8 to 1
Source Local garden centers

try these
Soft pink blooms *Scabiosa columbaria* 'Pincushion Pink'
Yellow flowers *Scabiosa columbaria ochroleuca*

Clematis
Clematis 'Rooguchi'

Clematis vines usually have leaves that will grip onto a trellis and climb their way to the top. This cultivar will need some help. But it'll be worth the time it takes to fasten it with some strips of fabric or twine. Once 'Rooguchi' starts blooming in early summer, it'll be going almost until frost.

The flowers are blue-purple, but may be paler in all-day sun, and darker with cool afternoon shade. Even the stems can have a purple-black tint. This clematis cultivar is in pruning group 3: It flowers on new growth, so each spring you can cut it down to within a foot of the ground. Or, at least trim it back to where you see new growth starting.

spring summer fall

Blooms Fragrant 2-in. blue-purple bells
Light Full sun to part shade
Size 6 to 9 ft. tall vine
Hardiness
Cold: USDA zones 3 to 9
Heat: AHS zones 9 to 1
Source Garden Crossings
www.gardencrossings.com
616-875-6355

try these
Deep-red flowers *C.* 'Niobe'
Lavender flowers *C.* Cezanne™ ('Evipo023')

top long-blooming perennials *continued*

Knautia
Knautia macedonica

If you grow lots of flowers, odds are you'll want to pick a few to bring indoors or share with a friend. Knautia makes a long-lasting cut flower. Plus, keeping the blooms picked makes room for more flowers. So even if you don't cut them to enjoy indoors, deadhead by cutting the spent flower stems down to the low mound of foliage. And make sure the soil is well-drained, especially during the winter: Knautias don't like wet feet or they'll rot.

Grow 'Mars Midget', the cultivar in the photo above, near the front of the border. It's a dwarf cultivar that will only grow 12 to 18 inches tall and wide.

spring — summer — fall

Blooms 2-in.-diameter ruby-red pincushions
Light Full sun
Size 12 to 24 in. tall and wide
Hardiness
Cold: USDA zones 5 to 9
Heat: AHS zones 9 to 1
Source Bluestone Perennials
www.bluestoneperennials.com
800-852-5243

looks **great with**

Highlight red flowers against gray foliage.
Artemisia *A. ludoviciana* 'Valerie Finnis'
Silver sage *Salvia argentea*

Red yucca
Hesperaloe parviflora

Arching spikes of narrow evergreen foliage give this perennial its Southwestern look. But the flower stalks that stretch in spring and bloom all summer are what will hold your interest. So will the hummingbirds that come to visit these colorful long-lasting flower spikes.

The architectural form and tall stiff flower stems make this a good choice for a focal point. Try one as a specimen in a rock garden that has well-drained soil. Or plant one in a striking or unique container to show off both the plant and the pot. Just make sure the soil drains quickly or the roots will rot. Once established, red yucca is extremely drought-tolerant.

spring — summer — fall

Blooms Shades of red
Light Full sun
Size 3 to 5 ft. tall, 3 to 4 ft. wide
Hardiness
Cold: USDA zones 6 to 11
Heat: AHS zones 11 to 1
Source Niche Gardens
www.nichegardens.com
919-967-0078

looks **great with**

Drought-tolerant and colorful perennials make good companions.
Chocolate flower *Berlandiera lyrata*
Blanketflower *Gaillardia* hybrids

102 *the* YEAR IN GARDENING www.GardenGateMagazine.com

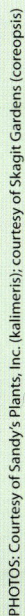

Kalimeris
Kalimeris pinnatifida

If you like baby's breath, you'll also like kalimeris. Sometimes called "false aster" or "double Japanese aster," the white flowers are a bit larger than those of baby's breath. But the plant has the same billowing habit that's terrific for visually knitting together neighboring clumps of perennials. And just like baby's breath, it's a good filler in cut flower bouquets, too.

Clumps spread slowly to form colonies, but kalimeris is not invasive. When it grows too far afield, dig a few sections from the edge to share with friends. And this insect-resistant and reliable perennial rarely needs to be staked — a plus for any busy gardener!

spring summer fall

Blooms 1-in.-diameter white
Light Full sun
Size 2 to 3 ft. tall and wide
Hardiness
   Cold: USDA zones 4 to 9
   Heat: AHS zones 9 to 1
Source Plant Delights Nursery, Inc.
   www.plantdelights.com
   919-772-4794

looks great with
Pair kalimeris with different shapes.
Daylily *Hemerocallis* hybrids (trumpets)
Blazing star *Liatris* spp. (spikes)
Garden phlox *Phlox paniculata* (round)

Coreopsis
Coreopsis 'Full Moon'

If you're new to gardening and a bit unsure about growing perennials, try 'Full Moon' coreopsis. Plant it in moist, well-drained soil and full sun. The first year you'll get a respectable show. But the second year and in following years, the pest-resistant foliage will be covered with flowers.

As the flowers fade, snip off spent blooms to keep the plant tidy. But, unlike some coreopsis, this one blooms well even without deadheading. And coreopsis is a source of nectar for butterflies. Plant several in one area and butterflies will be more likely to spot the large mass of color. 'Full Moon' coreopsis is also deer-resistant.

spring summer fall

Blooms 3-in.-diameter pale canary yellow
Light Full sun
Size 24 to 32 in. tall, 24 to 28 in. wide
Hardiness
   Cold: USDA zones 5 to 9
   Heat: AHS zones 9 to 1
Source Forestfarm
   www.forestfarm.com
   541-846-7269

looks great with
Blue makes a stunning color combo with yellow flowers.
Globe thistle *Echinops ritro*
Bluebeard *Caryopteris xclandonensis*
Sea holly *Eryngium* spp.

top multiseason shade

Multiseason Showoffs

Flowers are fantastic. But why stop there? Look for plants that let you have it all! It takes a bit of effort to get a new plant established and growing strong. You don't want to throw all that work away on a plant that only looks good while it's blooming for one week. What about the foliage, the form, the texture? There's more to having a great border than just bountiful blossoms.

That's where multiseason showoffs come in. Each of the 10 plants I'll show you here has something more to offer your garden. These plants will look fantastic long after their flowers have faded (and in many cases, before they bloom, too). I'll start with shade perennials, then sun perennials and annuals and finish up with a few great woody plants.

Look for hard-working foliage (the lungwort gets better after it blooms), unique seedheads (check out the poppies on page 107) and the ability to bring in the birds (love the dogwood on page 109). Speaking of birds, there's a little more to it than just plopping a plant birds like to eat just anywhere. Check out a few additional bird-friendly design tips on page 109.

Choose one of these plants to brighten a back yard corner or combine several to create a three-season garden. You have lots of options, and none of them involves a compromise! □

— *Kristin Beane Sullivan*

Jacob's ladder
***Polemonium* spp.**

Purple-tinged, tricolored, variegated, simple green… Jacob's ladder's foliage options alone are dizzying. Add to that its attractive spring blooms, and you have a plant that has something to show off in three seasons.

There are many species and cultivars of this shade perennial. That's Brise d'Anjou ('Blanjou') in the photos above. It's cold-hardy in USDA zones 5 to 8, but many cultivars and species will survive much colder areas — even to zone 2!

Want to keep it looking its best for months? Cut the bloom stalks back to the base as soon as they finish. This will encourage a fresh new flush of foliage growth.

Type	Perennial
Blooms	Blue, pink or cream in late spring
Light	Part shade
Size	8 to 36 in. tall, 6 to 24 in. wide
Hardiness	Cold: USDA zones 2 to 8 Heat: AHS zones 8 to 1
Source	Sooner Plant Farm www.soonerplantfarm.com

why grow it?
Arching ladderlike foliage comes in many colors. And in late spring, look for delicate blue, pink or cream flowers.

104 *the* YEAR IN GARDENING   www.GardenGateMagazine.com

perennials

Lungwort
***Pulmonaria* hybrids**

Yes, lungwort's blue, pink or white spring blooms are attractive. But check out that silver-speckled foliage! It's not just a feature of 'Bertram Anderson' in the large photo above. Almost all lungworts have silver on their leaves, ranging from "freckles" to being completely covered. This silvery sheen really lights up a dark corner.

In early spring, you'll need to cut off dead foliage to show off the oncoming blooms. Just be sure to wear gloves — lungwort has prickly leaves. When the flowers finish, cut back the stems to the base. The plant will send up an attractive mound of bigger foliage like the one in the inset.

Type	Perennial
Blooms	Blue, pink or white in early spring
Light	Part to full shade
Size	6 to 12 in. tall, 15 to 40 in. wide
Hardiness	Cold: USDA zones 3 to 8 Heat: AHS zones 8 to 1
Source	Bluestone Perennials www.bluestoneperennials.com 800-852-5243

why grow it?
These pretty flowers are some of the first to appear in spring. And the foliage shows off all summer.

Solomon's seal
***Polygonatum* spp.**

Solomon's seal brings elegance to a shady garden. Tall arching wands of foliage support white, bell-shaped blooms in late spring. In late summer, the blue-black berries in the inset appear. As a bonus, *P. odoratum pluriflorum* 'Variegatum', above, even has variegated foliage.

When you bring home a new plant, it's hard to imagine that the wimpy looking stem in a 4-inch pot will spread into a gorgeous clump. But give it time and some room, and it will. The more compost in your soil, the more quickly the plant will spread.

Plant Solomon's seal in early spring so it has plenty of time to settle in before winter. Just be careful with the brittle new shoots.

Type	Perennial
Blooms	White in late spring
Light	Part to full shade
Size	8 in. to 7 ft. tall, spreading indefinitely
Hardiness	Cold: USDA zones 3 to 9 Heat: AHS zones 9 to 1
Source	Lazy S's Farm & Nursery www.lazyssfarm.com

why grow it?
Its dramatic foliage even turns yellow in fall. Plus white flowers and dark berries add to the appeal.

top multiseason sun perennials and annual

Prairie smoke
Geum triflorum

This perennial's small, pink springtime flowers have a Dr. Seuss-like charm. You can see what I mean in the photo above. And when the flowers pass, they're replaced by the fuzzy seedheads you see in the inset. It's pretty clear where the name "prairie smoke" came from. These seedheads keep this plant looking good through summer.

Be sure to choose a spot with good drainage — root rot can be an issue in wet soil. Full sun is best, but prairie smoke will tolerate part shade, too. Meet these needs and this northern native won't require much attention. In fact, it'll probably self-sow, so you'll have a nice cluster of plants in a few years.

Type Perennial
Blooms Pink in spring
Light Full sun to part shade
Size 12 to 15 in. tall, 12 in. wide
Hardiness
Cold: USDA zones 3 to 7
Heat: AHS zones 7 to 1
Source Prairie Nursery Inc.
www.prairienursery.com
800-476-9453

why **grow it?**
Pretty pink flowers in spring and charming fuzzy seedheads through summer make this hard-working native a must-have.

Wild indigo
Baptisia **spp. and hybrids**

Tall spikes of blue, purple, white or yellow (like 'Carolina Moonlight' above) blooms add lively color to your spring garden. Flowers are followed by long, green seed pods (in the inset), which ripen to black and rattle when the wind blows. Plus, this is a plant with presence, at 2 to 4 feet tall and 2 to 3 feet wide.

Wild indigo grows slowly, so buy the largest plant you can find at the garden center, and don't expect much the first year or two. But give it room, because in a few years, you'll be impressed with its stature. Leave those interesting seed pods standing in fall and winter, then cut the stems back to the ground in spring.

Type Perennial
Blooms Blue, purple, white or yellow in spring
Light Full sun
Size 2 to 4 ft. tall, 2 to 3 ft. wide
Hardiness
Cold: USDA zones 3 to 9
Heat: AHS zones 9 to 1
Source Big Dipper Farm
www.bigdipperfarm.com
360-886-8253

why **grow it?**
This is one dramatic perennial — tall flower spikes, a great habit and fascinating seed pods.

Amsonia
Amsonia tabernaemontana

There aren't too many perennials with reliable fall color, but this is one of them. After its sky-blue spring flowers fade, you'll have a sturdy clump of trouble-free, almost shrublike foliage through the summer. Then fall comes, and you can see what happens in the inset — gold!

Don't worry if you don't see any sign of your amsonia poking through the soil in spring. It's later than most perennials to emerge, but once it does, it grows quickly.

Amsonia is also slow to take off after you plant, move or divide it. So it's a good idea to put it in a spot and leave it alone if you can.

Type Perennial
Blooms Sky-blue in late spring
Light Full sun
Size 2 to 3 ft. tall and wide
Hardiness
   Cold: USDA zones 3 to 9
   Heat: AHS zones 9 to 1
Source Busse Gardens
   www.bussegardens.com
   800-544-3192

why grow it?
Pretty spring flowers, sturdy, pest-free summer foliage and gold autumn color make this a multi-talented perennial.

Peony-flowered poppy
Papaver somniferum

It's hard to find a showier flower than this. Peony-flowered poppy has huge, 4-inch-diameter powder puff blooms for three or four weeks in early summer. And they're followed by gray-green seed pods that stand from summer to fall. Even better, these seed pods drop seeds that will come up for years to come, so you'll probably only need to plant this annual once!

When you're starting out, direct-sow peony-flowered poppy seeds (sometimes also sold as opium poppies) in the spring. Thin sprouts to stand a foot apart. You may need to stake them eventually because the flowers are so heavy.

Type Annual
Blooms Pink, purple or white in early summer
Light Full sun
Size 2 to 3 ft. tall, 1 to 2 ft. wide
Hardiness
   Heat: AHS zones 12 to 1
Source Select Seeds
   www.selectseeds.com
   800-684-0395. *Seeds*

why grow it?
Showy flowers, cool seed pods, flowers that plant themselves — what a great annual!

PHOTO: © Joan de Grey (wild indigo bloom); LOCATION: Powell Gardens (amsonia bloom)

www.GardenGateMagazine.com   *the* YEAR IN GARDENING   107

top multiseason shrub and trees

Virginia sweetspire
Itea virginica

In late spring, Virginia sweetspire is dripping with 6-inch wands of lightly fragrant white flowers. In summer, the fresh green foliage makes a stunning accent to summer-blooming perennials. Then in fall, that foliage turns burgundy-red and hangs on for weeks! 'Henry's Garnet' in the inset above has especially great fall color.

While it prefers moist, even slightly wet soil, this shrub can also handle some drought once it's established. Don't feed it — treat it too well and it'll sucker and form colonies. If you want to tidy it up, prune just after it flowers so it'll have time to set next year's buds.

Type Shrub
Blooms White in late spring
Light Full sun to part shade
Size 3 to 5 ft. tall and wide
Hardiness
  Cold: USDA zones 5 to 9
  Heat: AHS zones 9 to 1
Source Forestfarm
  www.forestfarm.com
  541-846-7269

why grow it?
Easy-care shrub shows off with white spring blooms and flaming-red fall foliage.

Serviceberry
Amelanchier **spp. and hybrids**

Serviceberry truly brings three-season color to any garden. In spring, you'll get lovely white star-shaped blooms, which are followed by red, blue or black berries in summer. This fruit is delicious — just get to it before the birds do! In fall, the foliage turns yellow, orange or scarlet.

You can grow serviceberry as a specimen with a single trunk, but its natural habit is to have several stems sprouting from the base, similar to the way a birch grows. This tree is great for a small garden — enough light gets through the leaves that you can easily grow other plants beneath it.

Type Tree
Blooms White in spring
Light Full sun to part shade
Size 10 to 30 ft. tall,
  10 to 25 ft. wide
Hardiness
  Cold: USDA zones 3 to 9
  Heat: AHS zones 9 to 1
Source Forestfarm
  www.forestfarm.com
  541-846-7269

why grow it?
It has clouds of white flowers in spring, tasty berries and eye-popping autumn leaves.

PHOTOS: © Neil Soderstrom (Virginia sweetspire inset); courtesy of Monrovia (serviceberry bloom)

108 *the* YEAR IN GARDENING www.GardenGateMagazine.com

BRING IN THE BIRDS WITH BERRIES!

I've just introduced you to serviceberry and dogwood, a couple of trees whose berries birds love. And simply having them in your garden will probably attract birds. But there are a few smart design tips that'll help you keep the birds safe and you happy.

HELP THEM EAT LOCAL You get home after a busy day, and your significant other says, "What's for dinner?" You agree that you don't want to cook. What's the first thing you do when you're hungry and decide to go out at the last minute? Hit your favorite neighborhood restaurant. Birds like to "eat local," too. If there are plenty of opportunities for both food and shelter in your yard, you'll get them to stick around. I like placing berry-producing plants next to evergreen trees and shrubs because evergreens are the popular housing choice for many birds, like warblers and nuthatches. Evergreens' dense foliage provides protection from predators and bad weather.

PUT OUT A SMORGASBORD Some birds love berries, but others are partial to nuts and seeds. So plant some seed-producing purple coneflowers and sunflowers near your flowering dogwood and serviceberry and you'll have even more entertainment.

SAVE A LIFE If a bird sees the reflection of its favorite food in your window, it'll zoom right into it. And if you've heard that sickening thud and seen a poor bird lying on the ground, you know how horrible that is. Help prevent these accidents by planting your bird-attracting trees and shrubs at least 10 ft. away from windows. You'll save the life of your favorite songbird and still get to enjoy the view.

NO ONE LIKES A MESSY EATER OK, this is for you, not the birds. Sure, a serviceberry dripping in blooms is gorgeous next to your front walk in spring. But picture it later, when the birds move in. Although no one likes a messy eater, birds just can't help it. How can I say this delicately? You'll see a mess on your sidewalk either before or after they eat the berries. And you don't want to track that into your house. So choose a spot away from sidewalks and patios so you can let the birds eat with abandon and no one will mind their bad table manners.

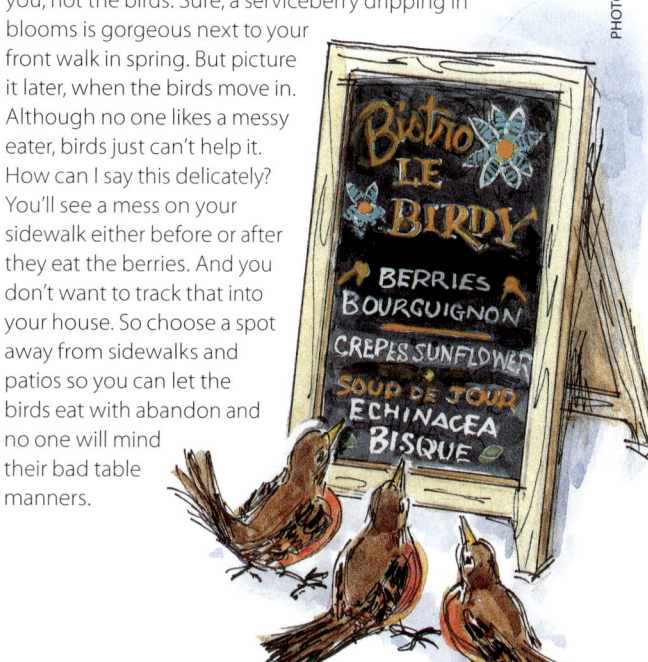

Flowering dogwood
Cornus florida **and hybrids**

Love spring color? Love birds? Then this dogwood is for you! In spring, tiny green flowers surrounded by petal-like bracts cover the tree. The species has white flowers, but on some cultivars and hybrids, such as Stellar Pink® above, the bracts are pink. In autumn the foliage turns scarlet and is accented by red berries that birds love.

Flowering dogwood does best in part or dappled shade. Give it a little extra water if you're in a drought to keep the leaves from turning brown. Dogwoods are prone to a blight, identified by purple-edged spots on the foliage. If trees in your area suffer, choose a spot with more sunlight and offer good air circulation.

Type Tree
Blooms White in spring
Light Part shade to full sun
Size 15 to 30 ft. tall and wide
Hardiness
  Cold: USDA zones 5 to 9
  Heat: AHS zones 9 to 1
Source Greer Gardens
  www.greergardens.com
  800-548-0111

why grow it?
Big dogwood flowers just say "spring has arrived." And who can resist colorful fall foliage and berries that bring the birds in?

Find out how we jazzed up this once-neglected bed with just a few plants on page 124.

before & after

transform *your* garden, we show you how

NEW AND IMPROVED! Sure it's a Madison Avenue cliche, but after flipping through the next few pages, you just might agree it applies here. These five garden makeovers are bursting with ideas for boosting curb appeal, adding lasting color, dealing with small spaces, and more.

Boost Your Curb Appeal **112**

This Color Won't Stop **116**

Create a Fantastic
Fall Entry Garden....................**120**

No Space is Too Small
for a Great Garden! **122**

Shape Up a Neglected Bed.......**124**

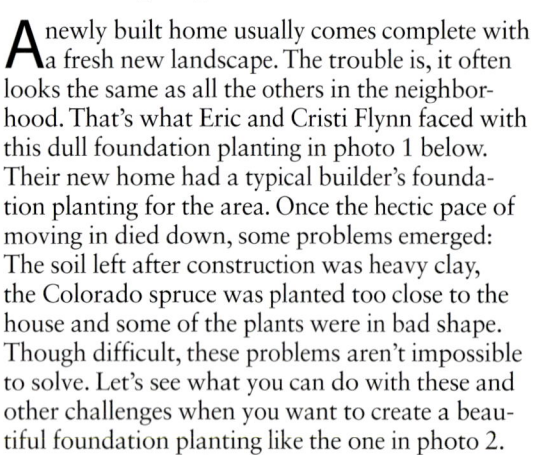

BEFORE & AFTER | FRONT YARD

boost your curb appeal

Botanical Names

Amur maple
Acer ginnala
Astilbe
Astilbe hybrid
Calibrachoa
Calibrachoa hybrid
Colorado spruce
Picea pungens
Begonia
Begonia hybrid
Hydrangea
Hydrangea paniculata
Spike blazing star
Liatris spicata

811 Know what's below. Call before you dig.

Not sure where your utilities are buried? Anywhere in the United States you can call 811 to set up a free appointment for someone to mark underground utility lines. (Each Canadian province has its own one-call number, listed in the phone book and online.)

(1) No frills foundation. This home had a builder's foundation planting typical for the area.

A newly built home usually comes complete with a fresh new landscape. The trouble is, it often looks the same as all the others in the neighborhood. That's what Eric and Cristi Flynn faced with this dull foundation planting in photo 1 below. Their new home had a typical builder's foundation planting for the area. Once the hectic pace of moving in died down, some problems emerged: The soil left after construction was heavy clay, the Colorado spruce was planted too close to the house and some of the plants were in bad shape. Though difficult, these problems aren't impossible to solve. Let's see what you can do with these and other challenges when you want to create a beautiful foundation planting like the one in photo 2.

SOIL SAVVY Before plants go in the ground, it's important to take care of the soil. But it's hard to get to the soil when it's covered by rock mulch, as this garden was. Rocks retain heat during the day and release it at night, causing soil to dry out quickly. Top that off with the extra heat from the surrounding concrete, and you have a place where plants will struggle. It won't be easy to shovel the rock out, but it's probably best to get rid of it. There may be landscape fabric beneath. While it's true it can keep weeds down, it also keeps out things such as leaves and other garden debris that nourish the soil, so you might want to take this out, too.

Here, there was a dying yew in the corner by the door. When you pull out a struggling plant like this, you might find that the topsoil has been stripped away during construction, leaving behind hard-packed clay and maybe even pockets of builder's sand. With clay soil, you have two choices — grow clay-tolerant plants, such as astilbe, spike blazing star and others, or amend the soil. In a small foundation area like this, amending the soil with lots of compost is a workable solution. When you're working around a lot of existing plants, you'll probably want to use a spade rather than a tiller to do this. Once your soil is improved, it's time to think about getting some new plants in the ground.

TREE TROUBLES At only 5 feet out from the house, the spruce tree on the corner was planted too close for its ultimate size. A full-grown specimen can get 40 to 60 feet tall and 10 to 20 feet wide — or more! Left alone, it would have eventually crowded the house, possibly damaging the siding, roof or foundation, so it had to come out. But trees add value to your property. In fact, the United States Forest Service has found that healthy, mature trees add an average of 10 percent to a property's value. In addition, trees cut energy costs so you don't want to eliminate trees altogether. Think about replacing potentially too-big trees with something more manageable, such as this amur maple. It'll reach about 20 feet tall and wide and can easily be pruned to size, if needed. When a lot of landscaping is done at once in an area sometimes plants aren't installed properly. This spruce

Amur maple

Turn the page for more on this foundation garden

Hydrangea

(2) Transformation complete! New trees, shrubs, perennials and annuals give a great street-side impression because they're colorful and in scale with the home.

had the burlap wrapping, wire and twine still in place around the trunk and rootball, in addition to a big air pocket full of water at the bottom of the hole. So if you notice trees or shrubs that are struggling, do a little digging to investigate. You may be able to save them by amending the soil, filling in air pockets or redirecting roots that are wrapping around themselves.

SHRUBS TO THE RESCUE Traditional foundation shrubs are often taken for granted. But they provide structure and interest for most of the year. And even if they aren't showy, their plain foliage is a good backdrop.

Adding a tall shrub like the hydrangea gives you flowers and a visual step between the house and lawn. Plus, bigger plants like this are easily seen from the street.

Finishing touches, such as the group of stylish containers near the front door, complete the sophisticated look of this garden. Check out "Container coordination" at right to find out how to make your home, garden and containers look unified.

Next let's focus on how to put together a plan for that small corner next to the front door.

Container coordination

By echoing colors and textures from the house and garden, these containers and the foundation planting look like they belong together. The colors of the containers and their ribbed texture complement the earth tones and rough shapes of the stone siding.

A few plants from the garden are used here but others wouldn't do well on this part-shade front porch. That creates an opportunity to try some new and interesting combinations, such as red hibiscus flowers and yellow calibrachoa.

spruce up a tight spot

Small spaces like this one trapped between a garage, the house and a concrete sidewalk can be difficult to deal with. The buildings and concrete all hold heat and the light is limited. And because it's so close to the entry, you'll want something attractive and colorful to greet visitors as they arrive. Taking care of the soil and getting rid of the rock mulch was a great place to start. And adding trees and shrubs for structure and seasonal interest all along the foundation was the next step. Now it's time to focus on what you can plant in the tight spot by the door. Annuals and perennials add that punch of color that creates a knock-out garden. The original planting didn't have much, so there was lots of room for improvement. Now the show starts in spring with pink bergenia blooms above red-tinged foliage. Later, bloody cranesbill, purple coneflower and chrysanthemums emerge. Annuals between the shrubs provide a steady supply of color all season.

MULCH MATTERS With the rock mulch gone, you need to cover the soil in some way to help conserve moisture in this hot spot. Don't throw the rock mulch away, though — it can come in handy. Check out "Saving stone" below for a great recycling idea. Organic mulch, such as shredded bark, is a good solution because it keeps weeds down and feeds the soil as it decomposes. Another organic solution is to plant a ground cover like the vinca in this garden. It shades the soil, keeps weeds

(3) A good-looking ground cover, such as the vinca here, softens the hard sidewalk edge, keeps weeds down and has pretty purple flowers in spring.

down and, to top things off, it blooms, too! As this spreading ground cover grows, it creeps out over the sidewalk, softening that hard concrete edge.

GET PLANTING The area above started out with a few yews and some hostas with crispy leaves. And since the soil needed some work anyway, it was a good time to remove one of the yews that was struggling and assess the situation. With a south exposure, those hostas were getting too much sun. If you notice that happening, move them to the more hospitable east side of the house. Start with structure plants, like this Japanese maple. It provides height, and those burgundy leaves are beautiful from spring to fall. Even after you put plants in the ground, don't be afraid to make changes. For example, the first rose, which was pink, just didn't go with the other colors. Now, a yellow-peach one is much better.

It pays to keep different perspectives in mind while you're planning the garden. While you can't see these yews from the street, you wouldn't want them too tall or they'd block the view in and out of the window. Plus, when visitors come to the front door and stand on the porch, that spot under the window where the yews grow is very obvious. Give the yews a quick clean up with an electric hedge trimmer every year to keep them the right size.

Whether you have a new home or not you can use these ideas to revamp your foundation planting so you have a landscape that stops traffic. □

— *Sherri Ribbey*

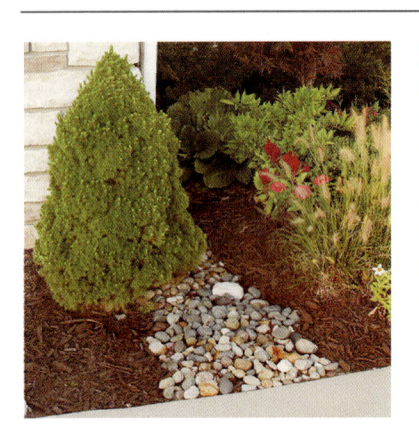

Saving stone

Most of the rock ended up under the deck in the back yard to keep weeds down. But this little ribbon of stone makes a mini dry-stream bed that directs water away from the foundation when it rains. It looks a lot better than a plastic downspout out to the walkway would. To do this, just make sure you build up the soil and rocks so you have a slight slope from the house down toward the sidewalk.

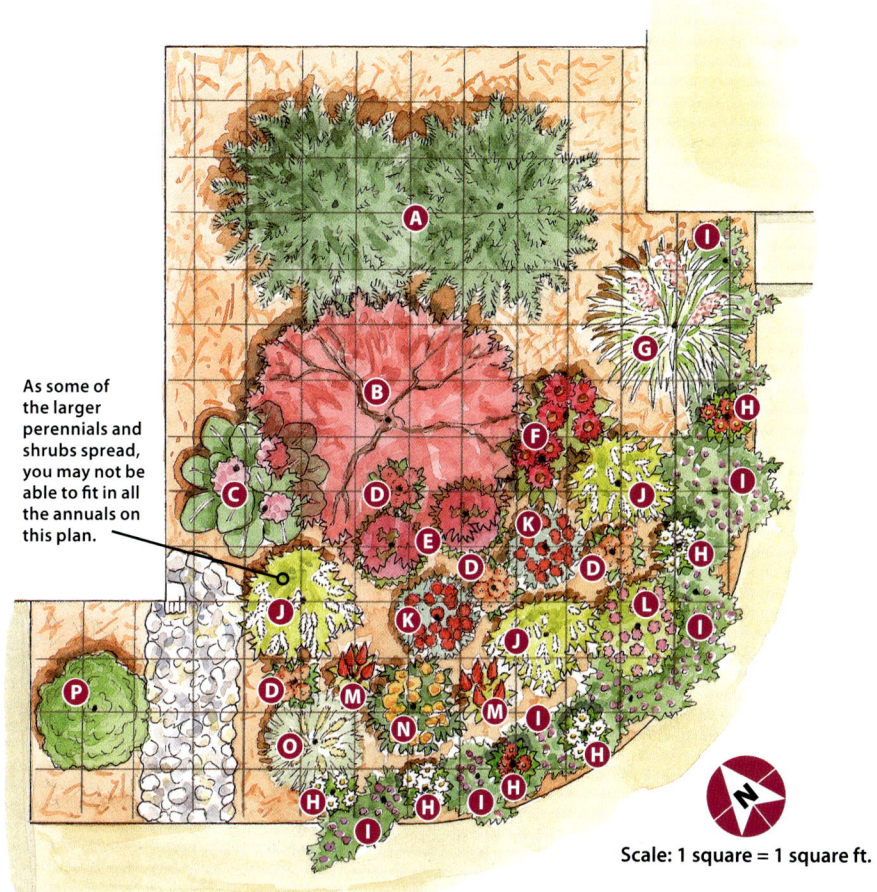

WARM, SUNNY CORNER

As some of the larger perennials and shrubs spread, you may not be able to fit in all the annuals on this plan.

Scale: 1 square = 1 square ft.

Code	Plant Name	No. to Plant	Blooms	Type	Cold/Heat Zones	Height/Width	Special Features
A	Spreading yew *Taxus* x*media* 'Densiformis'	2	NA	Shrub	4-7/7-1	3-4 ft./4-6 ft.	Needled evergreen; responds well to annual shearing
B	Japanese maple *Acer palmatum* Emperor I® ('Wolff')	1	NA	Tree	5-8/8-1	15-20 ft./15 ft.	Burgundy foliage all season; late to leaf out in spring; more cold-hardy than other varieties
C	Bergenia *Bergenia cordifolia* 'Winterglow'	2	Pink; spring	Perennial	4-8/8-1	12-18 in./12-18 in.	Evergreen foliage develops a red edge in cooler weather
D	Zinnia *Zinnia elegans* 'Dreamland Mix'	4	Mix; spring to fall	Annual	NA/12-1	10-12 in./8-12 in.	Water at soil level to prevent powdery mildew
E	Aster *Aster novi-belgii* 'Alert'	2	Red-violet; late summer	Perennial	4-8/8-1	12-15 in./12-15 in.	Dwarf variety won't flop; covered in flowers
F	Purple coneflower *Echinacea purpurea* 'Fatal Attraction'	2	Purple-pink; summer to fall	Perennial	3-8/8-1	18-24 in./12-18 in.	Fragrant; dwarf variety; petals won't droop; goldfinches feed on seedheads
G	Maiden grass *Miscanthus sinensis* 'Variegatus'	1	Red-pink; late summer to fall	Perennial	5-9/9-1	5-9 ft./4-5 ft.	Variegated foliage; red-pink flowers turn silver in fall; plumes last into winter
H	Zinnia *Zinnia* 'Profusion Mix'	6	Red and white; spring to fall	Annual	NA/12-1	12-18 in./9-12 in.	Water at soil level to prevent powdery mildew; attracts butterflies
I	Vinca *Vinca minor* 'Atropurpurea'	6	Purple; spring	Perennial	4-8/8-1	4-6 in./6-18 in.	Deer-resistant; can be invasive in some areas
J	Sweetspire *Itea virginica* Little Henry® ('Sprich')	3	White; late spring, early summer	Shrub	5-9/9-1	18-30 in./24-36 in.	Compact form; fragrant flowers in late spring; needs consistent moisture; red fall foliage
K	Chrysanthemum *Chrysanthemum* 'Five Alarm Red'	2	Red; late summer to fall	Perennial	5-9/9-1	14-24 in./20-36 in.	Cut plants back by half in early summer to encourage bushy growth
L	Bloody cranesbill *Geranium sanguineum* 'Vision Violet'	1	Magenta; summer	Perennial	3-9/9-1	1-2 ft./1-2 ft.	Cut back spent flowers for a second bloom
M	Celosia *Celosia plumosa* 'Castle Scarlet'	2	Red; spring to fall	Annual	NA/12-1	12-14 in./12-14 in.	Drought-tolerant; pest- and disease-free
N	Rose *Rosa* Flower Carpet® Amber ('NOA97400A')	1	Yellow-peach; spring to fall	Shrub	5-10/10-1	24-30 in./24-30 in.	Remove dead or damaged canes in late winter; deadhead to encourage more blooms
O	Fountain grass *Pennisetum alopecuroides* 'Hameln'	1	Buff; summer	Perennial	5-9/9-1	18-30 in./18-30 in.	Leave foliage standing for winter interest; cut back in early spring
P	Dwarf Alberta spruce *Picea glauca albertiana* 'Conica'	1	NA	Tree	2-8/8-1	8 ft./5 ft.	Slow-growing evergreen; provides winter interest; rarely needs pruning

BEFORE & AFTER | FRONT YARD

(1) A small corner bed is where this exuberant front yard started.

(2) When it was all shady, the garden was mostly hostas.

this color won't stop!
(but passersby will)

Running out of room to garden? Take your plants to the street! Here's how to create a color-filled front yard border from a shade garden that might be a little dull.

Of course, a garden is always evolving, and Kevin and Carol Venhaus' is no different. There wasn't much but lawn and mature trees 11 years ago. Photos 1 and 2 show how it started with a foundation planting. Over the years it expanded. The most recent version, in photo 3, has the front yard nearly filled with annuals and perennials of all types.

STREET SMARTS If you have big dreams for a garden,

(3) With a wide variety of colorful flowers and shade-tolerant foliage plants, this garden looks fantastic!

it's usually best to start with a small planting and see how it goes for a year or two. A smaller plot helps you get an idea if the garden style you'd like to use is going to work. That's especially important with a front yard garden since you want a nice view of your home.

The bed near the sidewalk started with a load of free fieldstone on the corner and was later expanded across the front of the yard. Stones positioned near the sidewalk hold soil in place and add to the garden's four-season appeal.

STONE PLACEMENT Want to try this look yourself? Here's how it all goes together: Starting next to the sidewalk, lay out a casual pattern of stones on the ground. You can butt them up to the sidewalk in a straight line or lay the stone out in an undulating line. Use a variety of sizes for a more natural look. Try to get a mix of about two-thirds larger to one-third smaller stones. "Rock stars" at right gives you a couple more tips for getting natural-looking rock formations in a bed.

You've probably noticed that this border has more than one row of stones in it. Some are stacked, some are dug in. You may want to level out a few areas for the upper tier of stones, which will also create a planting pocket here and there. Even if the stones are as tight to the sidewalk as you can get them, it's inevitable that weeds will find their way in. By leaving space for the garden plants to fill in, you may not have to battle the weeds as much later. When the stone settles and the plants grow, the wall will look like it's been there a lot longer than it really has.

As I mentioned, a rock-filled bed lets you tuck plants in front of and behind the stones. Don't be afraid to fill every nook and cranny. Speaking of plants, how do you choose whether you go with annuals or perennials? Kevin and Carol did quite a bit of experimenting before they came up with a ratio that works for them. A mix of about half easy-care perennials to half long-blooming annuals makes this bed show off all summer without much work.

TREE TROUBLE Based on all the tree trunks you can see in the photo at left, you might think that annuals or perennials wouldn't flower well in that much shade. And you're right. But years ago, one of the trees in the curbside strip was damaged by a storm and had to be taken out. It's amazing what a difference one tree makes. That full-shade garden suddenly had up to 6 hours of sun a day in some spots! That's plenty of light for lots of flowers, and, in fact, a little too much for some hosta varieties. It was time to rethink this front bed.

A front yard has different design needs than a back or side yard. Putting a shade structure, such as a pergola, here would block the view of the house, and a tree would take years to grow tall enough to cast any serious shade. With a front yard you want something that looks good fast. So the best solution was to move the hostas to a shadier spot and put in sun-loving plants. Now sun- and heat-loving plants like dianthus, sedum and gazania thrive with the reflected heat from the stones in some spots.

Don't be afraid to pull out plants that aren't doing well and try something different. In this garden, a struggling juniper was replaced with the good-looking container on the corner. You can't miss the dramatic foliage of that canna. The warm tones of the leaves, along with that of the terra-cotta container, echo all of the flowers nearby.

Interested in a garden like this for your own yard? Turn the page for the planting plan and some growing tips.

ROCK STARS

Here are two ways to get a casual, unstudied look in your rock placement: First, position all the stones in a bed so their stratification lines point in the same direction. Second, bury each rock so only a third of each one is showing. Put the broadest side down and the most attractive side facing out.

Bury ⅔ of your stones for a natural look.

Botanical Names

Canna
 Canna hybrid
Dianthus
 Dianthus hybrid
Gazania
 Gazania hybrid
Hosta
 Hosta hybrid
Juniper
 Juniperus hybrid
Sedum
 Sedum hybrid

Turn the page to learn how to grow this garden.

front yard color!

With a backdrop of cool green lawn and hostas, the warm colors at the front of this garden really pop. This mix of annuals and perennials is easy to care for and has a lot of showy color all season long.

So what's the secret to spring-to-fall color like this? Start with a foundation of long- and repeat-blooming perennials, such as the tall sedum, coreopsis and shasta daisy here. In spring, tall sedum takes a while to get going, but by summer the flowers are well on their way. Coreopsis and shasta daisies get going right away with long-lasting flowers. And if you deadhead them when they're done, they'll keep blooming until frost.

Once those reliable perennials are in place, fill the rest of the garden with your favorite mix of annuals for blooms from spring to fall. Some annuals can spread or sprawl so much they crowd out other plants. That's where those planting pockets we talked about earlier come in handy. The stones limit the roots and help hold foliage back enough so that other nearby plants can grow. It's almost like sinking them in their own containers.

No, your eyes aren't deceiving you. There are hostas and tall sedum thriving side-by-side in this bed. The fact is, the border isn't all sun or all shade. Check out the "Light meter" bar below the plan to see the amount of sun each part of the border gets.

Part-shade gardens don't have to be blah. In fact, with a little planning, it could be the most exciting garden on the block! □

— *Sherri Ribbey*

The area between the arrows is what you see in this photo.

'Blue Umbrellas' hosta and *H.* 'Albomarginata' usually grow 3 to 4 ft. wide. But because of nearby stones and plants, here they're smaller. If they grow wider than you want, slice off a side piece with a spade.

Light meter — 2 to 3 hours of sun

SHADE TO SUN GARDEN

Code	Plant Name	No. to Plant	Blooms	Type	Cold/Heat Zones	Height/Width	Growing Tips
A	Hosta *Hosta* 'Blue Umbrellas'	2	White; summer	Perennial	3-8/8-1	24-36 in./36-48 in.	Grow in shade for the best blue foliage
B	Coral bells *Heuchera* 'Palace Purple'	7	White; spring	Perennial	3-9/9-1	12-24 in./12-18 in.	Foliage is greener with less sunlight
C	Hosta *Hosta undulata univittata*	1	Lavender; summer	Perennial	3-8/8-1	10-18 in./18-24 in.	Also sold as *H. undulata*
D	Spurge *Euphorbia dulcis* 'Chameleon'	3	Chartreuse; summer	Perennial	5-9/9-1	12-18 in./18-24 in.	Reseeds; sap can irritate skin
E	Hosta *Hosta* 'Albomarginata'	1	Lavender; summer	Perennial	3-9/9-1	18 in./36-48 in.	Sun-tolerant with regular water
F	Yellow archangel *Lamium galeobdolon*	3	Yellow; spring	Perennial	5-9/9-1	12 in./18-24 in.	Can be invasive in some areas
G	Cosmos *Cosmos sulphureus* 'Cosmic Series'	3	Orange, yellow; summer to fall	Annual	NA/12-1	12-18 in./9-12 in.	Deadhead for a faster rebloom; reseeds; heat-tolerant
H	Gazania *Gazania* Daybreak Mix	17	Orange, yellow, white; spring to fall	Tender perennial	10-11/12-1	8-10 in./6-8 in.	Heat- and frost-tolerant; does best with good drainage
I	Tall sedum *Sedum* 'Autumn Joy' ('Herbstfreude')	2	Rust red; summer to fall	Perennial	3-9/9-1	24-36 in./18-24 in.	Attracts butterflies; leave plants standing in fall for winter interest
J	Begonia *Begonia* Dragon Wing™ Red ('Bepared')	2	Red; spring to fall	Tender perennial	10-11/12-1	12-18 in./15-18 in.	Overwinter inside as house plant; overwatering causes rot
K	Coreopsis *Coreopsis verticillata* 'Moonbeam'	3	Yellow; summer	Perennial	3-9/9-1	18-24 in./18-24 in.	Shear back by at least a third for a second bloom; needs good drainage
L	Zinnia *Zinnia* Profusion Series	16	Orange, white, yellow; spring to fall	Annual	NA/12-1	12-18 in./6-10 in.	Deadhead flowers for faster rebloom; attracts butterflies
M	Coleus *Solenostemon* 'Glennis'	1	Purple; summer	Tender perennial	10-11/12-1	24-36 in./12-18 in.	Pinch flowers off for showier foliage
N	Hosta *Hosta* 'Devon Green'	1	Lavender; summer	Perennial	3-8/8-1	18 in./18-24 in.	Shiny leaf surface reflects light in shade
O	Lamb's ear *Stachys byzantina*	6	Lavender; spring	Perennial	4-8/8-1	8-12 in./12-18 in.	Fuzzy silver leaves; likes it hot and dry

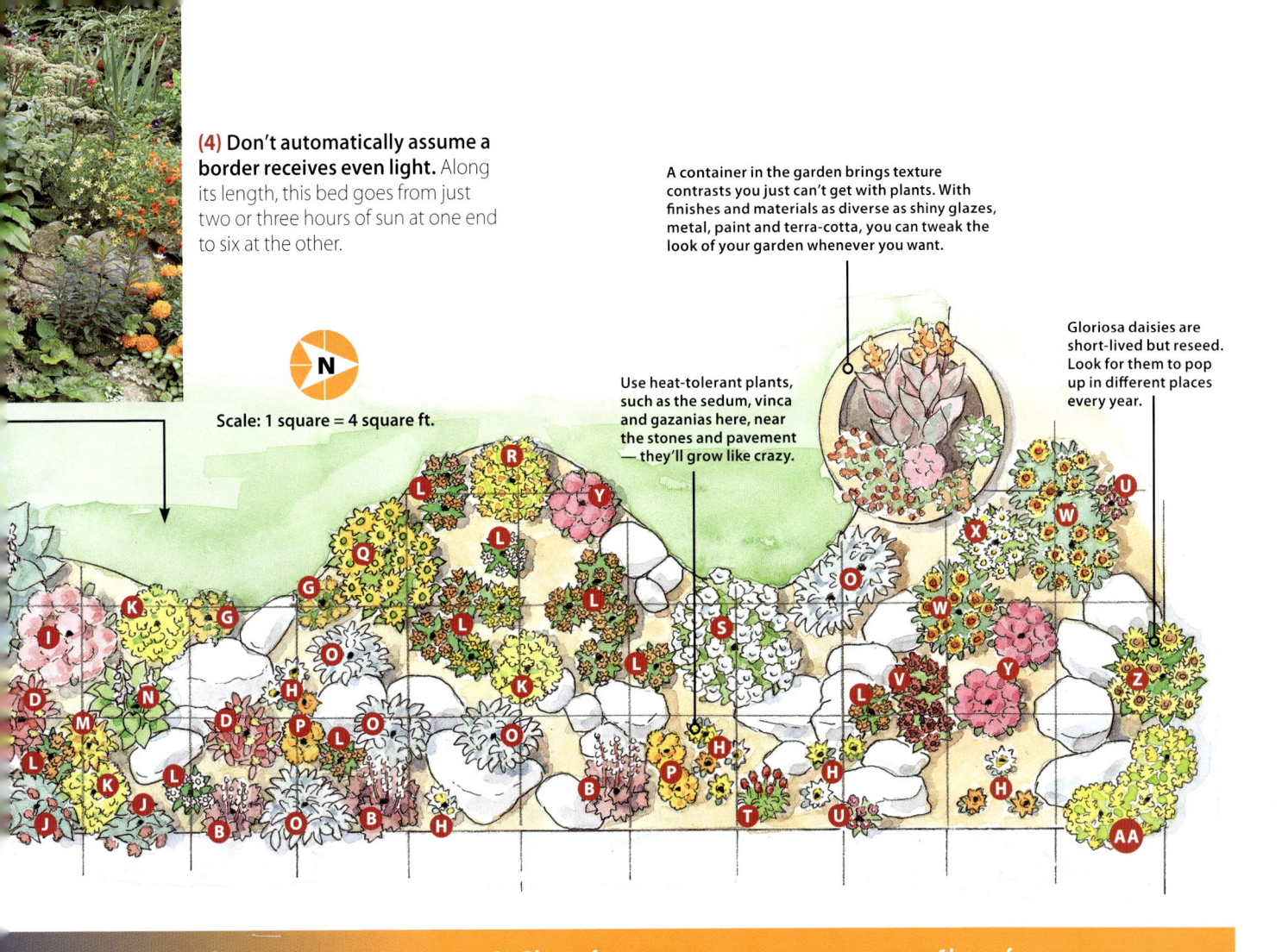

(4) Don't automatically assume a border receives even light. Along its length, this bed goes from just two or three hours of sun at one end to six at the other.

A container in the garden brings texture contrasts you just can't get with plants. With finishes and materials as diverse as shiny glazes, metal, paint and terra-cotta, you can tweak the look of your garden whenever you want.

Use heat-tolerant plants, such as the sedum, vinca and gazanias here, near the stones and pavement — they'll grow like crazy.

Gloriosa daisies are short-lived but reseed. Look for them to pop up in different places every year.

Scale: 1 square = 4 square ft.

3 to 4 hours of sun | 4 to 5 hours of sun | 6 hours of sun

Code	Plant Name	No. to Plant	Blooms	Type	Cold/Heat Zones	Height/Width	Growing Tips
P	Marigold *Tagetes erecta* 'Antigua Orange'	3	Orange; spring to fall	Annual	NA/12-1	12-16 in./6-10 in.	Large double flowers attract butterflies
Q	Gloriosa daisy *Rudbeckia hirta* 'Irish Eyes'	1	Yellow; summer	Perennial	5-9/9-1	24-36 in./24-36 in.	Short-lived perennial; yellow-green center; may reseed
R	Coreopsis *Coreopsis tinctoria*	1	Orange; spring to fall	Annual	NA/12-1	24-48 in./12-18 in.	Native wildflower; may reseed
S	Petunia *Petunia* Easy Wave® White	1	White; spring to fall	Annual	NA/12-1	6-12 in./30 in.	Spreading petunia; cut back if it gets leggy
T	Globe amaranth *Gomphrena* 'Strawberry Fields'	1	Red; summer	Annual	NA/12-1	18-24 in./12 in.	Good dried flower
U	Vinca *Catharanthus roseus* Hot Rose	2	Bright pink; spring to fall	Tender perennial	9-11/12-1	4-6 in./8 in.	Heat-tolerant; larger flowers than other varieties
V	Gloriosa daisy *Rudbeckia* 'Cherry Brandy'	2	Deep red; summer	Perennial	5-8/8-1	18-24 in./12 in.	Short-lived perennial; reseeds
W	Blanket flower *Gaillardia* Commotion® Frenzy	3	Red, yellow; spring to fall	Perennial	5-9/9-1	18-24 in./18-24 in.	More fluted petals than other varieties; heat- and humidity-tolerant
X	Shasta daisy *Leucanthemum ×superbum* 'Snowcap'	1	White; summer	Perennial	5-9/9-1	12-15 in./12-15 in.	Compact variety; good cut flower
Y	Sedum *Sedum spectabile* 'Hot Stuff'	2	Pink; summer	Perennial	3-9/9-1	10-12 in./12-15 in.	More compact than other tall sedums
Z	Gloriosa daisy *Rudbeckia hirta* 'Sonora'	1	Yellow with burgundy center; summer	Perennial	5-9/9-1	18-24 in./18-24 in.	Short-lived perennial; large flowers; may reseed
AA	Sneezeweed *Helenium amarum* 'Dakota Gold'	3	Yellow; spring to fall	Annual	NA/12-1	12-14 in./15-16 in.	Heat-tolerant; ferny foliage and mounded habit; reseeds

BEFORE & AFTER | FRONT YARD

make over your entry to
create a fantastic fall garden

quick tip
Hang a wreath on a wall with brick or siding hangers. No drilling required! Get these at www.improvements catalog.com.

The front garden in the "before" photo below needed help. It was a bit neglected, but passable, in spring and summer. By fall, however, it had become downright shabby. Daylilies and hostas were starting to look tired, with yellowing foliage and spent bloom stalks. Earlier, the container showed off a nice architectural hemlock. But now, the mud-spattered, off-kilter pot in the photo just holds a dead plant. One thing was still looking good, though — the New Guinea impatiens. Unfortunately, the first cold snap will take them down. This is definitely not the best look for a home's entry.

But just because it's fall doesn't mean you have to give up on the garden and wait until spring to clean it up. In fact, this colorful season offers some of the most pleasant weather for working outdoors. It doesn't take a lot of time or money to have a fall garden as nice as the one in the "after" photo. Get started by cleaning up what's there before adding anything new. Then take a look at existing plants to see what their needs are. The daylilies and the hosta at the far right had spent brown flower stems that needed to be removed. All it took was a quick tug on the stems to get them out of there. If you're more proactive and get to work while they're still green, just snip the stalks back with pruners. Cut near the base of the plant, down in the foliage, to keep plants looking tidy. With cleanup taken care of, you can see what holes need filling and go shopping.

In the few hours it took to buy some new plants and attend to a few other details, this garden went from weary to wow! Let me show you how I transformed this front entry garden. I learned a few things along the way and I'll share those tips with you, too. You can use them whether you're taking on a whole new look or only want to spruce it up a bit for fall. □

— *Sherri Ribbey*

Botanical Names

Flowering kale
Brassica oleracea

Impatiens
Impatiens hybrids

Pansies
Viola hybrids

Purple fountain grass
Pennisetum setaceum 'Rubrum'

Before

Rethink the decorating This entry looked a bit dreary and needed some punch. Nothing says fall like pumpkins. A few of them sitting on the stoop seemed like a natural. Especially since their shape and color go so nicely with the big round orange container already there.

The view from the sidewalk wasn't very inspiring — you couldn't even see the forest-green ice cream parlor table and chairs. So I pulled a buttery yellow metal chair out of the back yard. The brighter color and visual weight gave the chair more presence and was much easier to see. A couple of bright green birdhouse gourds on the seat added a nice touch of whimsy, too.

Create a focal point That tired orange container was just begging for something dramatic. All it needed was a plant with some height and architectural interest to turn it into a focal point. Lucky for me there was an end-of-season sale going on at a nearby garden center. I found this big purple fountain grass at a bargain price and bought it right away. Although some grasses, such as maiden grass, are cold-hardy as well as showy in fall, this particular cultivar isn't one of them. That doesn't matter as much here because in this zone 5 garden, a glazed container has to go inside before the ground freezes anyway to keep it from being damaged in the cold weather.

Make a sandwich Impatiens are pretty and the flowers last longer in cooler temperatures, but they turn to mush with the first freeze. To keep things colorful, sandwich them between cool-weather-loving pansies and kale. Go ahead and pull the impatiens when they go down. The kale and pansies will be there to continue the show. Shop early and you'll have the best selection of plants at the garden center: As fall wears on, pansies tend to outgrow their packs and get spindly and rough-looking. Interplanting early gives them a chance to put on some size before you pull the impatiens. There's an opportunity to change your color scheme here, too. See how the orange impatiens complement the purple pansies and purple kale foliage? It's an intense combo. But when the impatiens are gone, shades of purple and green create a more relaxing scene.

Stop the splash Nothing says "messy" like a dirty container. Every time rain fell, it splashed soil onto the orange pot. The remedy is simple: A once-over with a damp rag and wood mulch around the base. See how nice and shiny the pot looks now in the photo above? The mulch will help the garden bed, too. It'll protect plant roots from the alternating freeze and thaw in winter by keeping the soil temperature even.

www.GardenGateMagazine.com *the* YEAR IN GARDENING 121

BEFORE & AFTER | SIDE YARD

no space is too small for **a great garden!**

That narrow space along the side of the house is often one of the last places that gets attention, even when the rest of the garden looks great. After all, not too many people see it (including the folks who live there). As you can tell, this spot could use some work. Here are three ways to handle a space like this, whether you have a neighbor's house, a privacy fence or a driveway bordering your property. Believe it or not, these side yards are all less than 20 feet wide!

When you're putting in a path, consider how frequently you use it. If you use this area every day, choose a surface that's easy to clean and doesn't get slippery, such as concrete. If it's somewhere you just stroll occasionally, you can get more creative with the path. Now have a look at these options. You might find one that you like or use tips from all three! □

— Stephanie Polsley Bruner

Install a fountain near a window so you can enjoy the sound with the windows open.

HOUSE + HOUSE

The deep, dense shade between two houses can make it difficult to grow plants. But choose the right shade-loving plants and a few interesting details, and you'll create a welcome oasis.

Shade gardens often aren't too colorful, but that's where texture comes into play: Contrast bold-foliaged hostas with lacy ferns and Solomon's seal.

Add a fountain with splashing water to make this area seem cooler. It's also a great way to block outside noises. And let your neighbor help with your plans so you can both enjoy this shared space.

Last, don't forget to include a place to sit. A simple bench lets you slow down and enjoy this shady getaway.

Include a bench in your retreat so you can sit back and relax there.

Bold hosta leaves contrast with strappy spiderworts and fine-textured ferns. Colorful impatiens brighten up the shade.

ILLUSTRATIONS: Travis Rice

122   *the* YEAR IN GARDENING   www.GardenGateMagazine.com

HOUSE + FENCE

Rustling leaves, crunchy gravel… you'll take your time as you wander down these curving paths. At the end, you can even pause and do a little "interactive" gardening as you rake the gravel into a new pattern.

In a tiny space like this, it's a good idea to pick one theme and stick with it. Here, the gravel Zen garden, clumping bamboo plants and bamboo bench give an Asian feel.

Notice the large plants at the ends of the path. They keep you from looking too far ahead and help contribute to the feeling of seclusion. The bench with its back against the house, looking into the garden space does this, as well.

No zipping through this space! The curving paths in a Zenlike retreat encourage you to slow down and make your walk a journey.

Make a pea gravel bed. It's soothing to rake new designs in the ½-in. stones. And it's easy to maintain!

Even clumping bamboo can get away from you — plant it in a big tub with the bottom cut out to help it behave.

A hard-surfaced path keeps your feet clean and dry as you go from the driveway to the door.

Obelisks or trellises add height where there's no room for a small tree. Put cherry tomatoes on them if you have enough sun.

HOUSE + DRIVEWAY

Hot and sunny, with heat reflecting off the house and the driveway. Sounds like just the spot for some sun-loving herbs and vegetables. A few cherry tomatoes on obelisks are handy for snacks. Line the walkway with lavender so you can brush the leaves and release the scent as you walk along.

Most of us don't want a front yard full of runner beans, but here in the side yard, they're easy to get to, without being too noticeable. And if you cut an armload of salvias or irises, it won't matter if there's a hole in the garden for a while: It's the side yard. Best of all, this area is already enclosed by a house on one side and a low fence on the other, so if you have rabbits munching your lettuce, it's easy to fence the ends.

Ornamental grasses provide a visual barrier to the driveway, but they don't block much sun from the flowers and vegetables.

Botanical Names

Hosta *Hosta* spp.
Impatiens *Impatiens* hybrids
Iris *Iris* hybrids
Lavender *Lavandula* spp.
Salvia *Salvia* spp.
Solomon's seal *Polygonatum* spp.
Spiderwort *Tradescantia virginiana*

BEFORE & AFTER | BACK YARD

shape up a neglected bed

Botanical Names

Labrador rose
Rosa blanda

Juniper
Juniperus horizontalis

Yucca *Yucca filamentosa*

Sometimes, even the best gardening intentions get thrown off track. So whether you inherited the tangle of foliage and flowers or you let the bed go too long yourself (it happens to all of us!), it doesn't matter. Even the most neglected bed can be brought back to life. And it may not take more than a weekend to do it!

This lovely "after" photo, right, is what you'd expect to find in a garden magazine's test garden. Healthy plants, a crystal-clear fountain and plenty of color and texture to keep everything interesting. But take a look at our "before" photo — this particular section of our garden became overgrown in the past few years, and really needed a cleanup. A single yucca had multiplied and began taking over the whole left side of the horseshoe-shaped bed. The Labrador rose sent suckers out every which way, and the junipers looked tired and ratty.

So, it was time for me to get my hands dirty! First, I got a new pump for the fountain and, after cleaning a bit of debris from the water, I got it flowing beautifully again. After that, I gathered up a few common tools, drew up a plan of attack and got to work on the plants.

THE RIGHT STUFF To get this garden looking good again, I didn't need any unusual tools, although I did put pliers to work while weeding. Get all of your tools together and bring them to your work site, so you aren't running back and forth every time you need something different. I found both a spade and garden fork helpful for removing plants. Then I used a trowel, soil knife and pruners for the detail work on this job. While a project like this can be done in a weekend by yourself, having some help will make the process go much faster. Now turn the page, and I'll show you my plan for getting this bed back in shape, and how you can revitalize your garden, too.

(1) Green is a dynamic color, especially in the garden. But no garden should be entirely the same shade of green (like our "before" photo). Splashes of chartreuse help lighten up the dark greens. Add a few bright yellow and pale lavender flowers, and the "after" garden shines!

www.GardenGateMagazine.com *the* YEAR IN GARDENING 125

from messy to marvelous

With the evaluation done and all my tools ready to go, it was time to get to work on this messy garden bed. Take a look at the sketch below to see my vision for the project.

GARDEN BED In the photos, you can see that the bed is shaped like a horseshoe around a water feature. To make sure I didn't overlook anything, I worked around the horseshoe methodically, starting on the left and ending on the right. Don't get caught up in everything you need to do — focus on the task at hand, and worry about what's next when you get to it. The cleanup goes quickly!

REMOVING YUCCA Yucca is one tough plant! It grows from rhizomes and produces "pups," or small plants, right next to the parent. If you're serious about getting rid of an old yucca, you'll have to remove the rhizomes and all the other roots. Otherwise, the plant will come back. (Especially if you live in a frost-free area.)

Use your shovel to dig at the base of the plant. When it's loose, lift the yucca out of the ground. Yuccas have an extensive root system and will resprout from anything left behind. So be sure to pull out any roots you see at the edge of the hole. Because yuccas resprout so easily, it's worth the effort to dig out as many roots as possible. When you've removed everything, fill in the hole with soil. If you weren't able to get all the roots, cover the area with a piece of plywood for a year. This will block the light and kill any remaining roots. Conceal the temporary "bald spot" with a grouping of several containers.

Finally, don't put the roots and tubers you dug up into your compost bin. They break down too slowly, plus you run the risk of starting another yucca colony there.

There were a lot of rigid features in this garden — a rocky fountain, stiff evergreens and a path. Something light and swishy, like grasses, would help soften the mood.

I didn't want to tear out this old rose, but you couldn't see anything behind it. I decided to tame it with a bit of pruning and plant something taller behind it to frame the rose and add more visual drama.

This yucca concealed part of our waterfall, and its spiky foliage looked out of place in this setting of roses and evergreens. Blooming, mounding perennials would look better here.

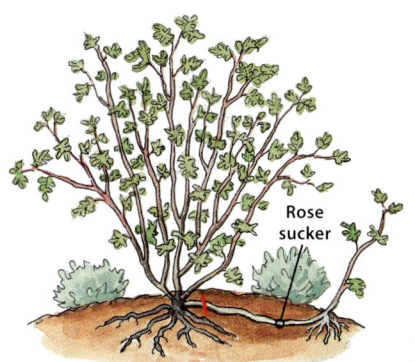

Cut suckers off as close to the main plant as possible.

ROSES Although Labrador rose is a low-maintenance and very disease-resistant rose, it has just one flush of blooms in late spring. And it spreads by suckers, which can pop up in unexpected places.

First, I needed to remove the suckers. The illustration above shows how an unwanted side shoot runs underground and takes root a few feet away. To get rid of it, pull the new plant out and cut it off with pruners as close to the base of the main plant as possible.

Once all the shoots are removed, you can prune the main plant. Most species roses bloom on old wood, so don't prune them back in early spring, like you would hybrid or shrub roses. Trim them up just after their blooms are spent. Remove any branches that are in the way or look too gangly.

WEEDING As I worked my way around the horseshoe, I came across quite a few weeds in this bed. Small ones, like common purslane, I just pulled out with my hands. But there were a few weedy saplings growing in there, too. Those were easy to remove with the help of a pair of pliers. Sure, pliers aren't a common garden tool, but they help you get a good grip on the small, thin trunks. Just grasp a sapling close to the base and give a good pull. It should come up easily. If the sapling is already on its way to being a small tree, cut it down and paint the stump with a brush and stump killer (available at garden centers and hardware stores).

EVERGREEN Three creeping junipers next to the fountain provide year-round color and interest, even during the coldest winters. But, just like any other plant, they can start to look a little wild if left too long. That was the case with these.

You can see in the illustration below how I cut back the lower branches of this juniper. Evergreens often form a thick mat of foliage on top that blocks sun from reaching lower branches, killing them. The easiest way to clean them up is to undercut them.

To undercut, lift a handful of foliage-laden branches, and take a look at what's growing underneath. If you see dead limbs, or sparse, struggling foliage, they're candidates for cutting back. But first, take the time to evaluate — with this branch gone, will the top side of the shrub still look OK? If the answer is yes, cut off the branch at the trunk with pruners or loppers. If the answer is no, leave the branch as it is.

Finally, to keep the juniper looking healthy and encourage a bit more growth, I lightly trimmed the tips of branches. To do this, look for an upward-growing stem along a top branch. Starting at the tip of the branch, follow it back 4 to 6 inches and cut it off. Cut the stem on the underside of the foliage so the overlap covers the cut and the pruned stem won't be visible.

Undercutting evergreens gives them a fresh, healthy look.

NEW PLANTS It only took me a few hours to clean up everything in this garden, and all of the existing plants were looking great. But the garden was still missing movement, seasonal interest and easy-care color. So I planted a large clump of maiden grass at the top of the horseshoe (behind the juniper) and another by the rose bush. Then I added the smokebush on the right. It has fuzzy clusters of pink flowers in summer and brilliant red-purple foliage in fall.

'Happy Returns' daylilies and 'Peter III' double asters filled the empty space where the yucca was. The daylilies rebloom all summer, for color from May to frost. And the asters' mounding habit echo the creeping junipers. 'Firewitch' dianthus will thrive in our rocky soil here, brightening the edge of the waterfall's basin.

Bulbs happily grow in the small spaces between stones.

For spring color in surprising places, I tucked small bulbs, like the grape hyacinth shown above, between the rocks around the fountain. Plant each bulb three times as deep as the bulb's height, and don't worry if the bulb isn't straight up and down — the bulb's shoots will work their way toward the sunlight.

To finish off the look, I added a glazed container filled with foliage plants to bring a new, smooth texture to the garden. And with that, the transformation was complete! ☐

— *Sherri Ribbey*

Botanical Names

Aster *Aster novi-belgii*
Common purslane *Portulaca oleracea*
Daylily *Hemerocallis* hybrids
Dianthus *Dianthus* hybrids
Grape hyacinth *Muscari armeniacum*
Juniper *Juniperus horizontalis*
Labrador rose *Rosa blanda*
Maiden grass *Miscanthus sinensis*
Smokebush *Cotinus coggygria*
Yucca *Yucca filamentosa*

Discover how you can create a garden worth exploring on page 158.

garden design
great *ideas* you can use!

IT STARTS WITH A DREAM. Then it goes down on paper, and finally it becomes a reality. We'll simplify the design process on page 130, then take you on a whirlwind tour of ideas to make your dream garden come alive. From designing for a particular season to incorporating fragrance, color, shape, and accessories into your garden, we share practical tips you can easily put to work yourself.

The Crowning Glory **130**	A Garden to Explore **158**
4 Tips for Fragrance All Year! **136**	Accesorizing Your Garden....**164**
Let the Sun Shine In! **138**	Winter Wonders **166**
Shape Up Your Garden **142**	Summer of Color **170**
Cheer Up with Chartreuse ...**144**	8 Simple Ideas to Fix This Skinny Back Yard......**174**
What You Need to Know About Fences....................**148**	Design Tips for Awkward Corners.............**178**
Create a Charming Cottage Garden Anywhere............**152**	Nearly No-Care Getaway....**180**
Six Plants, Three Beds..........**154**	Fabulous Combos Bring in Spring **182**
Easy Island Bed......................**156**	Did You Know........................**186**

DESIGN | BACKYARD

design your dream garden: part 3 — the final plan

Take your garden plan from paper to reality!
The Crowning Glory

We've come a long way together designing a new dream garden! See how the design has progressed and read about each step in the series of illustrations in "From the ground up" below. And if you missed the two previous articles, check out our Web extra.

Now I'm down to the final details of getting this design implemented. I've chosen a layout with straight lines because I think it uses the space better than my options with curving lines. There's also plenty of room for plants in this plan, especially in the back border. And the patio flows nicely across the back of the house, which was an important "want" in my new design. So, that means we're now up to choosing hardscaping and plants.

START BIG Start with large, visible hardscaping areas, such as the patio or pergola, to set the tone for a design. Even if you think you know what you want, consider a few options for each area. To help you get started, read over the "Material questions" in the box at far right.

For this garden I've narrowed my choices down to three material options for the patio, vegetable garden and pergola. Let me walk you through how I made decisions in "Weigh a few options" at right.

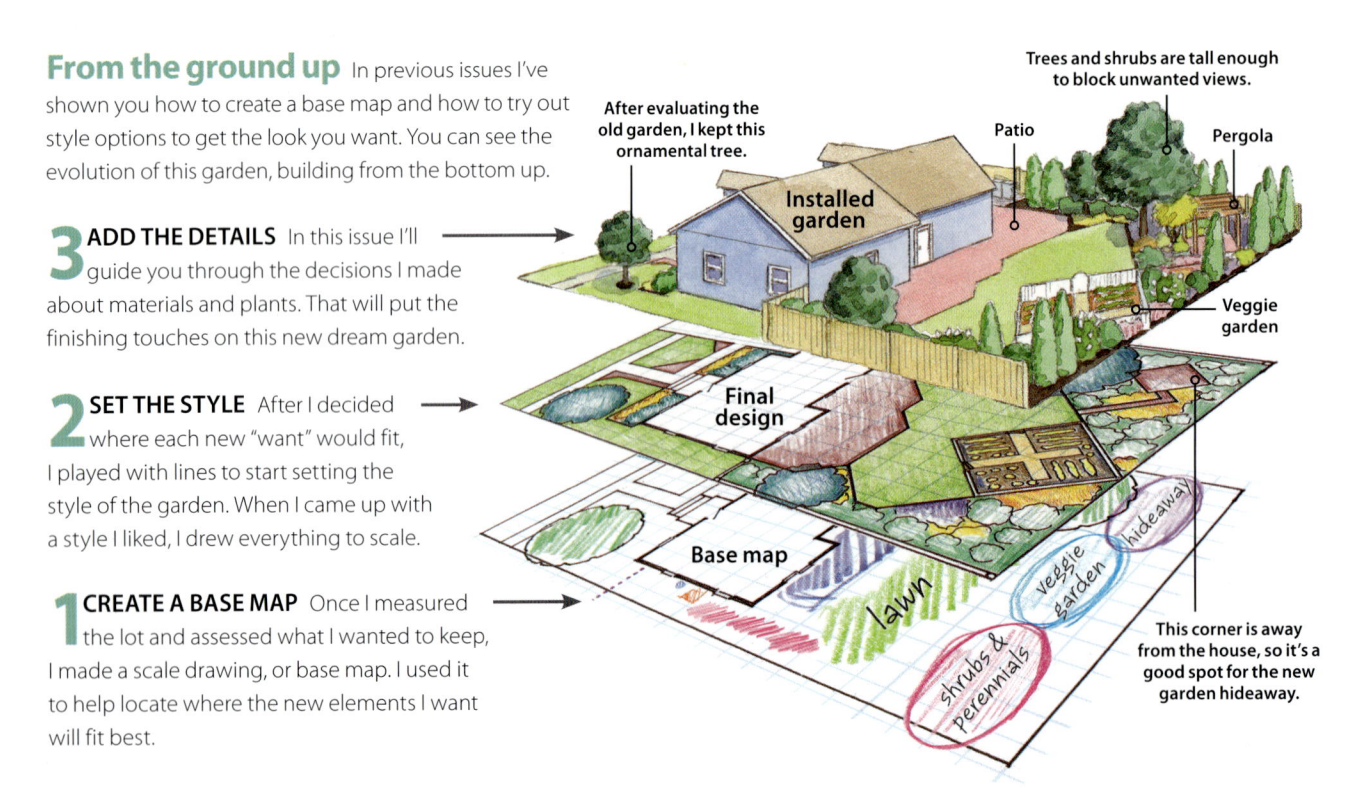

Web extra
Check out the *first two articles* in this design series.

From the ground up In previous issues I've shown you how to create a base map and how to try out style options to get the look you want. You can see the evolution of this garden, building from the bottom up.

3 ADD THE DETAILS In this issue I'll guide you through the decisions I made about materials and plants. That will put the finishing touches on this new dream garden.

2 SET THE STYLE After I decided where each new "want" would fit, I played with lines to start setting the style of the garden. When I came up with a style I liked, I drew everything to scale.

1 CREATE A BASE MAP Once I measured the lot and assessed what I wanted to keep, I made a scale drawing, or base map. I used it to help locate where the new elements I want will fit best.

After evaluating the old garden, I kept this ornamental tree.

Trees and shrubs are tall enough to block unwanted views.

Patio

Pergola

Installed garden

Veggie garden

Final design

Base map

lawn

veggie garden

hideaway

shrubs & perennials

This corner is away from the house, so it's a good spot for the new garden hideaway.

the YEAR IN GARDENING   www.GardenGateMagazine.com

Weigh a few options

Patio material

The patio in the back yard needs to be large enough for entertaining. And I want it to connect the kitchen and living room doors. That will make it easier to carry food and dishes. The materials need to be durable, but I need to balance the cost of the material with installation costs.

Paving brick

PRO Easy repairs; DIY project; lots of patterns and colors
CON Professional installation can be expensive

Concrete

PRO Quick to install; surface can be stamped and stained, like this one, to change the look; economical
CON Hard to repair if it cracks; probably needs to be installed by a professional

Dry-laid cut stone

My choice is stone
Limestone with smooth cut edges fits tightly together; this is also a good DIY project to save on installation costs

Vegetable garden fence

The veggie garden will be a focal point, so I want something around it that's good-looking and won't block the view. And, if it can help keep critters, such as rabbits, from getting to the garden, so much the better.

Iron

PRO Durable, won't rot; extremely long-lasting
CON Installation can be expensive; needs painting to prevent rust and keep it looking good

Split-rail

PRO Least expensive; almost no maintenance; quick and easy to install
CON Loose and open; no control of rabbits and other garden critters

Pickets

My choice is picket fencing
Will hide chicken wire for critter control; could go with a maintenance-free synthetic material if I want to avoid regular painting

Pergola

The pergola in the hideaway area needs to provide some shade and give a feeling of enclosure. But I don't want it to completely block the sunlight or air movement. And it would be best if the structure visually blended into its setting.

Metal

PRO Extremely long-lasting; almost indestructible
CON Expensive, would most likely involve some custom construction; frequent painting necessary

Rustic timbers

PRO Letting the timbers weather naturally means no maintenance
CON Hard to find treated or rot-resistant timbers, so may not be long lasting

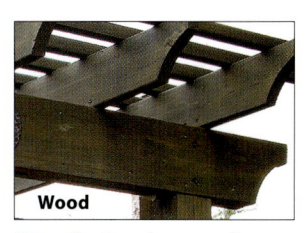

Wood

My choice is wood
Painted wood is an option, but I really like the low maintenance of unpainted treated or rot-resistant wood; easy to build and it'll last a long time

Material questions

☐ What's your budget? You can economize by doing some work yourself, or break the job into phases to spread out the cost.

☐ How much of the work do you plan to do yourself? Be realistic — some jobs, such as pouring concrete or laying a large brick patio, may be worth paying to have installed.

☐ What style are you working with? A painted fence has a more formal feeling than wood that weathers naturally.

☐ What's your winter climate like? Frost can heave concrete, cracking it.

☐ What's your time frame? If you need to get out of the mud now, make sure the materials you choose are readily available and can be installed quickly.

☐ Do you want to spend time maintaining the materials you choose? If you don't like to paint, go with wood that can weather naturally.

design your dream garden: part 3 — the final plan (continued)

DECIDE ON THE DETAILS

Sometimes it's the small details that really make a project stand out. Now that we have the three major materials chosen, it's time to move on to some of the smaller decisions. To help you get started choosing edging and mulch, check out "Material questions" below. Then, in the photos you can find out where I'm using all of these mulches and edging styles.

CLEAN EDGES Nothing keeps a garden looking better than well-defined edges. You can start simple with just a cut edge and upgrade it with metal, brick or stone, as time and money permit.

MULCH CHOICES Mulch is a time saver extraordinaire. With it, you'll spend less time weeding and watering. And a layer of mulch can make your plants healthier. Healthy plants are productive. Less work and more flowers — what more could you ask?

PERSONAL COLOR Choosing color is a personal thing. Let me walk you through how I chose the color scheme for this garden in "Color choices" at right. Then on the next pages, using this information, I've put together a detailed plan for my garden hideaway.

Material questions

- Is the area very visible, especially to visitors? If so, you may want to go with the most visually appealing choice.
- How much time do you want to spend maintaining the material you choose? Steel edging requires almost no maintenance while a trenched edge will need regular trimming.
- What style will you be working with? For example, a trenched edge and bark mulch are pretty universal. But a rustic stone edge may look out of place if you're designing a formal style garden.
- What's your budget? Not all materials cost the same. And if you want an expensive material in a very visible area, you may be able to economize in a spot people won't notice.

TRENCHED EDGE Around large beds and borders, this is an economical way to go. Dig a trench 4 to 6 in. deep and wide. Then fill the trench with loose mulch. Every year or so, use a sharp spade to clean up the edges.

STEEL EDGE When I need a sturdy edge to keep stone in place, such as around the service area, metal edging is the answer. While it may cost more than a trench, it's a good investment because it will last almost forever.

STONE EDGE Where I want a natural-looking edge, such as along the path to the hideaway, narrow slabs of stone are perfect. This material won't need much cutting if I use it for straight lines or gentle curves.

BARK MULCH Organic mulch is the best choice for keeping weeds down and soil moist around the shrubs and perennials. To keep bark mulch looking fresh, I can top it off every year or two.

STRAW MULCH I'll use straw for the vegetable garden. Look for bales that have shiny straw. Strands of green or brown indicate weeds. And straw breaks down quickly, so it can be tilled into the soil every year.

STONE MULCH I don't use stone around plants because it holds heat that stimulates plant growth before the weather settles. However, it's fine where I keep the garbage cans. Use landscaping fabric under stone to keep it from sinking into the soil.

This trenched edge is economical and easy to cut.

Repeating colors throughout the garden unifies the back yard.

Steel edging around the patio won't show but keeps the stones in place.

Color choices

Choosing a color scheme at this stage can help you unify the entire garden. I know I'm often tempted to buy the first interesting flower I find at the garden center, but then I remember my color scheme and stop to think if there's a spot where it will work. If not, I don't buy it.

COLOR LOCATIONS I could go with strong, bold colors. They'll stimulate and energize the scene, especially if I go with hot reds and yellows and contrast them with vivid purples and blues. But they may be better choices for the front garden where I want people who pass by to really notice the new garden. For the back yard I want something more calming and relaxing.

To help me get started on a color scheme, I looked at lots of photos. Photo 1 above inspired me to work with pastels in this back garden. Since the main planting area is quite a distance from the patio, where I plan on relaxing in the evening, I want at least some of the flowers to show in the low light. And since pastels are so calming I'll definitely want them in my hideaway area, too.

But I don't want a boring color scheme. A few punches of bright color are a good idea. In photo 2 the red daylily draws your eye. And in the hideaway you'll see designed on the next page, I've used a bright red rhododendron. Both only bloom for a limited time, but will attract lots of attention when they do.

In the illustration above you can see shades of pink, blue and purple. However, these colors are most noticeable when I'm close to them. Hot colors, such as yellow, red and orange, show more from a distance. I'll sprinkle in a few of these colors to add emphasis to the garden the way the red daylilies and yellow-edged hosta perk up the combination in photo 2.

LONG-LASTING COLOR Garden color doesn't have to be limited to flowers. Some foliage plants, like that gold-edged hosta, will add more interest. Foliage is a great way to keep a garden looking good between bursts of flowers. Colorful leaves last for most of the season. But they do more than simply add color. Just look at how the bright yellow foliage of the hakonechloa in photo 3 helps the deep tones of the pink geranium stand out more. While I like this grass, it's not hardy for me so I'll use hostas instead. The texture is different, but the color will still stand out.

Botanical Names

Daylily
 Hemerocallis hybrid
Geranium
 Geranium spp.
Hakonechloa
 Hakonechloa macra
Hosta *Hosta* hybrid
Rhododendron
 Rhododendron hybrid

design your dream garden: part 3 — the final plan (continued)

COZY **HIDEAWAY**

When I'm designing a new garden, or simply adding into an existing border, I make a list of options for the plants, just as I did for the hardscaping. I divide the list into heights, and then break it down into bloom time. That way I won't end up with everything in the garden maturing at the same height or blooming in the same season.

I've pulled the area around the hideaway out of the plan and shown you the detailed design. The goals for this area are to make it low maintenance and a peaceful spot for relaxing. That means I don't want lots of plants that need constant pruning, staking or deadheading. A thick layer of bark mulch will keep the weeds down. And I won't have to run the sprinkler in my retreat very often, either.

A sense of seclusion is important in a retreat. A pergola provides some shade but doesn't block the air movement like a large overhanging tree might. Some of the plants out away from the pergola, such as the oakleaf hydrangeas and arborvitae, are tall and dense to provide privacy. But closer in, most are shorter. They'll let sunlight and breezes into the hideaway.

The color scheme for my new garden is mostly cool and calm pastel salmon pink and white — I want to relax, not be stimulated. Intense colors, such as vivid red, tend to be energizing. I'll use these strong colors sparingly in my retreat and plant more of them in other areas, such as near the front door, where I want them to grab attention. A variety of textures, from the large hosta leaves to the delicate astilbe, will keep the view interesting even without much color.

MY THOUGHT PROCESS When I started thinking about a tree next to the pergola, I considered several options. I thought about a flowering tree, such as a dogwood, but decided it would grow too large. The foliage color on a 'Hakiro Nishiki' willow is very appealing, but it wouldn't give me much privacy. This fullmoon maple is a good size, the feathery branching provides enough screening, and I really like the brilliant red to orange fall foliage. Once the larger plants like this one are selected, I move on to medium sizes and eventually down to perennials and annuals.

Our design journey has come to an end. You now have the tools to create the garden of your dreams. And as you can see, all it takes is some time and asking yourself lots of questions. Now that you know how to do it, go ahead and design your dream garden! ◻

— Jim Childs

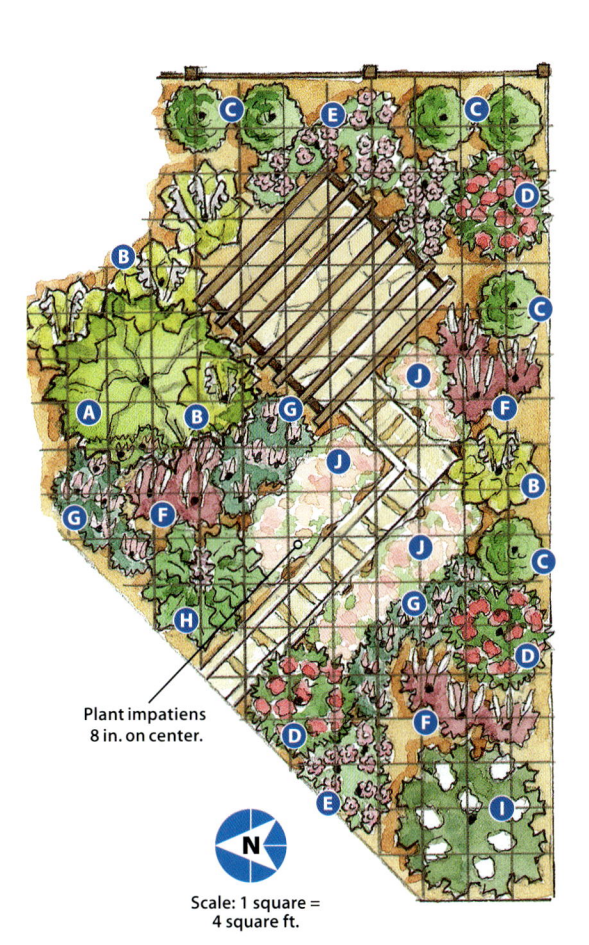

THE GARDEN'S PALETTE

Code	Plant Name	No. to Plant	Blooms	Type	Cold/Heat Zones	Height/Width	Comments
A	Fullmoon maple *Acer japonicum* 'Aconitifolium'	1	NA	Tree	5-7/7-1	8-10 ft./ 8-10 ft.	Deeply divided fernlike leaves turn brilliant crimson in autumn; low mounding habit
B	Hosta *Hosta* 'Sum and Substance'	5	Pale lavender; late summer	Perennial	3-9/9-1	2-3 ft./ 3-5 ft.	Very large leaves; will take several years to grow to full size; best gold foliage produced in part sun
C	Arborvitae *Thuja occidentalis* 'Emerald' ('Smaragd')	6	NA	Evergreen tree	4-8/8-1	15 ft./ 3-4 ft.	Narrow columnar form rarely needs shearing; bright green foliage year round
D	Rhododendron *Rhododendron* 'Nova Zembla'	3	Fuchsia-red; late spring	Evergreen shrub	5-9/9-1	6-10 ft./ 6-8 ft.	Large trusses of flowers; evergreen leaves add winter interest; mulch in summer to keep roots moist
E	Japanese anemone *Anemone hupehensis japonica* 'Pamina'	9	Rose-pink; fall	Perennial	4-8/8-1	28-36 in./ 24-30 in.	2- to 3-in.-diameter double flowers; slow to establish but can spread aggressively by underground rhizomes
F	Bugbane *Actaea simplex* 'Brunette'	9	White; late summer	Perennial	4-8/8-1	4-5 ft./ 1-2 ft.	Deeply cut dark purple-black leaves; fragrant bottlebrush flowers have a light purple tint
G	Astilbe *Astilbe* 'Sprite'	21	Pale pink; summer	Perennial	4-8/8-1	12-18 in./ 12-18 in.	Spring foliage has a dark bronze tint; requires moist humusy soil or it will go dormant in summer
H	Common bear's breeches *Acanthus mollis*	1	White; midsummer	Perennial	7-11/11-1	3-5 ft./ 2-3 ft.	Bold architectural foliage; an alternative is spiny bear's breeches (*A. spinosis*), cold-hardy to zone 5
I	Oakleaf hydrangea *Hydrangea quercifolia*	1	White; summer	Shrub	5-9/9-1	4-8 ft./ 4-8 ft.	Flowers change from white to pink to brown; foliage turns shades of purple and crimson in autumn
J	Impatiens *Impatiens* 'Tutti Frutti Mix'	105	Salmon-pink; summer	Annual	Annual/12-1	8-12 in./ 6-12 in.	Mix containing pastel shades of salmon and pink; constant bloom all summer; mulch to keep soil moist

Plant impatiens 8 in. on center.

Scale: 1 square = 4 square ft.

DESIGN | ALL AROUND THE YARD

4 tips for fragrance all year!

Wouldn't it be wonderful to have a garden filled with fragrance all year long? It sounds like a lofty goal, but after talking to Lucy Tolmach, director of horticulture for Filoli Center, I realized it's not only possible, but easy! (Filoli is a California estate that's part of the National Trust for Historic Preservation and known for very fragrant gardens.) Lucy shared her four best tips for designing year-round fragrant gardens, plus her favorite scented plants. See how each tip plays a part in the garden in our illustration below.

1 ADD BACKBONE The easiest way to work fragrance into the garden is through "backbone" plants. Backbones are trees, shrubs and woody perennials, usually long-lived and low-maintenance. Plus, many are fragrant! Do you want a hedge around your yard for privacy? A row of sweet-scented daphne might do the trick. How about some height in your island bed? Grow a climbing rose on an arbor. A rule of thumb for fragrance: Choose one scented backbone plant per garden bed, to avoid competing fragrances. If you grow more than one backbone in your yard, make sure each has a different season of fragrance.

2 ADD ACCENTS Once your backbones are in place, think back over each season. Are any still missing scent? Or do you want to enhance a particular plant? Use accent fragrances — perennials, bulbs and annuals that have softer scents to complement existing stronger fragrances. The heliotrope and alyssum in the illustration below accent the rose, with its strong, sweet old-rose perfume. Or plant grape-scented irises at the base of a mockorange. Want some ideas for every season? Check out "Four seasons of scent" at right. To find the most fragrant accents, look to old-fashioned cultivars, or buy species.

3 THINK OUTSIDE THE BED Fragrant plants aren't just for garden beds — they're also ideal for containers! The lavender in the illustration is a great option, but almost any plant, from an annual to a small tree, can thrive in a container. So choose your favorite fragrant bloomer, and find a pot that's big enough to hold it. Containers are portable, so you'll be able to show them off anywhere. Decorate your front stoop with pots of garden phlox. Grow fragrant stock in a window box below a living room window, so the scent wafts through the house as you relax. The options are endless!

4 PLAY WITH FRAGRANCE Sometimes, fragrance comes from unexpected places. Take sweet box, for example. Its small white flowers are easy to miss, but they bear a powerful fragrance. Tea olive is the same way. Choosing fragrant plants with small or hidden blooms is a great way to encourage friends and family to explore the garden to find the source of that scent. You might plant the crabapples in the illustration for the pretty spring blooms, but the bonus is that they're fragrant.

And don't forget about foliage. For example, bee balm leaves smell like Earl Grey tea. Pineapple sage smells like, well, pineapple. Scented geraniums have foliage that, when rubbed, can smell like peppermint, lemon, pine, chocolate and more.

Follow these four easy tips, and you'll have a garden full of enticing scents all year long! □

— *Amanda M.W. Glazebrook*

PHOTO: Courtesy of Filoli Center (Lucy Tolmach)

Crabapples offer fragrant flowers and colorful fruit.

'Hidcote Blue' lavender grows well in pots.

Fragrant William Shakespeare 2000™ roses are rebloomers.

Look for the species heliotrope for the best scent.

FOUR SEASONS OF SCENT

spring

Bearded iris *Iris* hybrids
Rhizome; pink, white, purple or yellow in mid- to late spring; full sun; 12 to 36 in. tall, 18 to 24 in. wide; cold-hardy in USDA zones 4 to 9, heat-tolerant in AHS zones 9 to 1

Common lilac *Syringa vulgaris*
Shrub; pink, purple or white blooms in midspring; full sun; 8 to 15 ft. tall, 6 to 10 ft. wide; cold-hardy in USDA zones 3 to 8, heat-tolerant in AHS zones 8 to 1

Crabapple *Malus* hybrids
Tree; red, pink or white blooms in spring followed by small fruits in fall; full sun; 8 to 25 ft. tall, 10 to 25 ft. wide; cold-hardy in USDA zones 3 to 9, heat-tolerant in AHS zones 9 to 1

Hyacinth *Hyacinthus orientalis* (in photo)
Bulb; blue, white, pink, peach or purple blooms in early spring; full sun; 6 to 12 in. tall, 3 to 5 in. wide; cold-hardy in USDA zones 4 to 8, heat-tolerant in AHS zones 8 to 1

Saucer magnolia *Magnolia xsoulangeana*
Tree; pink-and-white, cup-shaped flowers in early spring; full sun; 20 to 25 ft. tall, 20 to 30 ft. wide; cold-hardy in USDA zones 4 to 9, heat-tolerant in AHS zones 9 to 1

Silky wisteria *Wisteria brachybotrys*
Vine; 4- to 6-in.-long wands of pink or white midspring flowers; full sun; 10 to 25 ft. tall, spreading; cold-hardy in USDA zones 5 to 8, heat-tolerant in AHS zones 8 to 1

Hyacinth

summer

English lavender *Lavandula angustifolia*
Perennial; spikes of purple blooms in early summer; full sun; 1 to 4 ft. tall, 1 to 5 ft. wide; cold-hardy in USDA zones 5 to 9, heat-tolerant in AHS zones 9 to 1

Heliotrope *Heliotropium arborescens* (in photo)
Tender perennial; deep purple blooms from spring to fall; full sun to part shade; 18 in. tall and wide; cold-hardy in USDA zones 10 to 11, heat-tolerant in AHS zones 12 to 1

Mockorange *Philadelphus* hybrids
Shrub; white blooms in early summer; full sun to part shade; 3 to 10 ft. tall, 3 to 8 ft. wide; cold-hardy in USDA zones 4 to 8, heat-tolerant in AHS zones 8 to 1

Oriental lily *Lilium* hybrids
Bulb; white, yellow, orange, pink or red blooms in mid-summer; full sun; 4 to 8 ft. tall, 1 to 2 ft. wide; cold-hardy in USDA zones 3 to 8, heat-tolerant in AHS zones 8 to 1

Rose *Rosa* hybrid
Shrub or climber; wide range of colors and sizes; select carefully as not all are fragrant; cold-hardy in USDA zones 4 to 11, heat-tolerant in AHS zones 11 to 1

Sweet alyssum *Lobularia maritima*
Annual; flurry of small white, pink or lavender blooms from summer to fall; full sun to part shade; 3 to 9 in. tall, 6 to 12 in. wide; heat-tolerant in AHS zones 12 to 1

Heliotrope

fall

Bugbane *Actaea simplex*
Perennial; white bottlebrush blooms in late summer and fall; part shade; 3 to 4 ft. tall, 2 to 3 ft. wide; cold-hardy in USDA zones 4 to 8, heat-tolerant in AHS zones 8 to 1

Butterfly bush *Buddleja davidii*
Shrub; wands of blooms in pink, purple or white from summer to fall; full sun; 3 to 10 ft. tall and wide; cold-hardy in USDA zones 5 to 9, heat-tolerant in AHS zones 9 to 1

Moonflower *Ipomoea alba* (in photo)
Tender perennial vine; white evening blooms from summer to frost; full sun; 10 to 15 ft. tall, spreading; cold-hardy in USDA zones 10 to 12, heat-tolerant in AHS zones 12 to 1

Sasanqua camellia *Camellia sasanqua* 'Stephanie Golden'
Shrub; pink blooms from mid- to late fall; full sun to part shade; 10 to 20 ft. tall, 6 to 12 ft. wide; cold-hardy in USDA zones 7 to 9, heat-tolerant in AHS zones 9 to 1

Sweet autumn clematis *Clematis terniflora*
Perennial vine; flurries of small white blooms in late summer and fall; full sun to part shade; 20 ft. tall, spreading; cold-hardy in USDA zones 4 to 9, heat-tolerant in AHS zones 9 to 1

Tea olive *Osmanthus fragrans*
Shrub; small white blooms from fall to spring; full sun to part shade; 6 to 10 ft. tall, 6 to 8 ft. wide; cold-hardy in USDA zones 8 to 11, heat-tolerant in AHS zones 11 to 1

Moonflower

winter

Daphne *Daphne odora*
Shrub; white blooms in late winter and early spring; full sun to part shade; 18 to 48 in. tall and wide; cold-hardy in USDA zones 7 to 9, heat-tolerant in AHS zones 9 to 1

Japanese flowering apricot *Prunus mume*
Tree; pink to white flowers in winter or early spring; full sun; 10 to 20 ft. tall and wide; cold-hardy in USDA zones 6 to 9, heat-tolerant in AHS zones 9 to 1

Paperwhites *Narcissus tazetta*
Bulb; white or gold blooms in winter or early spring; full sun to part shade; 6 to 20 in. tall, 3 to 6 in. wide; cold-hardy in USDA zones 8 to 10, heat-tolerant in AHS zones 12 to 1

Sweet box *Sarcococca confusa*
Evergreen shrub; tiny white flowers in winter, followed by black berries; part to full shade; 3 to 6 ft. tall, 3 ft. wide; cold-hardy in USDA zones 6 to 9, heat-tolerant in AHS zones 9 to 1

Sweet violet *Viola odorata*
Perennial; blue, violet, pink or white blooms in late winter and early spring; part shade; 6 to 12 in. tall, 15 to 18 in. wide; cold-hardy in USDA zones 4 to 9, heat-tolerant in AHS zones 9 to 1

Witchhazel *Hamamelis xintermedia* (in photo)
Tree; yellow, orange or copper flowers in late winter; full sun to part shade; 6 to 20 ft. tall, 6 to 15 ft. wide; cold-hardy in USDA zones 5 to 8, heat-tolerant in AHS zones 8 to 1

Witchhazel

DESIGN | ALL AROUND THE YARD

(1) Lots of bright yellow, with touches of blue and gray, keep this garden warm even on a cloudy day.

Let the Sun Shine In!

Get the lowdown on how to create a colorful and spacious garden.

Botanical Names

Coleus *Solenostemon* hybrid
Coreopsis *Coreopsis* spp.
Hakonechloa *Hakonechloa macra*
Hosta *Hosta* hybrid
Lily *Lilium* spp.
Purple coneflower *Echinacea purpurea*
Purpleheart *Tradescantia pallida* 'Purpurea'
Russian sage *Perovskia atriplicifolia*
Sea holly *Eryngium* spp.
Yucca *Yucca filamentosa*

Most gardeners want their yards filled with as much color as possible. Mark Freeman is no exception. He uses a color palette of yellow and orange, with a few touches of blue and purple, to make sure his sunny Michigan garden always has a warm glow. But let's take a look at exactly how he keeps that color coming as long as possible.

LONG-LASTING COLOR Flowering perennials are one of the best ways to get lots of color. And this garden does use lots of those. You can't miss the lilies, coreopsis and Russian sage in photo 1. However, flowers aren't the only thing brightening up this scene. Splashes of gold 'Color Flash' yuccas in photo 2 carry the garden from one bloom peak to the next. And they're not alone: Hostas, hakonechloa, and even annuals, such as the purpleheart you see at the base of those yuccas, get in on the act, too. Why purpleheart? It makes a terrific color contrast to all of the gold foliage and it's an economical plant. Like many other foliage annuals, such as coleus, you can pick up and plant one or two, enjoy them in the garden and then overwinter them indoors. Take cuttings in spring, root them and you'll have lots of colorful plants to spread around next year.

Once you've found some hard-working plants you love, don't be afraid to use them in several places. This garden is an average-sized city lot. The photos you see here are in the front yard, but when you turn the page, you'll see some of the same plants carried into the back yard, too.

WIDE-OPEN SPACES Did you notice that most of the perennials and annuals in both of these photos are no more than waist high? Many of them also have a wispy habit you can see right through. Their low stature gives this sunny garden a wide-open feeling, making it appear larger than it really is.

138   *the* YEAR IN GARDENING   www.GardenGateMagazine.com

Front yard

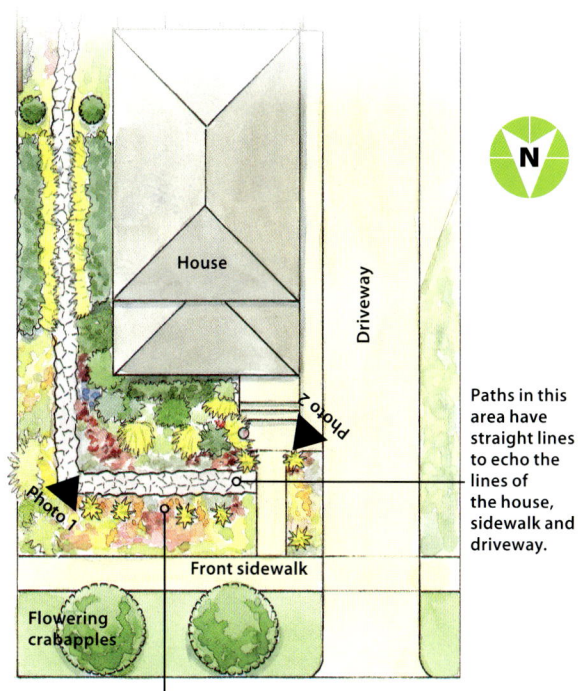

Paths in this area have straight lines to echo the lines of the house, sidewalk and driveway.

Except for two flowering crabapples, all of the plantings are kept low to give the feeling of wide open spaces.

INTERNATIONAL PRAIRIE

Translating an authentic prairie into the average-sized home property can be difficult — in a small area it may look rough and unkempt. That's why an "international prairie" may be better: Not all of the plants have to be native to your area. Just choose flowers that like full sun, and make sure your garden keeps a casual, unstudied look. The bed near the street is such a space. There's a closeup of it in the photo at right, too.

CHOOSE GREAT PLANTS The blue sea holly in this photo comes from Europe, but along with the native coneflowers, it keeps a prairie look. And don't shy away from named cultivars. What started out as white 'Fragrant Angel' coneflowers are reseeding to the shades of pink you see here. If you want to keep the flowers all the same, you'll need to deadhead. But a prairie is meant to evolve, so be flexible and the reseeders will keep your garden looking fresh and different each year.

MAKE TOUGH CHOICES Even though it's always on show, it's sometimes hard to keep a front-yard garden looking great. You want plants that are at their best all of the time. Often there's a lawn with shade trees to help tie the house into its setting and give a tidy, comfortable and cozy look. Shade trees help keep the area cool, too. Without large trees in a front yard, the spots near sidewalks, driveways and streets can get pretty hot. And it's usually quite a distance from the spigot to the street, so dragging a hose to water is kind of a hassle. To survive, let alone look good, the plants have to be drought-tolerant. Front-yard choices also have to take some abuse: It's inevitable that a few may get stepped on, or have a close encounter with a bicycle tire. And then there are dogs to consider. This is not a spot for your prized new hellebore!

This front garden takes advantage of plants that are drought-tolerant and sun-loving. Many of the choices here are prairie natives. But you don't need to be a purist. Some non-natives work well in these situations, too. Let me show you how to create a planting that keeps its natural spirit in "International prairie," above.

On the next pages you'll see more photos and learn tips on how Mark takes care of the garden. There are even specific tips on how he grows the spectacular clumps of hakonechloa you see in photo 1.

(2) Let in the sun! Low plants in the center with taller ones kept to the edges help this small garden feel spacious and wide open.

SIMPLE **BEAUTY TIPS**

You've seen how colorful this garden is. Here are some tips on how to keep yours healthy and looking just as good — without spending a lot of time doing it.

MULCH MATTERS Most of us couldn't keep up with watering and weeding if we didn't use mulch. Every spring these beds are topped off with a 1-inch layer of hardwood bark fines. It's a mix of 75 percent shredded wood and 25 percent bark. In photo 3 you can see that the texture and the dark color don't distract from the flowers and foliage.

Decomposing mulch actually pulls nitrogen out of the soil, robbing your plants of this nutrient. You can help offset this by sprinkling a very light application of nitrogen fertilizer over all the beds before you put the mulch down. But don't overdo chemical fertilizers or you'll harm the microorganisms that are helping plants absorb other nutrients. The mulch and the light feeding of nitrogen help all of the plants, including the striking clumps of hakonechloa, grow strong. Having trouble getting your hakonechloa to look this lush? Check out helpful tips in "Happy hakonechloa" at right.

LET INSECTS TAKE CARE OF THEMSELVES Several years ago this garden was badly infested with spider mites. Spraying had become a constant chore, and it was killing all of the beneficial insects, too. After struggling with the problem for a couple of seasons, Mark stopped using pesticides to see what would happen. It took a few years, but as the beneficial insects came back, they got rid of the spider mites. If your garden has a serious pest, try reducing or even skipping pesticides completely. You may find that beneficial insects return to take care of the problem for you.

THE PATH TO HAPPINESS Have you noticed that good paths often make great gardens? The surface can be as simple as the same mulch used in the flower beds. But the chunks of flagstone in photo 3 make an architectural statement. They're meant to be seen, and they unify the garden from front to back. The paths in the front yard use straight lines to mimic the lines of the street and house. In the back yard, the edges are gently curved for a less structured look.

These generous paths encourage folks to walk out into the garden and enjoy it up close. Being a hard surface, and wide, they're like a ribbon of patio extending out from the deck. And like a patio, in some areas they're wide enough for visitors to gather and enjoy the garden.

Botanical Names

Hakonechloa
Hakonechloa macra

JUST THE RIGHT FOUNTAIN A water feature is the crowning glory for many gardens. But a natural-looking stream is difficult to achieve in a small back yard. If a simple fountain fits the size and style of your garden better, go with that. Can't find just the right one? Cast your own!

The one in the center of photo 3 has four short pillars made from hypertufa, a mixture of equal parts of Portland cement, vermiculite and milled sphagnum peat moss. Mix it up in a tub or wheelbarrow and stir in enough water to moisten the mix enough that it resembles a crumbly brownie batter. Then pack it into forms and let them cure. These square pillars support a copper bowl, once part of a birdbath, that spills into a 16-inch-deep basin.

You can see exactly where the low fountain's placed in the garden in the illustration at right. It's set in a small bed in the center of the path so you can see it from the deck or enjoy it up close. Plus it's near enough to the small shaded sitting area that you can hear it as you're relaxing.

Well, we've come to the end of the tour of this garden. I hope you've discovered some tips you can use in your own yard! ☐

— *Jim Childs*

(3) Wide paths wind through the back yard, giving visitors more places to stand and enjoy the open feeling of this sunny garden.

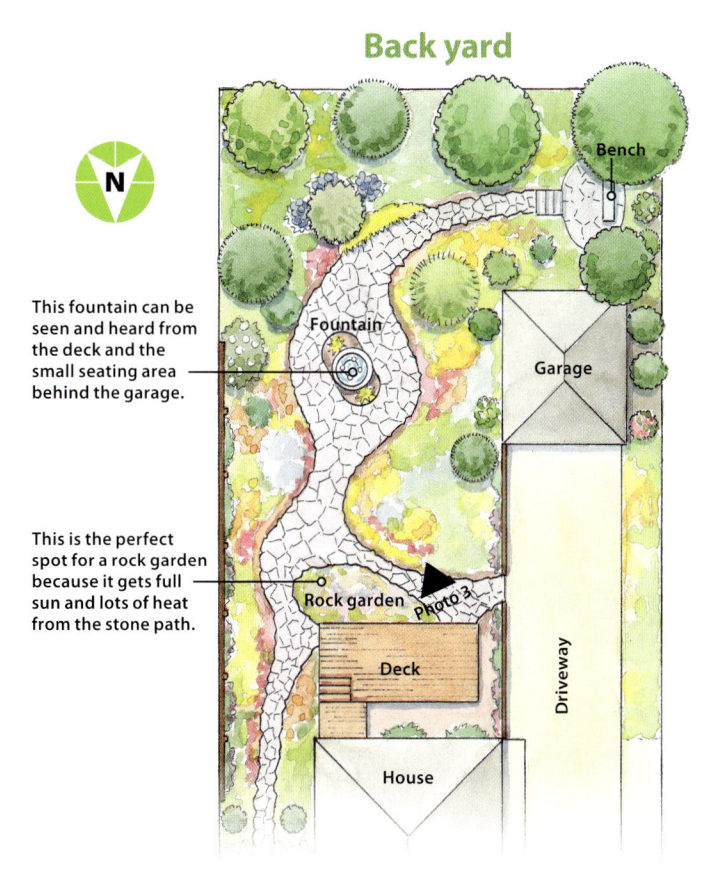

Back yard

This fountain can be seen and heard from the deck and the small seating area behind the garage.

This is the perfect spot for a rock garden because it gets full sun and lots of heat from the stone path.

HAPPY HAKONECHLOA

Want your hakonechloa to look like these? First, even though it's often listed as a shade grass, hakonechloa grows much denser with six hours of morning to early afternoon sun. Midafternoon sun will bleach out the color and scorch the leaves.

Second, after a couple of hard freezes, set your lawn mower as high as you can and mow down the foliage. Then spread a 1-in. layer of Milorganite® over each clump. It won't burn roots or foliage, and the microorganisms in the soil break the fertilizer down so the plants get off to a fast start next spring.

And finally, search out the most robust specimen you can find at your local nursery. If it looks wimpy in the pot, odds are it'll be wimpy in your garden. All of these clumps are descended from one healthy, lush plant purchased nearly 20 years ago.

DESIGN | ALL AROUND THE YARD

shape up your garden

Botanical Names

Astilbe *Astilbe* hybrid
Blanket flower *Gaillardia* hybrid
Boxwood *Buxus* hybrid
Canna *Canna* hybrid
Clematis *Clematis* hybrid
Feather reed grass *Calamagrostis xacutiflora*
Redbud *Cercis canadensis*
Russian sage *Perovskia atriplicifolia*
Snapdragon *Antirrhinum* hybrid

Do you keep looking at your garden, thinking that something just isn't right? Maybe it feels a bit wispy or messy, or maybe you've noticed that all the plants are about the same height. It probably needs structure! But what does that involve? Duane Hoover, horticulturist for The Ewing and Muriel Kauffman Memorial Garden, a garden open to the public in Kansas City, Missouri, can help.

A FIRM FOUNDATION What is structure? You might say that structural elements serve as a foundation or backdrop to your garden. Structure contrasts with surrounding plants and accentuates details like small flowers or colorful twigs. And when most of your garden is dormant, structure can add winter interest. Duane likes to add structure by including plants or hardscaping elements that are denser or taller — or both — than the plants around them.

But don't worry! You don't have to rush right out to plant a hedge or build a fence. There's an easy way to decide where your garden could use some structure, as you'll see in "Give structure a trial run" below. Try different combinations until you get it just right. Then take a look at the photos on the next pages for ideas on adding permanent structure.

SHAPE IT UP The first thing you notice about photo 1 is the fence, a great example of structure. Anything "constructed," whether it's a fence, a garden shed or the side of a garage, automatically adds structure. These elements are bigger and more solid than plantings, and they're in place year-round. They also add height — Duane recommends that most structural elements should be at least one and a half times taller than most of the surrounding plants, so that the structure doesn't disappear.

PLANT YOUR STRUCTURE Speaking of height, look at the upright clipped boxwoods in photo 1 and the tree in photo 2. They're taller than lower-growing plants in front of and beside them. And their dense, twiggy growth is a good contrast with looser, more open plants nearby. Clip evergreens into geometric shapes for more impact. (See our Web extra for Duane's favorite evergreens to add structure to home gardens.) And limb up small trees or large shrubs to expose enough bare trunk to set off surrounding plantings.

See how structure works? Go ahead and give it a try. It's just what your garden needs! □

— *Leslie Herring and Stephanie Polsley Bruner*

GIVE STRUCTURE A TRIAL RUN

Not sure if your garden needs structure...or where it should go? Duane recommends trying it out with a couple of bold-foliaged tropical plants in hefty containers. The Russian sage, feather reed grass and blanket flower in the top illustration are pretty together. But they're all airy and loose-textured. After you look at that for a while, it just seems messy.

In the bottom illustration, the canna's big leaves and dense texture break up the wispy, all-one-height planting, so you can see how a taller permanent plant (or two!) would add much-needed structure. The best thing about this technique is that you can move the containers around until you find just the right spot.

Airy, wispy, floppy... these flowers are pretty, but they need some structure.

Bold tropical leaves contrast with the lighter-weight plants nearby.

An asymmetrical group of containers lets you try out structure without drawing too much attention to one container.

142 *the* YEAR IN GARDENING   www.GardenGateMagazine.com

BACK IT UP A solid object, whether it's a privacy fence like this one, or a garden shed or the wall of a garage, automatically adds structure to a garden. And it's a great way to show off a plant like this purple clematis. Those sprawling stems look like artwork displayed against the fence.

MORE IS BETTER When you use evergreens for structure, plant several — one clipped evergreen will turn into a focal point instead of a structural element. In this yard, you can see that large boxwoods are spaced around the perimeter, including one raised up to a similar height in this container. Their dense, twiggy growth offers a pleasing contrast to the looser growth habits of the clematis, snapdragons and cleome in the beds.

DOWN IN FRONT Although most structural items or plants are tall, this row of small clipped boxwoods forms a definite dense "backbone" for this low-growing border. Even in winter, when the astilbe and snapdragons are past, you'll be able to see the shape of the border and appreciate the visual interest the boxwoods add. They'll also frame the container in four seasons, making it a gorgeous focal point.

DON'T FORGET THE OBVIOUS Next to a planting of light, airy grasses that are all about the same height, the trunk of this redbud tree really stands out. It's taller than the other plants, and it's solid, in contrast to their wispy texture. Limb up small trees or large shrubs to allow those sturdy trunks to take their structural place in the garden. (The rest of the tree adds structure, too, but it's most noticeable down at the level of smaller plants.)

Web extra Check out a **list** of Duane's favorite evergreens to add structure to any garden.

SET IN STONE Although it's shorter than the plants behind it, this boulder, with its size, density and permanence, is definitely structural. And while it could also be considered a focal point, its neutral color keeps it from taking over this scene.

DESIGN | ALL AROUND THE YARD

(1) Large containers are a good way to get chartreuse and other bright colors up close to the door.

4 ways to wake up any garden with this packs-a-punch color.

Cheer Up With Chartreuse

Like many bright colors, chartreuse is a jolt of energy. How do you harness it so it doesn't knock you off your feet? Let's take a look at four ways to make the powerful punch of chartreuse work for your garden.

1 BRIGHT ON BRIGHT The chartreuse door in photo 1 was bright and cheerful all by itself. Combined with chartreuse plants and some other bright colors, this becomes an entryway that makes you smile just to look at it.

Why do these elements work together so well? First, let's talk about placement. This doorway gets morning sun but is shaded by midday. That's a good place to use bright colors like chartreuse. Morning sun is less intense than afternoon light, so the chartreuse and orange are cheery, not in-your-face bright.

Now, about that red-orange. For maximum impact, pairing two high-intensity colors like this is really the way to go. It makes for an eye-catching combination, as each color actually makes the other appear brighter. If you're not all that wild about orange, then try chartreuse with hot pink or red-violet — either combo will be stunning.

2 FOCUS ON CHARTREUSE Speaking of eye-catching, you can't fail to see that bright chartreuse 'Frisia' black locust in the distance of photo 2, can you? That makes it a great choice for a focal point. What does that mean? Well, focal points are objects or plants that stand out, directing your attention to specific parts of the garden. A big tree like this one also serves as a great reference point — you can see it from many areas in the garden, so it helps establish a sense of space and location.

If you really want to make chartreuse pop, try it against a dark background, like the evergreens in the distance of the photo. This chartreuse locust would still show up against a stand of trees with lighter foliage, but it wouldn't have the impact that it does here.

While you're planting, include more chartreuse somewhere in the garden. It doesn't have to be a lot — in fact, it'll be more effective if you use it sparingly, because you don't want to distract from the main focal point. But that little clump of chartreuse spirea in the foreground is a nice visual link with the tree.

Want to see a couple more ways chartreuse can punch up your garden? Turn the page and keep on reading.

Botanical Names

Black locust
Robinia pseudoacacia
Spirea *Spiraea* hybrid

---

(2) A big splash of chartreuse like this locust is a focal point you can see from almost anywhere in the garden.

2 MORE WAYS TO **PERK THINGS UP**

Chartreuse isn't just for paint and trees. Let's take a look at how some smaller plants can add chartreuse charm to a garden.

3 FOLLOW THE TRAIL There are two great design secrets in the photo below. Can you spot them? Well, maybe not. Often, great design isn't all that noticeable! So what are these secrets? The first one is a basic design tip called "repetition," and it's simple. See how the clumps of chartreuse hakonechloa are repeated here and there along the edge of this border? Your eye follows them along the border, emphasizing the sweep and curve of the bed. Actually, there's also some great texture contrast, too, as the wispy hakonechloa stems trail in front of more upright plants with bolder foliage. That, paired with the bright color, makes these clumps even more eye-catching. (Besides hakonechloa, what plants have the best chartreuse foliage? Take a look at "A brighter shade of green," at left, for some of my favorites.)

So what's the second design tip? Well, this is a small garden, and this border is hiding a privacy fence. Placing a light color like chartreuse at the front of the border and backing it up with darker plants actually makes the border look deeper. The darker colors tend to recede, while the lighter color visually moves forward. It's a handy tip to know in a small area, or anywhere that you want to fool the eye into thinking you have a little more space than you really do!

And while we're speaking of light and dark, let's take a look at one last way chartreuse can perk up your garden.

A BRIGHTER SHADE OF GREEN

Black locust *Robinia pseudoacacia* 'Frisia' Tree; yellow-green foliage may turn orange in fall, fragrant white spring flowers; full sun; 30 to 50 ft. tall, 20 to 30 ft. wide; cold-hardy in USDA zones 5 to 9, heat-tolerant in AHS zones 9 to 1

Hakonechloa *Hakonechloa macra* 'Aureola' Grass; arching gold leaves with bright-green stripe; part shade; 1 to 2 ft. tall and wide; cold-hardy in USDA zones 5 to 9, heat-tolerant in AHS zones 9 to 1

Hosta *Hosta* 'Sum and Substance' Perennial; huge, puckered chartreuse leaves, pale-lavender flowers in midsummer; part to full shade; 30 in. tall, 60 to 72 in. wide; cold-hardy in USDA zones 3 to 9, heat-tolerant in AHS zones 9 to 1

Sweet potato vine *Ipomoea batatas* 'Margarita' Tender perennial; trailing vine that can cascade out of containers or act as a ground cover; full to part sun; 6 to 12 in. tall, 60 to 72 in. wide; cold-hardy in USDA zones 10 to 11, heat-tolerant in AHS zones 12 to 1

---

(3) Light colors in front and darker greens in back make this border look deeper than it really is.

GREEN GROW THE FLOWERS

Hydrangea *Hydrangea* 'Preziosa' Shrub; flowers open chartreuse, change to white then pink; part shade; 3 to 4 ft. tall and wide; cold-hardy in USDA zones 6 to 9, heat-tolerant in AHS zones 9 to 1

Lady's mantle *Alchemilla mollis* Perennial; flowers in late spring to early summer, deadhead to prevent reseeding; full sun to part shade; 10 to 18 in. tall, 18 to 30 in. wide; cold-hardy in USDA zones 4 to 8, heat-tolerant in AHS zones 8 to 1

Pineapple lily *Eucomis bicolor* Tender bulb; where not hardy, plant in spring for midsummer to fall blooms; full sun; 18 to 24 in. tall, 6 in. wide; cold-hardy in USDA zones 8 to 11, heat-tolerant in AHS zones 11 to 1

Zinnia *Zinnia elegans* 'Envy' Annual; double flowers attract butterflies; full sun; 18 to 24 in. tall, 12 to 15 in. wide; heat-tolerant in AHS zones 12 to 1

(4) Chartreuse flowers of lady's mantle and hydrangea brighten this shady area, making it look like it enjoys dappled sun.

4 FLIP ON THE LIGHT Have a dark, dreary corner that needs a little "oomph?" Chartreuse to the rescue! It reflects more light than plain old dark-green, and that makes it easier to see in a shady area.

Of course, there are plenty of plants that'll bloom and give you color in a shade garden. But chartreuse doesn't just add color; it adds the effect of extra light, as well. Take a look at photo 4. With those scattered dots and splotches of chartreuse, doesn't it look like dappled sunlight peeking in here and there? When beams of light shine down on "ordinary" green foliage, leaves look lighter and brighter. So chartreuse, which is lighter and brighter already, looks like it's out in the sun…even when it isn't!

When you're trying to lighten up a dark space, be sure to include several chartreuse plants, not just one. One spot of bright color will act as a focal point like the tree you saw earlier, and it will be the only thing you'll notice. But if the chartreuse is sprinkled all around the shady spot, it'll brighten the whole area. You'll be able to appreciate other details, like the small garden shed behind the planting in the photo.

Another thing you'll notice in this photo is that it's flowers that are doing the talking. As I mentioned before, you'll find plenty of plants with chartreuse leaves, like the yellow-green edges of the hosta in the photo. But surprisingly, there are actually plenty of yellow-green flowers, too, like the hydrangea and lady's mantle here. (Well, the hydrangea flowers are chartreuse before they're fully open, then they'll fade to white…which will also look great in a shady garden!)

Don't have a shady corner like this? Not to worry. There are chartreuse flowers for you, too. As you might imagine, they'll add a happy sparkle to a sunny garden, as well. Take a look at "Green grow the flowers," above, for a few glorious chartreuse flowers for shade and sun. And once you've picked some of your favorites, tuck them here and there in your garden, and see how they perk things up! ☐

— *Stephanie Polsley Bruner*

DESIGN | ALL AROUND THE YARD

What You Need to Know About Fences

5 ways fences can be functional *and* fabulous!

The old saying goes, "Good fences make good neighbors." But, in my view, it should also say, "Good fences make good *gardens*." That's because you can transform a so-so garden into an outstanding one by adding the right fence to the mix. And, on top of that, a good fence can do a lot more than stand around and look beautiful. Depending on your particular needs, a fence can fill any of a number of different roles: as a decorative backdrop, a boundary marker, a traffic director or something to block or obscure views. Let's take a look at some design considerations and the best features of each of these uses.

DECORATIVE BACKDROP You've probably heard that every garden needs vertical elements to spark visual excitement. A great way to do this is to add a fence. Though a short one like the one below won't provide any real privacy or security, it's very space-efficient. This one has a much smaller footprint than a tall plant does — important in a small garden.

And the fence's hard straight lines add a contrast to the softer lines of the plants, creating an instant frame or background for them. You can see that the flowers below have more impact against the neutral background of a fence that they would with a backdrop of lawn. In addition, ones with prominent posts like this create a pleasing repetition in a garden, which only adds to its appeal.

To use a fence as a decorative backdrop, be sure its look goes with your house. (The classic picket fence complements nearly all but very modern architecture.) But pick one that's open enough for the plants to show (and grow!) through so the fence also becomes an integral part of your garden's design.

BOUNDARY MARKER One of the simplest, and probably oldest, roles a fence can fill is to define the line between your property and your neighbor's. Many styles can do the job quite well. A fence that's acting as a boundary marker doesn't have to be solid, or even continuous, for that matter.

The board fence at right clearly outlines this gorgeous garden, but does it without precluding a friendly chat over the top of it with your next door neighbor. And the airy slats help slow down strong winds without completely blocking the view. On the other hand, sometimes, installing a simple post and split rails at the corners of your yard is all you need to mark the edges of your property and bring attention to the garden inside.

PHOTOS: Greg Ryan/Sally Beyer (decorative backdrop); © Jerry Pavia (boundary marker)

Decorative backdrop
This updated picket fence, with its natural-finished pickets and painted posts, is attractive in its own right. But it also complements the style and white trim of the house in the background. To anchor the fence, if you have the space, make the depth of the planting at least half the height of the fence.

Boundary marker
Painted a subtle gray, this handsome fence doesn't scream for attention, but gracefully defines the garden's boundaries. It gives you a logical starting place to begin to design plantings. The relatively low height of this board fence doesn't block the view. And its open-slat design allows air circulation to keep plants healthy.

MORE USES FOR FENCES

Botanical Names

Clematis *Clematis* spp. and hybrids
Honeysuckle *Lonicera* spp.
Penstemon *Penstemon digitalis*
Rose *Rosa* spp.
Silverlace vine *Fallopia baldschuanica*

In addition to providing an attractive background for plantings or marking the boundaries of your property, a fence can fulfill other purposes. Here are three more good uses for fences in your garden.

TRAFFIC CONTROL At the most basic level, fences are meant to keep people and/or animals either in or out of a designated space. A simple wire-mesh or chain-link fence is often the most obvious choice for a job like this. Compared to other types, these fences are affordable and not susceptible to problems from pests or decay. And they don't take as much maintenance as wood, bamboo or wrought iron. But there are some other benefits, too.

As you can see in the photo below left, this wire-mesh fence would certainly keep all but the most determined small child or dog in bounds. (There are even special wires you can install at the bottom to dissuade Fido from digging to freedom.) But it does it without blocking the view or creating pockets of stagnant air around your plantings. Want to enjoy the company of your neighbors, or a glimpse of the pretty yard next door? You'll still be able to see it through a fence like this. You can always plant a hedge or small tree if you change your mind down the road.

PRIVACY Sometimes there's a view you really need to hide, and nothing does that better than a privacy fence. Whether it's a standard stockade-style or the unusual one with horizontal boards at upper right, a tall fence can hide eyesores like a parking lot or busy street. It can also muffle outside noise. Planting a garden on the south side of your fence? A privacy fence may create a microclimate that lets you grow plants that aren't usually quite cold-hardy enough for your zone. On the other hand, a solid fence can make a windy spot worse by creating a back draft on the sheltered side of the fence. If you live where strong winds are common, an open style fence, which baffles the air, may be a better fit.

Of course, a privacy fence also blocks the view into the garden, a primary need when you're trying to create a safe and private retreat from the busy world outside. Dog owners benefit from this type of fence, too, as many dogs are less likely to bark at things they can't see — another way to preserve the quiet of your getaway!

SCREENING Maybe you need the height of a privacy fence (perhaps for a dog that jumps shorter ones), but you don't want a solid barricade. A tall lattice fence like the one at right is the perfect answer. It's great if you like a tall fence but don't want that closed-in feeling.

A fence that screens the view is also useful for dividing your garden into different "rooms." Even small gardens benefit from separating areas with different uses. Because the fence doesn't totally block the view, it can add a hint of mystery about what lies beyond. But a well-placed fence can also discourage people from stumbling into more private areas.

Traffic control

For the purpose of keeping pets or people in or out of particular areas, it's hard to beat a wire-mesh fence. This one looks tall, but is actually 42 in. high. Its open style won't make this small garden claustrophobic by blocking out the outside world. And because it's painted black, it easily blends into the garden background.

Privacy

Ready-made wood fence panels make installation simple and give instant privacy and security. Or choose a custom-built fence like this one, which boasts unusual horizontal panels instead of vertical ones. Spaces between boards allow air circulation.

Most privacy fences are 6 ft. tall, but you can attach a 2-ft.-wide lattice panel across the top for extra height. (Check with your local zoning laws first.) Then grow a climbing plant, such as this rose, along the top for a bit of colorful screening.

For a bit of extra privacy, grow a vine like this clematis on it. Not only does it enhance the beauty of the fence, but it also maximizes the planting area in your garden. And there's still plenty of air circulation, which can be important in a small, densely planted space.

Fences fill practical needs, but that doesn't mean they have to be boring. They can create an eye-catching or subtle background for your favorite plants, direct traffic, hide or screen a view. Now that we've explored different roles that fences can fill in a garden, you can choose the one that you'll enjoy in your own garden for years to come! ☐

— *Deborah Gruca*

Screening

Many clematis have leggy, bare stems at the bottom. Cover them up with lower-growing perennials, such as this penstemon. Other good woody-stemmed climbers to use are honeysuckle, with fragrant yellow, white or pink mid- to late summer flowers, or silverlace vine with its white late-summer blooms. The lattice lets a little extra light through, so you don't have the extremes of light and shade that you would with a solid fence.

DESIGN | ALL AROUND THE YARD

create a charming cottage garden anywhere

Botanical Names

Bee balm *Monarda didyma*
Coreopsis *Coreopsis* spp.
Flowering tobacco
  Nicotiana spp.
Larkspur *Consolida ajacis*
Maltese cross
  Lychnis chalcedonica
Marguerite daisy
  Argyranthemum frutescens
Masterwort *Astrantia major*
Queen Anne's lace
  Daucus carota
Rose *Rosa* spp.
Sea holly *Eryngium planum*

Don't you love colorful cottage gardens? This traditionally British garden style is not only pretty, but it looks doable. Want to know how to get that look with a North American spin? I talked with Stephen Westcott-Gratton, the author of *Creating a Cottage Garden in North America*, about this idea, and he shared some universal benefits and great how-to ideas.

EASY-GOING DESIGN If strict garden design rules and terms make you queasy, take heart! A cottage garden's loose, unpretentious look is simple to design. You need some sort of structure, such as a fence or hedge, enclosing a planting with lots of color and variety. Lay a few paths through the space and leave a small patch of lawn, at most, and you're done! And although a traditional cottage garden may have been in the front yard, there's no reason you can't use these same principles in any space. Is one plant spreading? Let it. Step in to intervene only if something starts to take over. See that pink foxglove leaning in photo 1? No big deal. Cottage gardens are casual that way. The plants in photo 2 are closely planted in clumps or drifts, not rows, with some bare spots left for tucking in spring bulbs, annuals or edibles.

LOTS OF VARIETY Though not large, the colorful border in photo 3 contains a wide mix of plants, including larkspur, coreopsis, roses and bee balm. Annuals, perennials and edibles all mingle happily in a cottage garden. Be sure to choose plants with a variety of heights, textures and bloom times. Plants native to your area work great because they grow well without much coddling. Those that reseed (but not excessively so) are traditional in cottage gardens, as are easy-care heirloom annuals, old roses and other plants that don't need a lot of

(1) A simple path like this is a snap to build, and reseeding plants, such as the blue love-in-a-mist, will quickly fill the space around the stones.

(2) Use lots of variety in a cottage garden. Tall yellow roses and scarlet Maltese cross contrast with shorter Marguerite daisies by the path. Mix up your flower shapes, too: Here, spikes, daisies and globes all mingle.

extra water. Don't forget to include plants that attract birds, butterflies and beneficial insects. Masterwort, Queen Anne's lace and sea holly are a few good examples. Check out four good plants for North American cottage gardens in "Colorful cottage garden favorites" below.

INEXPENSIVE PLANTS AND HARDSCAPING All of the easy-going plants I just mentioned will save you money because they're simple to get started in large numbers and they don't require much water or mulch. And when you can attract beneficial insects, like lady beetles and green lacewings, you won't spend a lot of cash for pesticides to keep plants healthy. You'll save money on hardscaping as well because the cottage style doesn't use a lot of manmade elements. A simple picket fence or arbor is perfect.

EASY-CARE BEDS Before you start, you'll ensure your plants are vigorous and disease-resistant by working plenty of compost or manure into the soil. Then space your plants close together. That way they'll shade the soil so there'll be less need to weed, mulch or water very often. Close planting also means you'll do less staking — sturdier plants can hold up their listing neighbors. And finally, because there are little or no turf areas, there's less grass to edge, mow, feed or water.

So there you have it. With the right plants and a few tips, you can enjoy that typically British cottage garden charm wherever you happen to garden!

— *Deborah Gruca*

(3) A simple picket fence is classic cottage garden style. This structure makes a great backdrop for the plantings on both sides of the fence. Want a softer look? Plant a hedge instead.

COLORFUL COTTAGE GARDEN FAVORITES

These four colorful plants are easy to grow in most of North America and reseed readily. Give them a try!

- **A** **Love-in-a-mist** *Nigella damascena* Annual; frilly blue flowers followed by interesting seedheads; 18 to 24 in. tall, 12 to 18 in. wide; heat-tolerant in AHS zones 12 to 1
- **B** **Borage** *Borago officinalis* Annual; edible blue flowers from early summer to early fall; 1 to 3 ft. tall, 10 to 18 in. wide; heat-tolerant in AHS zones 12 to 1
- **C** **Foxglove** *Digitalis* spp. Biennial or short-lived perennial; bell-shaped flowers in many colors in late spring to summer; 1 to 6 ft. tall, 1 to 2 ft. wide; cold-hardy in USDA zones 4 to 8, heat-tolerant in AHS zones 8 to 1
- **D** **Columbine** *Aquilegia canadensis* Perennial; red and yellow spring flowers; 9 to 36 in. tall, 10 to 18 in. wide; cold-hardy in USDA zones 3 to 8, heat-tolerant in AHS zones 8 to 1

DESIGN | ALL AROUND THE YARD

In these small beds, every plant counts!

Six Plants, Three Beds

You don't need a lot of plants or a big bed to make a lot of impact. I've taken six hard-working plants and mixed and matched them to create three simple beds for situations many folks have: along a driveway, around a mailbox and a small island garden.

When you're planning a short plant list like the one at right, start by choosing plants with flowers *and* pretty foliage. Then look for plants that don't get too huge — you don't want to spend all your time cutting a plant back to keep it in bounds.

DRIVE-BY GARDEN The narrow strip between two driveways needs tough plants that don't mind heat and an occasional dry spell. (This combination would be great for the parking strip between the sidewalk and the street, too.) Instead of planting a solid line of one plant down the center, cluster plants together in groups of three or four, and plant them at irregular intervals. That way, if one dies or gets too big, it won't throw off your whole planting.

CORNER POCKET Even a necessity can look great! A stepper in the middle of the snow-in-summer makes it easy to get close to the mailbox. There's no sedum in this plan — it attracts a lot of bees, which you don't want around a spot you have to step into. (The other flowers will only attract a few.) Weigela and phlox add plenty of color, as does the mandevilla growing on the mailbox.

EASY ISLAND An island bed can block a view, break up a sweep of empty lawn or serve as a focal point. Blue oat grass encircles an obelisk supporting the mandevilla. And weigela and sedum on the outside edge keep the blooming going strong from spring to fall.

Now what are you waiting for? Get started! ☐

— *Stephanie Polsley Bruner*

ILLUSTRATIONS: Travis Rice

Both snow-in-summer and sedum have attractive leaves, even when they're not flowering.

Drive-by garden

Plant list (Number to plant)

- **A** Weigela (9)
- **B** Blue oat grass (8)
- **C** Sedum (5)
- **D** Phlox (4)
- **E** Snow-in-summer (19)
- **F** Mandevilla (not included)

Scale: 1 square = 1 square ft.

Corner pocket

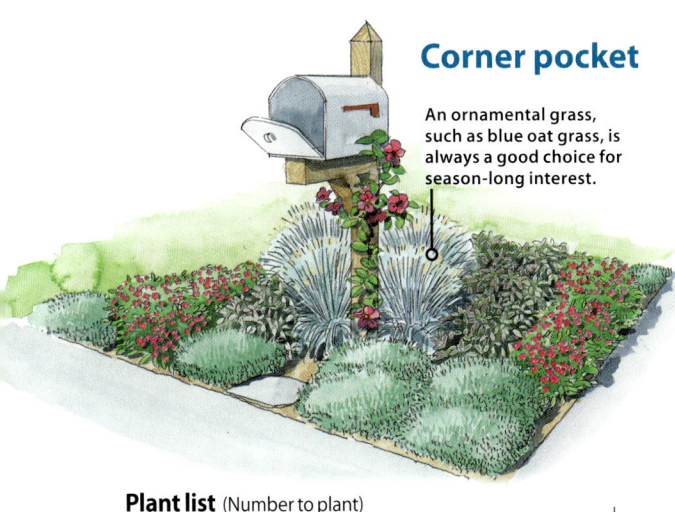

An ornamental grass, such as blue oat grass, is always a good choice for season-long interest.

Plant list (Number to plant)

- A Weigela (6)
- B Blue oat grass (5)
- C Sedum (not included)
- D Phlox (6)
- E Snow-in-summer (15)
- F Mandevilla (1)

Scale: 1 square = 1 square ft.

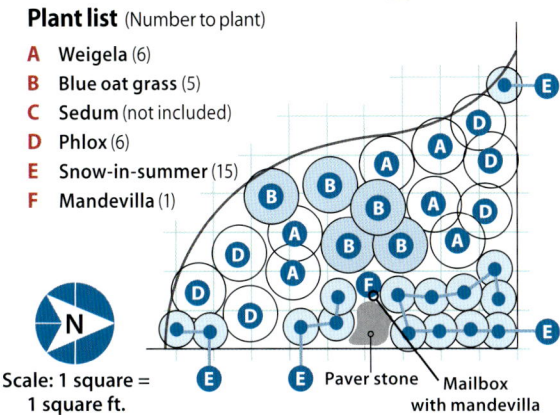

Paver stone — Mailbox with mandevilla

Easy island

Mandevilla looks great in the heat of summer, even when other plants start to droop.

Scale: 1 square = 1 square ft.

Plant list (Number to plant)

- A Weigela (6)
- B Blue oat grass (5)
- C Sedum (5)
- D Phlox (not included)
- E Snow-in-summer (not included)
- F Mandevilla (1)

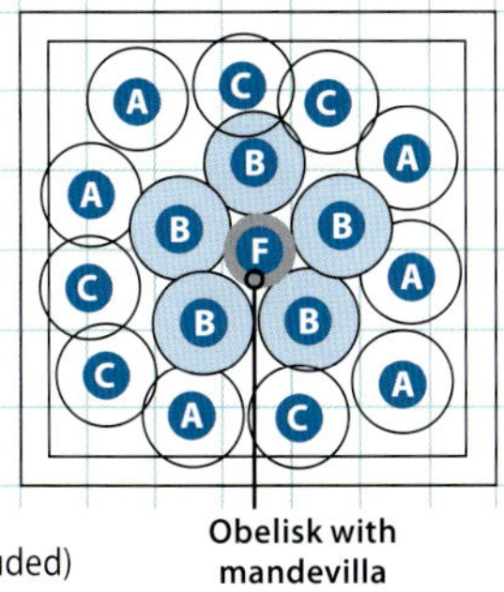

Obelisk with mandevilla

THE GARDEN'S PALETTE

A Weigela *Weigela* My Monet™ ('Verweig') Shrub; green, cream and pink foliage, pink early summer flowers; full sun to part shade; 12 to 18 in. tall and wide; cold-hardy in USDA zones 4 to 9, heat-tolerant in AHS zones 9 to 1

B Blue oat grass *Helictotrichon sempervirens* Ornamental grass; clump-forming, blue-green leaves topped with tan seedheads in early to midsummer; full sun; 2 to 3 ft. tall, 18 to 30 in. wide; cold-hardy in USDA zones 4 to 9, heat-tolerant in AHS zones 9 to 1

C Tall sedum *Sedum* 'Autumn Joy' ('Herbstfreude') Perennial; flat-topped rosy pink flowers in late summer to fall, succulent leaves; full sun; 18 to 24 in. tall and wide; cold-hardy in USDA zones 3 to 9, heat-tolerant in AHS zones 9 to 1

D Garden phlox *Phlox paniculata* 'Junior Dream' Perennial; bright pink-purple flowers all summer, compact, mildew-resistant cultivar; full sun; 18 to 22 in. tall, 18 in. wide; cold-hardy in USDA zones 4 to 9, heat-tolerant in AHS zones 9 to 1

E Snow-in-summer *Cerastium tomentosum* Perennial; white blooms in early summer, low mat of silver-gray foliage; full sun; 6 to 12 in. tall, 9 to 12 in. wide; cold-hardy in USDA zones 3 to 7, heat-tolerant in AHS zones 7 to 1

F Mandevilla *Mandevilla xamabilis* 'Alice du Pont' Tender vine; bright pink 4-in. blooms from early summer to frost; full sun to part shade; 3 to 20 ft. tall (smaller in containers or when grown as an annual); cold-hardy in USDA zones 10 to 11, heat-tolerant in AHS zones 12 to 1

PHOTOS: Courtesy of Spring Meadow (A); courtesy of Plant Delights Nursery, Inc. (D)

www.GardenGateMagazine.com   *the* YEAR IN GARDENING   155

DESIGN | ALL AROUND THE YARD

5 nearly no-care plants save you work

THE WEEKEND GARDENER · Garden Smarter

Easy Island Bed

Sometimes it's nice to have a garden that's as easy on the eyes as it is on the back. After all, there's nothing wrong with creating a bed that won't demand a lot of your time or effort. That doesn't make you a lazy gardener — just a smart one.

Having said that, a low-maintenance garden doesn't have to mean an all-evergreen-shrub border. In fact, look at this full-sun island bed. There are just five hard-working, easy-care perennials in it. I chose each plant for its good looks and lack of need for fussing. Then I tucked in a few low-care annuals here and there to fill in any gaps in the perennials' bloom times. To start the flowering even earlier, plant some spring-blooming bulbs around the perennials. Bulbs will thrive in a low-water bed like this because they hate being overwatered while they're dormant in summer.

Once this bed is planted, the hardest work is done and you can sit back and enjoy the flowers. In late spring, the bloody cranesbill has its big flush of pink blooms. It'll also rebloom on and off throughout the summer, but there's no need to deadhead the faded flowers. The 'May Night' salvia starts its own flower show in summer, followed closely by the spiky blue blooms of sea holly.

If, by midsummer, the weather gets very hot, you could freshen up the look of this garden by shearing the foliage of the bloody cranesbill lightly and cutting back the faded salvia blooms. (You may be rewarded with a few more of the deep blue flowers.)

Don't fret about losing those flowers, though. You'll still have the foliage of the 'Gold Bar' maiden grass and the burgundy sedum. And by late summer their flowers will make their entrances onto the scene. No deadheading needed here, either. They'll keep on blooming well into fall (highlighted by the red fall foliage of the bloody cranesbill). In fact, this pair doesn't really need anything more than to be cut back to about 3 inches high in early spring — which is a good time to do a general cleanup of the whole bed. So relax, you don't have to worry about doing that for quite a while! ☐

— *Deborah Gruca*

Tuck annuals, such as these 'Magellan Orange' zinnias, into any open spaces between the other plants. You'll be assured of constant color all summer long.

ISLAND IN THE SUN

PLANT LIST (number to plant)

A **Maiden grass** *Miscanthus sinensis* 'Gold Bar' **(3)**
Upright habit with horizontal gold stripes on leaves; burgundy fall flowerheads; cut the plant down to the ground in early spring before the new growth begins to emerge; full sun; 3 to 5 ft. tall, 2 to 3 ft. wide; cold-hardy in USDA zones 5 to 9, heat-tolerant in AHS zones 9 to 1

B **Sea holly** *Eryngium* 'Sapphire Blue' **(7)**
Spiny blue flowers in mid- to late summer with spiky foliage; long tap root makes it difficult to transplant, so be sure you know where you want it before planting; full sun; 24 to 30 in. tall, 18 to 24 in. wide; cold-hardy in USDA zones 5 to 9, heat-tolerant in AHS zones 9 to 1

C **Salvia** *Salvia* x*sylvestris* 'May Night' ('Mainacht') **(11)**
Long upright spikes of indigo blue flowers open in early to midsummer; will bloom for two months, if you keep it deadheaded; full sun; 18 to 24 in. tall, 15 to 18 in. wide; cold-hardy in USDA zones 4 to 9, heat-tolerant in AHS zones 9 to 1

D **Bloody cranesbill** *Geranium sanguineum striatum* **(10)**
Light pink flowers cover the plant in late spring; foliage takes on a reddish cast in fall; full sun to part shade; 6 to 9 in. tall, 12 to 18 in. wide; cold-hardy in USDA zones 3 to 8, heat-tolerant in AHS zones 8 to 1

E **Sedum** *Sedum telephium* 'Lynda Windsor' **(12)**
Dark burgundy leaves and stems on a tidy, compact plant; 2- to 3-in.-wide clusters of ruby flowers in late summer to fall; full sun; 12 to 18 in. tall, 12 to 16 in. wide; cold-hardy in USDA zones 3 to 9, heat-tolerant in AHS zones 9 to 1

Plant spring-blooming bulbs toward the center of the bed. Later, perennials will emerge and hide the fading foliage.

Scale: 1 square = 1 square ft.

(1) Create a focal point and a place to relax. The chairs you see here are in the large photo, too. Once you reach them you can rest and look back at the garden you've just passed through.

DESIGN | ALL AROUND THE YARD

A Garden to Explore

Borrow these design ideas to create your own beautiful yard.

Ever been traveling down the street and spy a garden you just had to explore? From the minute you first see this garden, you know it's going to contain intriguing things and have lots of places to investigate. And it's so inviting, how can you resist? I've checked with Chuck Beard and Charles Parrish. They won't mind if we take a quick tour of their Missouri garden.

ENJOY THE JOURNEY A straight line is the shortest, and often fastest, route from one point to another. But this generous path from the steet to the front door makes the journey much more enjoyable. A straight path would speed you along, but curves encourage you to slow down and look at the garden around you. And the bed shapes in the front garden all have curving edges to coordinate with the path, too.

Originally there was a large border across the front property line. And there was no break in it for a sidewalk from the street to the front porch. Visitors had to trudge up the blacktop driveway to get to the house. You can see it's along the west side of the garden in the illustrated plan at right.

So Chuck and Charles dragged the garden hose around to find just the right curve for the path from the street. What you see in the lead and photo 1 is the result. Its generous 5-foot width lets two people easily stroll side by side.

More than just a surface to walk on, this path is a visual ornament to the garden. While one color of brick would have been an option, this blend has a more relaxed feeling — kind of like a tweed jacket is more casual than a solid color. And these deep red and pale gold choices mesh beautifully with fall's color palette, too.

THE PATH LESS TRAVELED The small path in photo 2 greets visitors who walk up the driveway. Without it, folks, including the mail carrier, would have to cut through a shrub border, damaging plants and leaving a muddy path. But you'll save your plants, and your friends' shoes, if you can direct visitors onto a solid-surfaced path.

SHADE OUT THE WEEDS This front yard has a lot of trees and shrubs. But in late fall, rather than being a hassle, all those leaves can come in handy — chop them into mulch. This way they'll reduce weed problems next year.

(2) Take a shortcut to the porch. Guests, or even the mail carrier, will appreciate this charming informal path from the driveway.

Another thing that helps here is close planting. By summer, the tightly packed plants shade the soil, preventing weeds from popping up.

Now we're ready to move on to the next room. See the gazebo on the corner of the porch in photo 2? Use it as a reference point as we continue onto the next page.

Botanical Names

Boxwood
Buxus spp.

Pockets of annuals add color and change each year for a fresh look.

Before the brick path, guests used to walk up the driveway to reach the house.

Path

Evergreen boxwoods help guests find the path, even in the winter.

www.GardenGateMagazine.com · *the* YEAR IN GARDENING · 159

LEAD ON!

We're heading into the side garden now. It's just around the edge of the porch gazebo in photo 3 — let's explore.

SUBTLE STYLE CHANGE Since this area is more private and less traveled than the front walk, the path can be narrower, more like a hallway from one room to another. The same color blend of bricks you saw in the front yard is repeated to unify the two areas. And if you look at the illustrated garden plan at right, you'll see even narrower paths that are covered in wood mulch in this area. These are secondary to the main routes and they loop through the garden so you can explore. But you won't get lost — they all lead back to a brick path.

Mulch paths are fine for areas that don't get lots of use. However, organic materials tend to pack into the soil with lots of foot traffic. Eventually these paths need to be topped off or you could end up with a muddy mess. And if you opt for mulch, always go with shredded materials. Chips, especially large pieces, can be hard to walk on.

LET IT CLOSE IN ON YOU Unlike the front garden, where the plants along the path are low so you can see the house, here they gradually get taller. Walking through tall shrubs and trees gives you a feeling of being enveloped. Since you can't see too far into the distance, the screen of foliage creates curiosity about what may

(3) A curving path adds mystery because you aren't sure where you're headed.

Botanical Names

Canadian hemlock
Tsuga canadensis
Flowering dogwood
Cornus florida
Heavenly bamboo
Nandina domestica
Impatiens
Impatiens hybrids

(4) Get lost in your own garden by letting tall plants like the autumn-tinted flowering dogwood and red-fruited heavenly bamboo grow right up to the edge of the path.

160   the YEAR IN GARDENING   www.GardenGateMagazine.com

be ahead. Don't have room for a large planting of shrubs? A pergola with latticework sides and a heavy blanket of vines can give you a similar effect. Or if you have a structure that just seems plunked into your garden, grow a few vines on it to help it blend in.

Painting a garden structure a contrasting color, such as the bright white gate in photo 4, is a great way to create a focal point. Because it stands out strongly against the foliage, you know the white gate is the way to go. So let's head that direction and find out what's on the other side.

RELAX AND STAY AWHILE Walk through the gate and you enter a rectangular room. To the right in photo 5 you'll spot a screened porch. Imagine relaxing there on a summer evening, free of mosquitoes, as you enjoy the view into the garden. Enclosing this area with a hedge and creating a canopy of tree branches is a sure way to make a garden feel snug and protected. A hedge of evergreen Canadian hemlock will eventually be sheared to create an even denser screen.

Since you can see into every corner, you feel safe and secure. A fountain set dead center can be seen, and enjoyed, from every angle. The soothing sound of even the smallest water feature helps you relax. But we need to keep moving. There's a white arbor on the left in photo 5. It'll lead us into the next room. Let's go!

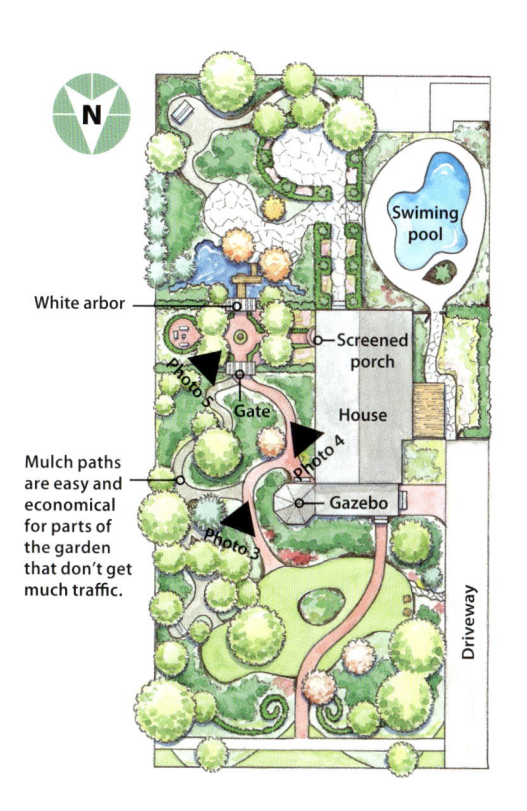

(5) Keep an area calm and relaxing by using lots of neutral green foliage and soft pastel flower colors, like these shades of pink and white impatiens. Save bold, vivid colors like red, bright yellow or orange for spots where you want to create excitement.

(6) Let the moss grow by keeping a shaded path moist. It'll make the path look like you're on a woodland stroll.

lead you onward, so you may not be sure which way to turn. Having that sensation will make this small area seem bigger because you can't see the boundaries, either. But don't worry — you won't get lost. See the house in the distance in photo 6? Follow the stone path and let's head that direction.

As you walk, notice how dense the plantings are. Large clumps of hydrangeas fill the area under a stewartia that's in its fall color. Unlike the front garden where clumps of annuals change each year, here the plantings remain pretty much the same. The seasonal changes of flowers and foliage are the focus. Even in winter, the structure and texture of the branches against a few evergreens create a pleasing scene.

A CHALLENGE TO SOLVE Keep moving toward the house and you'll step through a border to find a swimming pool. Not sure where you are? See the dark pot at the edge of the pool in photo 7? The path behind it is the same one you just walked up in photo 6.

Adding a swimming pool into a garden can be a challenge. It's large, and all that concrete is a strong contrast to the lush plantings. But an organic design like this fits the scheme better than a rectangular pool. Pots filled with plants bring the garden closer to the edge, too.

FIND THE RIGHT SPOT Chuck and Charles like to test the limits of the plants they grow. The key is to find just the right spot, or microclimate. It may take some research to find what the new "guest" will like, but they've had some good successes pushing the zones. This garden is on the line

A STYLE CHANGE

Seating areas tucked in a secluded corner encourage you to sit and observe the garden more often.

A koi pond adds interesting fish to look at and soothing water sounds to this part of the garden.

If you've been following along on the illustrated garden plan at left, you'll discover you're now in the back yard.

CHANGE IS GOOD A path of random pieces of limestone gives this part of the garden a rustic appeal. And the dense plantings without defined edges give you the feeling you've left the structure of a manmade garden and are out in a wild woodland. Even though the area is only about 60 feet square, there are no striking focal points in this part of the garden. There is not one distinct feature to direct your gaze and

162   the YEAR IN GARDENING   www.GardenGateMagazine.com

of USDA zones 5 and 6. Yet by cutting down the bananas and covering the stumps with several feet of mulch contained in a frame, the bananas, usually rated for warmer zone 6 or zone 7, survive. And scattered around the garden you also find heavenly bamboo, mondo grass and Japanese laurel. All of them grow best in warmer zone 6 and into 7. You'll find tips on how to push the limits in your garden in "Give them what they need" at right.

Like most gardens, there are areas in this one that are evolving. If you look at the illustration you'll notice that we didn't tour the area on the south side of the house. Perhaps next time? Like a good meal, a good garden always leaves you wanting more. □

— *Jim Childs*

GIVE THEM WHAT THEY NEED

Finding just the right spot for a plant is more than visual or the best soil type. Sun and wind play important roles in how well a plant thrives, too.

For marginally hardy plants, look for areas that are out of strong winter winds, often the south or east sides of your house. The bananas in photo 7 are a good example. Warmth from the foundation and the protection from cold winds are big pluses.

And consider the heat retention of a sunny stone wall or even a concrete sidewalk. Most folks might fill an area bordered by concrete with heat-loving annuals. But the concrete helps the fig in this photo survive. It holds heat radiated from the sun and keeps the fig's roots warmer than if it were planted in an open border.

Botanical Names

Banana
Musa basjoo
Common fig
Ficus carica
Heavenly bamboo
Nandina domestica
Hydrangea
Hydrangea spp.
Japanese laurel
Aucuba japonica
Japanese stewartia
Stewartia pseudocamellia
Mondo grass
Ophiopogon spp.

(7) Tropical plants look right at home next to a pool. And they can take the summer heat radiated from the concrete, too.

DESIGN | ALL AROUND THE YARD

accessorizing
your garden

See the detailed **planting plan** for both of these gardens.

PHOTO: Courtesy of Campania International

Have you ever purchased a piece of garden décor or an ornament to beautify your yard, brought it home and thought, "Now what?" That's not uncommon — I sure have. If you've ever struggled to make an ornament look just right, here are some tips to help. I'll take one simple yet striking piece — an urn — and show you how you could use it to achieve different effects in your garden.

Since the setting will be as important as the ornament, your first decision is how you want to stage the piece. Do you want it to be a focal point or something much less noticeable? You need to consider other focal points you may already have in the garden. Will adding another one make the scene look busy and confusing? The piece won't show up very well if it has to compete for attention.

A STAR IS MADE In the two gardens here, the 39-inch-tall urn is a star, or focal point, that quickly draws your eye. After you focus on it for a short time, your eye moves over the rest of the garden. But you will always come back to look at the focal point.

Getting the idea? You can really do a lot of different things with one simple ornament — it's all how you frame it. Let me give you more details on how to do that. ◻

— *Jim Childs*

The crown jewel

In a formal setting an ornament is often the center of attention. No matter where you stand in the garden, it's the focal point. If you're able to use a substantial enough piece, it's visible from a distance so it draws you into the garden, too. Although the urn is a neutral buff color, the shape and large size make it stand out. Plus there's just one urn and it doesn't have to compete for attention with other ornaments, so it has a bigger impact.

To call the most attention to your ornament, place it in the center of the garden and organize the plants as a frame around it. Use uncomplicated lines, like the straight edges and circle in this garden. In keeping with this simple approach, there are only four different plants in this garden. And other than white, there is only one flower color, a soft peachy rose. This simplicity also adds emphasis to the ornament as a focal point.

A lovely brooch

Here the ornament is in a more casual setting, partly because of its asymmetrical placement, and the variety of colors and textures around it. Your eye is still drawn to the urn, but it's more of an accessory, like putting a pretty pin on a lapel.

This urn's size is balanced by the masses of plants near it. The garden frames the urn, but it's a part of the garden rather than a separate entity. Since the urn is a neutral color, it's a strong contrast to the bright flowers surrounding it. That means it really stands out in this setting.

One of the nice things about this design style, and the one above, is that you can often put in a different ornament without ruining the balance. As long as the new piece is a similar size, or visual weight, you can swap ornaments for a fresh new look every now and then. And you can match or contrast the ornament with the color scheme to influence the impact, too.

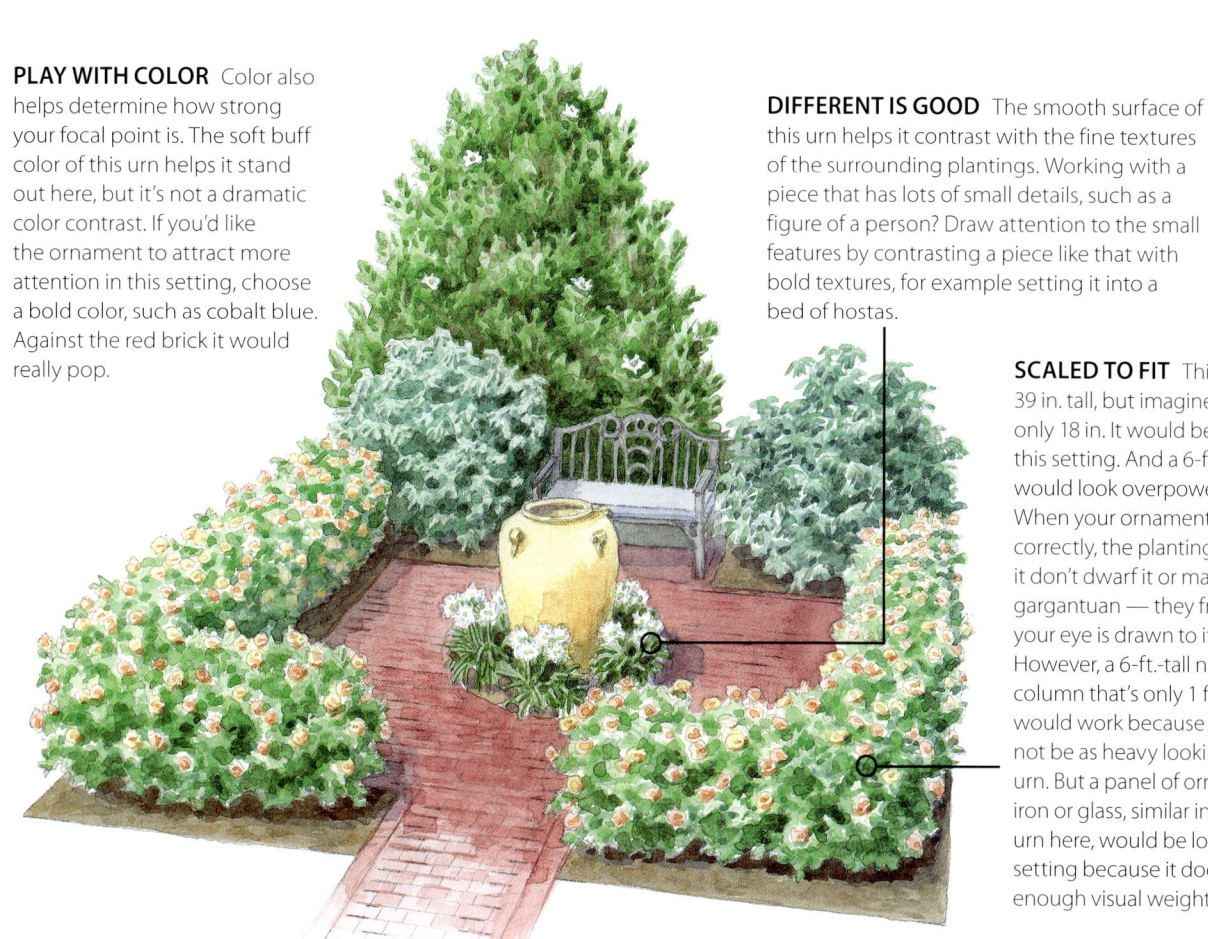

PLAY WITH COLOR Color also helps determine how strong your focal point is. The soft buff color of this urn helps it stand out here, but it's not a dramatic color contrast. If you'd like the ornament to attract more attention in this setting, choose a bold color, such as cobalt blue. Against the red brick it would really pop.

DIFFERENT IS GOOD The smooth surface of this urn helps it contrast with the fine textures of the surrounding plantings. Working with a piece that has lots of small details, such as a figure of a person? Draw attention to the small features by contrasting a piece like that with bold textures, for example setting it into a bed of hostas.

SCALED TO FIT This urn is 39 in. tall, but imagine if it were only 18 in. It would be lost in this setting. And a 6-ft.-tall urn would look overpowering. When your ornament is scaled correctly, the plantings around it don't dwarf it or make it look gargantuan — they frame it so your eye is drawn to it. However, a 6-ft.-tall narrow column that's only 1 ft. wide would work because it would not be as heavy looking as a 6-ft. urn. But a panel of ornamental iron or glass, similar in size to the urn here, would be lost in this setting because it doesn't carry enough visual weight.

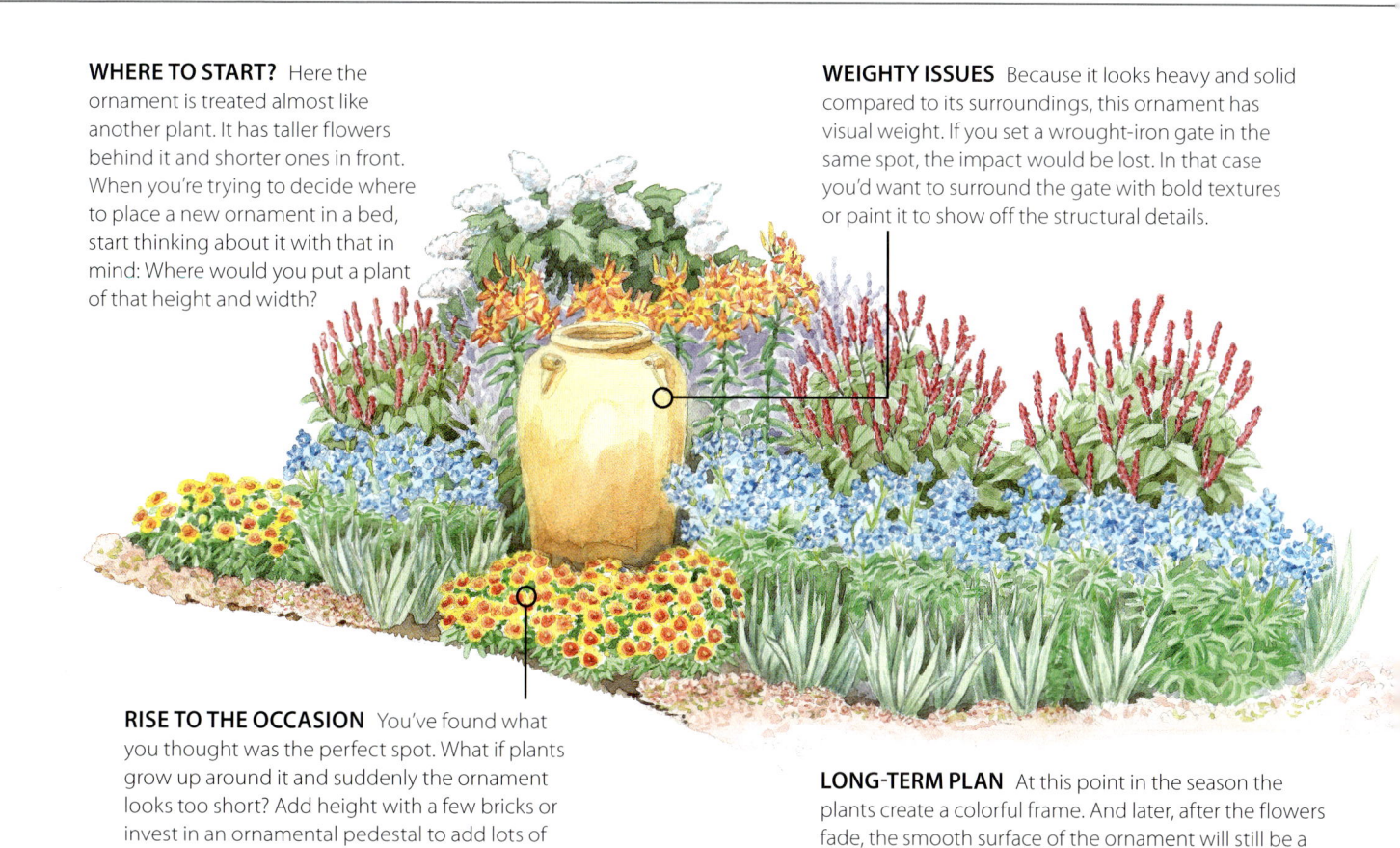

WHERE TO START? Here the ornament is treated almost like another plant. It has taller flowers behind it and shorter ones in front. When you're trying to decide where to place a new ornament in a bed, start thinking about it with that in mind: Where would you put a plant of that height and width?

WEIGHTY ISSUES Because it looks heavy and solid compared to its surroundings, this ornament has visual weight. If you set a wrought-iron gate in the same spot, the impact would be lost. In that case you'd want to surround the gate with bold textures or paint it to show off the structural details.

RISE TO THE OCCASION You've found what you thought was the perfect spot. What if plants grow up around it and suddenly the ornament looks too short? Add height with a few bricks or invest in an ornamental pedestal to add lots of impact to a small piece.

LONG-TERM PLAN At this point in the season the plants create a colorful frame. And later, after the flowers fade, the smooth surface of the ornament will still be a contrast to the foliage and it'll remain a focal point.

DESIGN | BACK YARD

Add color to your winter garden…it's easy!

Winter Wonders

Winter doesn't have to be drab! Can you believe this photo was taken in February? It has flowers, colorful foliage, nice hardscaping…all the elements of a great garden in any season. Creating your own winter wonderland is all about choosing the best plants for flowers, color and texture, and combining them with other hardscaping elements for a look you'll love. Oh, and one of the best things about winter gardens? They almost take care of themselves! Have a look at this nice front yard, then turn the page and I'll show you even more ideas for colorful winter gardens, no matter where you live.

Up close and personal

The smaller plants near the front of this beautiful entry planting allow you to see farther back into the garden. The taller evergreens back near the corner of the house block the view a bit, adding a sense of mystery about what might be around the corner. A simple fountain is a perfect first focal point. And the cool blue-gray of the house offers a neutral backdrop that lets the gentle flowers of the garden stand out.

Hellebore

WINTER-BLOOMING FLOWERS Can you believe there are even perennials and bulbs that bloom in winter? I will say that winter flowers tend to be on the subtler side, so I always think more is better. You'll have to look for three tiny winter aconite flowers along your path, but plant 100 of them and you'll see them from the street!

Hellebore *Helleborus niger* Perennial; white or cream midwinter flowers sometimes age to pink; part shade; 12 to 15 in. tall, 12 to 18 in. wide; cold zones 5 to 9, heat zones 9 to 1

Pansies *Viola* hybrids Perennial often grown as a cool-season annual; cheerful flower faces in many colors; full sun to part shade; 4 to 8 in. tall, 7 to 10 in. wide; cold zones 5 to 8, heat zones 12 to 1

Snowdrops *Galanthus nivalis* Bulb; nodding white flowers in midwinter; full sun to part shade; 4 to 9 in. tall, 2 to 3 in. wide; cold zones 3 to 9, heat zones 9 to 1

Winter aconite *Eranthis hyemalis* Tuberous perennial; yellow flowers in late winter; full sun to part shade; 2 to 3 in. tall and wide; cold zones 4 to 7, heat zones 7 to 1

PHOTO: Joshua McCullough DESIGN: Lisa Albert

GOOD BONE STRUCTURE In winter, the structure and lines of your garden become more apparent than ever because there's not as much foliage to cover it up. That's why clearly defined, crisp-looking bed shapes are a real plus. Focus on areas you can see from second-story windows — lines are always more apparent from overhead. A solid stone edging like this cuts a dramatic edge through this garden.

Witchhazel

WINTER-BLOOMING SHRUBS

I love the surprise of coming across a big witchhazel in full bloom in February. These charming little blooms don't mind a little cold rain, ice or snow. And they're not alone. There are plenty of shrubs that show off in winter.

Japanese pieris *Pieris japonica* White, pink or red blooms in late winter and early spring; full sun to part shade; 9 to 12 ft. tall, 6 to 8 ft. wide; cold zones 5 to 9, heat zones 9 to 1

Paper bush *Edgeworthia chrysantha* Small fragrant yellow flowers in late winter and early spring; full sun to part shade; 5 ft. tall and wide; cold zones 7 to 10, heat zones 10 to 1

Sweet box *Sarcococca confusa* White vanilla-scented flowers midwinter to spring; part shade; 3 to 6 ft. tall, 2 to 3 ft. wide; cold zones 6 to 9, heat zones 9 to 1

Winterhazel *Corylopsis glabrescens* Pale yellow blooms in late winter and early spring; full sun to part shade; 8 to 15 ft. tall and wide; cold zones 5 to 8, heat zones 8 to 1

Witchhazel *Hamamelis* x*intermedia* Yellow or orange blooms in mid- to late winter; full sun to part shade; 12 to 15 ft. tall and wide; cold zones 5 to 8, heat zones 8 to 1

FOLIAGE FOR FALL *AND* WINTER

Even perennials can be evergreen or in this case, ever-*red*! In cold winter climates, you probably can't count on coral bells (*Heuchera* spp.) every year — they may get buried under snow or desiccated by the wind. But their foliage can be gorgeous in winter. A quick clean-up of tattered, brown leaves every once in a while will keep them looking their best.

WELL-PLACED HARDSCAPING

Some garden ornaments last longer if you bring them indoors or protect them in winter. When you choose one to go near the house, look for a weather-proof metal or stone one so it can show off year-round. Since this garden rarely dips below freezing, this water feature is fine.

MORE WINTER BEAUTY

BARK AND STEMS
Here are four trees and shrubs with great form or colorful bark.

Harry Lauder's walking stick *Corylus avellana* 'Contorta' Deciduous shrub; twisted stems show up best in winter, yellow catkins in spring; full sun to part shade; 8 to 10 ft. tall and wide; cold zones 4 to 8, heat zones 8 to 1

Japanese kerria *Kerria japonica* Deciduous shrub; green stems in winter, yellow spring flowers; part shade; 2 to 10 ft. tall and wide; cold zones 4 to 9, heat zones 9 to 1

Red-twig dogwood *Cornus sericea* Deciduous shrub; bright red stems in winter, especially if pruned regularly, white flowers in spring; full sun to part shade; 3 to 10 ft. tall and wide; cold zones 3 to 8, heat zones 8 to 1

Tall stewartia *Stewartia monadelpha* Tree; peeling gray and red-brown bark, white summer flowers; full sun to part shade; 20 to 25 ft. tall, 15 to 25 ft. wide; cold zones 6 to 9, heat zones 9 to 1

Harry Lauder's walking stick

Variety makes things interesting
For the most impact, create a winter grouping. The beautiful form and bark of the tree below would be nice, but add to it all the different colors, textures and heights of the other plants, and wow! Group your winter showoffs together… you may not spend much time walking all over your yard admiring every nook and cranny. When you're choosing plant combinations for winter, look for lots of contrast: Big, leathery evergreen leaves make a great backdrop for thin red twigs, and bold, architectural tree branches highlight lacy blooms.

And finally, be sure to notice details. The Harry Lauder's walking stick at left casts beautiful shadows on the snow.

Red-twig dogwood

Tall stewartia

THE LAYERED LOOK The best winter landscapes have more than one thing going on at a time. Natural woodlands have layers of plants. Here there are flowers low to the ground and colorful stems and evergreen foliage a little higher.

"APPEELING" BARK The beautiful peeling bark of this tall stewartia waits patiently through spring, summer and fall while everything else shows off. Then in winter, it shouts, "Look at me!" Visit your local arboretum in winter to see which trees have beautiful bark. You can't always tell from young plants at the garden center.

PHOTO: Joshua McCullough LOCATION: Jane Platt Garden

Create a tapestry with evergreens

Evergreen foliage may be the single most important element in a winter garden. Even if it's too cold or snowy for flowers to show up, evergreens will still shine. But evergreen doesn't have to mean just plain old green. Check out the photo below to see burgundy, chartreuse, blue-green…you can have a whole tapestry of evergreen foliage. The list at right gives you an idea of the variety of shapes and colors out there.

Good design stands out in winter. Give your garden solid structure, include plants that show off in winter and invite in the birds. Then you can make your garden just as beautiful now as it is the rest of the year. ☐

— *Kristin Beane Sullivan*

DON'T FORGET THE BIRDS!
Since they don't drop their leaves, evergreens offer the best shelter for birds. Growing them is one way to get colorful entertainment in your garden year-round.

PRUNING POINTERS To shape them up or keep them in bounds, prune Sawara falsecypress before new growth starts in spring. But wait until the new growth candles stretch to pinch the tips of pines.

COLORFUL EVERGREENS Want a tapestry of color? Choose a conifer from each list below.

Burgundy foliage

Creeping juniper *Juniperus horizontalis* 'Youngstown' Spreading conifer; needles are green in summer, plum-colored in winter; full sun; 12 to 18 in. tall, 2 to 8 ft. wide; cold zones 3 to 9, heat zones 9 to 1

Arborvitae *Thuja occidentalis* 'Degroot's Spire' Pyramidal conifer; green needles turn bronze in winter; full sun to part shade; 20 to 30 ft. tall, 4 to 6 ft. wide; cold zones 2 to 7, heat zones 7 to 1

White cedar *Chamaecyparis thyoides* Red Star ('Rubicon') Columnar conifer; foliage is blue-green in summer, plum-colored in winter; full sun; 15 to 25 ft. tall, 8 to 12 ft. wide; cold zones 3 to 8, heat zones 8 to 1

Chartreuse foliage

Golden Japanese cedar *Cryptomeria japonica* 'Elegans Aurea' Pyramidal conifer; gold needles are most dramatic in full sun and cool weather; full sun to part shade; 10 to 30 ft. tall, 10 to 20 ft. wide; cold zones 6 to 9, heat zones 9 to 1

Juniper *Juniperus xpfitzeriana* Sea of Gold® ('MonSan') Spreading conifer; gold needles hold color well in winter; full sun; 3 ft. tall, 4 ft. wide; cold zones 3 to 9, heat zones 9 to 1

Leyland cypress *Cuprocyparis leylandii* 'Gold Rider' Pyramidal conifer; golden needle tips; full sun; 15 to 35 ft. tall, 10 to 15 ft. wide; cold zones 5 to 9, heat zones 9 to 1

Sawara falsecypress *Chamaecyparis pisifera* 'Lemon Thread' Dwarf mounding to pyramidal conifer; bright yellow, threadlike foliage; full sun to part shade; 3 to 5 ft. tall; 2 to 4 ft. wide; cold zones 4 to 8, heat zones 8 to 1

Blue-green foliage

Dwarf Alberta spruce *Picea glauca* 'Blue Wonder' Pyramidal conifer; blue-green needles; full sun to part shade; 6 ft. tall, 2 to 3 ft. wide; cold zones 2 to 8, heat zones 8 to 1

Weeping blue Atlas cedar *Cedrus atlantica* 'Glauca Pendula' Weeping conifer; drooping branches with blue-green needles; full sun; 15 to 25 ft. tall and wide; cold zones 6 to 9, heat zones 9 to 1

Dwarf Himalayan pine *Pinus wallichiana* 'Nana' Upright conifer; drooping, blue and green needles; full sun; 4 to 10 ft. tall, 4 to 8 ft. wide; cold zones 5 to 7, heat zones 7 to 1

DESIGN | BACK YARD

Learn how easy it is to have a stunning garden like this one.

Summer of Color

Botanical Names

Clary sage
  Salvia sclarea
Coreopsis
  Coreopsis spp.
Culver's root
  Veronicastrum virginicum
False indigo
  Baptisia australis
Gloriosa daisy
  Rudbeckia hirta
Hydrangea
  Hydrangea spp.
Queen-of-the-prairie
  Filipendula rubra
Russian sage
  Perovskia atriplicifolia
Spruce *Picea* spp.
Zinnia *Zinnia* hybrid

Why do some perennial borders make you slow down to examine them while others let you quickly look them over and move on? Connie and John Young's border in Minnesota is definitely one to slow you down. It has lots of design and care tips you'll want to use.

More than 10 years ago this border started out as a narrow bed along the edge of the back yard. Now it's evolved into the beautiful garden you see in this photo. Connie shared with me some of the things they've learned over the years. Let's take a closer look.

FADE IN AND FADE OUT Start by choosing plants that bloom at different times during the season. That way, there will always be something coming into flower as a neighboring plant finishes. Notice the false indigo at the far right side of this photo? It finished blooming several weeks ago and is already forming seed pods. After it was done, the queen-of-the-prairie took over. Now even its fluffy pink flowers are passing. It's time for the spikes of the Culver's root in the back to be the center of attention. Later, hydrangeas and grasses will take over the show. These perennials should be about a third to one-half of the flowers in your border. Then set "knitters" — plants that bloom for a long time — around these perennials to tie everything together. Russian sage, coreopsis and lots of annuals down front mean there will always be something in bloom in this garden.

Scattered around the photo you'll discover helpful tips you can learn from this garden to design your own. And on the next pages I'll share ideas about how to keep a border looking good.

Place a hardworking structure

This homemade obelisk contrasts with the plants around it, so it's an ornament that draws your attention. But it can also be moved around to act as a plant support for a floppy coreopsis or even help hold up the heavy heads of a hydrangea.

Provide protection

Wind can wreck a perennial garden. One of the first things planted in this garden was a row of spruces. It's there to add privacy and protect the garden from sweeping winds. And the dark green background really makes the colors in the border stand out, too. Don't have room for a row of large trees? A lattice-weave fence planted with ornamental vines will buffer the wind, take up almost no space and add a green backdrop for colorful flowers.

Wider is better

These beds were only 3 ft. deep when first planted. However, that's not enough space to create a good succession of bloom. Now the beds average 6 to 8 ft. deep, giving enough room to layer plants by height. And with more perennials to work with, it's easier to disguise one that's still to bloom or completely finished, too. To make maintenance easier, there are 12- to 18-in. stepping stones scattered among the perennials. They provide a place to stand as you work in your beds.

Make color work

At first glance, this border may look like it has a rather haphazard color scheme. But these colors work together because all of them are about the same intensity. To keep the reds and purples from looking drab and dreary, incorporate splashes of yellow to perk them up. And the yellows won't look as harsh in the summer sun next to the reds and purples.

Consider shapes

If all the flowers in this scene were the same shape and size, the view would still be colorful, but a bit boring. Mix them up, and the contrast makes it much more interesting. Notice how there are clumps of round flowers, like the big gloriosa daisies and zinnias and small coreopsis paired with spike-shaped Russian sage, Culver's root and clary sage? Of course you spot the color first, but the contrasting flower forms and sizes are what you spot next.

EASY CARE TIPS

You might think it takes a team of gardeners to take care of this garden, but the owners do the work themselves; it's truly a labor of love that keeps it looking good. And good design and well-thought-out plant choices make it surprisingly easy to care for.

MAKE GOOD CHOICES A garden filled with healthy plants always looks great. And it's easier to care for, too. Fill each bed with plants that have the same light and soil requirements. For example, everything in this border needs full sun and well-drained soil.

In the boxes below, find out why this garden isn't mulched, more about the brick walls and how pre-planting preparation got this garden off to a good start. And to the right, in "Design by trial and error," are a few of Connie and John's favorite plants, as well as three of their best tips on caring for any garden. □

— *Jim Childs*

Only mulch once
The only time any mulch is used in this garden is when young plants are newly set. Since sunlight still reaches the ground, mulch helps keep the moisture in the soil to get the new plant growing. Because the plants are set closely together, eventually they shade the soil, so it doesn't dry out very quickly. Plus, the shaded soil stays an even, cool temperature, perfect for the roots of most perennials. That means there really is no need to apply more mulch to these beds. By only putting it around your new plants, you'll be saving time and money, too.

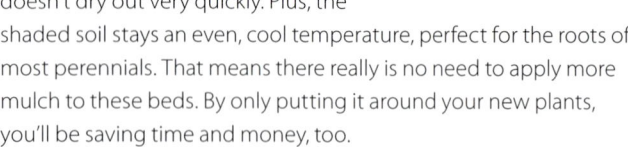

On the level with bricks
Classic brick edging defines these borders and gives them a neat and tidy appearance. But when you have a slope and want to level the beds so water won't run off quickly, bricks can do double duty. As the beds were dug, they were terraced to make them nearly level. Then the low walls of bricks were mortared together. The first row of bricks is only partly buried in the soil. But, even after 10 years of repeated freezing and thawing, the walls have held up with minimal repairs.

Solution to clay
Clay soil is the bane of many a gardener. But this garden is built on a bed of it. Raised beds and berms are options, but these beds aren't built up. They had the soil changed out. If you want to do this, before you bring any plants home, dig out about 12 in. of the clay and haul it away. Then fill the beds with a mixture of topsoil and compost. To keep the soil healthy, you'll also need to topdress the established beds with more compost every couple of years. While it's a lot of work, the soil makes this garden what it is today — beautiful!

Design by trial and error Trying to design a border can be a daunting task. You can start with a detailed garden plan, but to be honest, many of the best gardens evolve over time. And in reality the design is never really finished. Plants die or you find something new you want to try, so you have to take a plant or two out. That's part of the joy of a garden.

When it all comes together, friends will ooh and ahh. However, you don't have to tell them it was trial and error! You can simply say you used your knowledge and experience to choose the best plants and create your beautiful garden.

Because plants are like children, always growing and changing, the design of this garden has evolved over several years. In this photo and list you can see and learn about some of John and Connie's favorite plants.

A Queen-of- the-prairie *Filipendula rubra* 'Venusta' Perennial; pink blooms in early summer; North American native likes moist soil; full sun; 4 to 8 ft. tall, 2 to 4 ft. wide; cold-hardy in USDA zones 3 to 9, heat-tolerant in AHS zones 9 to 1

B Culver's root *Veronicastrum virginicum* Perennial; white blooms in summer; native plant stands well without staking; full sun; 4 to 6 ft. tall, 2 to 4 ft. wide; cold-hardy in USDA zones 3 to 8, heat-tolerant in AHS zones 8 to 1

C False indigo *Baptisia australis* Perennial; blue blooms in late spring; don't deadhead spent flowers, let the seed pods ripen for winter interest; full sun; 3 to 4 ft. tall and wide; cold-hardy in USDA zones 3 to 9, heat-tolerant in AHS zones 9 to 1

D Gloriosa daisy *Rudbeckia hirta* Perennial; blooms in shades of gold summer into fall; treat as an annual if you have trouble getting it through the winter, reseeds; full sun; 2 to 3 ft. tall, 1 to 2 ft. wide; cold-hardy in USDA zones 4 to 9, heat-tolerant in AHS zones 12 to 1

E Russian sage *Perovskia atriplicifolia* Perennial; blue blooms in late summer; cut to the ground each spring; full sun; 3 to 5 ft. tall, 2 to 4 ft. wide; cold-hardy in USDA zones 5 to 9, heat-tolerant in AHS zones 9 to 1

F Zinnia *Zinnia* Cut and Come Again Mix Annual; mixed colors of blooms summer into fall if you keep picking the flowers; full sun; 24 to 30 in. tall, 12 to 18 in. wide; heat-tolerant in AHS zones 12 to 1

G Coleus *Solenostemon* Kong™ Red Tender perennial, treat as an annual, pinch out flowers to promote more colorful leaves; full sun; 18 to 20 in. tall, 15 to 18 in. wide; cold-hardy in USDA zones 10 to 11, heat-tolerant in AHS zones 12 to 1

H Snapdragon *Antirrhinum majus* Solstice Rose Tender perennial, treat as an annual; mixed colors in spring, summer and fall; best in cool temps, pick flowers to keep the plant producing; full sun; 16 to 20 in. tall, 10 to 12 in. wide; cold-hardy in USDA zones 7 to 10, heat-tolerant in AHS zones 12 to 1

I Clary sage *Salvia sclarea* Biennial or short-lived perennial; shades of pink blooms in summer; deadhead most of the spent flowers to prevent excessive reseeding; full sun; 18 to 36 in. tall, 15 to 18 in. wide; cold-hardy in USDA zones 5 to 9, heat-tolerant in AHS zones 12 to 1

J Threadleaf coreopsis *Coreopsis verticillata* 'Moonbeam' Perennial; yellow blooms in summer; reblooms if stems are cut to the ground after first flush of flowers; full sun; 18 to 24 in. tall and wide; cold-hardy in USDA zones 3 to 9, heat-tolerant in AHS zones 9 to 1

THREE MAINTENANCE TIPS

☐ **WATER EARLY AND DEEP** This border is watered by the same system that irrigates the lawn. Run the sprinklers early in the day so the foliage has time to dry off before night. Give the bed about an inch of water per week, in one watering, to encourage the roots to grow deep into the soil, where they stay cool and moist. Light waterings bring the roots close to the surface where they will dry out faster.

☐ **KEEP FERTILIZING TO A MINIMUM** If you've put extra effort into the soil prep, fertilizing will be minimal. Apply a general-purpose water-soluble bloom booster, such as 15-30-15, twice during the growing season. Put on the first application in late spring as early perennials are setting buds or just starting to bloom. Apply the second, and last one, in midsummer to keep the perennials growing strong.

☐ **DO YOUR DEADHEADING** Take a bucket and shears with you every time you head out to the garden. Even if you're just going out to enjoy the flowers, you'll probably spot something that needs deadheading. Do a small task like deadheading, or even weeding, when you see it and it's less likely to feel like work.

DESIGN | BACK YARD

8 Simple Ideas to Fix This Garden

Learn great tips from the pros.

THE WEEKEND GARDENER — Garden Smarter

Would you spend more time in your back yard if only it were a more exciting and comfortable place to be? Perhaps yours is tiny, or even long and shallow, like the one at left. Well, take heart! I asked eight garden designers from all over to help take a space like this from cramped and boring to incredible. They each offered pointers on everything from hardscaping and design tips to plant choices. Read on to see which of these ideas might help you live large, even in a small space! □

— *Deborah Gruca*

Fewer plants = more impact

Dave Demers, CYAN Horticulture, Vancouver, BC

You can help a small space feel less cramped by limiting your plant palette. When you use too many different kinds of plants, it gives the scattershot effect in the "Don't" garden at right and creates a feeling of chaos that can be unsettling.

If you want it to feel as large as possible, use fewer types of plants instead. See how the "Do" garden below creates more impact in the same space with clumps of just a few plants? You'll get a more restful, well-planned look. And besides that, it simplifies garden tasks like deadheading and fertilizing.

DON'T plant ones and twos of lots of different plants — in a small place this only creates a chaotic, messy look.

**① **

DO limit your plant palette in a small space. Use masses of a few plants to give the garden more impact.

tough ground cover
Tuck in an easy-going evergreen ground cover for added color.

Corsican sandwort *Arenaria balearica* Perennial; tiny white spring flowers; sun to part shade; 2 in. tall, 12 in. wide; cold-hardy in USDA zones 4 to 7, heat-tolerant in AHS zones 7 to 1

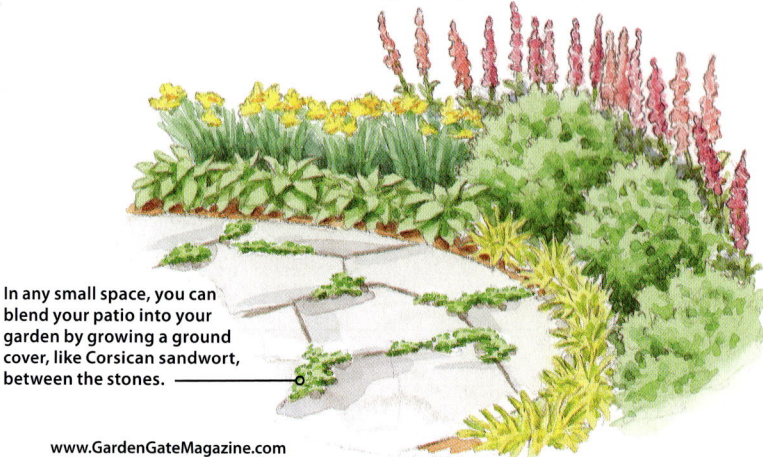

In any small space, you can blend your patio into your garden by growing a ground cover, like Corsican sandwort, between the stones.

PHOTOS: Courtesy of Dorothy Murray (before); courtesy of www.Stepables.com (Corsican sandwort)

174   *the* YEAR IN GARDENING   www.GardenGateMagazine.com

Design on an angle for a larger look

Anna Morgan, Anna Morgan Design, Stuart, FL

When you're laying out your patio and beds, set the lines at a diagonal to your house. In this garden, diagonal lines accentuate the distance from the seating area by the house to the cozy getaway in the back corner.

As you're seated on the patio, your eye is drawn to the focal point of the arbor at the far end of the yard, making the shallow space seem larger than it is. If the arbor were set perpendicular to the back fence of the yard instead, the arbor and getaway would be much closer to the house. This would only emphasize the shallowness of the yard.

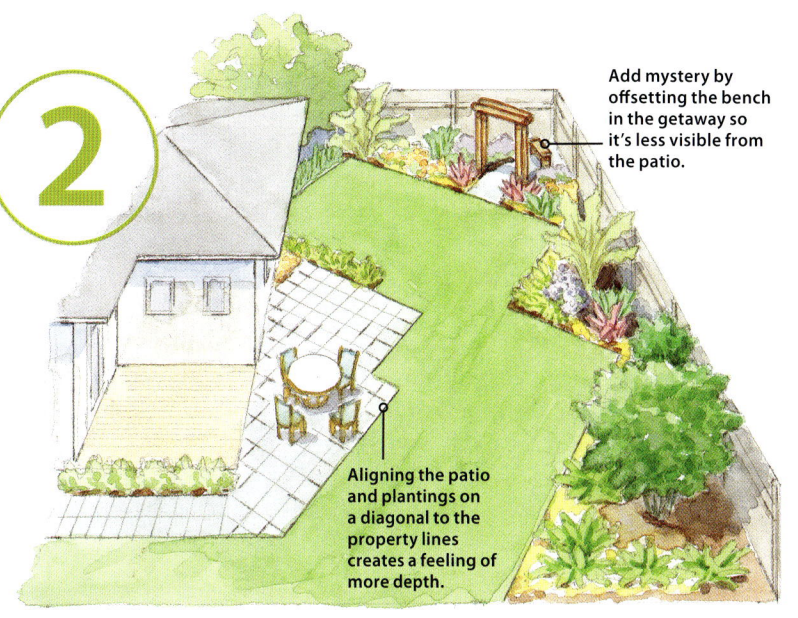

2

Add mystery by offsetting the bench in the getaway so it's less visible from the patio.

Aligning the patio and plantings on a diagonal to the property lines creates a feeling of more depth.

Frame the view to create depth

Linda Grieve, Perennial Gardens by Linda Grieve, Inc., Ankeny, IA

Remember that you also see your garden from inside your house. Here's a tip that will make it look as if a shallow back yard is much deeper than it actually is: Plant one or more small understory trees in front of a window that looks out onto the yard. Limb up the tree so there are just a few branches that frame the rest of the view. When you have to look through the tree's branches to see the view beyond, it seems like there's more distance there than if you had a wide-open, unobstructed view. At the same time, the trees provide a little shade and a sense of enclosure for the yard.

3

Branches frame the view from inside the house to create depth.

4

fragrant vine
Plant a fragrant vine to make any garden retreat more alluring.

American wisteria
Wisteria frutescens 'Amethyst Falls' Vine; noninvasive wisteria with fragrant, late-spring lavender flowers; sun to part shade; 20 ft. tall, 4 ft. wide; cold-hardy in USDA zones 5 to 9, heat-tolerant in AHS zones 9 to 1

Provide fragrant shade for relaxing

Troy Marden, Nashville, TN

Even a small garden can have a getaway. Tuck a couple of chairs into the corner opposite from where you enter the yard to make it feel more like a destination and to keep distractions to a minimum. Shade is important — a pretty umbrella is the quickest and easiest solution. Or, for added privacy and fragrance, plant 'Amethyst Falls' American wisteria on a simple pergola or arbor over your seating area. It's not invasive and blooms in late spring, so it isn't as likely to be killed by a late frost as other wisteria cultivars.

PHOTO: Courtesy of Monrovia Nursery (wisteria)

MORE DESIGNER TIPS

Give your patio some room
Tom Hoffman, Homestead Landscaping, Bondville, VT

A seating area in a small back yard can sometimes feel rather cramped. Spread out! Utilize the whole yard so you don't feel shoved up against the house: Place your deck or patio out from the house at least 3 feet and build a walkway to it. Make sure the walkway is a comfortable width — 3 to 4 feet is plenty. Surround the patio and both sides of the walkway with plants. You'll feel as if you're stepping out onto a dock that's "floating" in a sea of greenery and blooming flowers.

In Northern climates, choose a spot with a southern or western exposure that gets the most hours of sun, so you can enjoy the space earlier and later during the season. (Afternoon shade during hot months is ideal.) Be sure to include an open grassy area around the plantings if you need a place for pets or children to run.

5

Make the patio big enough so there's at least 2 ft. of space around the table and chairs so you can easily walk around them.

6

focal point
A plant with a strong architectural form grabs your eye.

Beaked yucca *Yucca rostrata*
Perennial; spikes of white flowers in late spring to early summer; spiky blue-gray foliage; full sun; 6 to 8 ft. tall, 4 to 6 ft. wide; cold-hardy in USDA zones 5 to 10, heat-tolerant in AHS zones 10 to 1.

PHOTO: © Charles Mann

Make your plants pop
Scott Calhoun, Zona Gardens, Tucson, AZ

Take a tip from a Southwest designer. Plants of the desert tend to be muted colors of gray and green. They're well-suited to dry conditions, but to prevent rot you can't crowd them together. So in a small garden, that means you won't have a lot of plants. To give them (and the space) more impact, choose architectural plants and display them in a dramatic way. Paint the wall behind a bright color that will show up well in the intense sun. The beaked yucca in front of the bright blue wall at left creates a focal point that makes the plant stand out and gives the garden real snap — a plus, no matter where you happen to live!

Create depth with curved paths

Michelle Derviss, Derviss Design, Novato, CA

Take a different approach to make a shallow space feel deeper than it is: Plan a widely undulating path. Doing this creates wide planting beds directly across from the narrower planting beds. Not only does the curved path at right *look* longer than the straight one, it *is* longer. This gives you more depth in a small space. Plant a variety of plants of different textures and sizes. In general, plant them shortest in front to tallest in back, but throw in a tall one here and there for more interest.

Place interesting focal points (whether plants, an urn or garden art) at the point of the largest curves in the path. You'll stop visitors for a little while before they continue down the meandering path.

7

DO place focal points at the curves of a winding path to add visual interest to this back yard and make the trip down the path even more enjoyable.

DON'T build a "bowling alley" path in a narrow space. Your eye goes straight to the end without pausing to enjoy the plantings on either side.

Make your back yard nearly no-care

Robin Leigh, Leigh Landscape Design, New Milford, CT

If you were standing in this back yard, you'd barely see the fence because of all the shrubs planted in this border. You might start to think that the yard just went on forever.

For a low-maintenance back yard like this, plant shrubs in casual groupings, with taller plants in back and shorter ones in front, as opposed to lined out in rows, to give the yard a natural look. It's tempting, in a small yard, to crowd plants in tightly. Instead, check the plant tag for the mature size of the plants, and give them enough room so they won't need constant pruning to fit the space you have. This also prevents a messy, crowded look that is magnified in a small space.

Use perennials or annuals, like the calibrachoa at right, to add splashes of constant color that you can change each year, or even each season, for a new look. Growing them in pots minimizes maintenance and brings the color up where you can easily see it.

bright color

Grow annuals or tender perennials in pots for a dash of color wherever you need it.

Calibrachoa *Calibrachoa* Superbells® Tequila Sunrise Annual; bright orange flowers; full sun; 6 to 10 in. tall, 24 in. wide; cold-hardy in USDA zones 9 to 11, heat-tolerant in AHS zones 12 to 1

Grow flowering annuals in containers to add bright touches of color throughout the garden.

Use shrubs of different sizes, shapes and foliage colors for a low-maintenance garden that looks good in all seasons.

8

DESIGN | CORNERS

Design tips for awkward corners

No matter how nice, nearly every garden has at least one awkward or neglected corner space. Maybe it's a small inward-facing corner on pavement, or perhaps that space around one of the outside corners of your house.

Carol Lindsay, of Design in a Day in Portland, Oregon, often designs gardens for clients who have small or tricky areas to work with. So I talked with her about ideas for turning unused corner spaces like these into real garden showplaces. Here are some of her tips.

OUTER SPACES All the angles of your home's roof, eaves and walls come together at the outside corners of the house. This tends to make your house look as if it's erupting out of the ground, as opposed to being a natural part of the landscape. Use curved bed shapes to soften these angles and help integrate the hard house materials with the plants of the garden and yard.

Entice visitors to venture around the corner by placing plants to obscure the view past the bed, so the entire thing can't be seen from any one spot. The hydrangea at left does that a little, but you could go with an even bigger and bulkier plant to increase the effect.

Use plants that are at least one half to two thirds the height of the house wall to keep the planting in scale with the house. So, for a one-story house with 12-foot walls, the plants should be 6 to 8 feet tall. And you've probably heard the tip about how deep to make a bed near your house. Imagine you could tip the house wall "flat on its face" into the yard. The widest part of your bed should be at least that deep.

PICKING PLANTS People tend to cut corners: Allow a path through the planting for visitors or the mail carrier to pass easily without trampling your beloved plants. Or use tough plants along the front edge of the border, like the creeping wire vine in the illustration. This ground cover can take the traffic in stride.

To give depth and unity to the whole planting, tie the bed to both walls by repeating plants or colors with vines on a trellis or plants in windowboxes. Beds on outside corners often encompass different exposures of sun and shade. For this reason, you may not be able to repeat plants throughout the bed, but you can still tie it together with a color scheme. The orange sedge on the shaded part of the bed at left echoes the orange coneflower in the sunnier area.

Sunny west side

- This hydrangea has been trained into a standard form.
- To disguise the downspout, paint it the same color as the house or trim. You could also plant tall plants or vines in front of it.
- Provide a path of steppers for visitors to cut through the bed.

Shady north side

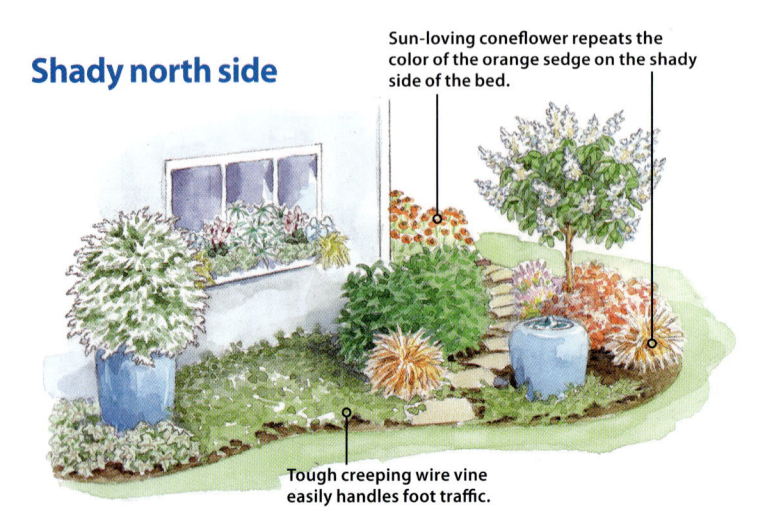

- Sun-loving coneflower repeats the color of the orange sedge on the shady side of the bed.
- Tough creeping wire vine easily handles foot traffic.

PHOTO: Courtesy of Chris Vestal

Inside impact

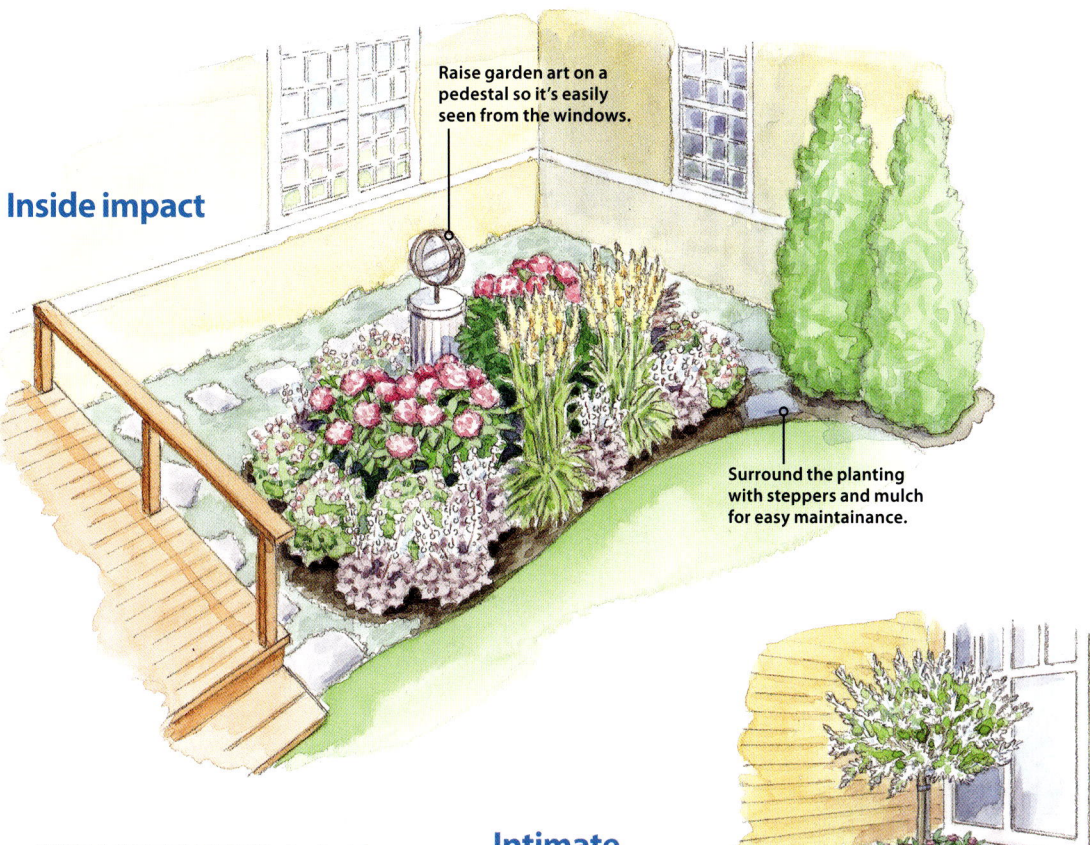

Raise garden art on a pedestal so it's easily seen from the windows.

Surround the planting with steppers and mulch for easy maintainance.

Intimate inside corner

Add different size river rock around pots to help "anchor" them to the surrounding patio.

Inside corners create echo chambers for water features.

INSIDE INFORMATION An inside corner is perfect for displaying a plant collection (in containers or in the ground) or a single focal point plant. For the most impact, choose a plant with outstanding color, texture or form that looks beautiful most of the year. Or try an interesting boulder or a few large containers, either planted or not. If you have the space, move the planting away from the house several feet, like the one in the illustration above. Then you can create a bed that can be viewed through the windows of two different rooms inside the house, as well as from the outside. You might like to include a pedestal that will raise a piece of garden art up where it can be easily seen from the windows.

Like to throw open those windows on a nice day? Inward-facing corners outside a private area of the house are great places for fragrant plants and water features. The walls of the corner help contain the fragrance close to the windows and amplify the sounds of moving water so you can enjoy them indoors.

And remember, because an inside corner is already closed in on two sides, it's a great opportunity to create a more enclosed, shady getaway. You could simply erect an overhead structure like a pergola or an arbor. Or by growing a hedge or roses on a well-placed lattice screen, you can create a private spot for a hot tub or even an outdoor shower!

In smaller areas — 8 square feet or less — keep the numbers and sizes of plants in balance with the space. The container grouping above has just five pots and a total of seven plants. If you want a shrub or tree, use smaller or slow-growing varieties. Why? If you crowd large or too many plants in, you won't be able to see any of them very well. And your plants may suffer from mildew from the lack of air circulation. Also, use mostly plants with smaller leaves, with a few large- or bold-foliaged ones thrown in for contrast. The combination will fit the scale of the corner best. Place plants with wispy or soft texture, like the willow standard, here, in the back to help disguise the hard vertical line of the corner. (See our Web extra for the complete plans and plant lists for all of these designs.)

Try these tips on those neglected corners around your house. Whether they're large or small, you can change them from awkward to awesome!

— *Deborah Gruca*

Botanical Names

Coneflower
  Echincaea hybrid
Creeping wire vine
  Muehlenbeckia axillaris
Hydrangea
  Hydrangea paniculata
Orange New Zealand sedge
  Carex testacea
Rose *Rosa* hybrid
Willow *Salix integra*

Web extra
See complete **planting plans** for these gardens.

DESIGN | CORNERS

9 easy plants + a couple hours a year = a gorgeous garden

Nearly No-Care Getaway

THE WEEKEND GARDENER · Garden Smarter ·

Have you ever seen a garden that just took your breath away? Have you wondered how much work it took to keep it looking that way?

This pretty corner planting is beautiful to behold. But, beyond that, it has easy-care features and plants that make it a snap to take care of. In fact, once this garden is planted, everything you need to do all year takes only a couple hours — and you could get by with even less. Here's what makes it so effortless:

EASY FLOORING See the landing with interlocking stones at right? This type of surface provides a solid foundation without a lot of maintenance — no need to interplant, and no weeds to pull!

NEARLY NO-CARE PLANTS The plants, too, are beautiful and simple to grow. Once established, they're very undemanding. (I've broken down the tasks in the checklist at right.) The perennials don't need any special attention to look good except a little deadheading if you like. None of the shrubs needs regular pruning, though where it's hardy, you might cut back the fatsia in spring if it gets too large. And the two trees bring year-round interest, with no maintenance needed (except a little fall leaf raking). Want a nearly no-care garden with more flowers? Go to our Web extra for another plan.

Even the busiest person can fit in an hour of tidying up a year. And if you're a meticulous gardener, even a couple hours still isn't bad — especially for such a gorgeous garden! □

— *Deborah Gruca*

THE GARDEN'S PALETTE

Code	Plant Name	No. to Plant	Type	Blooms	Height/Width	Cold/Heat Zones	Comments
A	Japanese maple *Acer palmatum* 'Shaina'	1	Small tree	NA	4-5 ft./3-4 ft.	5-8/8-1	Bright-red foliage in spring, turns deep red in fall; full sun to part shade
B	Brunnera *Brunnera macrophylla* 'Jack Frost'	13	Perennial	Light blue; spring	12-18 in./18-24 in.	3-7/7-1	Silver foliage with green veins; prefers consistent moisture; spreads slowly
C	Carex *Carex* 'Ice Dance'	28	Perennial	Pink; summer	1 ft./1-2 ft.	5-9/9-1	Dark green foliage with white edges
D	Dwarf sweet box *Sarcococca hookeriana humilis*	4	Shrub	White; spring	1-2 ft./spreading	6-9/9-1	Evergreen ground cover with deep green foliage; blue-black berries follow flowers; spreads slowly
E	Lace-cap hydrangea *Hydrangea serrata* 'Beni-Gaku'	2	Shrub	Pink to red; summer	3-4 ft./3-4 ft.	5-9/9-1	Blooms and grows best in moist soil in part shade; give regular moisture the first season as it establishes
F	Japanese stewartia *Stewartia pseudocamellia*	1	Small tree	White; midsummer	20-40 ft./25-30 ft.	5-8/8-1	Orange or red foliage in autumn; interesting bark; in hot climates, does best with afternoon shade
G	Hosta *Hosta* 'Blue Angel'	3	Perennial	Lavender; summer	30 in./36-48 in.	3-9/9-1	Giant, heart-shaped, blue-gray foliage; slow growing
H	Sweet box *Sarcococca confusa*	7	Shrub	Fragrant white; winter	3-6 ft./2-3 ft.	6-9/9-1	Evergreen; winter flowers followed by black berries; drought- and shade-tolerant
I	Fatsia *Fatsia japonica*	1	Shrub	Brown; spring	6-12 ft./6-12 ft.	8-10/10-8	Large, evergreen, glossy blue-green leaves

180   *the* YEAR IN GARDENING   www.GardenGateMagazine.com

Soft blue 'Blue Angel' hosta, silver 'Jack Frost' brunnera and white-edged green 'Ice Dance' carex provide summer color contrast.

A 2- to 3-in. layer of mulch keeps weeding to a minimum.

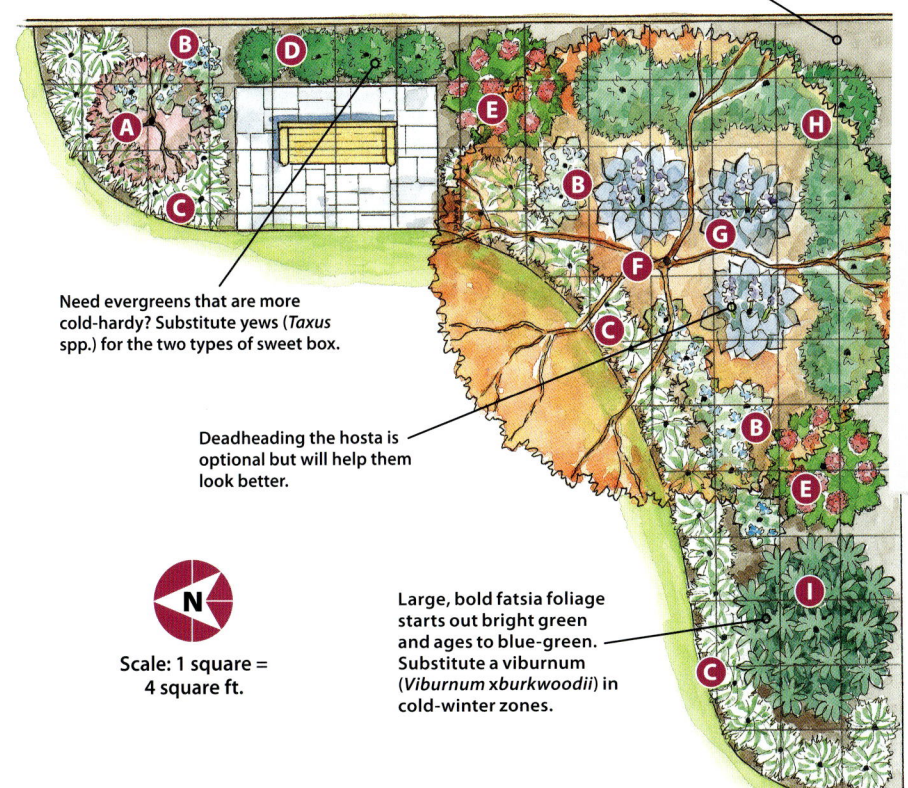

Need evergreens that are more cold-hardy? Substitute yews (*Taxus* spp.) for the two types of sweet box.

Deadheading the hosta is optional but will help them look better.

Scale: 1 square = 4 square ft.

Large, bold fatsia foliage starts out bright green and ages to blue-green. Substitute a viburnum (*Viburnum xburkwoodii*) in cold-winter zones.

The (Not Much) TO DO LIST

Here's an at-a-glance guide to everything you need to do (plus a few optional things) to keep this bed looking its best.

Spring

- ☐ **All plants** Clean up leaves and plant debris; sprinkle and scratch slow-release plant food into the soil around the crowns.
- ☐ **Carex** Shear plants back to 3 to 4 in. tall.
- ☐ **Shrubs** If you see dead or damaged branches, cut back sweet box (after flowering finishes) and fatsia. You can also remove any yellow fatsia foliage.

Summer

- ☐ **All plants** Water during extended dry spells (especially the first season after they're planted). Set a sprinkler or soaker hose on a timer to save time. Weed as needed.
- ☐ **Hydrangea and hosta** If you prefer a tidier look, remove faded flowers at their base.
- ☐ **Brunnera** To get fresh new foliage, use hedge shears to cut plants back by a third after flowering is finished.

Fall

- ☐ **Trees** Rake up and compost leaves.
- ☐ **Japanese maple** Cage the trunk if you have problems with critters.

Web extra See yet another low-maintenance **plan** for this corner bed.

DESIGN | GREAT COMBOS

Fabulous Combos Bring in Spring

Bulbs start your garden's season off with a bang!

Nothing matches the extravagant impact of bulbs blooming in spring. But you don't *have* to plant hundreds of them — even a few can create a great splash of color. Here are some simple tips on how to combine them with other plants for fabulous effects.

MATCH THE CONDITIONS This tried-and-true rule applies to any plant combination, and that includes ones with bulbs. For successful partnerships, choose plants that like similar growing conditions, such as light, soil and moisture. All of the combinations on these pages are examples of this. (Most bulbs like full sun and well-drained soil while they're blooming, with relatively dry soil in summer when they're dormant.) That way, all the plants thrive and the combination looks as beautiful as possible for as long as possible.

FOCUS THE COLOR Early in the season, before most perennials have emerged, the garden can be a bare landscape. For the most punch, pick a few smaller areas in the garden — perhaps ones that you see the most or are visible from the house — and concentrate several plants or bulbs in each. If you try to scatter the same number of plants over a larger area, you'll just dilute the effect.

COMPLEMENT AND CONTRAST How do you create the most impact with combos in a small area? Well, first be sure the flower colors don't fight with each other. A good way to choose effective combinations is to use similar colors, such as the purple and blue you see at right, or different shades of the same color, like red and pink. For a dramatic contrast, choose complementary colors, such as purple and yellow or orange and blue. And don't worry about sticking to the same flower color theme of your summer garden. Spring bulbs are usually long gone before summer flowers start to open, so you don't have to worry about how they'll look together.

Also, use contrast in flower shapes. The airy blue brunnera flowers at right really make the large purple tulips stand out. Think about contrast in the size of plants, as well. The foliage of the shorter brunnera frames the taller tulips. The hosta will grow larger and will continue to look good all season. It's a great anchor plant that'll also disguise the fading foliage of the tulips once their flowering is done.

Ready to see some great bulb combos? Take a look at "Pretty in purple" at right and then turn the page for more fabulous spring combinations. □

— *Deborah Gruca*

Pretty in purple For the most impact, choose a single flower color for your bulbs, like these purple tulips tucked in among brunnera and hostas. The rich color leads your eye to the front steps of the house where a pair of containers echo the hue. And the purple leans more toward blue than red, so it combines well with the airy blue flowers of the brunnera.

A **Brunnera** *Brunnera macrophylla* Perennial; tiny, airy light blue flowers rise above the foliage in spring; part shade; 12 to 18 in. tall, 15 to 24 in. wide; cold-hardy in USDA zones 3 to 7, heat-tolerant in AHS zones 7 to 1

B **Tulip** *Tulipa* 'Negrita' Bulb; large purple flowers in midspring; full sun; 12 to 18 in. tall, 3 to 6 in. wide; cold-hardy in USDA zones 3 to 8, heat-tolerant in AHS zones 8 to 1

C **Hosta** *Hosta fortunei hyacinthina* Perennial; green foliage and pale lavender flowers in summer; part shade; 12 to 18 in. tall, 18 to 24 in. wide; cold-hardy in USDA zones 3 to 8, heat-tolerant in AHS zones 8 to 1

D **Old-fashioned bleeding heart** *Dicentra spectabilis* 'Alba' Perennial; white heart-shaped flowers in spring, plant goes dormant in summer; part shade; 24 to 36 in. tall, 18 to 30 in. wide; cold-hardy in USDA zones 3 to 8, heat-tolerant in AHS zones 8 to 1

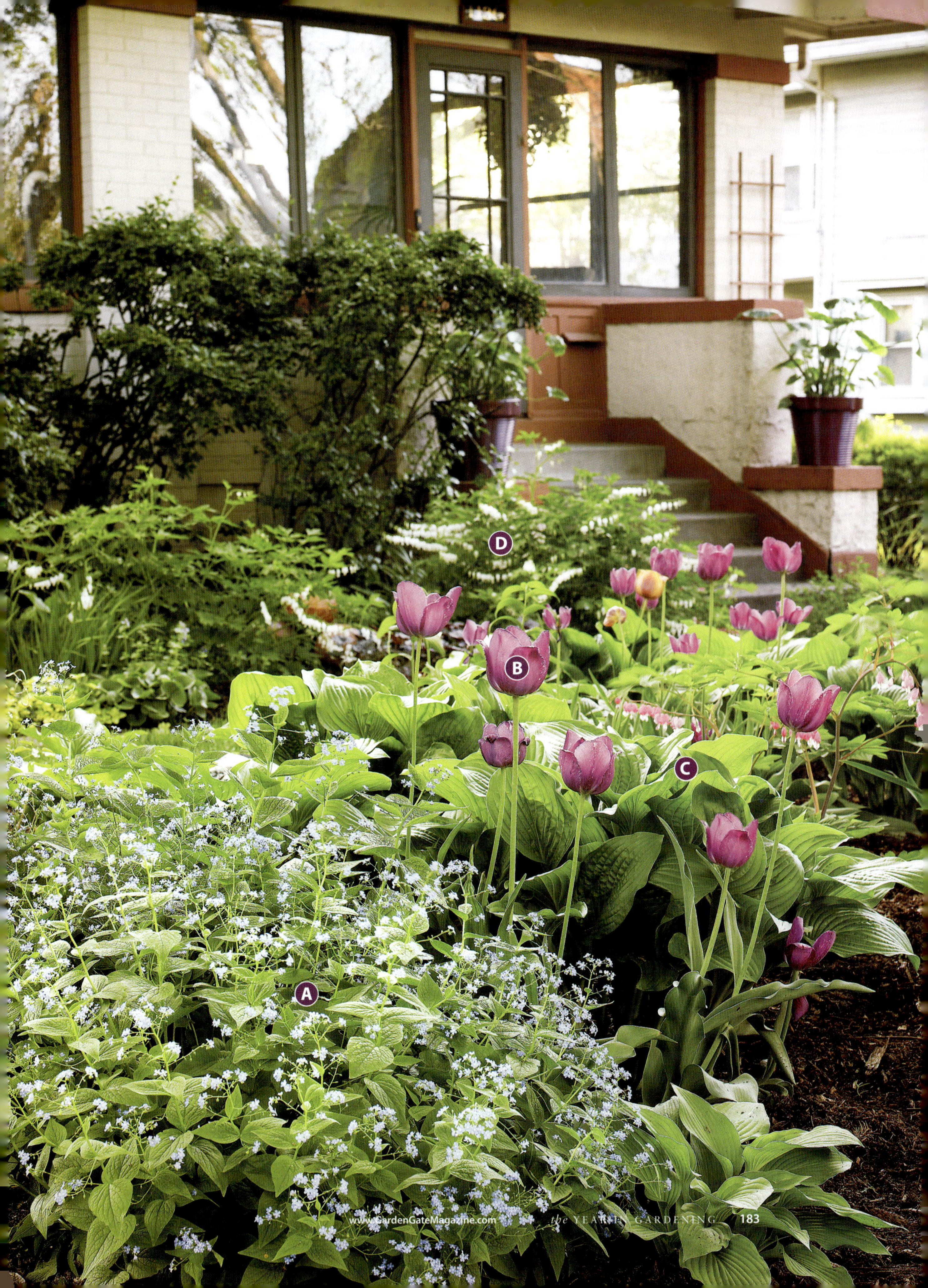
D
B
C
A

BULBS MAKE SPRING SING

Give them space One of the great things about spring-blooming bulbs is the ability of many of them to naturalize and form large colonies in just a few years. Both the daffodils and grape hyacinths here have filled in this border, producing loads of bright color for several weeks when not much else is blooming. So be sure to follow suggested spacing when planting bulbs to postpone the need for digging and dividing the plants.

A   **Fernleaf bleeding heart** *Dicentra* 'Luxuriant'   Perennial; pink to red flowers in midspring to summer; part shade; 12 to 15 in. tall, 20 in. wide; cold-hardy in USDA zones 3 to 8, heat-tolerant in AHS zones 8 to 1

B   **Grape hyacinth** *Muscari armeniacum*   Bulb; tiny clusters of blue to purple flowers in early spring; sends up new foliage in fall; full sun to part shade; 6 to 8 in. tall, 4 to 6 in. wide; cold-hardy in USDA zones 4 to 8, heat-tolerant in AHS zones 8 to 1

C   **Daffodil** *Narcissus* 'Pipit'   Bulb; yellow trumpet-shaped flowers with two to four flowers per stem in midspring; full sun; 14 to 16 in. tall, 4 to 6 in. wide; cold-hardy in USDA zones 4 to 9, heat-tolerant in AHS zones 9 to 1

D   **Daffodil** *Narcissus* 'White Medal'   Bulb; double white flowers in midspring; full sun; 14 to 16 in. tall, 6 in. wide; cold-hardy in USDA zones 3 to 8, heat-tolerant in AHS zones 8 to 1

Warm up spring Combining spring-blooming bulbs with spring or summer perennials is all well and good. But don't forget about shrubs and annuals. These plants bring their own distinct qualities to the mix that bulbs alone can't supply. Bright yellow tulips pick up the gold edges of this variegated euonymus, which will continue to provide structure and color in this bed throughout the seasons. Augment this planting with early season annuals, such as these violas, for even more long-lasting color.

A   **Viola** *Viola* 'Princess Mix'   Tender perennial; yellow, white, lavender or purple spring flowers; part shade; 4 to 8 in. tall, 7 to 10 in. wide; cold-hardy in USDA zones 7 to 9, heat-tolerant in AHS zones 12 to 1

B   **Tulip** *Tulipa* 'Golden Apeldoorn'   Bulb; golden yellow single flowers in midspring; full sun; 18 to 20 in. tall, 6 in. wide; cold-hardy in USDA zones 3 to 8, heat-tolerant in AHS zones 8 to 1

C   **Euonymus** *Euonymus fortunei* 'Canadale Gold'   Shrub; evergreen rounded leaves sport gold margins; part shade; 3 ft. tall, 4 ft. wide; cold-hardy in USDA zones 5 to 9, heat-tolerant in AHS zones 9 to 1

LOCATION: Atlanta Botanical Garden

Timing is tricky One aspect that makes spring combinations so exciting is their ephemeral quality. That fantastic, but brief, explosion of color is something to look forward to and enjoy while it lasts.

Here, sunny kerria and intensely hued redbuds bloomed shortly after this mass of white daffodils reached its peak. In other years, temperatures may start any of the blooms earlier or later so that the flowers open at different times, extending the spring show.

A   **Daffodil** *Narcissus* hybrid   Bulb; white or yellow trumpet-shaped flowers in early spring; full sun; 4 to 24 in. tall, 4 to 12 in. wide; cold-hardy in USDA zones 3 to 9, heat-tolerant in AHS zones 9 to 1

B   **Kerria** *Kerria japonica*   Shrub; yellow flowers appear in mid- to late spring; full sun to part shade; 6 ft. tall, 8 ft. wide; cold-hardy in USDA zones 4 to 9, heat-tolerant in AHS zones 9 to 1

C   **Redbud** *Cercis canadensis*   Tree; purple-pink flowers open before the leaves emerge in spring; full sun to part shade; 15 to 30 ft. tall, 20 to 30 ft. wide; cold-hardy in USDA zones 4 to 9, heat-tolerant in AHS zones 9 to 1

PERFECT PARTNERS

Not every combination needs lots of different plants to be pretty. Just two plants make up the combos here.

A large boulder provides part shade and shelter from the wind for the yellow trout lily and red primrose at right. Both plants will bloom the prettiest and longest with cool and moist conditions. You can grow primrose in a site that gets more sun if you give it regular moisture.

Good partners for the peony at far right also like moist, humus-rich but well-drained soil and full sun to part-shade conditions. Standing tall, 'Globemaster' allium, with its contrasting globe-shaped purple blooms, thrives here, as well. The flowers last three to four weeks in the garden. And later, the peony will hide the fading allium foliage.

A   **Primrose** *Primula* 'Wanda'   Perennial; red-purple spring flowers, evergreen or semi-evergreen foliage; sun to part shade; 4 to 6 in. tall, 12 in. wide; cold-hardy in USDA zones 3 to 8, heat-tolerant in AHS zones 9 to 1

B   **Trout lily** *Erythronium americanum*   Bulb; yellow flowers in early spring, goes dormant by late spring; part shade to shade; 4 to 6 in. tall, 6 in. wide; cold-hardy in USDA zones 3 to 8, heat-tolerant in AHS zones 8 to 1

A   **Peony** *Paeonia lactiflora* 'Garden Lace'   Perennial; light pink anemone flowers with yellow centers in mid-spring; part shade; 40 in. tall, 24 to 36 in. wide; cold-hardy in USDA zones 3 to 8, heat-tolerant in AHS zones 8 to 1

B   **Globe allium** *Allium* 'Globemaster'   Bulb; long-lasting 10-in. globes of purple flowers in spring; part shade; 2 to 5 ft. tall, 12 in. wide; cold-hardy in USDA zones 4 to 9, heat-tolerant in AHS zones 9 to 1

did you know...

product picks

Tuffits steppers

Throw pillows in the garden? Sure, especially if they're really Tuffits™ concrete steppers. Though they're sturdy enough to walk on, the surface is a bit uneven so you might want to save them for less-traveled areas. Or use one as a surprising garden ornament. There are several styles and colors — that's Xanadu in terra-cotta and Trojan in lilac above. The color is mixed into the concrete so it won't rub or wear off.

Bottom line They look so real!
Source Tuffits at www.tuffits.com or 707-778-8025
Price $35 each. Shipping prices vary according to weight and where you live. Expect to pay $15 to $25 each for shipping.

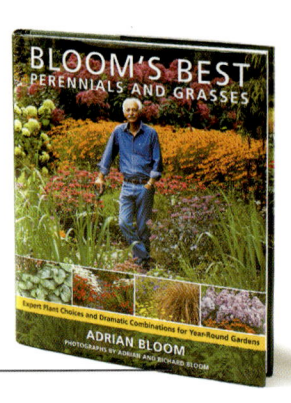

Bloom's Best Perennials and Grasses

Winter is the perfect time to settle in with a good garden book. The inspiring photos of beautiful gardens in this book from Adrian Bloom will get you dreaming about how your garden could look next summer. Then check out the plant profiles to help you choose which plants to use to achieve that dream. Finally, read the chapter with how-to techniques so you'll be successful at planting and caring for your new work of art.

Bottom line Beautiful photos and practical information help you plan for an inspiring garden of your own.
Source Local and online bookstores or www.GardenGateStore.com
Price $34.95; hardcover; 208 pages

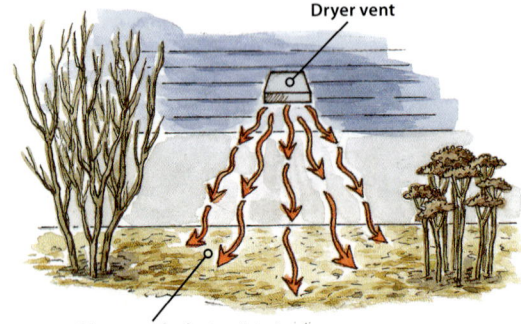

Dryer vent difficulties
Paul Manus, Idaho

Q Every year the shrubs I plant by my dryer vent die. What can I plant there?

A In winter, the hot air from dryer vents causes dramatic fluctuations in temperature, and that's what kills shrubs.
The illustration at left shows a "hot zone" created by a dryer vent. The higher the vent, the larger the hot zone. But lower vents create hotter zones.
Hardy perennials are usually fine set off to the sides. And so are deciduous shrubs that are cold-hardy in your garden. Don't plant anything that will block the vent or make it difficult to access for maintenance.

Patio umbrella trellis
Lark Kulikowski, Wisconsin

When Lark found an old, worn and tattered patio umbrella at a thrift store, she got an idea. Why not turn it into a trellis for her trumpet vine?

A plant as vigorous as the trumpet vine in the photo above needs a sturdy structure. So she made an umbrella stand using a galvanized pipe 3½ feet long with a 1½-inch diameter. She dug a hole and anchored it with concrete, leaving a foot of pipe above ground.

The illustration below shows how she attached a 5-foot-square piece of 2-inch hardware cloth to the umbrella's ribs. This provides something for the vine tendrils to cling to. It also helps the plant maintain its nice shape later in the season. There's no sagging in between the ribs. Since trumpet vine suckers freely, Lark let a couple of sprouts grow up around the post so the stems are intertwined. Any others that come up now get pulled out and given away or tossed on the compost pile. This vine has been growing steadily there for seven years. In a few more years you might not even see the post!

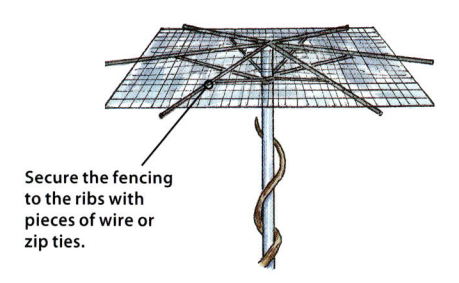

Secure the fencing to the ribs with pieces of wire or zip ties.

Save that arbor
Janet Cincotta, Massachusetts

After 15 years, the arch on Janet's arbor below was cracked and deteriorating. She hated to replace the whole thing because the sides were still in good shape. Plus, it would be tough to pull the panels out without damaging the climbing roses growing on them. Then she had an idea: Why not take the top off? So she did.

Later, at a craft store, Janet found four decorative birdhouses to use as finials for the remaining posts so they looked more complete. To add the birdhouses to the posts, she primed and painted them along with four square pine bases. She painted these to match the arbor, but you could choose different colors. When the paint was dry, she predrilled holes in the posts and used a 1½-inch screw to attach each base to its post. Then she glued each birdhouse to its base with a water-resistant wood glue, and her new trellises were finished!

After 15 years this arch was deteriorating and needed to be replaced.

Topped with decorative birdhouses, the arbor is now a pair of trellises.

Here's a smart way to bring a large yard into scale with your needs. Learn how to do it yourself on page 204.

design challenge
and drawing board
plans to solve *your* most challenging garden situations

PRACTICAL ANSWERS to common landscaping questions — that's what these stories are about. Learn how to design: a front entryway with easy-care perennials; a driveway bed that attracts butterflies; a border for the birds; a woodland retreat for contemplation; and more. It's all here!

Make it Easy on Yourself	**190**
Easy to Maintain	**192**
Bring in the Butterflies	**194**
Butterfly Bistro	**196**
Feeding Butterfly Caterpillars and Container Recipe	**198**
Birds, Welcome	**200**
Bird-Attracting Deck Planting	**202**
How to Tame a Big Space	**204**
Create a Woodland Retreat	**206**
Shady Haven	**208**
Pretty *and* Practical	**210**

DESIGN CHALLENGE | FRONT YARD

make it easy on yourself

Annuals are great if you want lots of flowers. But the problem is that they have to be replanted every year. That gets expensive, and it means a lot of work. Arlene Steffen of Nebraska used to brighten up the front of her house with flats and flats of petunias, but she's ready for a change. She'd like something easy to care for that only has to be planted once. Her garden needs perennials and shrubs!

Most perennials don't bloom all summer, as annuals do. But our plan makes it easy to get the right mix of spring, summer and fall bloomers…and unlike annuals, these long-lasting plants will add some winter interest! Best of all, most of them are available just about anywhere and they're low-care, too. You can buy small plants, tuck them in, and in a year or two, they'll fluff up to fill out your whole garden. You won't have spent a fortune buying them, either! Check out "Buy it small" at right for a list of perennials and shrubs that take off fast from small plants.

It's not just blooms that make this garden great. Vertical shapes help disguise the long, low, horizontal shape of the house. Evergreen shrubs and foliage plants keep things interesting even when there isn't a bloom in sight. A few decorative touches — planter boxes on the porch rail, a container grouping and a decorative trellis — dress up the area near the front door. Take a look at the illustration to see the finer points, then turn to page 192. You'll find a planting plan for the area closest to the door.

Standing tall
This long, low-slung house needs height! An arborvitae and a small crabapple tree at one end break the long line of the edge of the roof. But they won't get so tall that they'll loom over the house. Upright hollies repeated throughout the bed distract your eye from the strong horizontal line of the house even more. And don't forget about balance — the bulk of the house and garage to the right are balanced by grouping the crabapple and arborvitae close together at the other end.

PHOTO: Courtesy of Arlene Steffen

190   the YEAR IN GARDENING   www.GardenGateMagazine.com

More is better
Drifts or clumps of perennials are simpler to care for than the same plants scattered around the bed in ones and twos. If you need to do maintenance, like deadheading or fertilizing, you can do a bunch of plants at one time, instead of hunting around for each individual.

Use color wisely
Draw guests' eyes to the door with bright color. Concentrate flowering perennials around the steps, then bump up the impact with planter boxes on the railings. If you love annuals, tuck them into those planters and maybe some containers to sit on the sidewalk. It's easier to care for a couple of containers than an entire bed of annuals, and they'll still add great summer-long color.

Shrubs to the rescue
Any front-door planting benefits from shrubs because they'll give some bulk and structure year-round. Here, a group of spireas softens the edges of the steps, while adding a little bit of flower power, too. These small spireas have another benefit — they maintain a neat shape without much pruning, so the area around the front door will look tidy, not overgrown and messy.

Web extra See a complete *planting plan* for this foundation.

'Goldsturm' black-eyed Susan    'Rubinstern' coneflower    'Neon Flash' spirea    'Nikko Blue' hydrangea

Buy it small
Don't spend big money for big plants! These tough perennials and shrubs will grow quickly from the smallest sizes you can find. For example, buy a couple of black-eyed Susans in 3-in. nursery pots, tuck them into your garden, and you'll have full-sized plants in two years.

Perennials
Black-eyed Susan *Rudbeckia* spp.
Blanket flower *Gaillardia* hybrids
Coneflower *Echinacea* hybrids
Daylily *Hemerocallis* hybrids
Sedum *Sedum* spp.
Tall garden phlox *Phlox paniculata*

Shrubs
Arrowwood viburnum *Viburnum dentatum*
Hydrangea *Hydrangea* spp.
Sweetspire *Itea virginica*
Japanese spirea *Spiraea japonica*
Red-twig dogwood *Cornus sericea*

DRAWING BOARD | FRONT YARD

bright, beautiful…
and easy to maintain!

Digging, planting and pruning can be fun…but sometimes it's nice to have time to sit back and admire your garden, instead of having to fiddle with it season after season. Shrubs and perennials, instead of an annual planting, can give you that time to relax.

One thing to keep in mind, though: If you're making a break from planting all new annuals every spring, you don't want to end up with high-maintenance perennials instead! Of course, all shrubs and perennials have an advantage over annuals because you only have to plant them once. But there are shrubs that need meticulous pruning, and perennials that need constant deadheading and dividing to look good.

Don't worry — that's not the case with this plan! Feather reed grass, tall garden phlox, daylilies, and black-eyed Susans rarely need to be divided. Phlox and black-eyed Susans spread outward or reseed, so you may need to pull a few new shoots or seedlings to keep clusters in bounds. And while feather reed grass may eventually develop gaps in the center, it won't be for seven or eight years. A little bit of deadheading will help the phlox and the daylily rebloom and look tidier, but it's not absolutely essential. Leave the feather reed grass standing for winter interest, and don't cut back the black-eyed Susans — birds will eat those seeds in the winter.

As for shrubs, these spireas couldn't be easier to maintain. There's no nitpicky pruning, one branch at a time. Once they're done flowering, just shear back the spent blooms and the top 3 or 4 inches of growth. Before you know it, your spireas will be covered with fresh new leaves, and you may even get a few more blooms. And the upright hollies maintain their tidy shape with no shearing at all.

With all the time you'll have left over, you may choose to change things up a little bit, too. Don't be afraid to alter this plan to suit your needs. Leave a few gaps for your favorite annuals. Or tuck in bulbs among the perennials for spring color. (Another benefit to low-maintenance perennials and shrubs? You won't have to dig them up to divide them, so you won't disturb the bulbs when they're dormant.)

Have fun, relax and enjoy! □

— *Stephanie Polsley Bruner*

THE GARDEN'S PALETTE

Code	Plant Name	No. to Plant	Blooms	Type	Cold/Heat Zones	Height/Width	Special Features
A	Spirea *Spiraea japonica* 'Neon Flash'	7	Magenta-pink; late spring	Shrub	4-8/8-1	2-4 ft./2-4 ft.	Snip or shear off spent blooms to tidy plant; may have small rebloom in late summer
B	Tall garden phlox *Phlox paniculata* 'Laura'	8	Magenta-purple with white eye; midsummer	Perennial	4-9/9-1	3-4 ft./2-3 ft.	Lightly fragrant; water at base of plant to keep foliage dry and cut down on powdery mildew
C	Black-eyed Susan *Rudbeckia fulgida sullivantii* 'Goldsturm'	11	Golden yellow; mid- to late summer	Perennial	4-9/9-1	2-3 ft./1-2 ft.	Can tolerate drought, but foliage is healthier with consistent moisture
D	Daylily *Hemerocallis* 'Pardon Me'	11	Cranberry red; midsummer to fall	Perennial	4-10/10-1	18 in./12 in.	Reblooms; cut back spent flower stalks to encourage more flowers
E	Upright Japanese holly *Ilex crenata* 'Sky Pencil'	2	NA	Evergreen shrub	5-9/9-1	6-8 ft./2-3 ft.	Place in sheltered spot to protect foliage from drying winter winds
F	Feather reed grass *Calamagrostis xacutiflora* 'Karl Foerster'	3	Tan; midsummer to fall	Perennial	5-9/9-1	3-5 ft./1-2 ft.	Flowers earlier than most ornamental grasses; cut back hard in early spring to make room for new growth

Flowers on the top

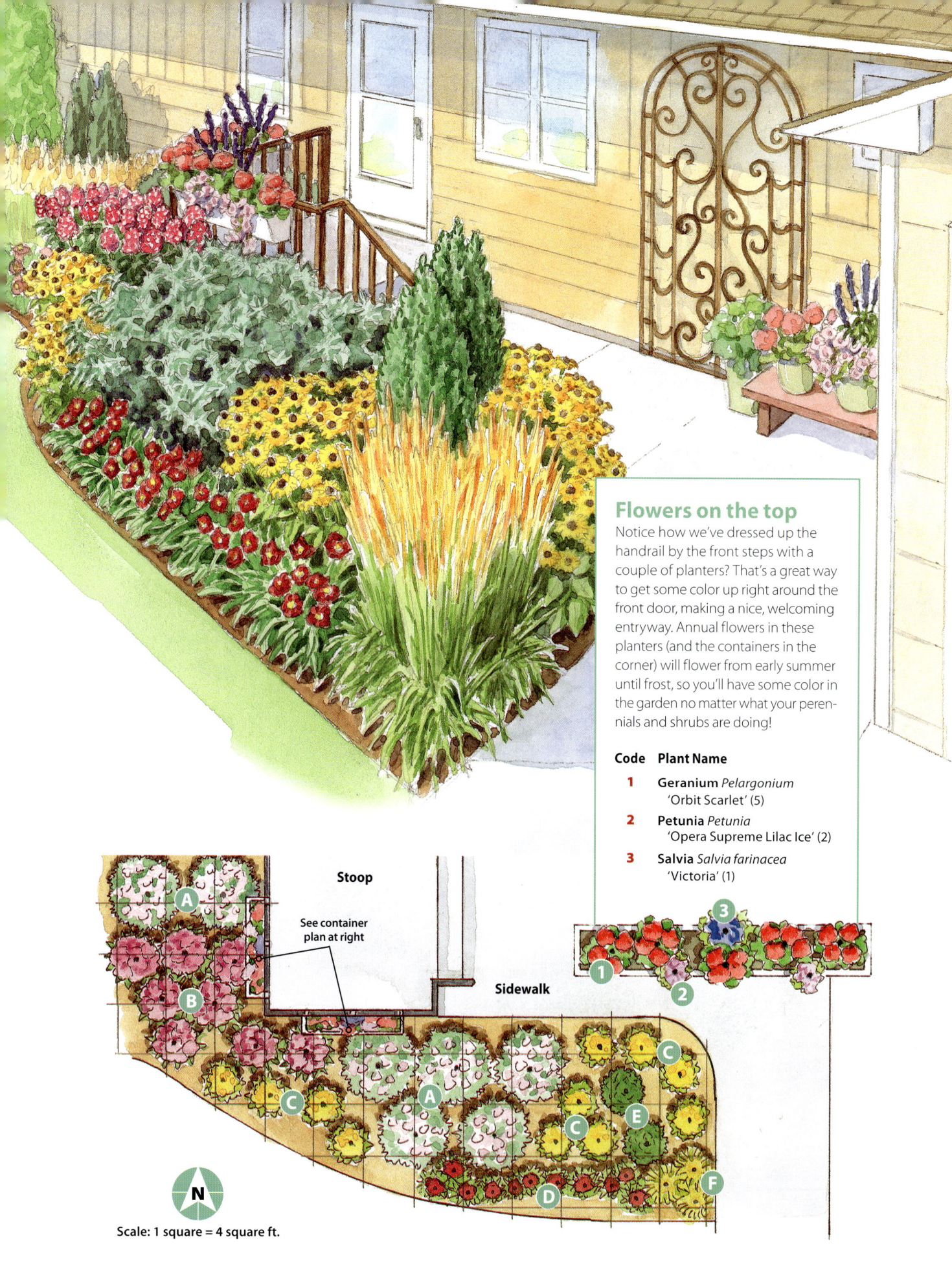

Notice how we've dressed up the handrail by the front steps with a couple of planters? That's a great way to get some color up right around the front door, making a nice, welcoming entryway. Annual flowers in these planters (and the containers in the corner) will flower from early summer until frost, so you'll have some color in the garden no matter what your perennials and shrubs are doing!

Code	Plant Name
1	Geranium *Pelargonium* 'Orbit Scarlet' (5)
2	Petunia *Petunia* 'Opera Supreme Lilac Ice' (2)
3	Salvia *Salvia farinacea* 'Victoria' (1)

Scale: 1 square = 4 square ft.

www.GardenGateMagazine.com *the* YEAR IN GARDENING 193

DESIGN CHALLENGE | FRONT YARD

brighten a dull drive and **bring in butterflies!**

Although gravel driveways are "greener" than their concrete counterparts, it's true they can look a bit untidy. The owner of this one wanted a way to dress up her driveway. So, I've pulled together some creative design ideas to make the whole area look fresher and more welcoming.

A vine-covered trellis makes this east-facing garage door look much more appealing. And shrubs along the foundation hide the blank wall. The rock garden to the right of the door just needs a few shrubs and some colorful flowers to give it more appeal. Finally, what better way to cheer up the entire yard than to add a colorful border that attracts butterflies? On page 198 you'll find five butterflies that are likely to visit this border. Would you like a plan for this entire side yard? Check out our Web extra. But before you do, let me show you some more smart design tips that make this side yard easy on the eyes, on the back and on the pocketbook. □

— *Jim Childs*

Serve food for caterpillars To get lots of butterflies, you'll want plants where the showy adults can lay their eggs and the caterpillars that hatch can eat and grow. And it doesn't hurt if the plants are easy to grow and are pest-resistant, like this lilac. Planted around and under it are the larval plants you see in the photos below, too. If you see a few chewed leaves, all of these plants will be fine. So don't bother spraying — you're raising future butterflies!

Virginia bluebells
Mertensia virginica

Columbine
Aquilegia canadensis

Common violet
Viola sororia

PHOTOS: Delilah Smittle (violet); Katie Downey (stone)

Make it butterfly friendly

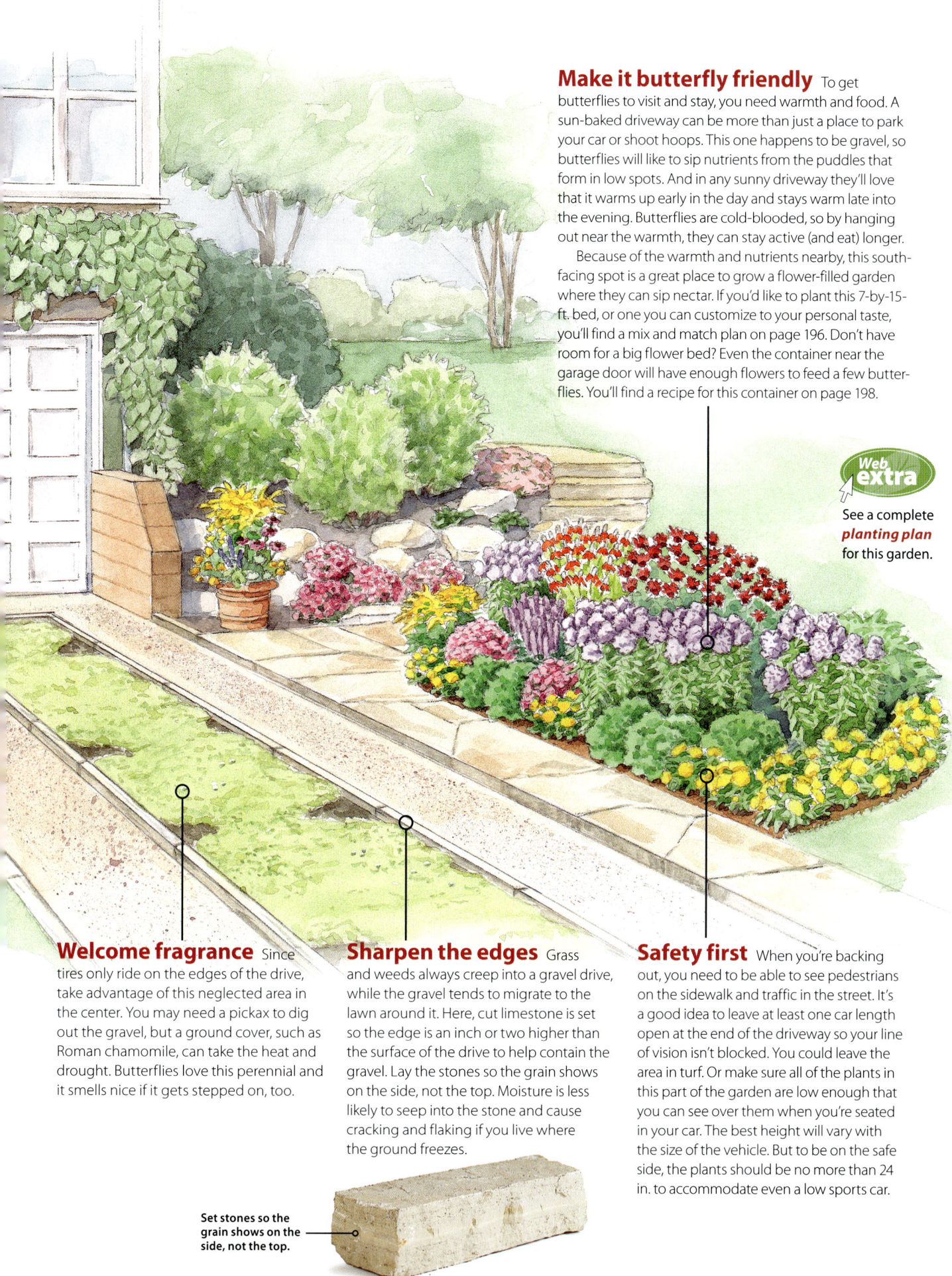

To get butterflies to visit and stay, you need warmth and food. A sun-baked driveway can be more than just a place to park your car or shoot hoops. This one happens to be gravel, so butterflies will like to sip nutrients from the puddles that form in low spots. And in any sunny driveway they'll love that it warms up early in the day and stays warm late into the evening. Butterflies are cold-blooded, so by hanging out near the warmth, they can stay active (and eat) longer.

Because of the warmth and nutrients nearby, this south-facing spot is a great place to grow a flower-filled garden where they can sip nectar. If you'd like to plant this 7-by-15-ft. bed, or one you can customize to your personal taste, you'll find a mix and match plan on page 196. Don't have room for a big flower bed? Even the container near the garage door will have enough flowers to feed a few butterflies. You'll find a recipe for this container on page 198.

Web extra See a complete *planting plan* for this garden.

Welcome fragrance

Since tires only ride on the edges of the drive, take advantage of this neglected area in the center. You may need a pickax to dig out the gravel, but a ground cover, such as Roman chamomile, can take the heat and drought. Butterflies love this perennial and it smells nice if it gets stepped on, too.

Sharpen the edges

Grass and weeds always creep into a gravel drive, while the gravel tends to migrate to the lawn around it. Here, cut limestone is set so the edge is an inch or two higher than the surface of the drive to help contain the gravel. Lay the stones so the grain shows on the side, not the top. Moisture is less likely to seep into the stone and cause cracking and flaking if you live where the ground freezes.

Set stones so the grain shows on the side, not the top.

Safety first

When you're backing out, you need to be able to see pedestrians on the sidewalk and traffic in the street. It's a good idea to leave at least one car length open at the end of the driveway so your line of vision isn't blocked. You could leave the area in turf. Or make sure all of the plants in this part of the garden are low enough that you can see over them when you're seated in your car. The best height will vary with the size of the vehicle. But to be on the safe side, the plants should be no more than 24 in. to accommodate even a low sports car.

the YEAR IN GARDENING

DRAWING BOARD | FRONT YARD

open your own
butterfly bistro

This garden is designed with two things in mind — it's colorful for you to look at, and it has lots of nectar for butterflies. Above and beyond that, all of the plants are tough, durable and easy to find, either in your local garden center or through a mail-order company. And while here it's planted along a driveway, which you can read more about on page 194, you could grow it in almost any sunny spot.

GIVE IT A PERSONAL TOUCH In the large illustration you can see the complete garden layout and where each plant is located. With each of the small illustrations, there's information on how big the plant will grow, where it's hardy, when and in what color it blooms, and how many you will need.

I've given you two options for each plant. For example, H1 is 'Cambridge Scarlet' bee balm, a perennial with scarlet-red flowers. But maybe you don't like the way bee balm spreads. Or perhaps you simply don't like red. Then go with H2, 'Coronation Gold' yarrow. It'll stay in a tidy clump and it's not red. As you make your choices, watch the sizes and number you need. While you will use 16 pot marigolds (A1), if you go with lantana (A2) you'll only need six plants to fill the same area.

However, butterflies need more than the nectar they'll get from this flowery garden. After the showy adult lays eggs, and the caterpillars, or larvae, hatch, they need food. On the next page I'll show you five colorful butterflies and share a few of their favorite larval foods, as well as information on regions where the adults are most likely to lay their eggs.

- United States Department of Agriculture (USDA) cold-hardiness zones
- American Horticultural Society (AHS) heat-tolerance zones

Don't know your zones? Find your heat and cold zones online at www.GardenGateMagazine.com/zones.

A1 Pot marigold
Calendula officinalis 'Candyman Yellow'
Annual with bright yellow flowers all summer
6-10 in. tall
12-15 in. wide
• Annual • 12-1
Plant 16

A2 Lantana
Lantana 'Radiation'
Tender perennial with scarlet and yellow summer flowers
12-15 in. tall
24-36 in. wide
• 9-11 • 12-1
Plant 6

B1 Peony
Paeonia lactiflora 'Elsa Sass'
Perennial with white flowers in spring
18-24 in. tall
24-36 in. wide
• 3-8 • 8-1
Plant 2

B2 False indigo
Baptisia australis
Perennial with violet-blue flowers in late spring
24-48 in. tall
24-36 in. wide
• 3-9 • 9-1
Plant 2

C1 Garden phlox
Phlox paniculata 'Katherine'
Perennial with fragrant pale lavender flowers in summer
24-30 in. tall
18-24 in. wide
• 4-9 • 9-1
Plant 5

C2 Gaura
Gaura lindheimeri 'Siskiyou Pink'
Perennial with pink flowers most of the summer
24-30 in. tall
24-36 in. wide
• 5-8 • 8-1
Plant 4

D1 Prairie coneflower
Ratibida columnifera
Perennial with small orange and brown summer flowers
24-36 in. tall
12-24 in. wide
• 3-10 • 10-1
Plant 3

D2 Zinnia
Zinnia 'Benary Giant Mix'
Annual with large colorful summer flowers
30-36 in. tall
12-15 in. wide
• Annual • 12-1
Plant 6

E1 — Goldenrod
Solidago 'Baby Gold' ('Goldkind')
Perennial with golden yellow flowers in fall
18-24 in. tall
8-12 in. wide
- 5-9 • 9-1
Plant 9

E2 — Tall sedum
Sedum 'Autumn Joy' ('Herbsfreude')
Perennial with pink flowers in fall
12-36 in. tall
12-24 in. wide
- 3-9 • 9-1
Plant 5

F1 — Aster
Aster novi-belgii 'Jenny'
Perennial with bright pink flowers in autumn
12-16 in. tall and wide
- 4-8 • 8-1
Plant 5

F2 — Coreopsis
Coreopsis verticillata 'Zagreb'
Perennial with golden yellow summer flowers
12-15 in. tall
12-24 in. wide
- 3-9 • 9-1
Plant 5

G1 — Blazing star
Liatris spicata 'Kobold'
Perennial with spikes of purple flowers in summer
18-24 in. tall
12-18 in. wide
- 4-9 • 9-1
Plant 13

G2 — Salvia
Salvia nemorosa 'Caradonna'
Perennial with deep-violet spires in summer
18-20 in. tall
12-18 in. wide
- 4-9 • 9-1
Plant 13

H1 — Bee balm
Monarda 'Cambridge Scarlet'
Perennial with scarlet-red summer flowers
24-36 in. tall
24-30 in. wide
- 3-9 • 9-1
Plant 3

H2 — Yarrow
Achillea 'Coronation Gold'
Perennial with gold flowers in midsummer
30-36 in. tall
18-24 in. wide
- 3-8 • 8-1
Plant 3

I1 — Parsley
Petroselinum crispum
Biennial herb with deep green leaves all summer that feed black swallowtail larvae
12-18 in. tall
9-12 in. wide
- 5-9 • 9-1
Plant 8

I2 — Verbena
Verbena 'Homestead Purple'
Perennial, can be treated as an annual, with rosy-purple flowers all summer
6-18 in. tall
24-36 in. wide
- 7-10 • 12-1
Plant 3

N — This bed is roughly 13 ft. long and 7 ft. wide.

www.GardenGateMagazine.com   *the* YEAR IN GARDENING   197

DRAWING BOARD: FRONT YARD

feeding butterfly caterpillars

Plant the garden on page 196 and you'll have plenty of nectar for butterflies — including the five above. But if you don't want them to eat and run, you'll need food for the caterpillars, too. And they can be picky eaters!

At least one of the butterflies above will visit almost any garden in North America. Want to know more about them? I'll share their favorite caterpillar foods, as well as how many generations of larvae you might see each year. And check out the maps to find out where you're most likely to spot each of these butterflies. □

— *Jim Childs*

1 EASTERN TIGER SWALLOWTAIL

Papilio glaucus With a wingspan of 3 inches, this butterfly is easy to spot from spring into late summer. And depending on how far south you live in its region, you may find up to three generations of caterpillars and adults per year.

Caterpillar favorites
Ash *Fraxinus* spp.
Black cherry *Prunus serotina*
Chokecherry *Prunus virginiana*
Common lilac *Syringa vulgaris*

2 COMMON BUCKEYE

Junonia coenia This 2-inch-wide butterfly is a wanderer. You may find adults further north, but the season may not be long enough for them to lay eggs and hatch caterpillars outside the areas shaded on this map. Common buckeyes can have up to three generations per year.

Caterpillar favorites
Plantain *Plantago* spp.
Snapdragon *Antirrhinum majus*
Verbena *Verbena* spp.

PHOTOS: © Bob Moul (2, 3, 5); © Phil Kelly (4)

198 *the* YEAR IN GARDENING www.GardenGateMagazine.com

container recipe

butterfly magnet

3 QUESTION MARK
Polygonia interrogationis
Since this butterfly overwinters as an adult in a tree hollow or underneath bark, you might spot one in early spring. While it occasionally sips nectar from a flower, it really prefers a juicy piece of rotten fruit. Its wingspan is 2 to 2½ inches wide and there can be up to three generations hatched per summer.

Caterpillar favorites
- Elm *Ulmus* spp.
- Hackberry *Celtis* spp.
- Nettles *Urtica* spp.

4 BALTIMORE CHECKERSPOT
Euphydryas phaeton With markings like a checkerboard, you can see where the name comes from. It has a wingspan of 1¾ inches up to 2¾ inches, with the larger ones being found in the southern part of their range. There are usually only one or two generations hatched per summer.

Caterpillar favorites
- Plantain *Plantago* spp.
- Turtlehead *Chelone* spp.
- White ash *Fraxinus americana*

5 BLACK SWALLOWTAIL
Papilio polyxenes These showy butterflies can have a wingspan of up to 3½ inches. They breed from late spring into late summer and can hatch two or three generations per year.

Caterpillar favorites
- Carrot *Daucus* spp. and hybrids
- Dill *Anethum graveolens*
- Parsley *Petroselinum crispum*

You don't need a huge garden to attract butterflies. In fact, this container is only 15 inches across, and it's packed with plants that'll have winged visitors fluttering around most of the summer. Late summer is its peak, as you can see here, but those salvias, coreopsis and lantanas will have attracted butterflies ever since they were planted in early summer.

Have you had problems getting a multicolored container like this one to look just right? The key is to pick one main color, like the yellow here, and make sure that at least two plants are displaying that color all the time. Dwarf goldenrod, coreopsis and lantanas ensure a continuous sunny yellow. Then pick some accent colors, like the pink and blue in this planting. Cluster those accent plants together, or pick some with big flowers — these coneflowers, for example. That way, the accent colors don't get lost or look like a mistake.

For immediate impact, start with good-sized plants and gently flatten the root balls a little as you plant to get everything to fit. As long as you don't break roots away from the crown, most plants don't mind this at all, especially if you give them a good drink of water right away! □

— *Deborah Gruca*

Tips for care
- Full sun
- Even soil moisture
- Feed monthly with a balanced water-soluble fertilizer

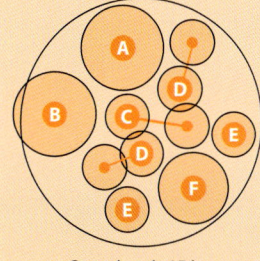

Container is 15 in. in diameter

Code	Plant Name	No. to Plant
A	Dwarf goldenrod *Solidago* 'Baby Gold' ('Goldkind')	1
B	Coreopsis *Coreopsis verticillata* 'Zagreb'	1
C	Purple coneflower *Echinacea purpurea* 'Ruby Star' ('Rubinstern')	2
D	Salvia *Salvia farinacea* 'Victoria'	4
E	Lantana *Lantana camara* 'Goldsonne'	2
F	Sedum *Sedum spectabile* 'Hot Stuff'	1

www.GardenGateMagazine.com *the* YEAR IN GARDENING

DESIGN CHALLENGE | BACK YARD

birds, welcome!

When she moved into her home in rural Vermont, Helen Bernard was thrilled with its location and the beautiful surrounding woods. She dreamed of a pretty, easy-care border that she could enjoy from her house and deck. But the mostly bare back yard sent her looking for design help. This colorful plan uses trees, shrubs, perennials and annuals that are easy to find and care for. As a bonus, the design also makes this zone 5 garden attractive to wildlife — especially birds.

MAKE IT BIRD-FRIENDLY To bring birds into your garden, you need to offer them food, shelter, water and nesting places. Feeders are a great start, but to attract the most kinds of birds to your yard, for more of the year, grow a mixed border of trees, shrubs and other plants. In addition to seeds, fruit and nectar, you'll be giving them places to nest and take shelter from predators and bad weather.

Aside from bringing in wild birds, there are lots of things that make this garden attractive to two-legged visitors. At right, read five tips that make this back yard easy to enjoy. And check out three birds that you might see in this garden in "Ones to watch," below. You'll find the plan for the bed around the deck on p. 202. For the plan and plant list for this entire back yard, visit our Web extra. □
— *Deborah Gruca*

Botanical Names

Annual sunflower
Helianthus annuus
Arborvitae
Thuja occidentalis
Bee balm
Monarda hybrids
Colorado spruce
Picea pungens
Goldenrod
Solidago rugosa
Purple coneflower
Echinacea purpurea
Serviceberry
Amelanchier xgrandiflora

Large trees Arranged from shortest to tallest, plants are placed in view of the house and deck. The larger Colorado spruce grows to the north side of the other plantings where it won't shade them out. In winter, the big evergreen will shelter the house (as well as the birds), offering some protection from cold winds.

ONES TO WATCH

Though these birds usually frequent open fields or forests, they often take advantage of back yard plantings and feeders. Using a combination of a tube feeder, a hopper and a suet feeder, you can attract a wide variety of birds. To encourage them to stay, place yarn, hair or shredded paper in an empy suet feeder for nesting materials.

Eastern bluebird *Sialia sialis* The 8½-in.-long bird is common near open areas along fields and golf courses bordered by trees. It nests in nest boxes and holes in trees and feeds on insects on the ground and berries. **Range** In summer: Eastern United States and southern Canada; In winter: Southeast United States and Mexico.

Northern mockingbird *Mimus polyglottos* Seen and heard in towns, suburbs and back yards, this 10-in.-long bird sings all day, even into the night, and can acquire a repertoire of hundreds of songs. It mainly eats insects, but also fruit, berries and seeds. **Range** Most of United States and southern Canada year round.

Evening grosbeak *Coccothraustes vespertinus* This 7-in.-long, brightly colored bird frequents coniferous or mixed forests. Its diet consists of small fruits, seeds and insects but it will readily feed at back yard feeders as well. **Range** Most of the United States and southern and western Canada year round.

PHOTOS: Courtesy of Helen Bernard (before photo); © Jeff Nadler (eastern bluebird); © Tom Grey (northern mockingbird, evening grosbeak)

A patch of lawn
During the growing season, grass is attractive to ground-feeding birds like robins and bluebirds. Keep it on the tall side — 2½ to 3 in. — and leave the clippings on the lawn. This will give these bug-eaters opportunities to hunt the insects and earthworms living there. A bonus: Most grass plants develop deeper roots when left tall, so you'll have a healthier, more drought-tolerant lawn, too.

Plan for the view
The backdrop greens of the tall arborvitae and big shrubs make the yellow annual sunflowers really show up from across the yard. That yellow, along with the goldenrod and the nearby red bee balm, echo the colors of the bed surrounding the deck. Place a pretty birdbath in front of the purple coneflowers where you can see the birds enjoying the water.

Leave it open
I've tucked the compost pile in behind the shrubs, where it's out of sight from the house but still easy to get to. A quick walk through the arbor and down the short 3-ft.-wide stone path and you're there. Don't cover your compost pile — birds are constantly foraging for food and nesting materials. They'll often find bits of plants, kitchen scraps or juicy earthworms for tasty snacks. Make sure to avoid meat or anything that might draw four-legged critters.

Add a little height
After it's established, the Colorado spruce will grow 12 in. a year. The serviceberry will take several years to reach its full 30-ft. height. So put up a structure, such as a trellis or arbor, to give the garden some vertical interest while you're waiting for your new trees to get big. When you sit on the deck you have a perfect view of the arbor that leads to a bench. And if you grow a fruit- or nectar-bearing vine on the arbor, you'll entice even more hungry birds that like to perch there.

Web extra
See a complete *planting plan* for this back yard.

DRAWING BOARD | BACK YARD

bird-attracting deck planting

Want to attract birds even in a small planting? Here's a plan designed to go around an intimate deck — though you can easily adapt it to any sunny outdoor space.

Farther out in this back yard on page 200, the Colorado spruce and the arborvitaes provide safe shelter even in the dead of winter. The plants in the design around this deck focus on offering lots of food to birds and butterflies. Shrubs and perennials make up most of it, with some annuals thrown in for extra color.

NEED SEEDS? This plan includes a few fruit-bearing shrubs. Spreading yew provides a green backdrop through the winter and red summer fruit. And rock cotoneaster flowers in early summer and produces fruit in late summer to fall. But this border concentrates on seed-bearing plants to minimize the mess on the deck. Threadleaf coreopsis, purple coneflower and ornamental millet add plenty of seeds to those offered in the birdfeeders. Hungry birds will eat the ripening seeds of bachelor's button, too. The seeds of this pretty blue annual are easy to sow outdoors in spring and the plants will self-seed around the garden.

DON'T FORGET THE HUMMERS Hummingbirds have plenty to feed on here as well. The flowers of the lilacs out in the yard will give these tiny winged wonders lots of nectar to eat in spring. And later, the red flowers of bee balm and two kinds of coral bells will keep them busy closer to the deck. This planting also has lots to offer butterflies all season. Even in fall, asters and goldenrod will give them a lavish buffet. □

— *Deborah Gruca*

Scale: 1 square = 4 square ft.

Attract a wide variety of birds by using a combination of a tube feeder, a hopper and a suet feeder. (Place yarn, hair or shredded paper in an empty suet feeder for nesting material.)

THE GARDEN'S PALETTE

Code	Plant Name	No. to Plant	Type	Blooms	Height/ Width	Cold/Heat Zones	Comments
A	Bee balm *Monarda* 'Jacob Cline'	5	Perennial	Red; early summer	3-4 ft./ 2-3 ft.	4-9/9-1	Erect stems; attracts hummingbirds; mildew-resistant; divide every three to four years in spring or fall
B	Threadleaf coreopsis *Coreopsis verticillata* 'Moonbeam'	9	Perennial	Pale yellow; early to midsummer	18-24 in./ 18-24 in.	3-9/9-1	Shear plant back by half in midsummer to encourage a smaller late-season rebloom
C	Ornamental millet *Pennisetum glaucum* 'Purple Majesty'	10	Tender perennial	Purple; early to late summer	48-60 in./ 9-12 in.	9-11/12-1	Striking dark purple stems and wide leaves; flower spikes have purple-brown seeds that birds like
D	Goldenrod *Solidago* 'Crown of Rays'	8	Perennial	Yellow; midsummer to fall	18-24 in./ 12-18 in.	5-9/9-1	Long bloom period; attractive to bees and butterflies; divide every three to four years
E	Aster *Aster* 'Wood's Light Blue'	7	Perennial	Blue; late summer to fall	12-15 in./ 12-15 in.	4-8/8-1	Mildew- and rust-resistant; compact habit needs no staking; attracts butterflies
F	Purple coneflower *Echinacea purpurea* 'White Swan'	10	Perennial	White; summer	24-36 in./ 18-24 in.	3-9/9-1	Drought-tolerant; leave ornamental seed heads for birds to feed on; divide every three to four years
G	Coral bells *Heuchera* 'Caramel'	2	Perennial	Light pink; summer	9-18 in./ 12-24 in.	4-9/9-1	Leaves emerge gray-red in spring and age to caramel; mulch after ground freezes to prevent root heaving
H	Coral bells *Heuchera* 'Purple Petticoats'	2	Perennial	White; early summer	12-18 in./ 18-24 in.	4-9/9-1	White spring flowers attract hummingbirds; dark purple, frilly edged leaves have best color with afternoon shade
I	Rock cotoneaster *Cotoneaster horizontalis*	1	Shrub	Pale pink; early summer	12-30 in./ 4-7 ft.	4-7/7-1	Small, pale pink flowers in early summer, red berries in late summer to fall; red-purple fall foliage; slow growing
J	Bachelor's button *Centaurea cyanus* 'Blue Boy'	13	Annual	Blue; summer to frost	24-30 in./ 9-12 in.	NA/12-1	Drought-tolerant; good cut or dried flowers; will self-seed
K	Spreading yew *Taxus* x*media* 'Densiformis'	1	Shrub	NA	3-4 ft./ 4-6 ft.	4-7/7-1	'Densiformis' is a female cultivar that produces red, fleshy fruit; spray with anti-desiccant to prevent winter burn

DESIGN CHALLENGE | BACK YARD

how to **tame a big space**

A big yard doesn't have to cause big headaches! My long, narrow lot has some challenges, including an awkward shape and a tangle of scrub trees and undergrowth at one end. But the right combination of trees, shrubs and easy-care perennials can turn it into a haven. With some suggestions from fellow *Garden Gate* editors, I've come up with a design that'll be easy to care for, and as attractive to birds as it is to humans. I'll share my design dilemmas and decisions with you, as well as some tips you can put to use in your own yard.

This back yard, behind a two-car garage, is a long rectangle, about 95 feet long and 57 feet wide. While previous owners kept the sunny front area mowed, no one had ever bothered to clean out the scrub trees in the back. Birds and small furry things love this wild back area. And actually, keeping the yard divided into two distinct sections — one a sunny lawn and the other a shady woodland — is a good design idea. If I tried to clear out the trees and create one big open area, this lot might end up looking like a lane in a bowling alley instead of a beautiful garden!

RING AROUND A YARD
While it's tempting just to chop this area in half, making two squares, a circle of lawn is more eye-catching. And the curve of the circle distracts your eyes from the straight lines of the lot edges, so the long, skinny shape of the yard isn't as noticeable. (Need help making your own "perfect" circle? Check out "Round 'em up" at right.)

THAT'S PRETTY WILD Across that circle of lawn, you'll see a rustic arbor leading to the wild area at the back. Quite a few houses are built next to "natural" areas like this. And it's always a dilemma — do you clear it out? Leave it alone? Actually, it's not as difficult as you'd think. Take a look at the existing trees (or get a tree professional familiar with local species to walk through it with you). Here, I plan to remove a few leaning boxelders, which have weak, easily broken wood. But I'll keep longer-lived trees, walnut and hackberries for an instant canopy. Then I'll plant a few understory trees, such as serviceberries, and shade-tolerant shrubs, such as snowberry. With just a little encouragement, they'll thrive in the shade, choking out weeds and covering bare soil. Once they're established, I'll only have to do occasional pruning to keep this area looking great.

FOR THE BIRDS People aren't the only creatures who'll enjoy both halves of this yard. The shaded back portion offers evergreens and tall trees for bird nesting sites. (See the plan for the wooded area on page 206.) And the sunny area in front has open space surrounded by trees, shrubs and perennials that provide fruit and seeds. Any garden can become a little more welcoming with some birdhouses and a feeder or two. Then you — and the birds — can sit back and enjoy your garden! □

— *Stephanie Polsley Bruner*

Web extra
See a complete **planting plan** for this bird-friendly back yard.

Challenge Our Designers

Is something about your yard giving you fits? Send a letter describing your landscape problems along with photos of the area. We'll choose a few, come up with ideas to make them work better and share them in future issues. Readers whose challenges are selected for publication will receive a one-year subscription or renewal to *Garden Gate* (not to mention some great garden advice!). Send your design challenge to:

Garden Gate Design Challenge Editor
2200 Grand Ave., Des Moines, Iowa 50312
Or e-mail us at gardengate@gardengatemag.com

Pick a theme This circular lawn is a bold statement, so make it look like you meant it! Continue the circular theme with a round vegetable garden and patio. And sweep a curving path off the edge to swing around to another circular patio deep in the wooded area.

Easy access Paths and destinations are important in any garden, but in a space this size, they're crucial. Gravel paths offer a mudproof walk, even after a rain. And cut-stone "floors" on the patios keep furniture level. This patio is about 14 ft. in diameter, just the right size for two people to relax in comfort.

Round 'em up Here's an easy way to mark a circle for a lawn or patio. In the center of the area, stick a stake firmly into the ground. Cut a length of string to the radius of the circle you want. (A circle's radius is the distance between the center and the edge.) Tie one end loosely around the center stake, and the other end to another stake. Stretch the string taut, and use the second stake to mark your circle. (Mark the circle more permanently with spray paint.)

Mark the circle with spray paint or flour.

Screen the view Fast-growing, tall perimeter plantings serve two purposes. They provide privacy and they blur the boundaries, so you're less likely to notice the long, narrow shape of this yard. Small ornamental trees are big enough to serve as a screen, but they won't cast too much shade across this sunny area.

www.GardenGateMagazine.com   *the* YEAR IN GARDENING   205

DRAWING BOARD | BACK YARD

create a woodland retreat

Instead of a wild wasteland, create a springtime retreat in a wooded area. You got a glimpse of the whole project in "Design Challenge" on page 204, so let's take a look at how it's done. It's easier than you think!

START AT THE TOP In a wooded area, you may want to leave a few existing trees, like the hackberries here. (You can see their bare trunks in the foreground in the illustration at right.) They'll add instant height and canopy. Plant a sycamore for its beautiful bark — it's far from the house and parking, so the big leaves and twigs won't create a litter problem. Then think about understory trees (shade-tolerant small trees that thrive under the canpoy of shade trees) for a natural forest look. Here, Canadian hemlock, an evergreen, and serviceberry, a spring-flowering tree, provide nesting spots and food for birds.

AT GROUND LEVEL Fill in around the trees with shrubs and perennials. Spring is the high point for a woodland garden, when ephemerals like bluebells pop up. For summer-long color, leave room for shade annuals like impatiens.

STROLLING ALONG With plants in place, you'll want to admire your woodland. A curving path ensures that it takes as long as possible to get to your destination. Speaking of paths, see the bridges? They're pretty *and* practical. This area is lower than the rest of the yard, and water moves through quickly after a heavy rain. A dry streambed channels the water so it won't wash out surrounding plantings. ("Wet and dry," below, gives some design tips for attractive dry streambeds.) Finally, a rustic pavilion is the perfect finishing touch. It doesn't even need a roof because there's plenty of shade back here. And it'll be a great place to sit and listen to the birds. ☐

— *Stephanie Polsley Bruner*

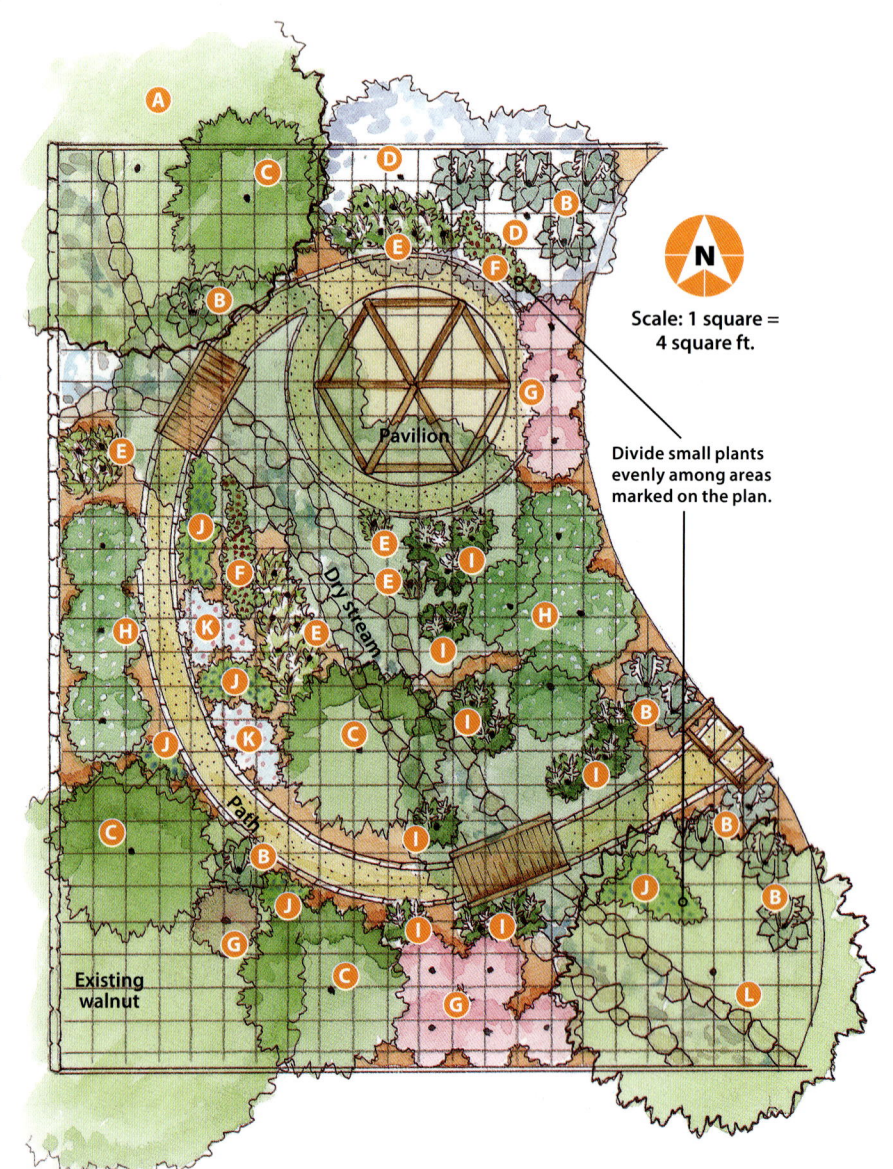

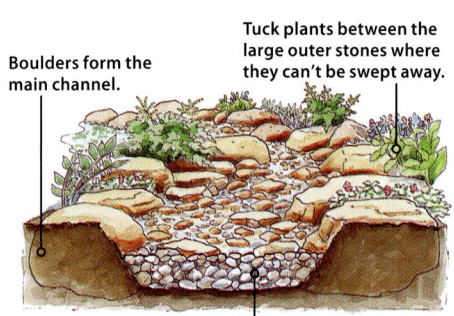

Scale: 1 square = 4 square ft.

Divide small plants evenly among areas marked on the plan.

Boulders form the main channel.

Tuck plants between the large outer stones where they can't be swept away.

Combine gravel with smaller stones for the center.

Wet and dry A dry streambed can look great even when it's not actually in use. Sink larger stones along the sides to form your main channel. Then fill in the center with smooth rocks or river gravel. Choose gravel with pieces that are all an inch or more in diameter, so it won't be washed away with a stream of water.

Leave existing hackberry trees to create instant canopy. They'll fill out when competing scrub trees are removed.

Tuck plants among the rocks of the dry streambed for a natural look.

THE GARDEN'S PALETTE

Code	Plant Name	No. to Plant	Blooms	Type	Cold/Heat Zones	Height/Width	Special Features
A	Sycamore *Platanus occidentalis*	1	NA	Tree	4-9/9-1	75-100 ft./75-100 ft.	Ornamental multi-colored bark; plant away from house and parking so large leaves won't create a litter problem
B	Hosta *Hosta sieboldiana elegans*	12	White; early summer	Perennial	4-9/9-1	2-3 ft./3-4 ft.	Grown for heavy, ribbed blue-green leaves
C	Canadian hemlock *Tsuga canadensis*	4	NA	Evergreen tree	3-7/7-1	40-70 ft./25-35 ft.	Branches become drooping and pendulous with age; best planted in part to full shade
D	Serviceberry *Amelanchier xgrandiflora* 'Autumn Brilliance'	2	White; spring	Tree	3-9/9-1	10-30 ft./10-25 ft.	Tolerates part-shade, understory setting; orange-red fall leaf color is best in more sun
E	Variegated Solomon's seal *Polygonatum odoratum pluriflorum* 'Variegatum'	20	White; spring	Perennial	3-8/8-1	24-30 in./24-30 in.	Flowers dangle beneath arching stems; medium green leaves with white-streaked margins; prefers consistently moist to wet soil
F	Columbine *Aquilegia canadensis*	25	Yellow and red; spring	Perennial	3-8/8-1	24-36 in./12-18 in.	Flowers attract hummingbirds; foliage looks good all summer as long as soil is consistently moist
G	Rhododendron *Rhododendron* PJM Group	9	Lavender-pink; spring	Broadleaf evergreen shrub	4-8/8-1	4-6 ft./4-6 ft.	Plant in site protected from wind to ensure winter survival; prefers good drainage
H	Snowberry *Symphoricarpos albus*	7	Pink; spring	Shrub	3-7/7-1	3-6 ft./3-6 ft.	Tiny spring flowers are followed by white fall berries; fruits hold on through much of the winter
I	Goatsbeard *Aruncus dioicus*	13	White; spring	Perennial	4-9/9-1	3-6 ft./2-4 ft.	Fluffy white plumes fade to brown; prefers part shade but will tolerate more sun if soil is consistently moist
J	Virginia bluebell *Mertensia virginica*	50	Blue; spring	Perennial	3-9/9-1	12-18 in./12 in.	Foliage goes dormant after blooms fade, so combine with perennials that will cover empty spaces later in the season
K	Spotted deadnettle *Lamium maculatum* 'Pink Pewter'	14	Pink; spring	Perennial	3-9/9-1	4-8 in./spreading	Prefers part shade and consistently moist soil to avoid scorched foliage; can cut back hard to refresh
L	Bald cypress *Taxodium distichum*	1	NA	Tree	4-9/9-1	50-70 ft./20-40 ft.	Feathery green needles turn copper-orange before dropping in fall; tolerates wide range of soil from dry to standing water

DESIGN CHALLENGE | BACK YARD

shady haven

Shade is wonderful…cool on a hot day and good for your skin! But it's frustrating when you want a garden full of flowers. And if deer regularly visit to browse, as they do in this townhouse garden, it makes a tough situation even worse.

Don't give up! With some careful choices for plants and hardscaping, you can turn even the shadiest spot into a flowery garden. And while there's no such thing as a completely deer-*proof* garden, you can choose plants that'll cause most deer to look elsewhere for a snack. (We'll tell you more about the plants on page 210.)

Let's look at how to transform this depressing back yard into a peaceful oasis. (And of course, if you live in a condo or townhouse yourself, make sure you check the association rules before you try this at home!)

GOODBYE, GRASS Make it easy on yourself. Grass struggles under trees, and it's a fight you're not going to win. This tear-drop-shaped patio echoes the unusual shape of the yard, and it'll give you a dry, solid surface underfoot. Depending on your budget or preferred look, you can make it from concrete (stamp or stain it for a custom look), pavers or even pea gravel held in place with edging.

FLOWERS EVERYWHERE Shade flowers often aren't as showy as their sunny counterparts, so mass them for more impact. They'll be easier to care for, too, because you can do one maintenance task, like deadheading, on a lot of plants at once. Many shade flowers turn up in shades of white, cream, purple and pink, and these are no exception. But colorful leaves, like the burgundy snakeroot, are a great way to get a little extra bang for your buck.

DRAT THOSE DEER! Pretty though they are, these plants have something better going for them. Almost all of them are things that deer avoid. (And we have an easy suggestion for a do-it-yourself fence option in "Fence me in," at right, too.) Punch things up with containers of annuals on the deck. Deer are less likely to get that close to the house. Even if they do, it'll be easier for you to discourage them, either with some fishing line across the opening (it's hard to see, and deer don't like bumping into it) or with some scent repellent sprayed on the edge of the containers.

A LITTLE PRIVACY, PLEASE The sheltering belt of shrubs that discourages deer also gives you a visual boundary, as does the section of picket fence along the property line with the next townhouse. Gardens that blend into a wooded area need a definite "edge" to show where the garden ends and the woods begin. And your perennials will show up better against a more uniform line of shrubs than they would against the looser texture of a woodland. □

— *Stephanie Polsley Bruner*

Web extra
See a complete *planting plan* for this deer-proof back yard.

Significant shrubs
Choose large shrubs, like these 5- to 10-ft.-tall bayberries, to provide privacy and protection from passing deer. Bayberries naturally form dense, twiggy thickets, and they're semi-evergreen, so they create a year-round barrier.

Exclamation point! A low-key, rustic obelisk makes a great focal point while still fitting into the easy-going feel of this garden.

Pick your battles It's tough to grow grass in the shade of big trees. Make it easy on yourself by installing a patio instead — it'll be low-maintenance and it won't be a muddy mess after a rain.

Choose carefully Although many shade-loving flowers bloom in spring, it is possible to find some, like monkshood, that bloom in late summer or fall. Astilbe's many cultivars bloom at different times, from late spring to midsummer, too, so you can pick several to keep the show going. Be sure there's one plant blooming from spring to fall, then add in a mix of perennials and shrubs with interesting foliage to keep this garden colorful all season long.

FENCE ME IN

A row of dense shrubs will go a long way toward keeping deer out of the garden. But while your shrubs get established, you might want a little extra barrier. If you don't want to build a solid privacy fence, there's a simpler alternative. Steel posts with heavy-duty black plastic (or even wire-mesh) fencing are easy to install and will keep deer at bay. You can take it down when your shrubs reach their full size or leave it in place — it'll practically disappear behind big shrubs and against a busy woodland backdrop. A deer fence should be 6 ft. tall at the very least. And it should be staked to the ground, because deer have been known to work their way under fences, too.

DRAWING BOARD | BACK YARD

You may notice gray, waxy berries on some of your bayberries. But they're small and hard, so they won't make a mess.

Monkshood's late splash of color will focus your attention on the fountain.

Burgundy foliage, like that of this bugbane, adds as much color to a shade garden as flowers would, and it lasts longer, too.

Scale: 1 square = 4 square ft.

Existing tree

Fountain
Patio
Air conditioner

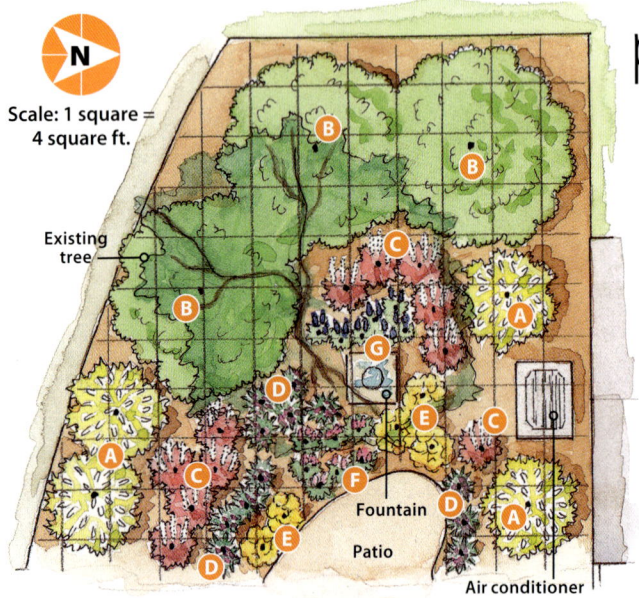

pretty and practical

In a small space, every plant needs to give 100 percent! Most gardeners like a plant to flower, but texture and structure are important, too, because leaves and shape last longer than blooms. In these plans, shrubs and ornamental grasses create a frame that sets off smaller, showier plants. And the shrubs and grasses give the garden year-round appeal, adding height, bulk and texture even in the winter.

Don't forget the "non-plant" features! Both these plans include a fountain with a strong, simple shape. It's beautiful whether it's bubbling among summer blooms or turned off for the winter and draped with a layer of snow.

Inside the row of shrubs and grasses, show off shorter perennials — they'll stand out against the backdrop, and they're protected from browsing deer, a problem in many gardens! This shade plan depends on plants with pretty foliage, like lady's mantle and 'Black Negligee' bugbane, for interest even when nothing's blooming. The sun plan

A SHOWY SHADE PALETTE

Code	Plant Name	No. to Plant	Blooms	Type	Cold/Heat Zones	Height/Width	Special Features
A	Virginia sweetspire *Itea virginica* 'Henry's Garnet'	4	White; late spring	Shrub	5-9/9-1	3-5 ft./ 3-5 ft.	Fragrant, drooping white flowers; fall foliage can be brilliant red, especially in full sun
B	Northern bayberry *Myrica pennsylvanica*	3	White; spring	Shrub	3-7/7-1	5-10 ft./ 5-10 ft.	Irregular, spreading shape; glossy green foliage is semi-evergreen; female plants produce waxy gray-green berries
C	Bugbane *Actaea simplex* 'Black Negligee'	11	White; late summer to fall	Perennial	4-8/8-1	4-5 ft./ 2-3 ft.	Fragrant white flowers sometimes tinged with pink; lacy dark-bronze foliage; prefers consistently moist soil
D	Spiderwort *Tradescantia* 'Concord Grape'	12	Purple; spring through summer	Perennial	4-9/9-1	9-12 in./ 12-18 in.	Grasslike foliage; cut back to ground after first flush of flowers to promote fresh new growth and small rebloom
E	Lady's mantle *Alchemilla mollis*	5	Chartreuse; late spring	Perennial	4-8/8-1	10-18 in./ 18-30 in.	Velvety gray-green leaves; cut flowers back after blooming to tidy plant and prevent reseeding
F	Astilbe *Astilbe* 'Country and Western'	7	Pink; early summer	Perennial	4-8/8-1	12-18 in./ 12-18 in.	Shiny dark-green foliage; cut back spent flower heads or leave them for late-season interest
G	Monkshood *Aconitum carmichaelii* 'Arendsii'	7	Blue; late summer to fall	Perennial	3-8/8-1	36-48 in./ 12-18 in.	An unusual color in late summer gardens; leathery, shiny leaves; all parts of the plant are poisonous

the YEAR IN GARDENING   www.GardenGateMagazine.com

The aromatic foliage of both bee balm and Russian sage make them unappealing to deer.

One clump of Indian grass wouldn't screen the view of the street, but a mass of them does.

You may prefer to cut back the seedheads of blue fescue to enjoy the simple mounds of blue-gray foliage.

features plants like Russian sage and 'Tiny Monster' geranium that just bloom on and on, so there's always something flowering.

Speaking of deer, there are no guarantees. Hungry deer will eat almost anything. But all the plants in both of these plans are ones that are usually deer-resistant. Of course, it's possible that the deer who visit your garden may be the only ones for miles who nibble the leaves of poisonous monkshood or actually enjoy the prickly delicacy of coneflowers. But at least these two plant lists will give your garden a fighting chance!

So pick up your spade and get digging. These simple plant combos can look great in any space. □

— *Stephanie Polsley Bruner*

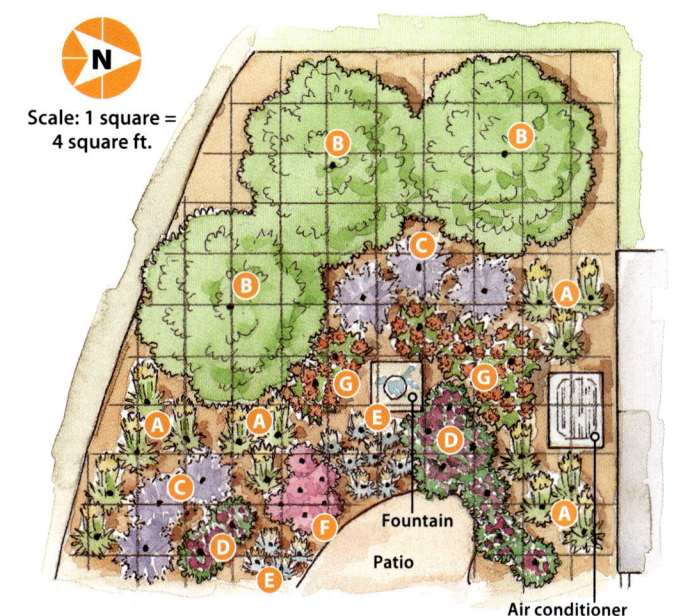

Scale: 1 square = 4 square ft.

A SUN-SAVVY PALETTE

Code	Plant Name	No. to Plant	Blooms	Type	Cold/Heat Zones	Height/Width	Special Features
A	Indian grass *Sorghastrum nutans* 'Sioux Blue'	15	Red-tan; late summer to fall	Perennial	4-9/9-1	5-6 ft./ 2-3 ft.	Gray-blue foliage provides a nice contrast with red-tan flowers; drought-tolerant once established, but prefers consistent moisture
B	Northern bayberry *Myrica pennsylvanica*	3	White; spring	Shrub	3-7/7-1	5-10 ft./ 5-10 ft.	Irregular, spreading shape; glossy green foliage is semi-evergreen; female plants produce waxy gray-green berries
C	Russian sage *Perovskia atriplicifolia*	6	Purple; midsummer to fall	Perennial	5-9/9-1	3-5 ft./ 2-4 ft.	Aromatic gray-green leaves; needs full sun and well-drained soil to thrive; cut back to ground in early spring
D	Geranium *Geranium* 'Tiny Monster'	9	Pink; spring to fall	Perennial	4-8/8-1	12-15 in./ 24-36 in.	Heavy flush of flowers in early summer is followed by light blooming until fall; foliage turns burgundy-red in fall
E	Blue fescue *Festuca glauca* 'Elijah Blue'	12	Tan; midsummer to fall	Perennial	4-8/8-1	8-12 in./ 12-18 in.	Blue-gray foliage color is best in full sun; clumps may die out in center and need to be lifted and divided every two to three years
F	Bee balm *Monarda* 'Petite Delight'	6	Pink; early to midsummer	Perennial	4-8/8-1	12-18 in./ 12-24 in.	Compact size; aromatic foliage; good disease resistance; deadhead for some repeat bloom
G	Coneflower *Echinacea* 'Tomato Soup'	6	Red-orange; midsummer to early fall	Perennial	4-8/8-1	32-36 in./ 32-36 in.	Huge, 5-in.-diameter flowers; cut back seed heads to prevent seeding or leave standing for winter interest

This cool-shade combo will delight all season long. See the recipe on page 228.

all about containers

grow your *best containers* ever!

EVERYONE LIKES A PRETTY CONTAINER GARDEN, but not everyone knows how to put together a showstopper. That's why we're sharing our tips here. From savvy plant shopping to resurrecting a tired container late in the season, we provide all the advice you need to succeed. And, of course, there are plenty of fresh recipes to try, too!

Plant Shopping...................... **214**
How to Wow with Containers................ **216**
Container Season is Here!... **222**
Disappointing Containers? Give Them a Makeover!... **226**
Windowboxes........................ **230**
Pansies in Pots: 3 Cool Looks...................... **236**
Ever so Exuberant................ **238**
Flowery Fall............................ **239**
Make a Tough Job Easier!.... **240**
Did You Know........................ **242**

CONTAINERS | BASICS

Plant Shopping

Buy or pass? Here's how to tell which plants are worth spending your money on.

Maybe it's spring, and you're heading out to the garden center for the first time, looking for that perfect plant that'll be the focus of a gorgeous summer container. Or maybe you're doing a little midseason bargain hunting, shopping for a few extras. Whatever the case, it's easy to get caught up in the spirit of plant shopping. But you don't want to come back home with a lot of less-than-super plants or a depleted bank account!

Let us walk you through a few to-buy-or-not-to-buy scenarios for plant shopping. We'll show you which plants to take home…and when to just say no!

Practically perfect! The impatiens in the photo below is healthy and compact, and it'll take off quickly in any container planting.

WHAT ARE YOU PAYING FOR? There's no point in paying for a lot of empty pot! The hosta on the left is healthy, but it's young and has been newly transplanted into a bigger container. Eventually it'll grow to fit the container, but it hasn't yet. Unfortunately, you'll pay the big-container price for a small plant, so pass on the plant on the left.

The hosta on the right is the same cultivar, but it's a much nicer specimen, in spite of the smaller pot size. Here's a plant that'll make an immediate impact in any container, and chances are, you won't pay as much for it, either. So the one on the right is a definite "do."

Compact growth and just a few blooms are signs that the plant hasn't been in the greenhouse too long. It'll have lots of energy to put into growing in your container.

You can see that there are healthy roots here, but this plant isn't rootbound, so it'll be able to take off quickly.

Speaking of container sizes, it only takes a quick glance to realize that the coreopsis on the left, above, is a much better bargain than the one on the right, even if they are the same size. What's the difference? The one on the left is probably an older plant that's had time to establish a better root system — and that means a better plant for your container. On the right, you're looking at a plant that's either very young or even possibly one with some root health issues. Pass!

www.GardenGateMagazine.com

It's easy to tell at a glance if a plant is rootbound. This many roots circling out of the drainage holes is not a good sign.

Buy the one on the left! You'll have to cut or break up that mass of roots on the plant on the right, which will set it back severely.

THE ROOT OF THE MATTER What's going on at the top of the plant is a pretty good indication of what's going on below the soil line. Above, the purple fountain grass on the left is big and healthy, with colorful leaves. On the right, you see a plant that's probably been in that container too long.

Just to prove our suspicions, we tipped these plants out of their containers. Take a look at those root balls at left. The healthy one, on the left, has plenty of roots, but they're not circling or forming a mass at the bottom. This plant will be able to take up water easily. The one on the right has a solid mass of roots at the bottom of the container, and that means it's not always getting enough moisture when it's watered. In a pinch, you could buy this plant and cut the root ball apart. The plant would recover, and might even thrive, but it'll take a long time — and you want that container to look beautiful right away!

Often, you don't have to pop the plant out of its pot to get an idea of the state of the roots. Take a look at the small photo above. If the plants' roots are circling out of the drainage holes at the bottom, that's a sign that it's pretty root-bound. Keep on looking!

OH, ROT! There's never a good reason to buy a plant that's showing signs of disease or decay. For one thing, the plant will disappoint you — even if it doesn't die outright, it will never look all that great. And for another thing, many plant diseases and fungus problems can spread from plant to plant, creating new problems in an otherwise healthy container.

We found both of these petunias on a bargain table in midsummer. The one on the left is starting to rot. See the black stems in the center? If you see discoloration or soft, mushy stems, just put the pot down and walk away! On the other hand, see how the one on the right has green stems all the way to the soil? It's a little leggy and it'll need some pruning and TLC to look its best, but if it's a plant you want and it's on sale, go ahead and buy it. It'll perk up!

PHOTOS: Brent Isenberger

www.GardenGateMagazine.com   *the* YEAR IN GARDENING

CONTAINERS | DESIGN BASICS

Simple, smart design ideas for container success!

How to Wow with Containers

Would you like your containers loaded with bright colorful blooms or do you prefer sophisticated studies in foliage textures? Well, with the huge variety of containers and plants available, the combinations you can create are limited only by your imagination.

This isn't a story about how to create or grow a good-looking container, though. I'd like to show you some great ideas for how to use your pots in your yard to draw attention, direct traffic, set moods and more. Along the way you'll see containers used as focal points, to mark transitions and to fill in unexpected gaps in the garden. Think you don't have any place to grow containers? I'll share some ways to enjoy colorful plantings in any space. To help you get each of these looks in your own yard, I've also included plans and plant lists for each pot.

1 MAY I HAVE YOUR ATTENTION, PLEASE… Pots make great accents or focal points to draw your eye. Whether it's filled with a combination of plants or a single specimen, an eye-grabbing container can direct attention to itself. A bonus? You can also use it to divert attention away from a less- than-attractive eyesore, such as a compost pile, utility area or your neighbor's garbage cans.

It's hard not to notice the bright green-and-yellow-striped pot in the yard in photo 1. The long arching leaves of this New Zealand flax echo the colors of its container and are showcased by the smooth expanse of green lawn surrounding it. Placed in the center of a long yard like this, it stops your eyes and effectively creates two smaller, more intimate garden "rooms." Instead of looking immediately at the far end of the yard, you'll pause, explore the closer space first,

Container is 16 in. in diameter

Look at me!
With its long, often brightly colored leaves, New Zealand flax is an easy-to-grow perennial that really calls attention to itself. Use a potting mix with lots of organic matter in it and don't let the plant completely dry out. If the lower leaves start to turn brown with age, simply cut them off near the base with sharp scissors.

Code	Plant Name	No. to Plant
A	New Zealand flax *Phormium* 'Yellow Wave'	1

216   *the* YEAR IN GARDENING   www.GardenGateMagazine.com

Step right up

A beautiful garden enhances any home, but to really make visitors feel welcome, use colorful container plantings to show them right to the front door. Growing these sun-loving annuals in terra-cotta pots of similar sizes simplifies care. All the pots will need water and fertilizer at about the same intervals.

Code	Plant Name	No. to Plant
A	**Oxalis** *Oxalis triangularis*	6
B	**Licorice plant** *Helichrysum petiolare*	4
C	**Geranium** *Pelargonium* 'Vancouver Centennial'	2
D	**Cape daisy** *Osteospermum* Soprano® Light Purple	1
E	**Licorice plant** *Helichrysum petiolare* 'Limelight'	1
F	**Petunia** *Petunia* Surfinia Sky Blue ('Keilavbu')	2
G	**Geranium** *Pelargonium* 'Mrs. Pollock'	1
H	**Sweet potato vine** *Ipomoea batatas* 'Margarita'	1
I	**Bacopa** *Sutera cordata* Cabana® Trailing Blue	1

Containers are 16 in. in diameter

Containers are 12 in. in diameter

Containers are 14 in. in diameter

and then move on to the area beyond the container. So the pot slows you down and lets you really enjoy the journey.

2 FOLLOW ME Directing traffic in your garden is another way to utilize containers. Whether they're pots of bright flowers or elegant foliage combinations, containers set the tone for each garden "room." You can also use pots to mark the transitions where visitors travel from one area to another. Notice how two sets of pots placed on either side of the steps in photo 2 give the entrance more weight than a single line of containers would. Repeating plant material and colors in the window-boxes draws your eyes to the house, as well. And from a practical standpoint, the pots of colorful flowers and foliage marking the entry alert strollers to slow down and watch their step as they approach the front door. When placing pots on steps, be sure to allow at least 2 to 3 feet of clear space to walk so you don't trip your garden guests.

Ready to learn more ways to design with containers in your garden? Turn the page.

USING CONTAINERS CREATIVELY

Call for the stand-in

Part to full sun and regular moisture keep the plants in the two containers on the left looking good. Can't bear to say good-bye at the end of the season? Overwinter coleus and Persian shield by taking stem cuttings in late summer and rooting them in moist potting mix.

Give the Japanese painted fern and sedge in the smaller pot to the right even moisture. In USDA zones 6 or colder, remove the fern and coral bells from the small pot and sedum from the large one and plant them in the garden in early fall to keep them through the winter.

Code	Plant Name	No. to Plant
A	Lantana *Lantana* 'Radiation'	1
B	Coleus *Solenostemon* 'Freckles'	1
C	Persian shield *Strobilanthes dyeriana*	1
D	Tall sedum *Sedum erythrostictum* 'Mediovariegatum'	1
E	Sweet potato vine *Ipomoea batatas* 'Sweet Caroline Purple'	1
F	Petunia *Petunia* Supertunia® Mini Blue	1
G	Coleus *Solenostemon* Color Blaze® Sedona	2
H	Japanese painted fern *Athyrium* 'Ghost'	1
I	Coral bells *Heuchera* 'Peach Flambé'	1
J	Irish moss *Sagina subulata*	2
K	Sedge *Carex oshimensis* 'Evergold'	1

Container is 12 in. in diameter
Container is 32 in. in diameter
Container is 22 in. in diameter

PHOTO: Brian Dobler (3)

3 FILL THE GAPS As anyone who grows plants can tell you, gardening is full of surprises. That perennial that bloomed so profusely and filled your border last year may succumb to a long hot spell this year. Or insect pests may damage it before you've even noticed they were there, leaving a hard-to-miss gap in the garden. Sometimes the void in a border results after spring-blooming plants or bulbs die back. Though the three container plantings in photo 3 seem close together, the spot where the largest one sits receives much more late-day sunshine than the smaller one on the right. The Japanese painted fern and coral bells in that smaller pot appreciate the same part-shade situation as the surrounding hostas.

In addition to filling unexpected spaces, pots come in handy for adding dashes of color in awkward spots that might otherwise be hard to garden in. Around the base of a shallow-rooted tree is an example. Not only is it hard to dig around the roots, but the tree greedily grabs any moisture in the surrounding soil. Simply place a pot in the spot. If the plants need a bit of sun for the best blooms, occasionally swap the pots with ones in a place with a little more sun. A few weeks will keep the flowers coming.

4 GROW WHERE THERE'S NO GARDEN Closing a gap in the garden is all well and good. But what if you don't have a garden at all? Don't despair. In fact, places that lack traditional garden spaces, like concrete-hemmed condos or city townhouses, need the fresh color and scent of plants even more. And

218   *the* YEAR IN GARDENING   www.GardenGateMagazine.com

Hot and sunny scene

The purple fountain grass, as well as the other annuals in this planting, can take the sun and heat well. But while they're tough, a few steps will lead to healthier and better-looking plants. Work water-absorbing crystals into the mix when you plant, check the soil daily and give the plants consistent moisture.

Containers are 16 in. on each side

Code	Plant Name	No. to Plant
A	**Purple fountain grass** *Pennisetum setaceum* 'Rubrum'	2
B	**Rudbeckia** *Rudbeckia hirta* 'TigerEye Gold'	2
C	**Dichondra** *Dichondra argentea* 'Silver Falls'	2
D	**Bigleaf coreopsis** *Coreopsis* 'Jethro Tull'	1
E	**Kale** *Brassica oleracea*	1
F	**Cockscomb** *Celosia* 'Dark Caracas'	1

Winning spring windowboxes

Open the windows to enjoy the soft fragrance of these nemesias. If you deadhead regularly, the plants will flower better and longer and they'll look tidier, too. When summer heat makes these spring plants start to fade, replace them with your favorite summer annuals.

Code	Plant Name	No. to Plant
A	**Calibrachoa** *Calibrachoa* Noa™ Tangerine	2
B	**Snapdragon** *Antirrhinum majus* Chimes™ Bronze	4
C	**Nemesia** *Nemesia fruticans* Compact Pink Innocence®	4
D	**Pansy** *Viola* 'Whiskers Yellow'	2
E	**Wallflower** *Erysimum* Citrona™ Yellow	2

Windowbox is 32 in. long × 8 in. wide

planting in containers is definitely the way to go in these spaces. But choose plants carefully. Concrete both reflects and radiates the sun's heat in a sunny spot like this. A layer of insulating bubble wrap lining the inside of these pots helps keep the roots and surrounding soil cooler.

The 42-inch-tall, narrow pots in photo 4 are in perfect balance with the space because they're large enough to be in proportion with the wide garage door and wall. Smaller pots would look dwarfed in this spot. Their strong vertical shape also helps counteract all of the horizontal lines created by the home's siding and stone. And they bring some much-needed color to this bland exterior. Breeze-tossed purple fountain grass flowers add movement and life to an otherwise static vignette.

5 GROW AT EYE LEVEL The cheery windowboxes in photo 5 demonstrate yet another advantage to growing in containers. You can place plants right at eye level, so you'll enjoy the view from a greater distance. And since you'll see the plants often, you're more likely to give them the consistent moisture that's so important to keeping them growing well. Repeating plants and containers like this helps break up the monotonous appearance of this long brick wall. Dashes of bright orange and other flower colors distract your eye from those strong light-colored lines of the mortar. Plus, these flowers aren't bee-magnets — not what you'd want next to a busy sidewalk.

And speaking of looking good, on the next pages I'll share how to use containers in groupings so you'll get even more impact in any garden space.

GREAT CONTAINER GROUPS

Some spaces — especially larger areas — practically scream for container groupings. How do you create an attractive combination of pots? Here are a few tips to create a container grouping that looks "put-together."

6 LET ME REPEAT THAT One of the keys to making a container grouping successful is to use repetition. Repeating similar colors, whether in containers or plants, creates a cohesive, unified feeling for your combination. See how all the pots in photo 6 share the same bold blue? Though the pot shapes vary, the consistent blue glaze not only catches your eye, but announces that these containers belong together.

While repeating colors or other elements in a grouping is good, a bunch of the same pots with the exact same selection of plants gets boring quickly. As when designing a single container, vary the sizes and shapes of your plants or pots to keep things interesting. And in a grouping, think about the old recipe that you use for a single pot — focal point, filler and trailer. Though the three pots below contain many of the same plants, the tall narrow pot with its upright mother-in-law's tongue gives the more rounded pots a needed vertical focal point. (It's standing on an overturned pot for a little extra height.) Arrowhead plant and euphorbias act as fillers, with burgundy sweet potato vines filling the role of trailers.

Think about how the containers and plants relate to their surroundings. In photo 6, red bricks and crisp white handrails evoke a clean, rather formal feel to the entry steps. Cobalt blue glazed pots match that mood and harmonize with the gray house paint, as well. Positioned to one side of the door, the group grabs your attention, while staying safely out of your path.

7 MATCH YOUR SPACE The three containers in photo 7 all hold bright-pink-flowering plants, but the pots themselves are completely different in shape, color and material. The variety in the pots

Three's company

Both Reiger begonias and mother-in-law's tongue are house plants. The begonias are short-lived, so when frost hits, toss them. But the mother-in-law's tongue will live for years indoors in a warm room with indirect light.

Code	Plant Name	No. to Plant
A	Mother-in-law's tongue *Sansevieria trifasciata*	2
B	Arrowhead plant *Syngonium* 'Neon'	2
C	Rieger begonia *Begonia* x*hiemalis*	1
D	Sweet potato vine *Ipomoea batatas* 'Sweet Caroline Red'	2
E	Angelonia *Angelonia* Angelface® White	2
F	Euphorbia *Euphorbia characias* 'Glacier Blue'	1

Container is 10 in. square

Container is 20 in. in diameter

Container is 16 in. in diameter

contributes an interesting contrast to the grouping and adds to the informal air.

With its comfortable furniture and view of the pretty white garden gazebo, the small patio elicits a relaxed atmosphere. Did you notice how the dark gray container repeats the color of the metal glider and the hanging basket? Or that the pink stripes of the cushions and the other pink flowers blooming at the far side of the back yard echo the flowers in the containers on the patio? They're just two more examples of how repetition creates a cohesive look and helps tie this grouping to the other elements in this cheerful vignette.

I hope I've been able to show you how easy it is to use containers in your garden. Whether you use a single stand-out plant to draw attention to itself, or a grouping of pots to brighten an area or guide visitors to the door, the possibilities are endless! ☐

— *Deborah Gruca*

Colorful companions

Before frost hits in fall, pull these containers indoors and store them in indirect light in a cool spot (low to mid-40s) until late spring. Then cut back the begonias and euphorbia and trim the lantana. Set the pots in a sunny spot (but protect them during cold snaps!) and water well.

Code	Plant Name	No. to Plant
A	**Lantana** *Lantana camara* 'Confetti' (trained as standard)	1
B	**Begonia** *Begonia* Dragon Wing Pink ('Bepapink')	6
C	**Euphorbia** *Euphorbia hypericifolia* Diamond Frost® ('Inneuphe')	3
D	**Begonia** *Begonia* BIG™ Rose with Bronze Leaf	2
E	**Begonia** *Begonia* BIG™ Red with Green Leaf	1

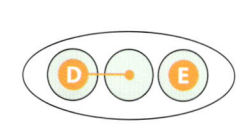

Container is 20 in. long × 11 in. wide oval

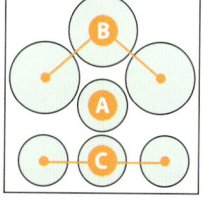

Container is 18 in. square

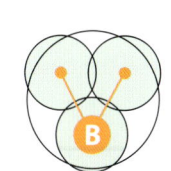

Hanging basket is 14 in. in diameter

CONTAINERS | RECIPES

Design your best containers ever with these 6 great-looking ideas.

Container Season is Here!

It's time to start planting containers! And there's nothing like a little extra inspiration to kick your creativity into gear. Take a look at two of our favorite recent designs and you'll see what I mean. Even though the plants we used are "everyday" varieties available from the local garden center, once planted, these combinations became superstars in our test garden.

For most containers, a basic soilless potting mix is a good place to start. The mix of perlite, sphagnum moss and peat drains well but still holds moisture.

Shade containers won't require as much watering as those in the sun. Hanging baskets like the one below can be a real challenge to keep watered, but moisture crystals can help. Once you've filled the container halfway with potting mix, sprinkle in a layer of crystals, then finish filling with potting mix.

We've shared a couple of our favorite containers here, but last year we challenged our readers to send us *their* best containers and got great results. On the following pages let's check out the reader containers we thought were real standouts.

Wonderful whites

This sun-loving container looks good from spring to first frost. Keep it watered though, since this hanging basket is only 10 in. square and dries out quickly. Deadheading geraniums helps keep the flowers coming. Remove spent blooms by following the stem down to its base and pinching it off. Globe amaranth flowers last a long time but if they start to look tired just cut them back.

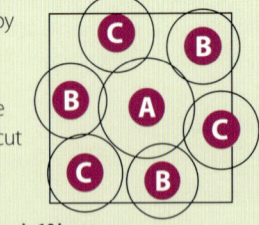

Container is 10 in. square

Code	Plant Name	No. to Plant
A	Geranium *Pelargonium* 'Maestro White Splash'	1
B	Globe amaranth *Gomphrena globosa* 'Buddy Purple'	3
C	Petunia *Petunia* Easy Wave™ White	3

✳ **handy tip**
White flowers look good even by moonlight. But if you hang this basket against a house with white siding, choose bright-colored geraniums and petunias so you'll be able to see the flowers.

If these trailing petunias get too long, cut them back to where they look good.

222 the YEAR IN GARDENING

Go ahead and plant this fern outside in the fall — it's cold-hardy to zone 5.

Classy shade combo

Coordinate flowers and foliage colors for a cool shade combo. This wishbone flower is almost due for some deadheading. So for more blooms, pinch the stems back to a leaf joint or where a pair of leaves emerge from the stem. And purple heart can take over a whole container, so go ahead and cut it back whenever you need to. This colorful trailer can take it.

Container is 20 in. long x 15 in. wide oval

Code	Plant Name	No. to Plant
A	Male fern	3
	Dryopteris filix-mas 'Undulata Robusta'	
B	Purple heart *Tradescantia pallida* 'Purpurea'	1
C	Wishbone flower *Torenia*	2
	Summer Wave® Amethyst	
D	Painted begonia *Begonia* 'Benitochiba'	1

✱ handy tip
Begonias like evenly moist but not wet soil or they'll rot. So let the soil dry out before you water this container.

Copper starts out shiny, but with exposure to the elements develops a patina like the container here. For a polished look, use a copper cleaner annually.

READER CONTAINERS

We're not the only ones who can put together a container — our readers do a great job, too. Here are our top picks from the 2010 container challenge. The editor's top pick receives a container from Campania, Organic Mechanics® potting mix, Speedy Grow™ growth accelerator and a box of annuals from Proven Winners! The best in sun, shade and whimsy will receive a soil knife and sheath along with our latest special interest book, *Containers Made Easy!*, Volume 3.

— Sherri Ribbey

Editor's top pick Terry Wolfel, CT

Wow! No one passes this part-shade windowbox without a second look. Though it looks like one long windowbox, there are actually four 26-in.-long boxes there. To keep the boxes from rotting, Terry uses smaller plastic liners inside. She fills each liner with potting mix, then mixes in moisture crystals, a heaping teaspoon of Osmocote® slow-release plant food and ¼ cup of Plant-Tone®, an organic plant food. Pinch the coleus back when you plant it to encourage branching. If it starts to get too tall for the box later, go ahead and pinch it again.

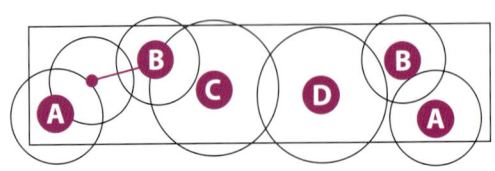

Each liner is 24 in. long x 6 in. wide

Code	Plant Name	No. to Plant per Liner
A	Creeping Jenny *Lysimachia nummularia* 'Goldilocks'	2
B	Caladium *Caladium* 'Florida Cardinal'	3
C	Begonia *Begonia* Dragon Wing® Red ('Bepared')	1
D	Coleus *Solenostemon* 'El Brighto'	1

Best sun Sandra Smith, PA

Bright yellow and orange flowers are the perfect welcome home on a hot summer day. This sunny combo needs consistent water to stay looking its best. Sandra gave it a quick drink each morning in the hottest part of summer so it wouldn't get too dry in the afternoon. The flowers here don't need deadheading but the creeping Jenny and sweet potato vine might need trimming back if they start to take over the container. To keep the black-eyed Susan vine growing up instead of over the edge of the urn, Sandra set a 45-in.-tall trellis in the back of the planter while the vine was still young.

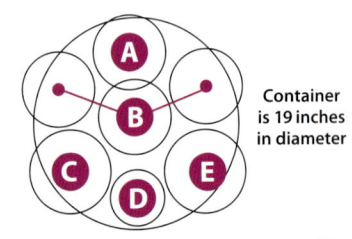

Container is 19 inches in diameter

Code	Plant Name	No. to Plant
A	Black-eyed Susan vine *Thunbergia alata*	1
B	Star daisy *Melampodium* 'Show Star'	3
C	Calibrachoa *Calibrachoa* Superbells® Dreamsicle	1
D	Creeping Jenny *Lysimachia nummularia* 'Goldilocks'	1
E	Sweet potato vine *Ipomoea batatas* 'Margarita'	1

Best shade Mimi Lang, PA

It's always nice to have low-maintenance containers. You can practically plant this one and forget it. A little extra watering during summer's heat will help keep it looking good. Shades of pink and a variegated vinca vine brighten whatever shady spot you want to put this in. Notice the tiny white dots near the pink impatiens? Those are the flowers of Diamond Frost euphorbia. Mimi liked how the delicate foliage and flowers wove between the larger plants. In full sun, Diamond Frost fills out to 12 to 18 in. tall, but with only a few hours of sun, its size is more modest.

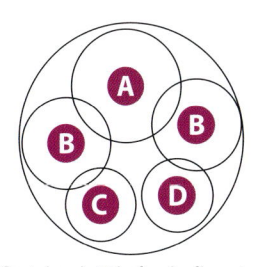

Container is 15 inches in diameter

Code	Plant Name	No. to Plant
A	Begonia *Begonia* Dragon Wing™ Pink ('Bepapink')	1
B	Impatiens *Impatiens walleriana* Dazzler® Blush	2
C	Euphorbia *Euphorbia hypericifolia* Diamond Frost® ('Inneuphe')	1
D	Vinca *Vinca major* 'Expoflora'	1

Best whimsy Lenore Erickson, WI

Some paintings look so real they seem to burst from the frame. Here's something that really does!

This project looks tough but it isn't. First you screw 1x4s together to make a box (Lenore's is pine, but you could also use treated wood). Then you staple 16-gauge wire onto it in a grid pattern and attach an old picture frame. The diagram below shows how to assemble the pieces.

Once you have the planting box assembled and the wire grid stapled in place, lay the box face down and pack a layer of moistened long-fiber sphagnum moss over the grid. Fill the box with potting mix and nail or screw the plywood back on. Flip it over and attach the frame to the box with L-brackets. Then plant a flat of Wizard™ mix coleus through the grid.

Water with a gentle spray from the hose. Or use drip irrigation as Lenore did by drilling two ¼-in. holes in the top of the box and inserting an emitter into each one. Display your artwork on a sturdy easel or lean it against a wall for a colorful show all summer.

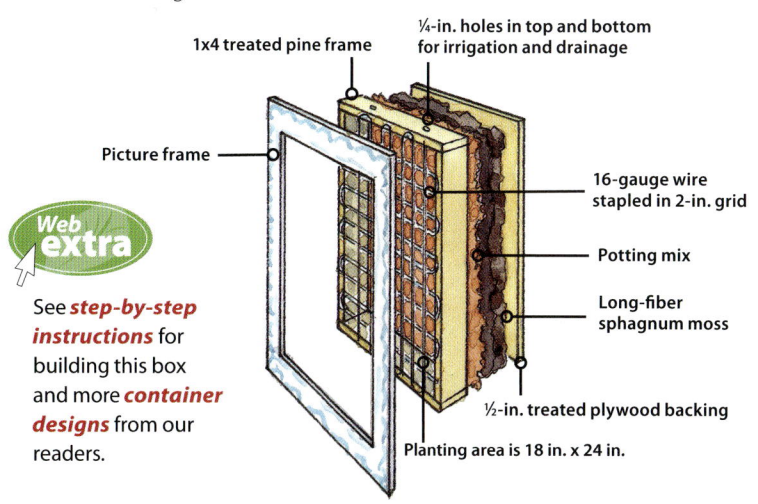

Web extra
See **step-by-step instructions** for building this box and more **container designs** from our readers.

Diagram labels:
- 1x4 treated pine frame
- ¼-in. holes in top and bottom for irrigation and drainage
- Picture frame
- 16-gauge wire stapled in 2-in. grid
- Potting mix
- Long-fiber sphagnum moss
- ½-in. treated plywood backing
- Planting area is 18 in. x 24 in.

CONTAINERS | BASICS

disappointing containers?
give them a makeover!

Botanical Names

Begonia
  Begonia hybrid
Fern
  Dryopteris hybrid
Feverfew
  Tanacetum parthenium
Jacob's ladder
  Polemonium caeruleum
Reiger begonia
  Begonia hybrid

Isn't container gardening rewarding? You visit the garden center, take home a few plants (after a little agonizing over which ones are just right), pot them up, step back and admire the view. At least that's what's supposed to happen. But sometimes I stand there with head cocked to one side, lips pursed and eyes narrowed, thinking, "This container just isn't working."

Good thing for me that gardening is one of those activities where do-overs are not only allowed but encouraged. That's what happened with this container: I "remodeled" it not just once, but twice!

You might not believe it, but the 'Black Coffee' begonia in photo 1 above started out as a few floppy leaves in a 4-inch pot a couple of years ago. Fortunately, it's easy to overwinter by positioning the container in a sunny window and watering the plant occasionally. Its enthusiastic growth dominated this large ceramic container by spring, and something had to be done.

Since I wanted to keep growing the begonia in this pot, I decided to divide it. That way I could replant part of it back into the container and save the new plants for other containers. Division won't work on tuberous begonias (the types with the big showy flowers.) But it's a good way to handle fibrous root types like this one. I'll show you how I divided 'Black Coffee' in "Get more begonias" below.

(1) Big and beefy 'Black Coffee' begonia was getting too large for this 20-in. green container.

'Black Coffee' begonia

GET MORE BEGONIAS

UP AND OUT In spring, use a soil knife or a trowel with serrated edges to cut around the dense root ball and gently pry it away from the side of the container. Try to get as much of the root ball out as possible.

LIFT AND DIVIDE What a big begonia! Take the plant out carefully because the stems are brittle and break easily. The base is woody so I used a soil knife to cut it into pieces. You can get a lot of smaller plants or opt for fewer, larger ones. If you see a gap between the stems, that's a good spot to start cutting.

Toss divisions that don't have roots.

SO MANY CHOICES Here are the results. Not all of these divisions are worth planting, though. Sometimes a chunk will fall apart into smaller pieces. If a piece doesn't have roots, toss it. The biggest divisions, like the one in the inset, can stand alone in a pot. I paired several smaller ones for more impact right away and grew the rest by themselves in 4-in. nursery pots.

(2) Newly planted 'Black Coffee' divisions are hard to see here in May. But the rest of the plants look good.

Once that chore was done, I replanted a couple of the begonia divisions near the center of this container, along with a fern, some Reiger begonias, a variegated Jacob's ladder and 'Golden Moss' feverfew. The initial results, in photo 2, weren't bad: In late May, when I planted it, the container had flowers, colorful foliage and interesting texture.

By the time photo 3 was taken in late June, the shine was definitely gone. 'Black Coffee' had taken off, but I realized it was hard to see against the dark green of the container. The colorful Reigers had rotted, the fern was getting ratty and the feverfew didn't grow or bloom in the cool weather.

But it was still early summer and I didn't want to pack it in just yet. So I looked around for ideas on how to improve my disappointing planting. I'll show you how things turned out on the next page.

POT IT UP Get those new transplants potted up right away so the roots don't dry out, and water deeply. Check the soil every few days or weekly, depending on how hot it is, and keep the soil evenly moist. The stems I'm cutting off here were broken in the move. I snipped them back to the base so they wouldn't be magnets for insects or disease.

(3) What a difference a month makes! In that time, although the two 'Black Coffee' begonias took off, the Reiger begonias and feverfew faded.

Turn the page to see how this container came out!

www.GardenGateMagazine.com   the YEAR IN GARDENING   227

Code	Plant Name	No. to Plant
A	Australian sword fern *Nephrolepis obliterata* 'Kimberly Queen'	1
B	Fuchsia *Fuchsia* Diva™ Cherry and White	2
C	Caladium *Caladium* 'Red Flash' ('Flash Rouge')	1
D	Begonia *Begonia* 'Black Coffee'	1
E	Impatiens *Impatiens* Fiesta™ Sparkler Cherry	1
F	Lilyturf *Liriope spicata* 'Silver Dragon' ('Gin-ryu')	3

Container is 20 in. in diameter.

better than ever

Wow! Switching out the plants in this container really made a difference. The colors in that earlier combo were all so similar that the planting looked drab. Plus, the 'Black Coffee' begonia was hard to see against the dark green container. But now with the variegated liriope in front of it and light green fern behind, the rich green-brown leaves really stand out. With fern fronds that remind me of fireworks and nonstop bloom from the impatiens and fuchsia, this planting is full of energy.

And not only does 'Black Coffee' look good in the big green container, it's also the star of this yellow one at right. Those divisions I put in the 4-inch nursery pots thrived and sure came in handy.

To keep both containers in peak condition, water and feed them regularly. I start with a slow-release fertilizer, such as Dynamite®. You can add your own to the soil or buy the potting mix that already has it mixed in. This supplies a steady stream of nutrients through the summer, even when it's rainy and you can't water in other fertilizers. For an added boost, water in a balanced liquid food at half strength every two weeks. Now I'll tell you more about each container.

Cool shade combo

Consistent moisture will keep the combo at left looking good all summer. Placing it where it gets no more than a few hours of sun will help, since the temperature will stay a little cooler there. It helps conserve water, too. And if you're planting (or replanting) later in the season, it's important to not let new plants dry out while they get settled in. On the other hand, you don't want too much water or the begonia may rot. Check the soil by inserting your finger up to the first knuckle in the potting mix. If it's dry at your fingertip, water.

Caladiums like warm temperatures and take a long time to get growing if you plant tubers directly in the soil. For big plants like these right away, buy them already growing in 4-inch pots. Or to save money, buy bags of tubers and start them indoors 4 to 6 weeks before your average last frost date.

Maintenance here is minimal. There's no need to deadhead impatiens — they take care of themselves. Fuchsias slow down and bloom less when summer gets hot, but they'll bounce back in the cool of autumn. If you don't want to wait on those fuchsias, go ahead and replace them with more impatiens. Liriope foliage sometimes gets brown at the tips in summer. Trim the brown off at an angle so it's not so obvious that the leaves have been cut.

Code	Plant Name	No. to Plant
A	Begonia *Begonia* 'Black Coffee'	1
B	Sedge *Deschampsia cespitosa* 'Northern Lights'	1
C	Variegated Swedish ivy *Plectranthus ciliatus* 'Troy's Gold'	1
D	Marguerite daisy *Argyranthemum* Butterfly ('Ulyssis')	1

Container is 12 in. in diameter.

Sunny days

Here's another way to provide enough contrast for the begonia leaves to show up: a light, bright pot. Most of the plants in the grouping above do just fine with full sun, but 'Black Coffee' begonia would burn in that intense light. Split the difference by putting this pot in morning sun for about 4 hours a day and they'll all be happy. Deadhead individual blooms of the Marguerite daisy. If you're in a hurry, shear the whole plant back by a third and it will grow back more compact and flowering in a few weeks. Swedish ivy can get big by season's end so don't be afraid to cut it back, too.

Keep an eye out for aphids; I noticed a few on the back side of the begonia leaves in early August. But a spray of water knocked them off for good.

Now that you've seen these two revivals, don't give up on your containers if they look less than beautiful the first time around. With a little patience and perseverance, they may end up being the best-looking containers you've ever had! □

— *Sherri Ribbey*

CONTAINERS | DESIGN BASICS

Our best tips for growing them anywhere (no window required).

Windowboxes

Nothing adds to a home's charm like a windowbox full of colorful flowers. But windowboxes can be more than just window *dressing*. Put them to work! For example, grow herbs outside your kitchen window and snip them for soup. Or include tall plants in your box to offer privacy while still allowing in some light. Photo 1 is a good example. Want to know the ins and outs of planning perfect windowboxes? Let me help. Then I'll take the boxes *off* the windows and use those same long, narrow planters in smart and great-looking ways all over the yard. If you like the boxes you see, I'll let you know what the plants are and show you some tips for planting, too.

CHOOSING A BOX You'll find hundreds of box options, both premade and custom. I think windowboxes are a great place to use synthetic materials. Plastic and fiberglass are lightweight, and won't require lots of painting or other maintenance. Plus you're usually viewing the box from a distance so no one will ever know whether it's real or faux wood or metal. Can you figure out what the ones in photos 1 and 2 are made of? They're both fiberglass.

SIZE CONCERNS A good rule of thumb is to match the length of the box to the width of the window, or the window plus the frame. If you have shutters, add 4 to 6 inches for the best-looking windowbox. But if you already have the shorter boxes in front of shutters, you can visually extend them with plantings. Notice in photo 2 how the petunias billow over the ends of the boxes? That makes the planter look wider than it really is, extending the length to the center of each shutter.

Mounting boxes in front of double windows and picture windows can present problems. A single one may be long and difficult to handle or very heavy when filled with soil. It's often easier to use a series of boxes to cover the width. Keep the box ends at the edges of the window or near the center of the shutters, for a well-proportioned look, and grow plants that vine or billow over the gaps.

BE REALISTIC ABOUT MAINTENANCE There are a lot of places windowboxes would *look* great, but not all of them are easy to access. If you want second-story boxes, you'll probably need to open a window, and possibly take out a screen to hang them. Even

PHOTOS: Brian Dobler (1, 2)

PLANT THIS CONTAINER
A **Cilantro** *Coriandrum sativum*
B **Ivy geranium** *Pelargonium* Tornado™ Red
C **Heliotrope** *Heliotropium arborescens* 'Fragrant Delight'
D **Salvia** *Salvia splendens* 'Picante'
E **Ivy geranium** *Pelargonium* Colorcade™ Cherry Red

(1) Measure before you install. Most windowboxes are 8 to 10 in. deep and at least that wide. Allow for that when you position the mounting hardware so the box won't interfere with the operation of the window. This one slides to the side. But if it cranked out, the height of the box and the plants would get in the way.

PLANT THIS CONTAINER

- A **Petunia** *Petunia* Surfinia® Rose Vein
- B **Angelonia** *Angelonia angustifolia* Angelface® White
- C **Marguerite daisy** *Argyranthemum frutescens* 'Butterfly'
- D **Petunia** *Petunia* Surfinia® Candy Cane
- E **Mealy cup sage** *Salvia farinacea* 'Victoria'
- F **Geranium** *Pelargonium* Fidelity™ L Magenta
- G **Petunia** *Petunia* Surfinia® Sky Blue

first-story boxes can present a challenge: Prickly foundation shrubs can be tough to reach over or through. Lightweight potting mix keeps windowboxes from being too heavy, but it also means they dry out very quickly. In hot, dry weather that means you may be watering every day, or even twice a day. And if you don't have a water hookup nearby, you'll have to haul (and hoist) watering cans. So be sure to hang windowboxes where you can keep them looking great without too many hassles.

HARDWARE HOW-TO Many ready-made boxes come with basic mounting hardware. Some hang on hooks; others rest on brackets. But you may have to customize your method to your situation. However you hang your windowbox, get the sturdiest mounting hardware you can find. A 48-inch-long wooden box can weigh 100 pounds or more after you water it. So look for steel hooks, and brackets made of steel, iron, cast aluminum or wood. Later I'll share some information on mounting brackets as well as other helpful windowbox gadgets.

GIVE IT BREATHING ROOM To save your siding or paint, leave some space between the wall of your house and the box. This will allow air to circulate

(2) How do you plant? At this height it's easier to fill the boxes from inside rather than haul a planted box up a ladder or through the house. On a first floor window, the choice is up to you, but a full box can be very heavy.

and prevent excess water running down the siding and staining it. A small scrap or two of 1-inch-thick wood, fastened to the back of your box, is all the spacer you need.

Did you know you can get all the beautiful benefits of a windowbox whether or not you have a window to hang it on? Turn the page to see how.

WINDOW(LESS) BOXES

Don't have a spot for a windowbox? There are still plenty of ways to use long planters in your garden. Let me show you a few locations where you can add them.

ADD COLOR IN A TIGHT SPOT You have a lovely porch where you like to sit and relax, and you'd like a planter there. But sometimes a porch can be a bit narrow: Narrow windowboxes are perfect for tight spaces like this. Although there *are* windows in photo 3, they are pretty low to the ground in this case, so windowboxes might not work well. Plus the blank wall between the window and door could really use some interest. I could have hung a box on the wall, but decided to use a raised planter instead since it could easily be moved to make more space for entertaining.

A partly shaded, protected porch is a great spot to move a few houseplants outside in warm weather. Leave the plants you'll move back inside in their own pots. Set them into a windowbox and fill around the pots with soil. Tuck in a few annuals around them to dress up the planter and you're set for the summer.

RIDE THE RAILS Planter boxes are also a creative DIY project to dress up a deck or porch. And they take up almost no floor space. I showed you earlier how a windowbox on your house can help screen a window to create privacy. But you can use that same principle on your deck or porch. Perhaps the spot where you like to relax has a view into the neighbor's kitchen window or is easily seen from the street. In that case, strategically placed boxes can help.

Use trailing or draping plants to screen below the box. The sweet potato vines in photo 4 block the view from the street so people seated on this shaded porch can't be seen. Is your deck lower than the neighbor's windows? Grow lots of tall flowers or foliage in the planter to create a living screen. In most cases, you don't need or want *complete* privacy. It's just nice to have a little separation from the rest of the world when you're sitting down. That's why hanging a box on a deck or porch railing works so well — it's the perfect height.

DIRECTIONAL PLANTINGS A patio that's level with the lawn is easy to navigate. However, sometimes it's good to direct visitors to the best place to step. An edging of containers is a great way to mark where you do (and don't) want people to walk. And since the planters are narrow, they won't take up valuable patio space. You'll need at least two boxes, or if the patio is large, you may want more.

The concrete planters in photo 5 are about 2 feet long and 1 foot wide. Unlike windowboxes, in this situation there's no need to worry about the weight. In fact, heavier is often better. Heavy planters won't tip over in the wind or if they get bumped.

To make the boxes visible, so folks don't trip over them, fill them with substantial plants. Small shrubs up to 2 feet tall, such as the arborvitae in these boxes, are a good size for planters because they're easy for visitors to see. But don't go much taller or the plants will look out of proportion to the height of the container. Planters like these are also good at the edge of a porch or deck that has no railing. They'll prevent people from accidentally stepping off.

> ### PLANT THIS CONTAINER
> - **A** Torenia *Torenia* Summer Wave® Blue
> - **B** Fanflower *Scaevola* Whirlwind® White
> - **C** Fittonia *Fittonia argyroneura* 'Bianco Verde'
> - **D** Peace lily *Spathiphyllum* 'Domino'
> - **E** Oxalis *Oxalis* Charmed™ Jade

(3) A raised planter is the perfect spot to show off your houseplants while they spend the summer outdoors. And if you need more floor space for a party or gathering, it's easily moved out of the way.

(4) Boxes on railings can be hung on the side like this one using brackets. If you want more height, fasten the box directly to the top of the railing.

Unlike boxes on the side of your house, these planters will often be seen up close. You'll want to keep them groomed and looking as good as possible. One way to do that is to swap the plants occasionally, especially as they begin to look tired or the seasons change.

Liners are a good way to keep a fresh look. For each of your planters, pick up at least two inexpensive plastic windowbox liners. They'll need to be slightly smaller in length and width so they fit inside the planter. Fill one liner with flowers and slip it into place. A few weeks later, plant up another one and have it growing before you're ready to move it into place. When the first batch of flowers begins to look ratty, you'll be ready to lift it out and slip in the new one; you won't have to wait for the new plants to fill in.

On the next page I'll show you an easy planting technique that helps keep a planter looking fresh all season. And you'll find information on five of my favorite gadgets that make taking care of wall-mounted windowboxes easier.

PLANT THIS CONTAINER
A **Sweet potato vine** *Ipomoea batatus* 'Margarita'
B **Cape primrose** *Streptocarpus saxorum*
C **Impatiens** *Impatiens* Super Elfin Pastel Mix
D **Fuchsia** *Fuchsia* Shadow Dancer® Yolanda

PLANT THIS CONTAINER
A **English ivy** *Hedera helix* 'Eva'
B **Arborvitae** *Thuja plicata* Golden Spire ('Daniellow')
C **Begonia** *Begonia* BabyWing™ Pink
D **Wax begonia** *Begonia xsemperflorens cultorum* 'Prelude White'

(5) Boxes at ground level direct guests where to step off this stone patio. Make sure the boxes are set at least 2 ft. apart so people can comfortably walk between them.

QUICK CHANGE!

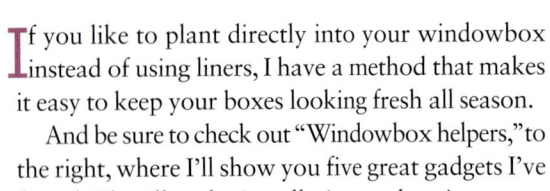

If you like to plant directly into your windowbox instead of using liners, I have a method that makes it easy to keep your boxes looking fresh all season.

And be sure to check out "Windowbox helpers," to the right, where I'll show you five great gadgets I've found. They'll make installation and maintenance much easier. Then you'll be ready to get outside and start planting next spring! □

— *Jim Childs*

Landscape fabric
A lining of landscape fabric keeps soil from washing out of the seams of a wooden box. Cut it carefully, and overlap seams so it covers the corners and drainage holes — anywhere soil could wash out. If your box is plastic or metal, you probably will only need to put fabric on the bottom to cover the drainage holes.

Potting mix
Whether you hang it on the house or set it on the ground, lifting or supporting a soil-filled planter can be tough. Choose a lightweight potting mix to make the task easier. The mix also promotes lots of healthy root growth. However, if you're planning to use drought-tolerant plants in the box, add bark mulch in the bottom to keep them from staying too moist.

Nursery pots
Make it easy to swap plants in and out by setting several empty plastic pots into the box. Fill the planter with a couple inches of potting mix, set the pots in place and fill in around them. Now you can slip potted plants into the container without disturbing others in the box. But remember, unlike a container where all of the plants are together, growing this way means you'll need to water each pot separately.

Out of the box

You don't have to plant the whole box with empty containers. Tuck in just a couple of them. Plant most of your selections directly in the box and slip in some planted pots to keep the scene changing over the growing season.

Mulch Not only will it help hold in valuable moisture, but mulch also gives the box a neat and tidy look. Once the pots are in place, cover everything with a thin layer of mulch. You'll want to use a finely shredded bark so it is in proportion to the size and scale of the box.

WINDOWBOX HELPERS

Make growing gorgeous windowboxes easier with these five gadgets.

1 SIDE PLANTING WINDOWBOXES These plastic-coated wire frames are fitted with a coconut fiber liner. What makes them unique is the planting holes along the sides. They allow you to get even more cascading color from your container. Pamela Crawford's side planting windowboxes and liners are available in many lengths from Kinsman Company, 800-733-4129 or at www.kinsmangarden.com.

2 WICKINATOR The storage reservoir of PVC tubes is easy to fill with water. A series of wicks pulls the water from the tube and into the soil so plants have a steady supply. Well, they will as long as you fill the tubes occasionally! The Wickinator comes in many sizes from Flower Window Boxes at 678-455-8797 or at www.flowerwindowboxes.com.

3 SIDING HOOKS These clips slide under the overlap and hang on the nailing edge of metal or vinyl siding. Each clip holds about 12 pounds: Weigh the filled and watered container to see how many clips you need. And the clips can be repositioned easily. They're available from Kinsman Company, 800-733-4129 or at www.kinsmangarden.com.

4 ADJUSTABLE RAILING BRACKETS These brackets from Garden Treasures® give you lots of options. And you don't need any special tools or woodworking ability to install them on metal or wooden railings. Find them at Lowe's.

5 WATER WAND WITH ROTATING HEAD Switch the angle and flow to make it easier to water boxes at different heights or across foundation plantings. This Flow-Control Watering Wand is available at www.GardenGateStore.com.

CONTAINERS | RECIPES

pansies in pots: 3 cool looks

The fastest way to cheer up a cool spring, fall or (if you live in the Deep South) winter day is to add pansies. These container favorites are available in just about any color imaginable — and many color combinations, too! Some flowers are solid-colored while others have "blotches" of a contrasting color. Blooms with prominent whiskers (tiny lines of color radiating from the blooms' centers), picotee (petals edged in a different color) and even ruffled petals are easy to find. Every year, new shades and patterns are introduced. Planting them has never been so fun!

Pansies are technically perennials, but they're short-lived, so most people treat them as annuals. In any case, they make versatile, cool-weather plants for sun to part-shade pots.

The photos here show they work equally well whether you tuck several of one variety into a terra-cotta pot or mix them with other plants in a hanging basket or glazed pot. Thriving in well-drained soil in full sun to part shade conditions, pansies love the cool weather of spring and fall. See "Tidy up!" below for a tip to keep them looking good. But when the weather starts to get warm, they often get leggy and stop blooming well. At that point tear them out and toss them. ☐

Botanical Names

Calibrachoa
  Calibrachoa hybrids
Gazania
  Gazania hybrids
Flowering kale
  Brassica oleracea
Snapdragon
  Antirrhinum majus
Sweet pea
  Lathyrus odoratus

Mass planting ▶

1 IS THERE ANYTHING PRETTIER THAN MASSES OF PANSIES? These beauties look good planted with other flowers, but they look great massed together on their own! That's because, more often than not, pansies are multicolored (the ones above have shades of orange, gold, bronze, burgundy and purple — and that's just in one cultivar!). Plus, most modern pansies have a compact, dense habit that really fills in a container. Be sure to pack them together for a full effect right away.

While the pots above hold just one cultivar, you could fill a container with several cultivars of pansies for even more color. To encourage more blooms, snip back the stems of spent flowers. And when the pansies are done for the year, replant the containers with succulents or other heat-loving plants.

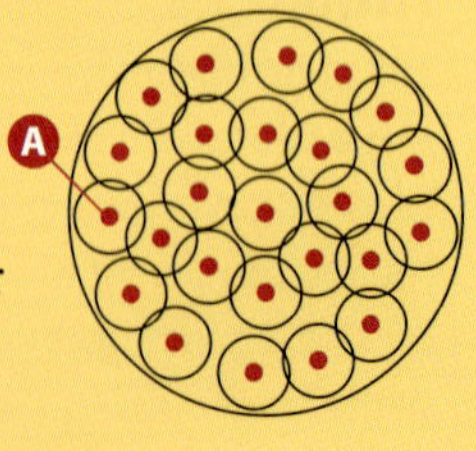

PLANT LIST (number to plant)
A Pansy *Viola* 'Mulberry Shades' **(25)**
Container is 16 inches in diameter

TIDY UP!

PANSIES FLOWER MORE WHEN THEY'RE DEADHEADED. If you have just a few plants, snip off the spent flowers. Wait too long, and they'll start to develop seed pods (which sap the plant's flower-making energy). If you have a whole pot of pansies, shear them all back at once.

It's easy to confuse this seed pod with a new bud. Look closely before deadheading to make sure you don't cut a flower-to-be.

Old-fashioned favorites ▶

2 PANSIES ARE TRULY TIMELESS Add them to an old-fashioned planting. Matched with fragrant stock and ferny lotus vine, they create a spring container that would have felt as comfortable in the 19th century as it does in the 21st.

Looking for another classic, late-winter-to-spring pairing? Grow sweet pea vine up a trellis in a container, and plant pansies at its feet. Or, for an old-fashioned fall, pair pansies with kale and snapdragons — they'll look good until the first hard freeze, or very late into the fall.

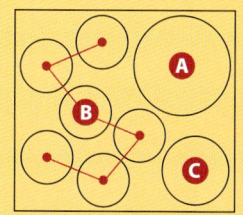

PLANT LIST (number to plant)
- **A** Stock *Matthiola incana* 'Hot Cakes White' **(1)**
- **B** Pansy *Viola* Frizzle Sizzle Mix **(6)**
- **C** Lotus vine *Lotus berthelotii* **(1)**

Container is 8 inches × 9 inches

◀ Seasonal switcheroo

3 PANSIES TAKE A SUMMER HIATUS You might see that as a disadvantage, but look at it as an opportunity to give a container a makeover! In this spring hanging basket, the pansies will fade once summer kicks in. But the purple heart and ivy won't. That makes it the perfect makeover candidate. When the pansies are done, pull them out and replace them with white calibrachoas (to keep the same look) or yellow gazanias (for a vibrant complementary color combo). Plant up several pots with one spring plant so you can give your whole yard a makeover in an afternoon!

PLANT LIST (number to plant)
- **A** Pansy *Viola* Whiskers White **(3)**
- **B** Purple heart *Tradescantia pallida* **(3)**
- **C** Ivy *Hedera helix* 'Duck Foot' **(3)**

Basket is 12 inches in diameter

the YEAR IN GARDENING

CONTAINERS | RECIPES

ever so exuberant

There is nothing shy about this container. With billows of coleus and calibrachoa, feathery plumes of fountain grass and a shouting orange begonia, it demands attention. And it'll look better and better right up until frost. With all of those exuberant plants, a low-key wooden planter box is a good idea. You can plant straight into it as I did, or tuck plants into a large plastic pot, then slip the pot into the wooden planter. (The plastic liner will help the wooden box last longer.)

Trailing coleus grow even faster than the upright kinds, so don't be afraid to pinch or cut them back a few inches at a time as needed. (The cuttings root easily if you stick them in potting mix, so it's a great way to get a few extra plants for other containers.) This begonia is one of my favorites, so we always bring it inside to overwinter as a house plant in a sunny room (but not right in a window, or the leaves might scorch). It gets a little straggly inside, but I prune it back about halfway in spring, and it's ready to delight again.

love this look?

Want to try this container in a sunny spot? The grass and calibrachoa will be just fine in sun. Swap a chartreuse sweet potato vine for the coleus and a blazing-red zinnia for the begonia, and it'll add a blast of color to any sunny garden.

Code	Plant Name	No. to Plant
A	**Purple fountain grass** *Pennisetum setaceum* Graceful Grasses® Red Riding Hood	1
B	**Coleus** *Solenostemon* 'Red Trailing Queen'	2
C	**Calibrachoa** *Calibrachoa* Superbells® Coral	2
D	**Winged begonia** *Begonia* 'Orange Angels'	1

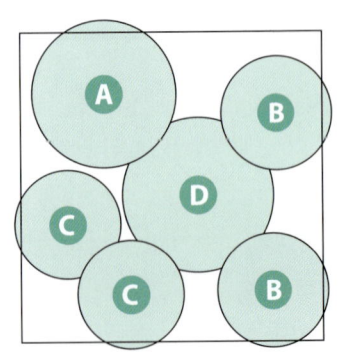

Container is 14 in. square

flowery fall

It happens to me every fall. As soon as the weather starts to cool down, I get a renewed urge to garden. This container planting is a snap to put together and take care of. What could be better?

The oblong copper tub was the inspiration for this combo. A few bright-orange chrysanthemums from the garden center play up the color of the tub. I added plum-colored coral bells in front and red euphorbia to the right to complement the warm flowers and break up the masses of blooms. The spiky purple-tinted blades of the maiden grass tie it neatly to the other leaf colors and give height contrast. Finally, I added a small St. John's wort with red-tinged berries for texture.

Whether this pot's in sun or shade, it doesn't matter, since it's just a short-term container. And for the same reason, don't bother to fertilize these plants either. In fact, there's no need to even plant this container up. Just set the pots in the planter and save yourself some time.

Keep a close watch on the soil in the pots so the plants don't dry out. The St. John's wort is a good moisture indicator — when you see it start to wilt, water the plants. This planting is out in the open, where rain can collect in the tub, so I used a nail to punch two or three drainage holes in the bottom. If it's going to be on a porch or other covered spot, skip the holes and protect your porch from the draining water. There, safe from hard rains and frost, the flowers of the mums will last much longer, too, so you'll get more mileage out of this cheery combination. □

— *Deborah Gruca*

Code	Plant Name	No. to Plant
A	Coral bells *Heuchera* 'Plum Pudding'	2
B	Chrysanthemum *Chrysanthemum* 'Pelee'	1
C	Maiden grass *Miscanthus* 'Purpurascens'	1
D	St. John's wort *Hypericum* Ignite™ Red	1
E	Chrysanthemum *Chrysanthemum* 'Fire Island'	2
F	Euphorbia *Euphorbia dulcis* 'Chameleon'	1

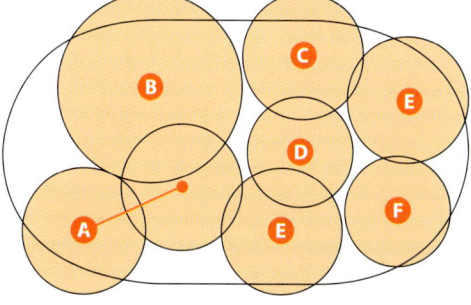

Container is 21 in. long × 14 in. wide × 7 in. deep

Tips for care

- Full sun to part shade
- Even soil moisture
- No need to fertilize

CONTAINERS | BASICS

make a tough job easier!

Botanical Names

Alternanthera
  Alternanthera spp.
Impatiens
  Impatiens hybrids
Licorice vine
  Helichrysum petiolare
Rocky Mountain juniper
  Juniperus scopulorum

(1) Trim or pull the plants you don't intend to keep. Then slide the soil knife down along the inside edge of the container to loosen the roots clinging to the inside.

Whether you're doing an end-of-summer cleanup or renovating an overgrown container, there's always the question of what to do with the plants. You can pull annuals and toss them on the compost pile. But what about perennials, grasses, shrubs or small trees that you want to keep? You can't just yank them out of the soil because that'll tear the roots apart. And most plants survive a move better if the root ball stays intact.

I plant a lot of big containers in the *Garden Gate* test garden. Over the years, I've developed a pretty good method for getting those big plants out of containers without damaging the plant's root ball, the container…or my back!

First, find a spot to work on mulch or grass, because you're less likely to crack or chip your container on a forgiving surface. Then spread out a tarp to catch loose soil and gather your tools. I like to use a soil knife, a small, short-handled spade, a rubber mallet and two pieces of 2x4 to keep the container from rolling.

Let's get started! I'll walk you through how I emptied this container, saving the small Rocky Mountain juniper to plant in the garden.

TRIM AND LOOSEN First, get rid of plants you don't plan to keep. It's OK to pull shallow-rooted annuals like impatiens, but some, like the licorice vine and alternanthera in photo 1, have big, deep root systems. Give these plants a gentle tug — if they don't come out easily, cut them off. Don't yank on them because that could tear apart the root ball of the plant you want to keep. Your goal is to get that root ball out in one piece, with plenty of soil still around the roots!

Once the small plants are out of the way, loosen the soil around the edge of the container with the soil knife. Tiny hair roots may have attached themselves to the rough inside of the container, so they'll need a little coaxing to let go.

240   THE YEAR IN GARDENING   www.GardenGateMagazine.com

ROCK AND ROLL You've loosened the soil at the top of the pot, but you need to get the soil and roots loose around the bottom. Tip the pot on its side, and tap gently along the sides and bottom with the rubber mallet to loosen those roots that are attached to the inside of the container. Tap a few times, then roll the container part way, and tap the new area. (In photo 2, you'll see how to use those pieces of 2x4 as blocks so the container can't roll away from you.) Continue tapping all the way around the container, rocking it from side to side as you go. See how there's a little soil falling out? That's a sign that the root ball is working loose, but it's not falling apart. You may need to do a couple of complete rotations of the pot to get the root ball completely free around the edges.

WORK WITH CARE Now it's time to dig a little deeper, so you'll need to use your short-handled spade. Guide it along the inside wall of the container, as I'm doing in photo 3, instead of cutting into the roots. Roll the container gradually, working the spade in along the edge at every stop. It's OK to pry a little with the spade, but don't apply too much pressure or you may break the rim of your pot. (You'll probably need to roll the container completely over a couple of times, digging and prying as you go.) As you roll, you'll start to work the root ball out of the container. It's tempting to pull on the top of the plant, but you'll run the risk of pulling the root ball apart, or even yanking the plant loose from most of its roots. Instead, just support the top of the plant, as I'm doing in the inset, as you gently ease the root ball out.

CATCH THE BALL Almost there! The root ball is almost all the way out of the pot. In photo 4, see how I've tucked my knee under the trunk of this tree? When I finally pull the root ball all the way out, the tree won't slap down hard against the ground, which could break branches or loosen the soil from the root ball. Don't be afraid to get dirty — you'll end up hugging that root ball as you ease it onto the ground. Once it's out, you can use the tarp as a work space to pot it into another container, or drag the tarp carefully to where you'll put the plant in the ground. Another container successfully emptied, and a plant saved to enjoy elsewhere in the garden! ▫

— *Marcia Leeper*

(2) Rock the pot from side to side as you tap with the rubber mallet. Sections of 2x4 stop the pot from rolling too far, and they won't chip the pot, either.

(3) Carefully pry around the edge of the pot, supporting the base of the plant as you wiggle it free.

(4) Once the root ball is out of the container, use the tarp to drag it to its new location. Or repot it right there on the tarp — it'll catch the loose soil.

did you know...

Boat planter
Maureen Williams, Texas

What do you do with an old boat that's not safe to put in the water anymore? Make it into a planter, of course! Maureen had a leaky old metal johnboat (the type with a flat bottom) sitting in the yard of her lakeside home. Once the boat was moved to its final resting spot, she put some edging and mulch around it to set the area apart from the rest of the yard. Then Maureen put soil between the bench seats and added plants. She set a few containers with mums on the bench seats to add a little height to her "container." A cascading plant, such as sweet potato vine or Wave™ petunias, spilling over the boat's edge helps it seem more a part of the landscape.

If you don't have a boat, you can still get creative with your planters. Anything will do — a purse, an old shoe, even a teakettle. Whatever you use, the most important thing is to be sure there are a few drainage holes. Use a drill, an awl or a screwdriver to drill or punch holes in the item you're using. Otherwise, your plants may sit in water and rot.

Watering top to bottom
Ann Fink, Minnesota

Keeping flower pouches well-watered in the summer is tough. So Ann came up with this clever idea that makes it easier to get water along the entire length of the pouch. She uses those plastic tubes that keep the clubs separated in a golf bag.

Ann starts out by measuring her flower pouch and cutting a tube so it's about 3 inches longer than the pouch. That done, she uses a ¼-inch drill bit to drill holes in the tube. She starts a few inches from the top of the tube, drilling all the way through to the other side. Then she rotates the tube a quarter turn, measures down an inch and drills through the tube again. She repeats the turning and drilling along the length of the tube so it looks like the illustration at right.

Once that's done, it's time to "plant" the watering tube in the middle of the pouch. Ann starts by putting a few handfuls of potting mix in the bottom of the pouch. Then she stuffs a paper towel in the bottom of the tube to slow down the water and force it out the drilled holes. She protects the top of the tube with a small plastic pot to keep the potting mix out and continues to fill the pouch with soil. Finally, she plants it up. Later, when it's time to water, it's easier to find and pour water into the tube if it's a few inches above the soil.

The holes along the length of the tube help moisten the soil for all the plants, not just the ones at the top.

Make sure the golf tube sticks up a couple of inches above the soil so it's easier to find.

Holes along the length of the tube get water to all the plants in the bag.

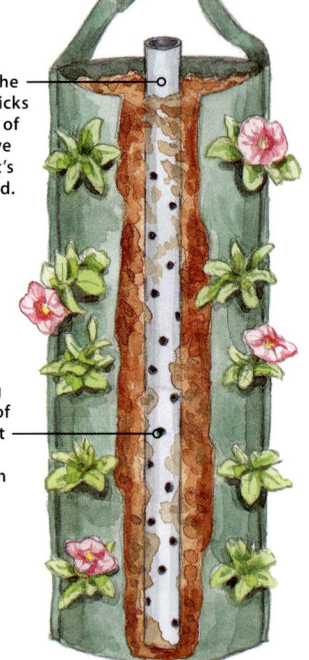

Pine basket
D.C. Harrison, Ohio

When it's time to fill those hanging baskets this year, don't bother buying a liner. Do what D.C. Harrison does and line your basket with pine needles! He just picks up a tangled mass of needles from under his trees and works them together in his wire frame baskets until they're about 2 inches thick. D.C. has found that Scotch pine needles (*Pinus sylvestris*) work best. The short, stiff needles hold together well. When he's tried white pine needles (*Pinus strobus*), the soil falls right through.

Cork feet
Pauline Crinnan, Massachusetts

Using pot feet to keep containers up off the deck prevents stains. But that can get pricey. Pauline found an inexpensive solution — wine corks! Whether they're natural cork or made of synthetic materials, the pot feet last a long time. Check out the illustration and you'll see how easy it is to assemble one: Just four corks that are held together with four wood screws.

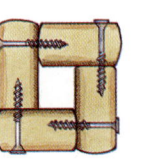

Line the screw up with the hole made by the corkscrew.

Wet vac redo
Adiana Pulliam, Missouri
You can never have too many containers — that's Adiana's policy. So when the motor on her wet vac burned out, she thought, "Why not turn it into a container?" And since the lower half that holds the water has wheels, it would be portable, too! Adiana removed the lid with the motor and hose and set that aside. Then she drilled five holes in the bottom of the 12-gallon tub that used to hold the water. To make it look nice, she got some granite spray paint from the local craft store and covered the whole thing. After that, she sprayed a coat of waterproof sealer to keep the paint from deteriorating. Now she has a good-looking large container that's easy to move wherever she wants it.

Keep squirrels out
Candi Glancy, Texas
Squirrels and new container plants don't mix — just ask Candi. She kept losing the small plants she put in her containers to the pesky creatures. Then she got an idea. She removed the front grille from a non-working fan and placed it on top of the container — it was a perfect fit. Now the squirrels can't get to the soil and upend her seedlings! So Candi's plants survive and grow up through the tines. The squirrels just have to dig somewhere else.

An old fan grille keeps squirrels from digging up new plants.

Bundle up!
Valdean Schultz, Minnesota
Valdean was looking for a quick way to protect her beautiful hanging basket from a light frost. So she turned to something she had on hand — a hooded sweatshirt! See how simple it is to do in the photo above? Just hang the hood on the shepherd's hook, pull the hood drawstring and tie it tight. Then bring the body of the sweatshirt around the container, zip it up and stuff the sleeves in the pockets. Your container is tucked in for the night. The next morning the sweatshirt comes off until the next frost.

PHOTO: Doug Appleby (container sweatshirt)

did you know... (CONTINUED)

product picks

Succulent Container Gardens

You may have grown sedum, hen and chicks, yucca or other succulents. Flip through the pages of this new book and you'll meet other, more unusual members of this family, such as crassula, echeveria and aeonium. And they all look great in containers. But this isn't just a book of photos. There are plenty of design ideas along with tips for growing these fascinating plants. In addition, you'll find a section on nonsucculent plants that make good companions.

Bottom line Great inspiration and how-to help for growing great-looking succulent containers.
Source Local and online bookstores and GardenGateStore.com
Price $29.95; hardcover; 248 pages

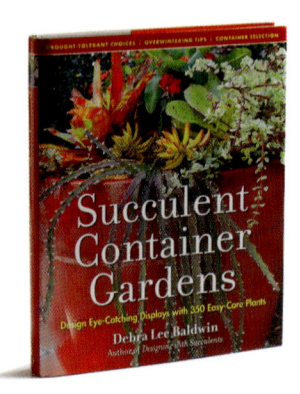

Two-Tier Plant Hanger

Get a multilevel display using two of your own containers and the two-tier hanger. Made of rustproof aluminum, each hanger is 21 inches long and is easy to use. Just make sure the combined weight of the plants, containers and soil doesn't exceed 40 pounds. To use, slip the hanger with the loop up through the drainage hole of the top pot. Then slip the hanger without the loop into the bottom pot. Plant them up, hook them together and you're ready to go.

Bottom line This easy-to-use hanger is great for two-story decks and other tall narrow spaces.
Source Lee Valley Garden Tools at www.leevalley.com or 800-871-8158
Price $15.95

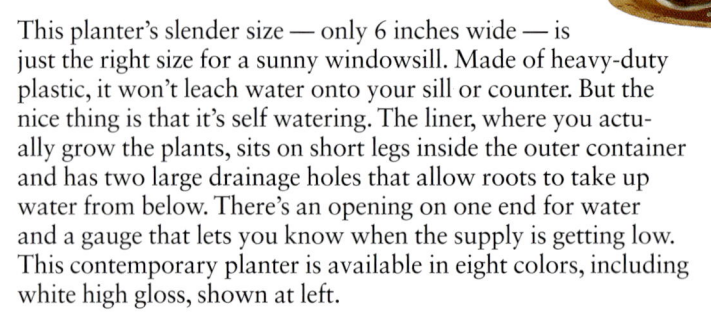

Windowsill planter

This planter's slender size — only 6 inches wide — is just the right size for a sunny windowsill. Made of heavy-duty plastic, it won't leach water onto your sill or counter. But the nice thing is that it's self watering. The liner, where you actually grow the plants, sits on short legs inside the outer container and has two large drainage holes that allow roots to take up water from below. There's an opening on one end for water and a gauge that lets you know when the supply is getting low. This contemporary planter is available in eight colors, including white high gloss, shown at left.

Bottom line It's a good-looking planter that makes caring for your plants easier.
Source Lechuza at www.lechuza.com or 877-532-4892
Price $34.95

Watering pointers
Marilyn Davis, California

Q I tried to water, but water is pouring out the bottom of the container and the mix is still dry. What's happening?

A Most potting mixes contain peat moss, which holds water well when it's wet, but when it gets completely dry, it can be hard to rehydrate. Too-dry potting mix often forms a "crust" on top of the pot, so water rushes off it. And dry mix also contracts, pulling away from the sides of the pot, so water runs through the container without ever getting to the plant roots. You'll have to break the crust and loosen the soil so it will start to absorb water again. See how we're poking holes in the mix with a pencil, below? After you do this, add water. Revisit the container in an hour and add more, until the mix has absorbed plenty of water. If you're really having a tough time, set the container in a tub of water for half an hour or so, so the potting mix can absorb moisture through the drainage hole.

Use a pencil (or a fingertip!) to break through crusted soil so water can seep into soil more easily.

Increase the humidity around a Christmas cactus to keep the buds from dropping and help make the blooms last longer, too.

Blooming holiday
Shirley Bigalk, Iowa

Q Some years my Christmas cactus sets buds, other times not. And lots of the buds drop off before they open. Why?

A Just because it has "cactus" in the name doesn't mean this winter-flowering house plant will like hot and dry conditions.

A healthy Christmas cactus (*Zygocactus* spp.) may bloom several times during the year but flowers most during the short days of winter. To make sure buds form by Christmas, in mid-October move the plant to a spot where it gets bright daylight, but no artificial light at night. The plant needs six to eight weeks in 12 to 14 hours of uninterrupted darkness each day. And the temperature should stay between 50 and 55 degrees F even at night. But it can be a few degrees warmer during the day. A window in a spare bedroom or basement, where lights are not turned on frequently, is a good place.

Once the plant sets buds, you can move it out of the dark room, but keep it cool. Water is being added to the pebble-filled saucer in the photo above to increase the humidity around the plant. Don't let the pot sit directly in the water or buds will begin to drop and the roots will rot. When the top inch of the soil feels dry, water thoroughly until water runs out of the pot.

After the flowers are gone, keep the plant on a sunny windowsill. Late winter is the time for repotting, but don't do it every year — a pot-bound Christmas cactus will bloom best.

Too much fertilizer
Lisette Paul, Maryland

Q Oh, no! I think I over-fertilized! What should I do?

A Don't panic — just flush out the container with water right away. Let water run through the container for several minutes to get the extra nutrients out of the potting mix. If the container is small enough to pick up, set it over a bucket or saucer to catch the run-through. You can "recycle" that diluted fertilizer on other containers or on your garden.

In spite of flushing out the extra fertilizer, you may see some burned leaves anyway, like the ones below. If you do, pinch or prune the damaged areas out. Move the container into shade, and give it plenty of water — you want to avoid stressing the plant as it recovers from the excess fertilizer.

Plants can recover from fertilizer burn, but you may have to pinch back damaged leaves.

One way to save money is to start your own perennials from seed. Learn how on page 256.

gardening basics

how to *grow* the garden you've always wanted

INSPIRATION AND IDEAS only go so far. That's when another "I"—Instruction—comes in handy. We've got tools and techniques to make your gardening experience more rewarding. There are tips on everything from saving time and money to dealing with pesky bugs and weeds. It's what you need to know to keep your garden looking its best.

Our Top 10 Tips to Save Money and Time	**248**
Get Started with Spring Cleanup	**250**
Enjoy More Flowers!	**252**
Starting Perennials from Seed and Save Money	**256**
Success with Bare-Root Perennials	**258**
Fall is for Planting Cool-Season Vegetables	**262**
What's Your Fall Garden IQ?	**264**
Do Home Remedies Really Work?	**268**
Spring Weed Alert	**270**
9 Bugs to Stop Now!	**274**
Slugging it Out with Slugs	**278**
Is That Critter a Friend or Foe?	**280**
The Best Sprinkler for You and Your Plants!	**282**
Make Over a Stark Patio	**284**
Elegant Ornaments	**288**
Did You Know	**290**
Pests to Watch	**304**
Beneficials to Know	**305**
6 Weeds to Know	**306**
Know Your Zones	**308**

BASICS | SMART GARDENING

Our top **10** tips
Save Money and Time

THE WEEKEND Garden Smarter GARDENER

Does saving money and time in the garden sound good? Hey, I'm with you! With all we have to do every day, gardeners are very clever about coming up with ways to save on the work and expense of growing plants. Through the years, I've found many. Here are 10 of my favorite money- or time-saving tips on tools, plants and supplies.

1 BUY INEXPENSIVE WATERING TOOLS Don't buy high-priced watering tools, such as wands, nozzles or sprinklers. Even the expensive ones will spring leaks, so save your money and buy cheap ones instead. Replace worn rubber washers where the tool connects to the hose to minimize leaks. And buy a good brass hose connector like the one below. The shutoff lever saves you trips back and forth to the faucet, and brass means it'll hold up for many years.

Invest in a good brass hose connector — skip the high-priced attachments.

2 PAY NOW, SAVE LATER Good-quality tools can make gardening tasks easier and go more quickly. But you don't have to pay a lot for *every* tool you use. Do invest in well-made trowels, spades and pruners — the tools you use most often. You'll save yourself the frustration and lost time of fixing bent, broken or non-working parts. Buy from companies that stand behind their products, such as Sears®, which will replace any Craftsman® gardening hand tools purchased there.

3 GO FOR BROKE When you shop for bagged mulch or soil, ask for broken bags. Employees usually pull damaged ones off to the side, and stores are often more than willing to get rid of them at a reduced price.

While you're at the store, look for chipped or cracked terra-cotta or glazed containers, as well. You can get several years' use from a slightly damaged pot, and often the plants will hide any defects. Most managers will haggle with you for a lower price, especially near the end of the season.

4 SPOT TREAT WEEDS If you don't have lots of broadleaf weeds in your yard, don't apply weed killer to the entire lawn. Instead, buy liquid ready to use with a hose-end sprayer and spot-spray weeds rather than applying granules with a drop spreader. You'll save time, and the liquid spray works better anyway. It dries quickly and starts to work right away, while the granules must be applied to wet grass and then have dry weather for 2 to 4 days afterward. The chart below shows how you can save even more money if you can buy the liquid concentrate, mix it up and spot treat weeds with a tank sprayer. You'll cover the same area for a fraction of the cost. And for any liquid herbicide, since you spray only where you need it, you'll use less, which is better for the environment.

Cost to cover 5,000 sq. ft.:
 Granules $23.99
 Liquid, ready to use
  (spot spraying) $11.50
 Liquid concentrate
  (spot spraying) $6.50

5 DON'T THROW OUT YOUR POTTING MIX Anyone who plants up large containers knows how expensive it can be to fill one with potting mix. Well, unless your plants had disease problems during the year, you don't have to empty your big pots completely at the end of the season. Remove just the top 8 to 12 inches of mix — the depth the roots of most annuals will reach. In spring, use a trowel to loosen up the mix left in the bottom of the pot, refill it with fresh mix and plant!

248 *the* YEAR IN GARDENING   www.GardenGateMagazine.com

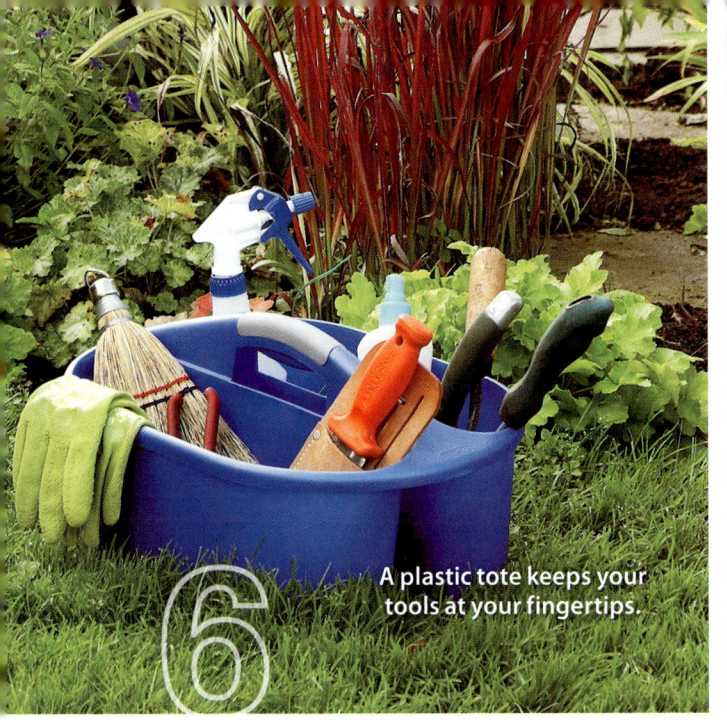

A plastic tote keeps your tools at your fingertips.

Nearby foliage hides the nursery pot support.

PHOTOS: Brent Isenberger (1 and 8)

6 KEEP 'EM TOGETHER A good way to save money on tools is to not lose the ones you have. Keep the hand tools you use most in a lightweight cleaning tote. Totes with openings are easy to clean with a spray of the hose.

7 START PERENNIALS FROM SEED Want a lot of perennials, but don't need them right away? Save money by buying seeds and starting your own plants right out in the garden. Wait until well after the last frost (in fact, you can start them as late as the middle of summer), and plant them in prepared, well-drained soil in the garden. Be sure to keep the seedlings moist. It helps if you plant them where they'll get a little shade during the hottest part of the day. In fall or the following spring, move the plants to their permanent homes.

For the best selection buy seed online. Coneflowers (*Echinacea purpurea*), pinks (*Dianthus* spp.), salvias (*Salvia* hybrids) and black-eyed Susans (*Rudbeckia* hybrids), are all easy to grow. Some plants will bloom the first year, but most will take two to three years to reach full size and bloom. If you're willing to wait, you'll save big.

8 SUPPORT IT YOURSELF Save cash and make your own stakes and supports. Push prunings from woody plants into the soil to hold up floppy plants. Make small trellises or obelisks from the dried canes of large ornamental grasses. Or make your own plant supports from black nursery pots. I made the one above for a leaning sedum. Cut off the bottom of the pot and sink it into the ground around your plant while it's small. The rolled top edge of the pot protects the stems as they lean.

9 START A TOOL CO-OP Have friends or neighbors who like to garden as much as you do? Get together with them and share large or expensive tools that you don't use often. Tillers, chipper/shredders and chainsaws can certainly make a job easier, but are pricey to buy or rent. If you share the tools, you all get to use them without crowding the car out of your garage or draining your bank account.

10 WHAT'S THE BEST BUY? You might think that you'll save money at the garden center by buying small plants rather than large ones. However, that's not always the case. So compare the plants and prices before you decide. I paid $6 for the coreopsis in the gallon container below. You can see that before planting I could easily divide it into three good-sized plants, making the cost of each one $2. Meanwhile, a 4-inch pot of the same (but much smaller-sized) plant costs $4. And if I divide the larger plant right away, it'll save me a bit of work, as it will be longer until the plants need dividing again.

I hope at least one of these tips will leave you with a little more spare change in your pocket and the time to enjoy it!

— *Deborah Gruca*

Look closely— you might find two or three plants in a bigger pot!

$6 or $4

BASICS | SMART GARDENING

get started with spring cleanup

After a long winter indoors, the first thing any gardener does is inspect the garden... what made it through the cold weather? What's coming up? And finally, is it time to start spring cleanup?

You want to get those new shoots off to the best possible start. But just as you use the right tools and techniques for cleaning counter tops or taking fingerprints off mirrors in your house, you want to use the correct methods to clean up plants, too. Depending on the plant's growth habit, stem and leaf texture and more, you may need to tread lightly. Or it may be OK to just rip in there and make the dead leaves fly! Some plants, like coneflowers or black-eyed Susans, are easy — whack off the dead tops, and you're set to go. But some plants prefer more specialized techniques. Let me show you three methods for cleaning up those plants that need a little extra care. ☐

— *Marcia A. Leeper*

Careful cutbacks

When you're dealing with a perennial with evergreen or semi-evergreen foliage, take care. You can't just pull at the old foliage because it's still alive and attached. But you need to remove those tattered leaves and make room for this year's new growth.

Before you cut, reach into the clump of plants and gently pull out loose debris so you get a good view of the base of the plant. Next, cut off the old growth. See how I'm reaching right down to the base of the bergenia in the photo? That way, I can be sure I'm cutting old stems, not disturbing new shoots. Sometimes I use household scissors instead of pruners — the long, narrow blades can reach into tight spaces more easily. You'll be rewarded a few weeks later by the flowers and fresh growth in the inset.

PLANTS TO CUT BACK WITH CARE
- **Bergenia** *Bergenia cordifolia* (in photo)
- **Coral bells** *Heuchera* spp. and hybrids
- **Epimedium** *Epimedium* spp.
- **Hellebore** *Helleborus* spp.
- **Pinks** *Dianthus* spp.

A few weeks later blooms and new growth appear.

If necessary, push leaves aside so you can see where to cut.

A springy metal leaf rake will remove dead leaves without damaging plant crowns.

Really rake them over

Your rake is another go-to tool for spring cleaning. For ground cover perennials that spread quickly, like this lamb's ear, the fastest cleanup is a vigorous once-over with a rake. (Use a bamboo rake or a springy metal leaf rake, not a heavy, rigid garden rake.) It'll get rid of dead leaves and stems, and these perennials will relish extra air and light. This is a simple technique — just get that rake in there and go to work. How much is enough? Well, you don't have to get every single bit of old foliage or stem. And it's OK to yank out an occasional new shoot, but you don't want to start seeing bald patches. Once you get that dead stuff out, stand back! These plants fill in quickly, and in a few weeks your plants will look like those in the inset.

Do keep in mind that this technique doesn't work so well for vining ground covers like vinca. Stems will tangle around the rake, and you'll pull out too much new growth.

PLANTS THAT LIKE A STRONG HAND ON THE RAKE
- **Bugleweed** *Ajuga reptans*
- **Dalmatian bellflower** *Campanula portenschlagiana*
- **Lamb's ear** *Stachys byzantina* (in photo)
- **Lily-of-the-valley** *Convallaria majalis*
- **Ribbon grass** *Phalaris arundinacea*

In a few weeks, lamb's ear will fill in.

Fluff them up

If you live where there's snow cover, lifting and "fluffing" is a necessity. Perennials with long, trailing stems, like this variegated creeping speedwell, tend to get packed down over the winter, so you need to let a little air in around the stems. I've found that when I do this, I see faster new growth in spring, and before I know it, I have the fresh green foliage and flowers in the inset. This is actually a pretty simple technique. Wiggle the tines of the rake, points up, under the mat of stems and "fluff" them a little. The key is to keep it gentle — you don't want to pull stems loose from their roots, just lift them clear of the mud and debris. If you need to remove dead leaves that collected on top of the plant, rake them out gently with your fingers once you've loosened everything up.

PLANTS TO LIFT AND FLUFF
- **Candytuft** *Iberis sempervirens*
- **Creeping sedum** *Sedum* spp.
- **Creeping speedwell** *Veronica prostrata* (in photo)
- **Spotted deadnettle** *Lamium maculatum*
- **Thyme** *Thymus* spp.

In late spring bright new growth shows off and blooms.

Use care when you pull the tines back out of the plant after you've "fluffed."

BASICS | SMART GARDENING

Prune your spring-blooming shrubs now.

Enjoy More Flowers!

Web extra
Learn *pruning tips* for 20 more shrubs.

If you want more color from your spring-blooming shrubs, now's the time to start planning. You may be surprised to find that pruning is the most effective way to encourage your shrubs to bloom better. However, pruning can be a frightening task — will you hurt your plants? The answer is no — not if you do it the right way. And this isn't hard to do. Let me show you how to prune 18 spring-flowering shrubs to encourage more and bigger blooms next year. Then check out our Web extra for tips on 20 more flowering favorites.

TIMING IS CRITICAL The most important thing to remember is to do your clipping right after the flowers fade. The reason is that these shrubs need time to form the buds on new growth for next year's flowers. If you cut too late, you'll miss out on the blooms for a year. And if you prune them back too much, you may lose the flowers for a year or so, too. But don't worry, I've included illustrations showing you the simple pruning techniques you'll use.

HOW TO DEADHEAD A SHRUB Deadheading, which you see in the illustration below, means snipping off just the spent flowers. Often on a deciduous shrub, you can even see the new leaves sprouting at the base of the dying flowerhead. This makes the decision of where to cut easy on shrubs with large flowers, such as lilac or viburnum.

Spring is also when you should deadhead evergreens, such as rhododendron and mountain laurel, but don't take off too much. They are often slower growing than their deciduous counterparts and take more time to recover. With your fingers, grasp each spent cluster of flowers at the base and give it a twist to snap it off. Do it early in the day, before the sun wilts the stems, and you'll find they come away easily. Next, I'll share tips for thinning shrubs that have lots of small flowers. *continued >>*

Snip or pinch below the flowerhead, leaving the new leaves.

Deadheading is the technique to use on shrubs with large flower heads, such as lilacs.

Camellia *Camellia japonica* **and hybrids**

TAKE A LOOK This broadleaf evergreen blooms in very early spring with individual red, pink or white flowers. A spot out of harsh wind, with moist soil and part shade, is ideal. A camellia can grow 3 to 20 ft. tall and 3 to 10 ft. wide. It's cold-hardy in USDA zones 6 to 8 and heat-tolerant in AHS zones 8 to 1.

GROW MORE FLOWERS Deadhead the spent flowers to keep the shrub tidy and direct more energy into buds for next spring's flowers. Don't worry if you can't reach them all; simply removing the majority will promote better blooms next year.

Deutzia *Deutzia gracilis*

TAKE A LOOK Lots of small white bells line the stems of this shrub. It grows 1 to 3 ft. tall and 1 to 5 ft. wide and prefers full sun to part shade. It's cold-hardy in USDA zones 5 to 8 and heat-tolerant in AHS zones 8 to 1.

GROW MORE FLOWERS Cut all of the stems down to just a couple inches to grow lots of flowers. The plant will stay shorter if you do this, so if you want height, only take out some of the stems. And if these early spring flowers are ruined by late frost, cut them off so you'll get an even bigger burst of blooms next spring.

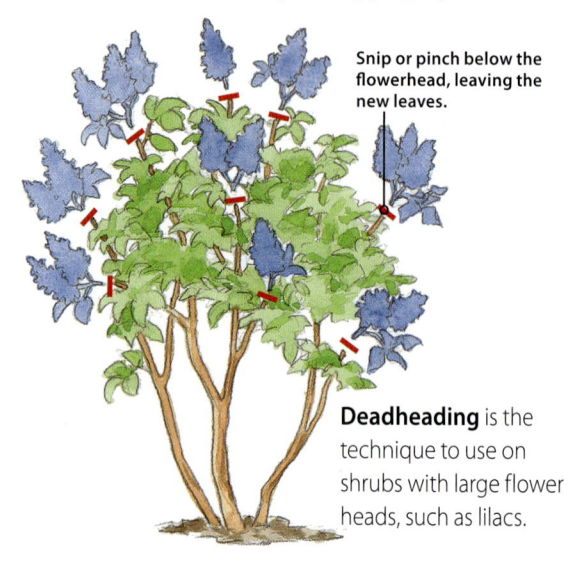

the YEAR IN GARDENING   www.GardenGateMagazine.com

Common lilac *Syringa vulgaris*

TAKE A LOOK Common lilac blooms best in full sun. You'll find lots of purple, pink, red and white cultivars that can grow from 8 to 15 ft. tall and 6 to 10 ft. wide. It's cold-hardy in USDA zones 3 to 8 and heat-tolerant in AHS zones 8 to 1.

GROW MORE FLOWERS To keep this midspring flowering shrub from growing tall and lanky, deadhead the spent flowers. As soon as the flowers fade, snip out the brown heads. If you want to keep the plant even shorter, this is also the time to trim a few stems back a bit lower, to a side branch.

Corneliancherry *Cornus mas*

TAKE A LOOK Tufts of early spring flowers, some of the first to be seen, sprout along the stems. Tolerant of part shade to full sun, this treelike shrub can reach 15 to 25 ft. tall and wide. It's cold-hardy in USDA zones 4 to 8 and heat-tolerant in AHS zones 8 to 1.

GROW MORE FLOWERS Thinning some of the branches back to a main stem every couple of years produces more flowers and makes them easier to see, too. But don't overdo it; the flowers are followed by shiny red fruit in summer. They last well into fall unless eaten by visiting birds.

Daphne *Daphne xburkwoodii*

TAKE A LOOK The leaves are interesting, but it's the fragrant pink midspring flowers you'll want. Find a spot in part shade with well-drained soil for this 3- to 4-ft.-tall and 3- to 6-ft.-wide shrub. It's cold-hardy in USDA zones 5 to 8 and heat-tolerant in AHS zones 8 to 1.

GROW MORE FLOWERS This shrub is noted for having some dieback, so start by removing all of the dead wood. The spent flowers will drop off, but deadhead the entire shrub with hedge shears, lightly trimming the tips of the stems. That produces more side branches to hold more flowers next spring.

Flowering quince *Chaenomeles japonica*

TAKE A LOOK Clusters of red, pink or white flowers line the stems of this full-sun shrub. Growing 4 to 8 ft. tall and 4 to 10 ft. wide, flowering quince is cold-hardy in USDA zones 5 to 8 and heat-tolerant in AHS zones 8 to 1.

GROW MORE FLOWERS After flowering quince blooms in midspring, thin out several of the oldest stems right down to the ground. For the biggest flower clusters along the main stems, cut back some of the small side branches in late summer, too. That sends more energy into fewer flower buds so the flowers end up larger.

Forsythia *Forsythia xintermedia*

TAKE A LOOK There are lots of forsythia cultivars, some with hardier buds than others, so look for one recommended for your area. Growing 6 to 10 ft. tall and 10 to 12 ft. wide, this early-blooming shrub flowers best in full sun to part shade. It's cold-hardy in USDA zones 4 to 8 and heat-tolerant in AHS zones 8 to 1.

GROW MORE FLOWERS No pruning means a ragged look and few flowers. Each year cut at least a third of the branches to the ground. Shorten the rest of the stems by as much as half and forsythia will maintain lots of long stems that will be covered with flowers.

Fothergilla *Fothergilla gardenii*

TAKE A LOOK White bottlebrush flowers have a slight honey scent and last a long time in cool spring weather. Fothergilla grows 3 to 4 ft. tall and wide and is cold-hardy in USDA zones 5 to 8 and heat-tolerant in AHS zones 8 to 1.

GROW MORE FLOWERS The flowers are at the tips of branches, so you could simply deadhead. But cut a bit further back to a leaf, and you'll get more flowers in midspring. Plus, you'll make sure this loose, casual shrub keeps a fuller habit and in fall you'll have more colorful foliage, too.

MORE SPRING SHRUBS!

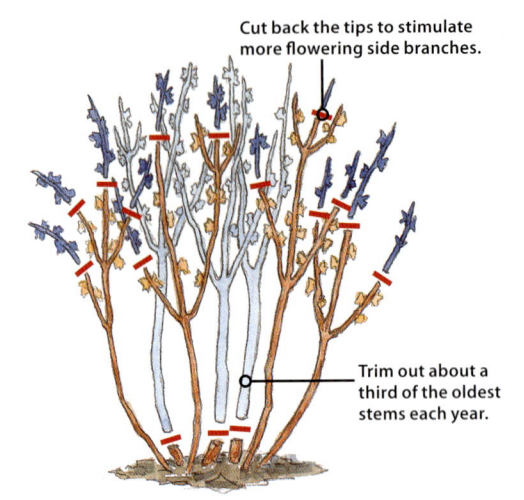

Cut back the tips to stimulate more flowering side branches.

Trim out about a third of the oldest stems each year.

Thinning works best on shrubs that produce lots of flowers along their stems, such as forsythia.

TIPS FOR THINNING It would be very tough to deadhead all of the individual flowers on a forsythia, mockorange or deutzia. For shrubs like these, which have lots of small blossoms along the branches, you'll want to remove a few of the older stems. Cut about a third of the stems down to within a few inches of the ground. The new stems that result from making these cuts will produce the best flowers over the next two to three years. Then, as those stems mature, you take some of them out every year to make room for more new growth. This technique is called "thinning," and I've shown you how to do it in the illustration above.

Spring is a gorgeous time of year, and flowering shrubs are a big part of that beauty. To help you add more of these colorful plants to your garden, check out the three plans on our Web extra. □

— *Jim Childs*

Web extra See **three plans** that feature spring-blooming shrubs.

Fringeflower *Loropetalum chinense*

TAKE A LOOK The midspring flowers are small, but there are lots of them. Best in part shade to full sun, you'll find cultivars that grow between 4 and 10 ft. tall and wide. Fringeflower is cold-hardy in USDA zones 7 to 9 and heat-tolerant in AHS zones 9 to 1.

GROW MORE FLOWERS Thinning out a few older stems is your best bet. That's especially true if you prefer a natural, informal look. Want more structure? As the flowers fade, prune the ends of the stems back, even shear them. You'll keep the form tidy and have loads of flowers next year.

Gardenia *Gardenia jasminoides*

TAKE A LOOK More flowers mean more fragrance, and that's what this part-shade shrub is all about. 'Kleim's Hardy' above blooms in mid- to late spring and grows 3 to 5 ft. tall and wide. And unlike the more tropical varieties, it's cold-hardy in USDA zones 7 to 11 and heat-tolerant in AHS zones 11 to 1.

GROW MORE FLOWERS Deadhead spent flowers, but if you miss a few they usually drop off cleanly. Snip off a few tips or errant branches to clean up the shape. That also grows more side branches for a denser plant and more branches mean more flowers.

Mountain laurel *Kalmia latifolia*

TAKE A LOOK Give this beauty a spot in full sun to part shade. And make sure it has some room to grow. You'll find a range of sizes from 3 to 15 ft. tall and wide. This native evergreen is cold-hardy in USDA zones 4 to 9 and heat-tolerant in AHS zones 9 to 1.

GROW MORE FLOWERS Like many rhododendron relatives, mountain laurel does not like heavy pruning. Pinch out the spent flower clusters with your fingers and you're done. If the shrub is spindly with few flowers, thin out no more than a third of the stems to grow more flowering branches.

Rhododendrons and azaleas *Rhododendron* spp. and hybrids

TAKE A LOOK Some are evergreen, some are deciduous — but all of them have colorful flowers. Most appreciate part shade, but will tolerate full sun. You'll find lots of species and cultivars, growing from 2 to 15 ft. tall and 3 to 15 ft. wide. They are cold-hardy in USDA zones 4 to 9 and heat-tolerant in AHS zones 9 to 1.

GROW MORE FLOWERS Deadhead by plucking off the spent flower heads. Keep the form neat and tidy by snipping off any errant stems now, too. But don't overdo it, or you may lose the flowers for next spring.

Koreanspice viburnum *Viburnum carlesii*

TAKE A LOOK Pale pink flowers with the scent of carnations — you'll surely want more! This midspring blooming shrub grows 4 to 6 ft. tall and wide in full sun to part shade. It's cold-hardy in USDA zones 4 to 8 and heat-tolerant in AHS zones 8 to 1.

GROW MORE FLOWERS Deadhead, but instead of just cutting off the spent flowers, cut further down the stem to a set of leaves. That will stimulate more side branches that will be tipped with flowers next spring. This shrub will produce clusters of berries, but they aren't showy, so you won't miss them.

Mockorange *Philadelphus* hybrids

TAKE A LOOK Loads of fragrant white flowers signal the end of spring. There are lots of cultivars in lots of sizes, ranging from 3 to 10 ft. tall and 3 to 8 ft. wide. Mockorange prefers full sun to part shade and is cold-hardy in USDA zones 4 to 8 and heat-tolerant in AHS zones 8 to 1.

GROW MORE FLOWERS Thin out a few of the oldest stems, those that are two years old or more, to make way for new ones that will bloom more heavily. Then snip the ends off a few of last year's new stems so the plant produces more flowering side branches.

Ninebark *Physocarpus opulifolius*

TAKE A LOOK Many cultivars have colorful leaves, but those pale pink to white flowers are very nice. There are cultivars that grow from 1 to 8 ft. tall and 2 to 8 ft. wide. Plant this durable shrub in full sun to part shade. It's cold-hardy in USDA zones 2 to 7 and heat-tolerant in AHS zones 7 to 1.

GROW MORE FLOWERS Thin this shrub by removing a few of the oldest stems down to the ground. If you're a shy pruner, start with ninebark — you can't go wrong. Stimulate more flowering side branches by trimming back a few inches of last season's growth.

Sweetshrub *Calycanthus floridus*

TAKE A LOOK Unusual-shaped late-spring flowers have a sweet fragrance. Preferring part shade or full sun, sweetshrub can grow 5 to 10 ft. tall and wide. Sweetshrub is cold-hardy in USDA zones 4 to 9 and heat-tolerant in AHS zones 9 to 1.

GROW MORE FLOWERS Thin out a few of the oldest, thickest stems each spring. If sweetshrub grows too tall, shorten some of the tallest stems to force more side growth, too. These new side branches will produce more flowers.

Vanhoutte spirea *Spiraea xvanhouttei*

TAKE A LOOK An elegant late-spring-bloomer, it can become a tangle with flowers only at the tips of the branches. Growing 5 to 8 ft. tall and 6 to 10 ft. wide, it tolerates full sun to part shade. Vanhoutte spirea is cold-hardy in USDA zones 3 to 9 and heat-tolerant in AHS zones 9 to 1.

GROW MORE FLOWERS Every year or two, thin out up to a third of the oldest, thickest stems. A fountain of white is what you're aiming for, so shorten back tall stems that are sticking straight up. That will force them to branch more and arch better.

Witchhazel *Hamamelis xintermedia*

TAKE A LOOK Fragrant witchhazel flowers are small so they're best enjoyed up close. Plant this shrub in part to full shade. Cultivars bloom from late winter to early spring and can grow 6 to 20 ft. tall and 6 to 15 ft. wide. All are cold-hardy in USDA zones 5 to 8 and heat-tolerant in AHS zones 8 to 1.

GROW MORE FLOWERS Relax! Witchhazel will bloom fine with absolutely no pruning. But if you must, only remove a branch here and there. You don't want to create a dense tangle of branches or you won't be able to see the flowers.

BASICS | SMART GARDENING

Make a small depression for each seed with a pencil.

Tap the tray to settle the seeds.

PHOTOS: Doug Appleby

start perennials from seed and save money

Botanical Names

Hardy hibiscus
Hibiscus moscheutos

Lavender
Lavandula angustifolia

Purple coneflower
Echinacea purpurea

Want a lot of plants for a little money? Start seeds. Before you dismiss the idea as too much hassle, check out my guide at right. I'll show you the easiest plants to start, and give you a few tips to make even the most challenging seeds take off faster and more reliably. I've grown thousands of seedlings over the years and have learned quite a bit in the process. The most common problems, sowing seeds too deeply and overwatering, are often the easiest to overcome. Let me share my tips. □

— *Marcia A. Leeper*

An easy start

Some seeds are so easy, they almost start themselves: I don't even bother planting more than one seed in a cell. Purple coneflowers and many other perennials will even bloom the first year if you start them in late winter or early spring.

I simply make a small indentation with a pencil in each cell, then drop the seed into my moistened, sterile seed-starting mix. I don't cover the seeds with soil, but see how I'm gently tapping the tray in the photo above? This way a little loose soil drifts over the top of each seed. It gives the seed a little light, but not too much, and allows air to reach the seed, too.

You can see them start to grow roots before they send up leaves. Even though it's tempting, don't try to poke the roots deeper into the soil. They'll find their own way, and leaves will soon appear. Keep the seed-starting medium moist, but not wet, and you should see seedlings emerging before a week is up. Harden them off to outdoor temperatures and plant anytime after they are 3 to 4 inches tall.

PLANTS TO TRY

These perennials all germinate quickly. Once they're up, just keep them moist.

Blanket flower *Gaillardia* ×*grandiflora*
Tickseed *Coreopsis* spp.
Shasta daisy *Leucanthemum* ×*superbum*
Rudbeckia *Rudbeckia* spp.

A few shakes with a small piece of sandpaper is all it takes to rough up hibiscus' seed coat.

A tough coat to crack

Sometimes a seed needs a little help to germinate more quickly and reliably. Hardy hibiscus seeds have a tough coating that can make them take what seems like forever to germinate. And if they sit in damp seed-starting mix too long, the seeds can get moldy and rot. Help them get up and growing quickly by scarifying, or roughing up, the hard seed coat.

In the photo above I'm dropping the seeds into a jar with a piece of medium-grit sandpaper. Then I closed the lid and gave it a few shakes. This took just enough of the hard surface off so moisture from the seed-starting mix could penetrate into the embryo and get it growing. Another way to soften up a seed coat is to soak it in water. Just a few hours will do the trick for most hard-coated seeds, but soaking time varies, so check the seed packet for any specific recommendations.

PLANTS TO TRY

Each one of these plants will germinate better if you scarify the seed coat.

Hollyhock *Alcea rosea*
Lupine *Lupinus* spp.
Mallow *Malva sylvestris*
Baptisia *Baptisia australis*

Constant vigilance

Finally, there are some seeds that don't just need a *little* help: They need *a lot* of help. Lavender can be finicky. Here's what I do to get mine off to a good start. First, lavender seeds are so tiny they look like dust. I can never tell how many seeds I'm planting, so I make a small depression in each cell of a pack and just sprinkle a little "dust" into it. I don't cover the seeds but keep the medium moist, just like I do when I'm starting any seeds.

The first two leaves, the *cotyledons*, sprout, then the first set of true leaves. Once the lavender seedlings have true leaves, I carefully scoop the clump out with a spoon and move it into a cell pack of potting mix. Most plants grow happily in seed-starting mix for quite a while, but lavender hates being wet, so I like to move it into potting mix. It doesn't hold as much moisture as seed-starting mix does, and I don't water until the potting mix is dry. Check out the difference between the two above.

When the seedlings grow a few leaves, you can start thinning. Don't pull, though. So you don't damage roots, use scissors or small pruners to snip all but the best-looking seedling out of a clump. As the seedlings grow, they'll look tall and skinny, and have little curly tops. Pinch the curly tops out to get the lavender to grow bushy.

Start seeds in moist seed-starting mix.
Once they're growing well, move your seedlings into drier potting mix.

Thin seedlings to one plant per cell.
Pinch out stretchy tops to encourage a bushy habit.

PLANTS TO TRY

Delphinium *Delphinium* spp. Buy seeds packed for current year — fresh seeds germinate best; germinate with no lights
Lily *Lilium* spp. Place the seed packet in a plastic bag and refrigerate. Each species needs cold treatment for a different length of time.
Columbine *Aquilegia* spp. Slow to germinate. Refrigerating seeds for a month before planting can help.

BASICS | SMART GARDENING

Everything you need to know to grow plants like a pro.

Success! with Bare-Root Perennials

Botanical Names

Asparagus
Asparagus officinalis
Clematis
Clematis hybrids
Daylily
Hemerocallis hybrids
Four o'clocks
Mirabilis jalapa
Hosta *Hosta* hybrids
Phlox *Phlox* hybrids

Have you ever opened a box of perennials that you ordered and thought that they were dead? I did the first time I bought bare-root perennials. Fortunately, I had a friend with mail-order experience to reassure me: Bare-root perennials are actually dormant, so they're shipped without soil and don't always have foliage. I like buying bare-root because it's economical and I can find varieties that aren't at the local nursery. Hostas and daylilies are two of the most common plants sold this way, but you can find a lot of others, too. Check out "Where to find bare-root perennials" below for some good sources.

Once you have the plants, here's how to get bare-root perennials off to a fantastic start.

HOW DOES IT LOOK? As soon as your plants arrive, whether they're from a mail-order nursery or the store, open the package and look over the contents. You'll probably see a bunch of tangled roots. "Get to the root of things" at right shows that even the healthy ones may not be pretty. Healthy roots are plump and solid-feeling and may or may not have green top growth. Don't worry if a few roots or stems are broken. You can trim those back to healthy tissue and the plant will be just fine.

Keep an eye out for moldy, rotten or shriveled roots. Too much moisture can cause rot, which results in plant material that's soft or smelly. You might also notice mold. The gray or white stuff isn't anything to worry about. But fuzzy blue mold indicates rot, and you might as well toss the plant.

Even with good packing material, plants that sit too long or get too hot will dry out. So if your order looks flaky and dry or feels light and hollow, you have a dud.

We've all seen those displays in the big box stores selling bare-root hostas, clematis and others. They can be a good buy, but make sure to get your favorites early. The longer they sit in a warm store, the drier those roots are going to get. And since the plants are usually sealed in a bag and packed with peat moss, it's hard to tell what you're getting.

If there's a problem with your order, hang on to the plants and your receipt and get in touch with the place you purchased them from right away. They can walk you through whatever return or refund process they have.

NOW WHAT? It's time to get on with the business of planting. If you don't have time now, get the plants back into their original packing material and seal it up. Store the whole thing for up to a week in your refrigerator crisper, where it will stay cool and slightly humid. A large order is hard to get in the fridge but an unheated garage or porch will work, too, as long as it stays between 33 and 40 degrees. Now you might be wondering, "How in the world do I get these plants to grow?" Good question. Turn the page to find out.

WHERE TO FIND bare-root perennials

So where do you get bare-root perennials? Big box stores carry them in early spring, or check with a local nursery. They may be willing to order for you if you let them know early and can order a large enough quantity. But you'll also get good selection and product from mail-order nurseries, such as:

Busse Gardens
www.bussegardens.com
800-544-3192. *Catalog $3*

Jung
www.jungseed.com
800-297-3123. *Catalog free*

GET TO THE ROOT OF THINGS

Are you wondering whether that package of bare-root perennials is really going to grow? Look over this collection of good and bad roots so you'll know if what you bought is worth the trouble.

Good to go These asparagus have plump roots and are ready to go into the ground.

— Roots

Crown

Growth

Packaging matters Good packaging is important. It keeps the roots from drying out during shipping. The wood chips in this order of daylilies were still moist and the roots were in good condition.

Dried out These pale-looking phlox got too dry as they sat in the store. They look shriveled and feel flaky and lightweight. Don't bother potting up roots like these.

Crown

Growth

Dry crown

Good growth? Don't worry about the funny-looking new growth on these four o'clocks. They'll look better once you get them in some soil and light.

This white or gray is just surface mold, which isn't a problem. However, fuzzy blue mold is. It causes rot, and more than likely the plant won't survive.

Where is it? It's difficult to see what you're getting with bagged bare-root plants, especially if the bag is opaque like this one. These clematis were so small and desiccated, it was hard to find them. Once potted, they didn't grow.

Roots

www.GardenGateMagazine.com   the YEAR IN GARDENING   259

GET THOSE ROOTS GROWING

Watch our *video* on planting bare-root perennials.

You can pot up bare-root perennials or plant them directly in the ground. It all depends on the situation. Either way, you're going to want to check the plant over for any broken or damaged roots. The daylily in photo 1 had a few broken roots, so I pruned them off. Leaving a dead root to rot on the plant offers an easy place for disease to take hold. Crown rot is one of the biggest problems you might face when starting bare-root perennials. I'll tell you more about it in "Crown rot" below.

Next, soak the roots in a bucket of water. I added a few drops of fish emulsion fertilizer in photo 2. I think it gives plants a boost to start growing.

Pot 'em up

The most common reason for potting up bare-root plants is because the weather and the soil are still too cold for them to go outside. But you might also want to baby an expensive or temperamental plant by closely controlling the moisture and light levels. Or maybe it's summer already and hot temperatures would be a big shock for your young plant. Growing it in a pot in a cool, shady spot for a while might help ensure its success.

Let me show you the best way to get plants going in a nursery pot. Then check out our Web extra video for even more help.

GET A GOOD MIX When it's time to plant, make sure to use a soilless potting *mix*, not soil. Most mixes are made of sphagnum, peat and perlite, which drain well. While getting too dry is a problem for packaged plants, rotting is the biggest concern once they're planted. So at this point, it's better to have dry soil than wet soil.

PLANTING TIME While your plant is soaking in the bucket, get a nursery pot that's a little larger than the root mass so there's room for roots to grow. Choose a pot that's big enough that you don't have to bend the roots to get it to fit. Now fill the pot part way with the potting mix and tap the bottom on the work surface to settle it. Then add the plant, fill the pot the rest of the way and tap it again to settle. I planted the daylily in photo 3 so the crown (that's the spot where the roots and green growth come together) is right at soil level. If it's set too low, water can pool there and the crown will rot.

Don't worry about yellow leaves like the ones below. That's normal — the plant just didn't get enough light in storage or shipping. It will green up in a week or so. Water your new perennial until water runs through the holes in the bottom of the pot. To firm the mix around the roots, wait 20 minutes and water again. Use a watering can with a rose for a gentle flow that doesn't wash the soil away. Remember, you don't

Crown rot

Symptoms of crown rot vary, but generally plant growth is stunted and the leaves and crown turn brown or mushy. You need to get rid of these fungus-infected plants, but the tricky part is where. Compost piles don't get hot enough to kill the fungus, and you shouldn't bury the plant because that might spread the problem. So if your city allows, send the plant away in the trash or burn it. Since crown rot fungus spreads by pieces of root or infected organic material, scrape all the soil off the tools and back into the area where the infected plant was growing. Then clean the tools with soap and water. You can still plant there, but choose another perennial or shrub instead, as fungi tend to be host-specific.

1 Trim broken roots to prevent disease.

2 Soak roots in water for an hour.

3 Make sure the crown is at soil level to avoid rot.

want the plant to rot so there's no need to water again until you see green growth sprouting.

POTTED PLANTS Once your plant is potted up, it needs a place to grow. In spring, if temperatures are still around freezing, keep it inside where it's cool, 60 degrees or so. Avoid air vents that can dry out potting mix and foliage too quickly. A sunny windowsill should provide enough light, even if there aren't any leaves yet. Usually within a couple of weeks you'll see new green growth, so you can start watering with a weekly dose of fish fertilizer or a half-strength solution of balanced liquid fertilizer. When there's vigorous growth on top, your plant is ready to go into the ground.

Once the soil is warm and dry enough to work, your plant can go outside. Give it a sheltered shady spot to start with so sun and wind don't damage the new leaves.

In the ground

Tough plants like daylilies and hostas won't mind if you take them from the box and plant them in the ground, as along as all chance of frost is past. I planted the daylily in photo 4 directly in the garden last spring. This process is similar to potting up, but there are a few differences. Let me show you.

GET DIGGING Clean up and soak the plants, just as you do before potting up. While the plants are soaking, dig a hole a little wider than the root mass of the plant you're putting in the ground. Notice how I made a mound of soil in the center of the hole in photo 4? That gives the plant support and a place to spread out the roots. Water the empty hole before you plant to help settle the soil. Then place the plant on the mound and make sure the crown is even with the soil's surface. If the crown is too low, it can rot. Refill the hole with soil as I'm doing in photo 5. Now it's time to water. I like to use a watering can with a rose like the one in photo 6 so the soil isn't washed away.

AFTER CARE Keep your new perennial going strong by watering it about once a week if it doesn't rain — more often if it's hot. Even sun perennials do better with a little shelter from the hottest part of the day for a few weeks until they get established. Place a laundry basket over the top of the plant for a few hours in mid- to late afternoon each day. Once new growth starts, scratch compost into the soil a few inches out from the crown to feed the plant.

Pests aren't any more of a problem than they are with other plants. So keep an eye out and treat accordingly. Some plants, such as coral bells or this daylily, will take right off. Others, such as hostas, may sit for a while. They're just slower to get established, so be patient. It won't be long, though, and those humble brown roots will be great-looking new plants. □

— *Sherri Ribbey*

BASICS | SMART GARDENING

fall is for planting
cool-season vegetables!

Gardeners are fearless. The weather forecast says cold temperatures are on the way, but to Barbara Damrosch, author of *The Garden Primer*, the gardening season is far from over. There's still time to grow a few tasty vegetables — no matter how small an area you have to work with. Here are her tips on crops you can sow from seed in early fall and still reap a harvest.

WHY PLANT IN FALL? Although they need a spot in full sun, there are plenty of vegetables that don't need lots of heat. Spinach, lettuce and radishes, among others, grow best in the warm days and cool nights of early fall. And, unlike spring when the ground is cool, the soil in your garden is nice and warm — perfect for a fast sprout. However, be aware that as the daytime temperatures fall, the growth on fall crops may slow down.

Another advantage is that there are usually fewer insect pests as the temperature goes down. Cold-blooded insects are entering winter dormancy. Even most weeds are growing more slowly. In general, fall crops will have fewer weeds to compete with for nutrients.

You may have less watering, too. While fall crops do need moisture, water doesn't evaporate out of the soil as quickly as it does in the blazing heat of summer. And speaking of heat, it's over. You'll want to get back into the garden and enjoy the cool weather, too.

RECIPE FOR SUCCESS Look for veggies that stay low to the ground. They take advantage of the radiant warmth stored in the soil. After a sunny day, even as the air temperature drops, the soil will stay warm longer into the evening.

At right are five of Barbara's favorite fall crops and her best tips for growing them. You'll find how deeply to sow the seeds, how long before you'll see sprouts and about how many days before you can harvest. However, growing may take a bit longer in fall than in spring. Why? Although seeds often germinate more quickly in warm soil than they do in cool spring soil, dropping air temperatures may make it take longer for the crop to mature.

Always read catalogs or the seed packets to see how many days a particular cultivar will take before it's ready to harvest. To find out when to plant for fall, a good rule of thumb is to count back about that many days from your average first frost date to start them. The chart below left can help. For example, in USDA zone 5, the first frost usually arrives in the middle of October. Radishes need about 21 days to reach harvest. That means you can sow radish seeds in late September. But don't be afraid to start later…you could end up with a longer than average fall and lots of extra produce. For the price of a few seeds, it's worth the gamble.

KEEP THEM COOL However, don't worry *too* much about frost. Unlike tender annuals, such as tomatoes, once these five crops are up and growing, they can take some cold. They won't grow as much in cold weather, but all of them will keep producing until the ground begins to freeze. That's usually at least several weeks after a frost hits. But before that, if you want to keep your plants warmer, and growing faster and longer into the fall, cover them up at night. You'll find some tips on the best way to protect your plants in "Cold cover-up" at right.

Winter is on the way. No matter where you live, the temperature is getting noticeably cooler. But that doesn't mean you have to stop gardening, or eating tasty homegrown veggies!

— *Jim Childs*

AVERAGE FIRST FROST

USDA cold-hardiness zone	Average first frost date
1	July 15
2	August 15
3	September 15
4	September 15
5	October 15
6	October 15
7	October 15
8	November 15
9	December 15
10	December 15
11	No frost

Find your zone at www.GardenGate Magazine.com/zones.

Spinach Sow spinach seeds a bit more thickly for a fall crop than you would in spring. If the soil is still very warm, it may reduce germination. And keep the soil moist, either by extra watering or spreading an organic mulch as soon as the seeds are up and growing. Pinch off a few leaves to eat when they're just an inch or two long. Or wait and cut the whole rosette later. Another benefit of mulch is that it keeps the leaves cleaner.

SOW ½ in. deep
GERMINATION 7 to 14 days
HARVEST 25 to 35 days

Leaf lettuce Lettuce seeds won't germinate if the temperatures are in the 80s. And later, if the weather turns hot and you see your lettuce wilting, a piece of row cover over the seedlings will cast some cooling shade. The board in the upper right of the photo above is propped up on the sunny side of the row.

Fall is ideal for baby lettuce leaves. Pluck a few from the edges when they're about 2 in. long. Or wait until all of the leaves are larger and cut the entire plant at the main stem.

SOW ¼ to ½ in. deep
GERMINATION 7 to 14 days
HARVEST 28 days

Radish Radishes are fast! That makes them perfect for fall planting. Whether you choose a classic round cultivar or oval-shaped 'French Breakfast' in the photo above, they'll mature in 21 to 26 days. If the larvae of root maggots feast on your spring radishes, plant a fall crop. This pesky critter isn't active at this time of year so you won't have to share the harvest. Just make sure to keep the soil moist. Your radishes will have a much better flavor if you do.

SOW ½ in. deep
GERMINATION 4 to 12 days
HARVEST 21 to 26 days

Tatsoi Not familiar with this veggie? You can use it raw like lettuce or cooked like spinach. Most folks think it has a light "cabbagey" flavor. Maybe you don't want to devote lots of space to something you're not familiar with. If so, sprinkle a few seeds in with another leaf crop, such as lettuce.

Harvest by pinching off a few leaves here and there or waiting until there's a dense rosette like the one in the photo. Then you can either cut or pull the entire plant.

SOW ¼ in. deep
GERMINATION 7 to 14 days
HARVEST 21 days

Beets For a fast start, soak the seeds. Just a few hours will help, or overnight is better. Sow them an inch apart and keep the bed moist. Thin the sprouts by pulling them out of the soil, or snip them off with scissors. Tender young sprouts like the ones in the photo above will make a tasty salad. As the beets mature, keep them watered — if the soil gets too dry, the roots may end up being hard and woody.

SOW ½ in. deep
GERMINATION 5 days
HARVEST 30 days for full size greens; 50 days for baby roots

COLD COVER-UP

During the day, soil stores heat from the sun. As the sun goes down and the air temperature drops, heat leaves the soil. A fabric covering can hold that warmth closer to your plants when it gets cold. Even a sheet or piece of floating row cover — available at garden centers or www.gardeners.com — will work. For the best protection, keep the fabric from touching the plants. If it gets wet it can transmit the cold from the air to the leaf and damage it. In the photo below, the cover is supported by an overturned wire basket. To capture the most heat, put the covering on just as the sun goes down in the evening. Be sure to remove it after the sun comes up.

What's Your Fall Garden IQ?

Most of us are creatures of habit. I admit that once the calendar's page turns to October, I'm compelled to start checking things off my garden's to-do list. But then I started brushing up and learned that most of the things I did in fall to clean up or tuck in really should have more to do with the weather than with a specific date. I discovered that by making a few simple adjustments in timing or technique, I could help my garden grow better! And not everything means more work or time — some of these improvements are actually easier and take less time!

If you, too, find yourself racing through your to-do list every fall, you should take our quiz. It'll help you decide if you're tackling your fall tasks at the right time and in the right way. You might even find some new ways to save time and effort! □

— *Kristin Beane Sullivan*

Botanical Names

Ash *Fraxinus* spp.
Bermudagrass *Cynodon* spp.
Boxwood *Buxus* spp.
Crabapple *Malus* hybrids
Kentucky bluegrass *Poa pratensis*
Locust *Robinia* spp.
Maple *Acer* spp.
St. Augustinegrass *Stentaphrum secundatum*
Sycamore *Platanus occidentalis*
Tall fescue *Festuca arundinacea*

What's the best way to mulch fall-planted perennials?

A Tuck them under a heavy layer of mulch the first chance you get.
B Once your first frost hits, mulch them.
C Wait until the ground freezes (or at least gets about as cold as it will get).

Wait. Cover them too early and they won't have a chance to harden off slowly to colder temperatures. It's not necessarily the cold that damages vulnerable plants, it's the cold/warm/cold cycles that sometimes happen in winter. So wait until the soil is good and cold, then mulch so it stays that way until spring. Shredded leaves, wood mulch and straw are all good choices. When you start to see new growth next year, pull the mulch back so your perennials don't have to fight their way through the cover. (But keep some handy so you can toss it back on plants to protect them from a late cold snap.) *The answer? C.*

How should you tackle the leaves that fall from your big maple tree?

A Rake every last one up as soon as you can.
B Rake them off your lawn but don't go too crazy in the perennial beds.
C Leave them alone. What the wind doesn't blow away will be good mulch!

Large leaves that mat down, like those of maples or sycamores, should come off the lawn because they can suffocate your grass over the winter. If you have some leaves in your perennial borders, it's not a big deal, but knee-deep is too much. Small-leafed trees, such as ash, locust or crabapple, aren't such a worry. Their leaves will probably break down before they have a chance to smother anything. Want to use your leaves as mulch? Chop up the big ones with the lawn mower or a shredder. *The answer? B.*

ILLUSTRATIONS: Mavis Augustine Torke
PHOTOS: Doug Appleby (1, 2, 3)

What's the last tool you should put away after fall cleanup?

A Hose
B Rake
C Shovel

It's true that in fall and winter plants don't dry out as quickly as they do in summer, but they still may need water. Check the soil and if it isn't frozen and feels dry, you should water, whether it's October or January. In fact, if your ground doesn't freeze, you probably shouldn't even put your hose away! But be sure to disconnect and empty the hose after each use when a freeze is a possibility. Water freezing inside the hose could cause it to burst. *The answer? A.*

How can you make sure your lawn looks passable without putting much effort into it?

A Better stick with the program: Feed in early spring, early summer, late summer and late fall.
B Put down a slow-release fertilizer once a year in fall and let it do its work all year.
C Feed in late spring and summer.

Long and slow feeding is a good way to keep a healthy lawn without much effort. The issue is, do you have a cool-season grass or a warm-season grass? Cool-season grasses, such as Kentucky bluegrass and tall fescue, stop growing but don't turn completely brown in winter. They're what most Northern lawns have. Warm-season grasses, such as Bermudagrass and St. Augustinegrass, are most common in the South, and they turn a straw color in winter.

To feed a cool-season grass just once, do it in fall after the grass has gone dormant. This will keep the grass green later in fall and let it green up earlier in spring. Feed warm-season grasses once in late spring and again in summer to keep the growth going.

If you have a healthy lawn, weed killers may not be necessary — so if you can find a fertilizer without the weed killer, choose that. *The answer? Cool-season grasses: B; warm-season grasses: C.*

You found a great deal on a boxwood but discover it's rootbound. Was this a bad purchase?

A Yes. Take it back to the garden center.
B This never happens to you — you pull all plants from their pots at the nursery to check their roots before you buy them.
C No, it'll be OK if you loosen them up.

Any of these answers may be right. If the roots of any perennial, tree or shrub are so tightly packed that you can't even find soil, take the plant back if you can. But roots that are circling inside the pot aren't *necessarily* a deal killer if the plant is healthy. In photo 1, this boxwood's roots are circling inside the pot, but I was able to loosen them. If I'd left them alone, they'd probably continue to grow that way, and the plant could eventually strangle itself.

Before you loosen a root ball, be sure the soil and roots are moist. This will keep roots pliable and easier to work with. I poked my fingers into the bottom of this root ball and teased the side roots out with my hands. As I worked, some pieces broke off. See the pile of debris in photos 2 and 3? That's no big deal. Most of the roots are still intact. You can even make three or four vertical slices around the outside to loosen the roots if you need to. You want the plant to have the shaggy look in photo 3 when you're finished. *The answer? A, B or C.*

FALL GARDEN IQ (continued)

The tree's successfully planted. Should you mulch it in?

A No. It wasn't mulched in the container, why does it need mulch in the ground?
B Yes, pile it up around the collar to protect the trunk and roots.
C Yes, spread a layer over the roots.

A 2- to 4-inch layer of organic mulch spread over the trees' roots is plenty to keep roots insulated from the freeze-thaw cycle that damages plant roots. Be sure to start about 6 inches away from the tree's trunk so you don't invite pests. How do you know if you're covering the roots? If it's a new tree, you'll just be covering the planting hole area — which, by the way, should be twice as wide as the size of the root ball. It isn't uncommon to see "volcanoes" of mulch piled up around young trees in the winter. This is a good way to attract rodents and insect damage, but not such a great way to protect the tree. In fact, if voles are a problem in your area, you may consider skipping the mulch altogether — they love to tunnel in soft mulch. *The answer? C.*

Do put a 2- to 4-in. layer of organic mulch over a newly planted tree's roots to protect them from winter damage. Start 6 in. away from the trunk to keep pests at bay.

Don't pile mulch against the tree's trunk. It attracts insects and gnawing rodents to make a home in or eat your new tree.

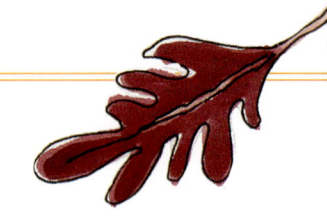

At the sales counter, the clerk asks you if you need some bone meal to feed the bulbs you bought. Do you?

A Yes. It's the traditional way to feed bulbs.
B No. It only attracts squirrels and other digging pests.
C No. You're growing tulips as annuals.

Bone meal used to be a common bulb food, but now there are lots more options. And it does seem to attract rodents and digging dogs. Bone meal only contains phosphorous, not any other nutrients that bulbs need. And putting fertilizer in the hole with the bulb can be risky because there's a chance the fertilizer could burn the roots. The most earth-friendly way to feed perennial bulbs is to topdress with compost in fall and spring. If your flowers aren't blooming like they should, you might want to put a slow-release bulb fertilizer on top of the soil in fall. That's when the roots are most actively taking up nutrients. Oh, and if you're growing them as annuals, don't bother. *The answer? B or C.*

The bulbs start showing up in the garden center around Labor Day. Isn't that too early to plant?

A No. If they're in the garden center, it must be the right time for my area.
B Yes. Wait until after the first frost.
C Yes. October 15 is the time to plant bulbs.

The fact is that roots don't start forming until the ground temperature reaches 50 degrees. Plant too early and your bulbs may rot with fall rains. So wait until at least your first frost, or a couple of weeks of night temperatures of about 40 degrees F. Keep in mind that small bulbs, such as snowdrops or fritillarias, can go in a bit earlier because they may dry out in storage.

It's all right to buy early for good selection, just store them with good air circulation. Open up the bags and keep them in a cool spot in your house. *The answer? B, for most bulbs.*

Planting a big tulip bulb at three times its height seems like a lot of work. Is it really necessary?

A No. The bulbs' roots will eventually pull the bulb to the correct depth anyway.
B Yes. It protects the bulb from cold temperatures and digging pests.
C Yes. Most tend to perennialize better when planted deeply.

Deep planting will help a tulip get through the winter better in cold climates. And pests like voles and squirrels tend to dig only in the top 3 to 4 inches of soil. So deeper planting does help with both of those problems. If you don't have either of these issues and you're just growing your bulbs as annuals, you can probably get by with skimping on planting depth.

But here's an interesting additional fact: It helps them perennialize better, too. After a few years, tulips (except the Darwin hybrids) love to break apart into daughter bulbs, which won't be big enough to flower. The deeper you plant them, the greater the soil compression on the bulb and the less able they are to break apart and reproduce themselves. This means that the original bulb will last longer and keep sending up its beautiful flowers. So if you can't dig an 8- to 10-inch-deep hole, don't worry, just pile soil on top of the planting area to make up the difference! *The answer? B and C.*

A friend tells you how much she admired your foxtail lilies earlier this year. You have plenty to share. What should you do?

A Tell her when the clump starts to look overcrowded, she'll be the first one you call to get divisions.
B Tell her to come back in the spring and you'll give her a division.
C Get out the spade and start digging.

Fall is a great time to divide spring-blooming perennials, such as foxtail lily (*Eremurus* spp.) but with a few qualifiers: First, make sure the day's not a hot one, and second, you shouldn't expect the ground to freeze for 4 to 6 weeks yet. Either of these circumstances could make for a tough transition.

But there's no need to wait until your perennials suffer to divide them. If they're spectacular now, there's a good chance they'll be past spectacular in the next few years. Take pre-emptive action. You'll know when plants start to decline and need division — they'll generally look worse in the center than at the edges, sometimes even dying out in the middle.

Although in general, I divide spring-bloomers in early fall and fall-bloomers in spring, both are fine for most plants. Bulbs (like foxtail lily) and fleshy-rooted perennials really do best if you divide them in fall. *The answer? C.*

DIVIDE THESE PLANTS IN EARLY FALL
- Foxtail lily (*Eremurus* spp.)
- Iris (*Iris* spp.)
- Moss phlox (*Phlox subulata*)
- Oriental poppy (*Papaver orientale*)
- Peony (*Paeonia* spp.)
- Pulmonaria (*Pulmonaria* spp.)
- Sweet woodruff (*Galium odoratum*)

BASICS | PROBLEM SOLVER

do **home remedies** really work?

We've all read those handy tips about using do-it-yourself home remedies for the garden. They're often made with things that you're likely to have around the house, such as dish soap or garlic. You've probably even read some of them in *Garden Gate*! But do these things really work? Jeff Gillman, a horticulture professor at the University of Minnesota, started to wonder. So he decided to find out which remedies work, and why. He tried dozens of the concoctions himself. Then he wrote *The Truth About Garden Remedies*. I thought his work was interesting so I asked him to share some information with us.

It turns out that while some remedies don't live up to the hype, others can be dangerous to the environment or even your health if you use them incorrectly. The remedies in this chart are those that Jeff found really *did* work, although even those may have a few drawbacks. For example, have you ever used hot peppers to repel insects? It works great, especially against whiteflies and mites, and may even help keep deer and rabbits at bay. But don't touch your eyes after you've been handling them or the burning sensation will remind you why they're called "hot peppers." For more details on these and a few other do-it-yourself recipes, check out the chart at right. It contains seven items you have around the house that you can use to keep your garden happy and healthy. And make sure to read "Don't use these!" for a few home products you *don't* want to use.

The home remedies here are just the beginning. Get your own copy of Jeff's book at www.GardenGateStore.com so you can find the real science behind growing healthy plants.

— *Sherri Ribbey*

Star ingredient

BUTTERMILK
[used as foliar fertilizer]
The idea High-protein foods are high in nitrogen. As the milk decomposes, it releases nitrogen to the plant.

EGGSHELLS
[used as fertilizer]
The idea Eggshells contain calcium, which is released as they break down in the soil.

DISH SOAP
[used as insecticide]
The idea The soap dissolves an insect's waxy coating, causing it to dehydrate and die.

GARLIC
[used as insect repellent]
The idea Garlic contains a couple of compounds that kill or repel insects.

HOT PEPPERS — JEFF'S FAVORITE
[used as insect repellent]
The idea If the peppers are hot to human taste, it will be too hot for the insects, too.

MILK [used as fungicide] — JEFF'S FAVORITE
The idea Researchers think that lactoferrin (a protein found in milk) deters fungus.

MOUTHWASH
[used as fungicide]
The idea It kills the smelly stuff in your mouth so it should kill the fungus on the leaf, too.

Will it work?	Is it worth using?	Recipe
Yes, but it's expensive to use in this manner. Plus, it doesn't have as many nutrients as commercial fertilizers.	Sure, why not? It's a good way to get rid of leftovers, but on a regular basis you'll get better value for your money with commercial fertilizers.	1 part buttermilk to 4 parts water. Spray 1 to 2 cups on the leaves of a medium-sized plant or shrub.
Yes. Crushed shells do add small amounts of calcium, as well as phosphorus, potassium and magnesium. They add sodium, too, but not enough to harm the plants.	Go for it! You were just going to throw them away anyway. **✱ Add them to your compost pile, too!**	Crush four or five eggshells per plant and mix them into the potting mix or garden soil once a year. Or pour 2 cups of cooled water from hard-boiled eggs onto the soil every week or two.
Yes, it works on aphids, mites, thrips and others. It's less effective on caterpillars and beetles. The problem is the soap can also strip away the waxy coating on leaves and damage or kill the plant.	This one's iffy. Dish soap works, but each batch from the manufacturer can be different. Even tiny variations can result in burned foliage. Commercial brands of insecticidal soap are more reliable.	1 Tbsp. per gallon of water. Apply whenever you see pests (but do it in early morning or on a cloudy day to avoid burning leaves). Test each batch on a leaf or two, and after a couple of days, check the foliage for damage.
Yes. It's most effective against whiteflies, aphids and beetles. **✱ The smell can last up to a week in the garden and repels deer at the same time.**	Yes, if you don't mind the smell.	Blend one garlic bulb into 2 cups of water, strain and spray on leaves and stems. Thoroughly cover both upper and lower parts of the leaves and stems to keep insects away.
Yes. The active ingredient, capsaicin, can repel insects. Hot peppers work especially well on whiteflies and mites. **✱ If you add dish soap, prevent burning foliage by spraying early in the day or when it's cloudy.**	Definitely worth using. And a hot pepper repellent may even keep deer and rabbits from nibbling.	When insects show up, get out your blender. Add ½ to 2 cups of hot peppers to 2 cups of water, blend, strain and spray. Cover all parts of the leaves and stems. (Adding ¼ tsp. dish soap helps the spray stick to the leaves.)
Yes. But apply it before blackspot actually develops.	You bet! **✱ Whole, 1%, 2% — it all works.**	Thoroughly spray the upper and lower surfaces of the leaves with milk every week.
Yes. It's not as good as a commercial fungicide, but it works better than most homemade remedies against blackspot and powdery mildew.	It works, but you risk burning the foliage, and commercial fungicides do a good job without the worry.	Mix 1 cup of ethanol-containing mouthwash with 3 cups of water and spray weekly. Spray a small area first to be sure it won't damage the plant's foliage.

Don't use these!

When it comes to home remedies, some ideas sound good but don't really work. Here are a few products you should steer clear of.

SPONGES It seems to make sense — cut up a few inexpensive sponges, toss them in the potting mix, and they'll help hold water.

Why not? In Jeff's testing, the sponges didn't hold any more moisture than the potting medium, and they actually seemed to make the soil dry out more quickly.

BEER Beer is made of natural ingredients, so it must be good food for plants, right? Not really.

Why not? Beer does have carbohydrates, protein and a few trace minerals that plants like. But it also contains alcohol, which inhibits growth. So why does the alcohol in beer cause problems but the alcohol in mouthwash doesn't? An alcohol spray evaporates quickly, but when it's taken up by plant roots, it causes trouble.

TOBACCO Tobacco has been used as a home remedy to fight insects for years because it works. But there are some major drawbacks.

Why not? First, tobacco varies in potency so it's hard to get the formulation right. Too strong and it kills the insect *and* the plants. Second, the tobacco you use could be host to Tobacco Mosaic Virus (TMV). This is a deadly disease for peppers, tomatoes, geraniums and many other plants. The curing process for tobacco doesn't kill TMV. So spraying plants with tobacco can introduce a disease that's more of a problem than the insect you're trying to kill.

BASICS | PROBLEM SOLVER

Get these pests out of your garden now!

Spring Weed Alert

To everything there is a season — and that's as true of weeds as it is of lovely flowers. Like the annuals and perennials you carefully tend, weeds appear at specific times of year. Learn when to expect them and you're better prepared to identify and get rid of them.

CAST OF CHARACTERS Let's take a look at nine weeds that show up each spring. You'll find them in a wide variety of garden situations. Some invade areas that are worked up frequently, while others pop up in soil that's been undisturbed for several years. Most are annuals that sprout in spring, flower, set seed and die before summer. A few are "winter annuals" — they sprout in late summer or fall and overwinter as seedlings. Then when the weather warms enough in spring, they start growing again, set seed and soon die. The three weeds to the right are perennial; they're always there, just not showing off. But because of early fast growth or spring flowers, I've included them here.

All of these pests can be found throughout much of the United States and into Canada. And when it comes to getting rid of them, there's always more than one way to do it. Chemicals are effective and useful options. But, like many gardeners, if you want something organic, check out "Earth-friendly tips" below. While these methods may take more time and effort, they're safer for you and the environment. ☐

— *Jim Childs*

EARTH-FRIENDLY TIPS

There are lots of chemical weed killers out there. Selective ones take care of broadleaf weeds in a lawn without harming the grass. And nonselective herbicides kill everything. But what if you don't want to use chemicals?

ATTACK WITH ORGANICS Corn gluten, usually put down in spring at the rate of 10 to 20 pounds per thousand square feet, will prevent seeds from germinating. But like any preemergent herbicide, if you break the barrier it forms, seeds will still sprout. Look for corn gluten granules or powder at local garden centers.

Household vinegar will *sometimes* kill weeds, especially if you mix in a bit of dishwashing detergent to make it stick on the leaves longer. Apply vinegar in full sun on a hot day to get the best results. It's nonselective so don't spray it on plants you want to keep. I find it works best in cracks in sidewalks and patios. Be aware that many weeds can recover and will need a second or third application.

USE A LITTLE MUSCLE What's the safest, most effective organic way to get rid of weeds? Manual removal. In most of my flower beds, I like to get down on my hands and knees and use a soil knife or a hand hoe. Each lets me work close to stems and roots and neither one harms the environment or nearby plants.

Many perennial weeds resprout if you don't remove every piece of the root from the soil. The sturdy blade and serrated edge make a soil knife, in the top photo, great for deep roots.

For most annuals and biennials, I like to use a hand hoe, in the lower photo. It has a sharp blade to slice off weeds like this annual bluegrass just below the surface of the soil. Because you're not disturbing the soil much, you're not likely to turn up many weed seeds.

Soil knife

Hand hoe

Purchase the tools above at **www.GardenGateStore.com**

PERENNIAL WEEDS

Yellow woodsorrel
Oxalis stricta

WHAT IT LOOKS LIKE If yellow woodsorrel has something to lean on, it can grow to be 20 in. tall. But it's usually more mounding to sprawling. It has tiny yellow flowers almost all of the growing season. Each leaflet is shaped like a small heart.

WHERE YOU'LL FIND IT You'll find yellow woodsorrel in flower beds, lawns and even containers. It grows in most any kind of soil, but tends to be less aggressive in fertile soil. And it tolerates both sun and shade.

HOW YOU CAN GET RID OF IT The stems break easily, making it difficult to pull. But it's easy to hoe out the shallow roots, and large areas of it can also be controlled by herbicides. This perennial spreads by seeds and underground rhizomes.

GOOD TO KNOW Each leaflet folds up at night. When touched, the ripe seed pods explode to shoot the seeds great distances.

To get all of the roots out, pull yellow woodsorrel when the soil's moist.

Feathery seedheads are a good way to identify this weed in spring.

Crown vetch
Coronilla varia

WHAT IT LOOKS LIKE Crown vetch grows up to 2 ft. tall. It has a dense, sprawling habit with stems that can be 5 to 6 ft. long. Pink flowers are followed by 3-in.-long seed pods.

WHERE YOU'LL FIND IT You'll find this pest in full sun to part shade in rocky or rich soil. Once used to control erosion along roadways, this weed escaped and is forcing out native plants.

HOW YOU CAN GET RID OF IT Dig crown vetch out of established gardens or use a selective herbicide in turf areas. It's a perennial, so for the best control, apply herbicide in fall, before the leaves go dormant, and again in spring as the leaves emerge. Repeated mowing also keeps this weeds from producing seeds.

GOOD TO KNOW Although it's still being sold and planted, you do not want this near your garden. It can spread quickly with seeds, root and stem pieces, and it's tough to get rid of.

Foxtail barley
Hordeum jubatum

WHAT IT LOOKS LIKE Growing up to 3 ft. tall, this upright grass has wispy seedheads that look iridescent in the sunshine.

WHERE YOU'LL FIND IT Foxtail barley can grow almost anywhere with full sun and well-drained soil.

HOW YOU CAN GET RID OF IT Dig this perennial from the soil or apply a non-selective herbicide in the spring as the flower heads begin to show.

GOOD TO KNOW Foxtail barley spreads by seeds and roots. Each seed has wiry bristles with tiny barbs that grip onto clothing or fur to help it travel to new locations.

WINTER ANNUAL WEEDS

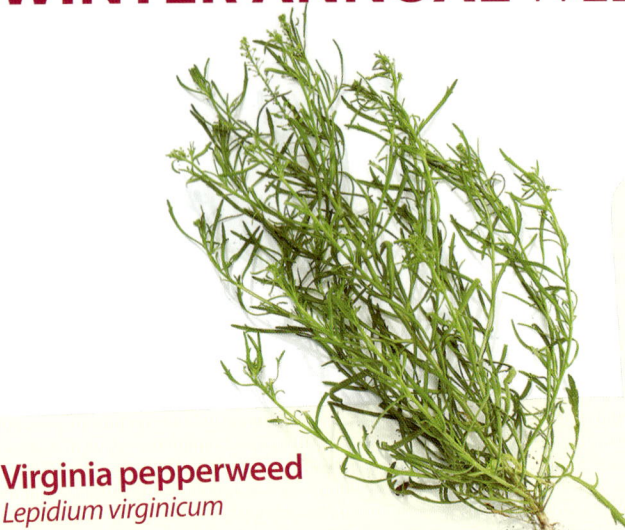

Virginia pepperweed
Lepidium virginicum

WHAT IT LOOKS LIKE Virginia pepperweed grows up to 24 in. tall, with an upright shape and lots of branches. The small white flowers are followed by flat round pods.

WHERE YOU'LL FIND IT You'll find this weed in perennial beds and shrub borders with full sun and dry soil, rarely in lawns.

HOW YOU CAN GET RID OF IT This winter annual is easy to hoe out or pull.

GOOD TO KNOW Seeds shoot out of the pods when raindrops hit them and can live in the soil for 30 years or more. Because of the narrow leaves, it's also called peppergrass.

These leaves get the seedling through the winter. As the flower stems stretch in spring you'll find narrow leaves.

Annual bluegrass
Poa annua

WHAT IT LOOKS LIKE The dense, low-spreading tufts of this fine-textured grass grow only 2 to 12 in. tall.

WHERE YOU'LL FIND IT This weed is found mainly in sunny, moist areas of flower beds or in lawns.

Shallow roots mean this weed is easy to pull.

HOW YOU CAN GET RID OF IT Apply preemergent herbicides to the lawn in the fall and again in the spring to keep this winter annual's seeds from germinating. In other garden areas, pull or hoe it out before the seeds form.

GOOD TO KNOW Annual bluegrass can produce viable seed 24 hours after the flower is pollinated. In the fall you'll spot small tufts like you see in this photo. In spring, as soon as the weather warms up, they resume growing and quickly start producing seeds.

Go after the fall growth of annual bluegrass and you'll have less to do in spring!

Field pennycress
Thlaspi arvense

WHAT IT LOOKS LIKE Upright branches sprout from a low rosette of leaves, growing 4 to 24 in. tall. It may have fibrous roots, a shallow taproot or both. Flat clusters of small white spring flowers quickly stretch into tall bottlebrushes lined with bulging disc-shaped seed pods.

WHERE YOU'LL FIND IT Field pennycress is usually found in vegetable and flower beds. It grows tallest in full sun and tolerates almost any type of soil.

HOW YOU CAN GET RID OF IT Hoeing or pulling is generally effective at getting rid of this winter annual. And most types of herbicides will help get field pennycress under control.

GOOD TO KNOW Seedlings overwinter as a small rosette before sending up flower stalks in spring.

This fall rosette of leaves disappears in spring. But the leaves along the stem of a mature plant look much the same.

PHOTO: Brent Isenberger (bluegrass)

ANNUAL AND BIENNIAL WEEDS

Pennsylvania pellitory
Parietaria pensylvanica

WHAT IT LOOKS LIKE Growing 6 to 18 in. tall, the underside of each leaf is slightly fuzzy. At first glance, the narrow upright form looks broader because Pennsylvania pellitory often grows in dense colonies.

WHERE YOU'LL FIND IT Although it prefers part shade, you'll find it in full sun if the soil never dries out.

HOW YOU CAN GET RID OF IT The shallow, fibrous roots are easy to pull. But herbicides are effective if you need to eradicate large stands of this annual.

GOOD TO KNOW The green flowers along the main stems have no petals and are barely noticeable. But it reseeds rampantly, especially in areas that are tilled annually. If you miss pulling a few weeds, red admiral butterfly caterpillars will enjoy eating the leaves.

The fleshy hollow, almost translucent, stems make this weed easy to identify.

Waterpod
Ellisia nyctelea

WHAT IT LOOKS LIKE The first thing you'll notice is that each leaf is deeply cut and pale green. Growing less than 12 in. tall, waterpod has a taproot. Pale blue to white flowers are about ¼ in. in diameter and are followed by rounded seed pods in late spring.

WHERE YOU'LL FIND IT It's usually in cultivated or lightly mulched areas, but rarely in lawns, in full sun to part shade.

HOW YOU CAN GET RID OF IT This annual's shallow tap root is easy to hoe out or pull.

GOOD TO KNOW Also known by the common name "Aunt Lucy," this native weed prefers fertile soils. The first spot you may find it is next to your compost pile.

Dig out this weed before you see flowers so it won't have a chance to set seed.

Dame's rocket
Hesperis matronalis

WHAT IT LOOKS LIKE Growing up to 5 ft. tall, but usually under 3 ft., it has an upright form with large straplike leaves that become progressively smaller toward the top of the stem. In late spring it blooms with fragrant lavender or white flowers.

WHERE YOU'LL FIND IT Often found in shrub and perennial borders, dame's rocket prefers undisturbed soil in full sun to part shade.

HOW YOU CAN GET RID OF IT A taproot makes pulling difficult, so dig it out or use an herbicide. This biennial spreads by seeds and roots.

GOOD TO KNOW Dame's rocket is often confused with garden phlox because of the similar flower clusters at the top of the stems. However, phlox flowers have five petals and dame's rocket flowers only have four.

BASICS | PROBLEM SOLVER

Don't let these nasty pests take over your garden!

9 Bugs to Stop Now!

Even if you could, you wouldn't want to destroy *all* the bugs in your garden. Most of them are harmless, and some even help your plants with pollinating or keeping other pests in check. That's why I'm not usually too concerned if a few of my plants have some holes in the leaves. I'll resort to pesticides for a particularly bad outbreak, but usually I just keep an eye on things, and most problems resolve themselves.

That said, when I come across one of the nine bugs I'm about to show you, I'm a little more vigilant. Why? When they show up just as hot weather hits, plants may already be stressed by heat, drought or because they've just put a lot of their energy into blooming. So they're especially vulnerable to attack.

Of course, I try to keep my plants as healthy as possible by improving the soil, watering deeply during dry spells and keeping weeds and debris to a minimum. This gives them the best shot at withstanding insect attacks. But sometimes that's not enough.

Here are nine hot-weather pests you're likely to run into, what plants you'll find them on and what to do when you spot them. I've given earth-friendly ways to deal with these pests, including organic means and natural predators, plus a few chemical controls, in some cases. The idea is to use the control that keeps the pests' damage at a level you're willing to live with, while doing the least amount of harm to the environment.

But not all scary-looking bugs are harmful. I'll also share three creepy-looking insects, found in nearly all of North America, that you will actually *want* to see in your garden. ☐

— Deborah Gruca

Aphid

FAVORITE PLANTS There are thousands of different aphid species, and most attack a specific kind of herbaceous or woody plant, such as rose, maple, juniper and apple or the zinnia at right.

WHAT'S THE DAMAGE? Aphids, like the orange adults here, pierce and suck out sap, especially on stems and tender new growth. This causes stunted growth and leaf curling, distortion and yellowing. The sticky honeydew aphids produce promotes the growth of sooty mold, a black fungus that forms on plants and nearby surfaces. They also spread viral diseases between plants.

WHAT'S THE PLAN? Don't overfertilize plants or you'll cause lots of lush new growth that aphids love. Knock them off with a strong jet of water or spray the insects thoroughly with insecticidal soap. Or prune off infested stems and dispose of them in the trash. Aphids can be controlled by parasitic wasps, lacewings and ladybugs, available from mail-order and online sources, such as www.gardensalive.com.

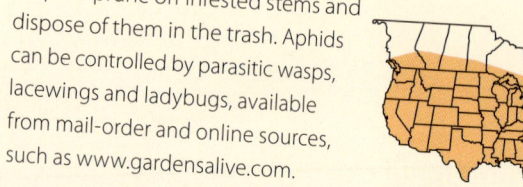

These aphids are orange, but they can also be yellow, green, white, black or even pink.

Scale

FAVORITE PLANTS More than 200 species of these sap-sucking insects attack many shrubs and trees (including evergreen, deciduous and fruit).

WHAT'S THE DAMAGE? Crawlers hatch in late spring and move around briefly before they start to suck sap from tender growth. They soon form the protective shells you see on the stem at right. Leaves turn yellow and drop. Usually damage is minimal for mature trees, but can stunt or kill young ones. Scale insects secrete sticky honeydew, which promotes sooty mold growth.

WHAT'S THE PLAN? Lady beetles, parasitic wasps and soldier beetles will feed on scale. Purchase these from many mail-order sources. For small numbers, remove the adults with a cotton swab dipped in soapy water or rubbing alcohol. Suffocate adults and eggs by spraying with horticultural oil while the plant is dormant. Cut back and destroy branches with heavy infestations.

Scale are harder to get rid of once they secrete these waxy coverings for protection against predators. It's easiest to tackle them while they're in the immature "crawler" stage.

Leafhopper

FAVORITE PLANTS Leafhoppers belong to one of the largest families of insects. They feed on scores of plants, including grasses, vegetables and herbaceous and woody plants.

WHAT'S THE DAMAGE? Adults and nymphs feed on plant sap in leaves and stems throughout the growing season. The leafhopper at left is an adult — you can tell because it has wings. Nymphs are about the same size — ⅛ to ⅓ in. long — but don't have wings. A toxin they inject often causes white or yellow stippling on leaves before they curl and fall off. Leafhoppers can also spread viruses and bacteria as they move between plants.

WHAT'S THE PLAN? Spiders, assassin bugs and robber flies, as well as birds and lizards, prey on leafhoppers, so small populations aren't usually a problem. Spray insecticidal soap on all surfaces of plants, including the undersides of leaves, to kill large infestations.

Whitefly

FAVORITE PLANTS Several shrubs and trees (especially citrus) and most types of house plants or greenhouse-grown plants.

WHAT'S THE DAMAGE? Because of their short month-long life cycle, whiteflies can multiply quickly during warm weather or any time on indoor plants. Larvae suck the sap from young leaves, which turn yellow and die. To check for whitefly, brush the foliage and watch for a white cloud rising from the plant. The 1/16- to ⅛-in. adults leave a sticky honeydew that promotes sooty mold. Whiteflies also transmit several plant viruses.

WHAT'S THE PLAN? The photo at right shows both larvae and adults on the bottom of a leaf. Rub eggs and larvae off the undersides of leaves or blast them off with a strong jet of water. If that doesn't work, spray all surfaces of plants with insecticidal soap once a week for several weeks to kill multiple generations of this pest.

the YEAR IN GARDENING

MORE NASTY BUGS

Colorado potato beetle
Leptinotarsa decemlineata

FAVORITE PLANTS Potato, pepper, eggplant and tomato

WHAT'S THE DAMAGE? The larvae and the ½-in.-long adults chew large, ragged holes in leaves, flowers and fruit. Heavy infestations can kill plants.

WHAT'S THE PLAN? Start looking for the adult beetle at left in early spring on vulnerable plants. You'll see more as the summer goes on. For a few beetles, handpick insects and drop them in soapy water. If you see several on a plant, spread a white drop cloth beneath it and gently tap the plant. Destroy adults and larvae that fall onto the drop cloth and also check the undersides of leaves for the yellow-orange egg masses and send them away in the trash. The B$_t$ strain *Bacillus thuringiensis* var. *tenebrionis* and insecticides containing neem control adults and larvae when applied as soon as you spot them.

European earwig *Forficula auricularia*

FAVORITE PLANTS Ornamental plants, such as butterfly bush, dahlia, clematis, hollyhock, rose and zinnia, and edibles, such as beans, beets, lettuce, strawberries and potatoes

WHAT'S THE DAMAGE? You may notice the small, ragged holes in leaves, fruit and tender shoots made by earwigs, but no insects. The ½-in.-long brown-red adults at right hide during the day in plants, debris or cool, moist, dark areas near woodpiles and buildings, including your house. In addition to fruit, leaves and shoots, they also eat other insects, such as mites.

WHAT'S THE PLAN? Inspect plants after sunset with a flashlight to find earwigs and carefully knock them off into soapy water. Remove hiding places, like plant debris, especially around buildings. Place short sections of hose as hiding places to trap insects during the day and empty into soapy water daily. For larger numbers, use an insecticide like carbaryl (Sevin).

European earwigs have large rear pincers. Reach into the wrong flower and they'll use them to deliver a painful pinch!

Rose chafer *Macrodactylus subspinosus*

FAVORITE PLANTS Turf grass, roses and many other ornamental plants

WHAT'S THE DAMAGE? In spring to summer ½-in.-long pale green to tan adults chew large, irregular holes in leaves, fruit and flowers. Although this one's on a pink dianthus, they're especially attracted to white flowers, too. Larvae cause minimal damage as they feed on grass roots in fall.

WHAT'S THE PLAN? If you've had problems before, water beneficial nematodes into lawn areas in spring or fall to kill larvae. When you see the adults, handpick them in early morning or at dusk when they're moving slowly. Or make a trap by setting white buckets filled with an inch of soapy water near affected plants. The bugs, attracted by the white color, will drown. For large infestations, use organic pesticides, such as neem, insecticidal soap or pyrethrum.

PHOTOS: © Neil Soderstom (Colorado potato beetle, rose chafer); courtesy of Whitney Cranshaw, Colorado State University, Bugwood.org (earwig)

276 *the* YEAR IN GARDENING

Squash bug *Anasa tristis*
FAVORITE PLANTS Squash, pumpkins, cucumbers, watermelons and raspberries

WHAT'S THE DAMAGE? Nymphs and adults spread disease and suck juices from leaves, vines and fruit. Leaves develop pale green to yellow specks, which grow into larger brown patches, and finally die. Plants can quickly wither, turn black and die.

WHAT'S THE PLAN? Rub off the orange egg clusters you see at right as soon as vines stretch in midsummer and pick off and destroy any adults or nymphs. Place boards around the plants for the ⅝-in. brown or gray adults to hide under during the day, then dispose of them in the trash. Squash bugs are hard to control with insecticides, though tachinid flies and wolf spiders are natural predators (and can be found in most gardens).

Get rid of these eggs. They'll just hatch into more squash bugs. Also remove the adults, as well as plant debris where adults overwinter.

Harlequin bug *Murgantia histrionica*
FAVORITE PLANTS Squash, corn, cabbage, beans, asparagus, okra and tomatoes

WHAT'S THE DAMAGE? Nymphs and adults suck juices from stems and leaves, leaving irregular-shaped, light-colored spots.

WHAT'S THE PLAN? In the northern parts of their range, watch for adults to emerge the first warm days in spring. (They remain active all year in areas with mild winters.) For small populations, handpick adults before they lay eggs. Continue to watch for adults through summer. The ¼- to ⅓-in. black adults sport orange, red or yellow markings, as in the photo at left. Remove and destroy the black-and-white keg-shaped eggs found on the undersides of leaves. Spray plants with horticultural soap when bugs first appear, following label directions. At the end of the season, remove plant debris from gardens where adults overwinter.

CREEPY CAN BE GOOD

Praying mantis

Lady beetle larvae

Wheel bug

The best way to attract beneficial insects to your garden is to limit your use of pesticides. These three ugly insects are good to have around — so don't squish any you see!

PRAYING MANTIS Typically green or brown, these insects prey on aphids, beetles, caterpillars, leafhoppers, flies and wasps. Unfortunately, they also sometimes eat butterflies and bees (as well other praying mantises!).

LADY BEETLE Both adults and the larvae, like the one in the photo, feed on aphids, potato beetles, whiteflies, mealybugs, spider mites and scales. You can purchase beetles to augment the ones already in your garden.

WHEEL BUG The wheel bug is an assassin bug that preys on insects that include aphids, hairy caterpillars, fall webworms and sawflies. It injects a paralyzing toxin into its victims. Don't handle it — its bite can hurt!

PHOTOS: Courtesy of Whitney Cranshaw, Colorado State University, Bugwood.org (squash bug); courtesy of Russ Ottens, University of Georgia, Bugwood.org (harlequin bug); courtesy of ShawnOlson.net (wheel bug)

www.GardenGateMagazine.com *the* YEAR IN GARDENING

BASICS | PROBLEM SOLVER

Slugging it out with slugs

(1) Check citrus rind traps every day so slugs don't have a chance to drift back onto your plants.

(2) Tuck a 1- or 2-ft.-long piece of board under plants to create a moist, shady hiding place that'll attract lots of slugs.

Strolling through the garden, you find your hostas looking like Swiss cheese. What could have committed such a crime? The likely culprit: slugs. These slimy, rasp-toothed rascals love moist, shady conditions and lush new growth. These globs of goo are hard on hostas, but they aren't picky — you'll find them on other plants, too.

I've wrangled a lot of slugs in the *Garden Gate* test garden and have a few control tips to share. Of course, you can use slug bait. Most of today's baits aren't as toxic as the old formulas used to be. But I'd rather stick with nonpoison options when I can. These four low-impact techniques do a good job of keeping slugs away from my most prized plants, and there's nothing in these methods to harm beneficial insects, pets or people. Read on, then head on out to the garden to rid your garden of these slimy pests!

Traps

Instead of picking slugs one by one from your plants, use food or hiding places to collect them in one place, then drop them into a bucket of soapy water, feed them to your chickens or (eek!) squash them underfoot.

LET THEM EAT ORANGES Slugs love citrus! Buy inexpensive oranges or grapefruit (you don't need the nicest fruit) for slug traps, or use rinds left over after you've squeezed some orange juice. Leave the citrus halves near vulnerable plants — the slugs usually hop off the hostas and hustle over to investigate this new offering. Check your citrus traps about once a day. Throw spent rinds in your compost pile, but remove the slugs first!

I'M SO BOARD A board on the ground in a shady spot might not look like much to you, but to slugs, it looks like a great place to spend the day. Slugs are active at night, but during hot days, they retreat under mulch, rocks…or board traps. Check the trap in the afternoon, when slugs are enjoying their siesta under your board.

the YEAR IN GARDENING   www.GardenGateMagazine.com

(3) Don't let any leaves touch the ground outside the copper barrier, or slugs will use them to get onto the plant.

Stretched-out copper scrubbers are an economical alternative.

Barriers

Once you've coaxed slugs away from your plants, you don't want them sneaking back on to tender leaves the minute your back is turned. These easy barriers will keep the pests at a distance.

SHOCKING RESULTS! When slugs come in contact with copper, it gives them a shock — scientists think that the slug slime reacts with the copper to produce the jolt. You can purchase copper strips and tape just for use in the garden. They'll last for years, and you can reuse them. I like to use the strips around tender young plants, to give them a chance to get established. But you can use the strips around larger plants, too. Just be sure that no leaves touch the ground outside the copper strip, as slugs can use them as "bridges" to reach the rest of the plant. It's a good idea to shine up your copper strips once in a while — research indicates that bright, shiny copper is more effective than strips that have begun to corrode.

Want a cheap alternative to copper strips? I've also had good luck with copper pan scrubbers (like Chore Boy® brand) from the grocery store. These copper mesh bundles can be pulled out into long, thin ribbons and pressed into the soil around the plant, as I did in the inset for photo 3. (Pin them in place with landscaping pins if you're having a hard time keeping them in contact with the soil.) When using these scrubbers, I think the sharp edges are just as unpleasant for the slugs as the copper itself. Make sure that the ends overlap so there's no gap to let slugs in.

DIATOMS TO THE RESCUE Yes, I said diatoms. Diatomaceous earth, a white powdery substance, is made up of the crushed shells of fossilized diatoms, tiny hard-shelled algaelike plants. What does that have to do with slugs? Well, diatomaceous earth is abrasive. It creates tiny cuts in the soft underbellies of slugs and snails, causing them to dry out and die — no more holes in the hostas!

Lightly sprinkle diatomaceous earth under the dripline of hostas and other shade plants, just like you'd put cinnamon sugar on toast. You'll need to reapply it after rain, because it washes into the soil. Be careful when you apply it, though — you don't want those tiny abrasive particles in your lungs, so be sure to wear a dust mask and gloves.

There you have it. These four easy-to-use methods will keep slugs (as well as their better-protected relatives, snails) from doing their worst to your prized plants. And you won't have to worry about storing poisonous slug bait in the garden shed, either!

— *Marcia Leeper*

(4) Make sure you completely surround the plant with a 5- or 6-in.-wide band of diatomaceous earth.

Botanical Names

Hosta
Hosta hybrids

did you **know?**

Scientists estimate there are several hundred species of slugs in the world, although no one knows for sure. Slugs can range from ¼ in. to 7 in. long, in shades of gray, brown, black, orange, yellow and white. Most slugs eat plant material and leaf litter, but some also eat (gasp!) other slugs.

BASICS | PROBLEM SOLVER

is that critter a friend or foe?

We have plenty of critters at our test garden. Some we coexist with peacefully and enjoy having around. Others cause us all sorts of problems. Take, for example, chipmunks. While it's true their antics are entertaining, they dig up container plantings and undermine retaining walls. Here are six well-known animals we've dealt with. With each one we've included information about where you could encounter them, what kind of damage they can do and why you just might want to keep them around. Finally, there are tips on handling the situation if you still want to banish them from your garden. □
— Kristin Beane Sullivan and Jim Childs

Rabbits

Few predators and plenty of food have made the rabbit population explode.

LOVE 'EM They are fun to watch, especially the babies as they leave the nest and strike out on their own.

What to do If rabbits have found good food, they'll stick around. Putting out rabbit pellets, available from pet and feed stores, may help keep them fed and away from your favorite plants.

HATE 'EM Rabbits seem to be able to eat their weight during one night of foraging. And they don't restrict themselves to just one season. They gnaw shrubs to nubs and nibble and girdle tree bark in winter. Then in spring and summer they gobble vegetables, annuals and perennials.

What to do Commercial repellents, such as Ro-Pel®, Rabbit-Scat® or Liquid Fence®, help. Surrounding a favorite bed with wire fencing, such as chicken wire or hardware cloth, is your best, most reliable bet. Be sure to bury the bottom edge 6 to 12 in. so rabbits can't burrow their way under it. And the wire needs to be at least 4 ft. high so they can't hop over it. The openings in the mesh should be no more than 1 in. in diameter so the youngsters can't crawl through for a nibble.

Woodpeckers

These entertaining birds don't just keep to themselves. Especially in winter, look closely at a mixed flock of nuthatches and chickadees — you might see woodpeckers running with the crowd!

LOVE 'EM Woodpeckers drum on trees to attract mates and claim territories. As long as they don't start to work on your home's siding, the sound is pleasant. And they're little pest control machines, eating tent caterpillars and bark beetles, among others.

What to do Plant plenty of trees for these woodland-loving birds. Of the common woodpeckers, the downy woodpecker (in the photo) is the most likely to visit a feeder stocked with suet or black oil sunflower seeds.

HATE 'EM The springtime drumming isn't all that destructive, but it often happens in early morning. If it's outside your bedroom window, it's pretty annoying. Although the problem isn't typically widespread, when woodpeckers excavate for insects in wooden buildings or trees, it can be extremely damaging.

What to do Woodpeckers are persistent once they've identified a territory so it can be difficult to get rid of them if they've moved in. Bird netting stretched between the eave and wood siding seems to be a good way to keep the birds from getting into that space. If they've started to excavate one of your favorite trees, wrap the injured area with ¼-in. hardware cloth, plastic mesh or burlap to get them to move on.

PHOTO: © Jay Gilliam (downy woodpecker)

Squirrels

You'll find squirrels most anywhere there are trees to climb and food to eat. They often build their nests in high branches, hollow tree cavities or in buildings.

LOVE 'EM Their antics are always fun to watch. They chase each other, racing up trees and telephone poles and jumping from tree to tree.

What to do Give them their own feeder where they can eat seeds, grain and nuts.

HATE 'EM Eating, stealing and digging are just a few of the problems squirrels cause. They eat mostly nuts, seeds and berries (frequently at bird feeders). They also sometimes eat plants and even eggs and baby birds.

What to do Metal baffles on bird feeder poles are helpful at protecting seed. All-metal birdfeeders and storage containers with tight-fitting lids can't be gnawed through. Lay wire mesh over planted areas to prevent digging.

Chipmunks

Usually found in wooded areas, chipmunks, or ground squirrels, have adapted to urban living. Look for tunnels near retaining walls, foundations, between tree roots and in dense plantings.

LOVE 'EM Chipmunks are entertaining to watch and they do eat slugs and insects.

What to do They can make a feast from almost any kind of seed you put out for them.

HATE 'EM When they tunnel around plants, the roots dry out. Digging and tunneling can cause retaining walls to collapse. Chipmunks dig up and eat newly planted seeds and bulbs, as well as tender young plants and fruits.

What to do Trapping may be your best option. Protect newly planted areas with hardware cloth placed over the soil to prevent digging. Spraying Wilt-Pruf® on containers' edges can keep chipmunks from climbing in and digging.

Bats

You won't see bats during the day. But as the sun goes down, they're out hunting.

LOVE 'EM Bats consume thousands of insects, even in a single night.

What to do Plants that bloom at night draw insects, and bats will stick around to eat the bugs. Avoid using insecticides that might kill their food sources. Dark hidden areas, such as old sheds, are great for daytime rest. And if you want to put up a bat house, learn what you need to do in our Web extra.

HATE 'EM Bats generally try to avoid humans and their living areas, but they can carry diseases. Their appearance, as well as their erratic flight patterns, can startle or frighten people. And no one likes a bat in the house — even the cute little brown one in the photo.

What to do Ignore them as much as possible. But if they get into your home, open doors and windows to let them out. Then plug any holes where they could re-enter. Bats can bite, so always wear heavy gloves for protection if you have to handle one.

Web extra If you want bats to "hang" around, put up a bat house. Check out *our tips* on where to place it.

PHOTOS: © Steven Nordmeyer (squirrel); © Adam Mann Environmental Solutions & Innovations, Inc. (bat)

Garter snakes

Garter snakes live in brush piles, stone walls and areas with dense weeds or long grass, or in other words, damp areas where there's a food supply.

LOVE 'EM Snakes eat slugs, small mammals, such as mice, and even other reptiles. But garter snakes don't damage structures or other property — and they're not poisonous.

What to do Provide dark, cool rock or brush piles where they can hide.

HATE 'EM It's the surprise factor that gets most folks. And some snake species *are* dangerous. Learn to identify your local garter snakes so you can tell the difference. Colors and markings vary regionally, but nearly all have this characteristic striping pattern.

What to do Odds are, after you spot one, you won't see it again unless it has a steady food supply, so try to ignore it since it is beneficial. Still don't like them? Mow long grass and remove brush and rock piles where they hide.

BASICS | PROBLEM SOLVER

the best sprinkler
for you — and your plants!

New plants need a lot of water. And even drought-tolerant, established plants may need a drink now and then. Soaker hoses and drip irrigation are great for long-term watering. But many shrubs and perennials just need a splash of water once in a while. In our test-garden tool shed, I keep several sprinklers. That way, I can pick the one that'll work most efficiently for a specific situation, without running up a huge water bill or wasting water on the sidewalk or driveway.

Speaking of efficiency, it's easy to test how much water a sprinkler puts out. Set several empty straight-sided, shallow cans, all the same diameter, around the area. (I've found that tuna cans work well.) Run the sprinkler for 20 minutes, then measure the water in each can with a ruler. Adjust the water pressure or the time until you get about an inch of water (what most gardens need every week). This is also a good way to make sure that your sprinkler is delivering water to all the thirsty plants. If some plants are getting shorted, move the sprinkler until it's watering evenly, with no tall plants in the way of the water droplets.

Let's look at my three favorite types of sprinklers, plus the best uses for each one. Then pick the one that works best for your garden needs! □

— *Marcia Leeper*

Lush lawns

In areas with ample rainfall, you don't really need to water the lawn all the time, so an irrigation system may be overkill. But if you're trying to get seed or new sod established, you'll save yourself time and money if you can deliver water over a broad area quickly. That's when a good old-fashioned oscillating sprinkler can really come in handy. The overhead spray reaches a large area. And it delivers a fairly even amount of water across the spray path, as long as there are no tall plants to obstruct it. Most oscillating sprinklers are adjustable, allowing you to water areas of different widths, so look for one with easy-to-understand adjustments. After all, you don't want to waste money watering the sidewalk! Some have light plastic frames, but I like a heavy, all-metal one like the one above, because the extra weight keeps it from tipping over.

To cover a large area quickly, set the sprinkler in the center, and adjust the throw to the maximum side-to-side movement.

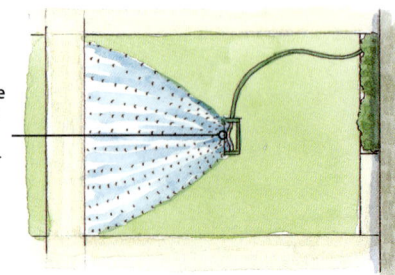

Absolutely adjustable!

Need to water a large area of garden beds? A rotor sprinkler is my go-to choice for bigger borders and beds, because it's super-adjustable. You can set the angle so it sprays in full circles, or just wedge-shaped segments. And you can adjust the shape of the spray pattern, too, so it waters only the flower beds at the perimeter or the adjoining lawn as well. Overhead watering gets leaves wet, so I use this sprinkler early in the morning, to give foliage a chance to dry during the day, cutting down on mildew problems. You also don't lose as much water to evaporation if you get it done early.

There's one spot on the lawn where I can put the sprinkler and set it to hit almost all of the perennial border, so I mark that spot with a golf tee. When it's time to water, I stab the spike on the bottom of the sprinkler into the ground right next to the tee. (Just push the tee down far enough that you can mow over it.) Some of these sprinklers don't have the spike on the bottom, and rest on a wide base instead, but they work just the same way.

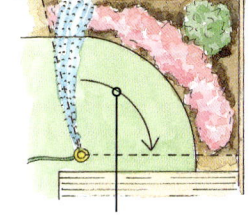

Set the angle so it waters anything from a narrow area to a complete circle.

Here, the sprinkler is set to water only the perimeter border, but it can also be adjusted to water the lawn as well.

Down to earth

I especially like these stationary or spot sprinklers for watering under shrubs or in annual beds. The low profile keeps the water down at the base of the plant so the leaves stay dry, which cuts down on mildew and other fungal diseases. They're water-savers, too, because watering close to the ground makes sure that all the moisture hits the soil, instead of evaporating into the air. Do keep in mind, though, that you'll need to move these a little more frequently than other sprinkler types because they don't reach as wide an area. But there's nothing to adjust, so they're easy to move.

You'll find similar-shaped sprinklers in different weights and materials. But this metal one is heavy, so I can give it a swing and toss it gently out into the bed without having to climb in among the plants. That's definitely handy when I'm watering these roses! You might see this style in circle or triangle shapes, too. The spray pattern may be a little different, although I find that they all tend to water roughly in a circle. So don't worry too much about picking the "right" shape — they'll all work just fine.

No fancy controls on this sprinkler! Adjust the water pressure to make the spray pattern larger or smaller.

CUT BACK ON CHLORINE

Some research shows that chlorine in water may harm plants, killing good soil bacteria and changing soil pH, which affects how plants take up nutrients. You can keep your garden extra healthy with a chlorine filter. I like this CuZn GardenMate® filter because you change out the inside cartridge, instead of the whole thing. According to the retailer's Web site, one cartridge lasts through about 20,000 gallons. Buy it at www.friendsofwater.com (866-482-6803). The filter is $69.96 and the refill cartridges are $26.95.

BASICS | PROBLEM SOLVER

THE WEEKEND GARDENER · Garden Smarter

Create a relaxing retreat.

Make Over a Stark Patio (in 2 Weekends!)

Before

✱ handy tip Mix up the etching solution in a dark-colored watering can. Then you can easily see when the white granules have completely dissolved.

Concrete is a wonderful building material. But new concrete often has a stark, sterile look. Doesn't that newly poured patio in the before photo stand out? Since this area is basically the entry to the house, it needs to look more inviting. But how do you warm up a blindingly white new patio and make it blend into the yard? With a little concrete stain, some well-placed furniture and a few good-looking pots, it's not too difficult. Although the transformation you see on page 286 is pretty dramatic, it only *looks* like a lot of work. It's something you could easily tackle in a couple of weekends, and still have plenty of time left. Let me show you how.

First weekend

1 CLEAN IT UP Whether you have a newly poured patio or an old one, concrete stain is a great way to change it up. For a new surface, wait about a month for it to cure completely. As long as older concrete isn't sealed, chipped or crumbling, you can stain it, too. I wanted a warm natural color so I chose a concrete stain kit from Rust-Oleum® called "Earth Brown." The kit included etching solution, stain, sealer and a small pump sprayer. But there are lots of kit options available; it's really just a matter of choosing a finish you like.

The first step is to clean and etch the concrete. Use a hose with a spray nozzle to remove the dirt. Then mix up the etching solution in a watering can. Etching solution prepares the surface to take the stain and is caustic, so be careful not to get any on your skin. Sprinkle it on a small area (about 4 square feet) at a time so you can scrub the solution in with a stiff-bristled brush before it dries. After scrubbing the patio, rinse the entire surface well to get all traces of the solution off.

Although the etching solution isn't supposed to hurt plants, I also rinsed the area around the new

1 Etch the concrete so it'll take the stain better. Use a long-handled brush so you don't have to scrub in the solution on your hands and knees.

2 Apply stain using small circular motions. Carry a rag to catch the larger drips.

boxwoods planted near the patio with plenty of water. They weren't harmed, but if I were to do this project again, I'd plant the boxwoods *after* I stained, just to be on the safe side.

2 APPLY THE STAIN When the patio is dry, open the can of stain and mix it thoroughly with a stir stick. To prevent clogging the sprayer nozzle, pour the stain through a paint filter to strain it as you're pouring it into the tank. Then close the tank and give it a few pumps to pressurize it.

Start at one end of the patio and work your way across, using small circular motions to spray on the stain. I wanted an uneven, almost splotchy effect rather than a solid coating, so I didn't mind the occasional drip from the sprayer. But sprayers do tend to drip, so keep a rag handy for cleanup. After the stain dries, you can easily see any lighter areas. Go over them with another light coat of stain if you want to even out the color a little more. Afterward,

✱ quick **touch-up**

Your patio's stain may get scratched or scraped by an enthusiastic snow shovelling or something heavy being dragged across the surface. Do an easy spot repair by lightly scrubbing the affected area with a wire brush to remove the sealer, and applying another coat of stain. (There's no need to mask it off — the stain will only stick to the brushed area.) When the stain's completely dry, apply more sealer to protect the new finish!

rinse out the sprayer with water and wait several hours until the stain is completely dry. Using the sprayer again, apply a coat of the sealer to protect the finish and let it dry.

That's about enough for one weekend. Now take a break. Turn the page to see what the second weekend holds.

YOUR RETREAT!

4 Position an easy-to-make screen and a tilting umbrella to provide shade and privacy.

3 Create a place for you and your visitors to relax with comfortable, weather-proof furniture.

Second weekend

3 COMFORTABLE AND RELAXING At 9 by 24 feet, this slab has plenty of room for a large landing, but it isn't really large enough for a dining table and several chairs. That's OK because a patio at the back of the house is used for dining. I wanted this patio to feel more like a living room. So I chose four brown wicker-look chairs and matching tables to make a cozy place to gather at one end of the patio. It's a good idea to leave 18 to 30 inches of space between the front of chairs and a coffee table to make it easy to move around. All these pieces are comfortable with a slightly modern style that goes well with the look of the house. Though large and inviting, they're in perfect proportion to the space.

A weather-proof rug under the coffee table helps tie the pieces together and echoes some of the flower colors. There are all kinds of options for weather-proof area rugs out there these days, and the prices are coming down every year. I love them because you can just hose them down when they start to look dingy. (Buy a rug that's more than half the size of the seating area, so it doesn't look too small.)

Door mats are always a good idea, but there's not much room at the top of the steps for one. I decided to move this one down onto the patio. The only problem: I couldn't find one I liked that was big enough to fit the space. For these 4-foot-wide steps, the typical 18-by-30-inch door mat looked wimpy. But two mats side by side were perfect. To keep the coir mats together and in place, flip them over and stick on a length of heavy-duty double-sided tape where the edges meet. Pull off the tape's paper backing and set the mats in place face up. You'll need to replace the tape every once in a while.

For ambience, I found an outdoor table lamp and some candle holders I liked at a local home improvement center. Want to see how I kept working with this patio until the accessories and other elements were just right? Check out the slide show in our Web extra.

Web extra Watch a *slide show* of this patio transformation.

Mother-in-law's tongue

Add color and mark the entrances to the house and yard with matching pairs of containers.

✳ **inside out** Feel free to use your indoor plants in patio containers. You can bring these striped mother-in-law's tongues back in the house in fall.

4 SHADE AND PRIVACY Even with the furniture and plants in place, this patio had a problem with privacy. Don't you hate it when you're relaxing on your patio and you can see your neighbor talking on the phone in his kitchen? Here, the far end of the patio is only a few steps from the neighbor's door. The remedy: A screen. To make this one, screw together three cedar frames and attach them to 4x4 cedar posts sunk into the ground. I've stapled shower curtains in the frames. Change the style instantly by choosing a different shower curtain.

And finally, you can prevent the sun from blinding you no matter where you're sitting and at any time of day with a freestanding patio umbrella. Move it around the patio and tilt it so it works for you. It's also great for providing a little privacy, especially if your neighbors have second-story windows.

5 PLENTY OF PLANTS No patio would be complete without plants, right? Lots of containers of colorful annuals and perennials add movement and life. If you grow no other containers, start with a matching pair flanking the steps into the house. They'll mark the door and dress up the area near the entry. Then, wherever you have an entrance or an exit, add another smaller pair.

The path out to the yard in photo 5 is just a simple stepping stone set in mulch. But the matching terra-cotta urns really dress it up. This second pair echoes the shape and flower colors of the larger ones, but takes up much less space. Terra-cotta is a good theme for containers because no matter what shape or size, as long as they're all of the same material, they seem unified. And the warm terra-cotta color blends nicely with the other earth tones on this patio.

Isn't it amazing what two weekends and the right plants and furnishings can accomplish? A stark concrete slab is replaced by a welcoming, comfortable space where you'll want to spend many more weekends with your family and friends! ☐

— *Deborah Gruca*

BASICS | PROJECT

Elegant ornaments you can craft in an hour!

Simple Beauty

These ornaments sparkle in the light and bring new colors and textures to the garden. Plus, they're fun to make! Find unique votive holders and candy dishes in flea markets, antique stores or even your own attic, and put them together. Then stick one or two in a planted container or bed, and sit back and watch them glisten in the sun.

MATERIALS
- 2 to 4 pieces of vintage glassware
- ½-in. copper pipe, cut to the length you want with a copper tubing cutter
- Copper pipe fittings
- Copper wire
- Epoxy (we used E6000® brand)

1 EXPERIMENT Play around with your glass pieces to see what looks and fits together best. Pair unique textures and different colors. Also consider the shape of the surfaces and how the pieces will glue to one another. Then, when you find the combination you like, wash and dry each piece.

2 ASSEMBLE THE ORNAMENT Following package instructions, use epoxy to glue together your glass pieces. Apply the glue carefully (you don't want to get it all over your ornament). Then try not to move the pieces — most epoxies take 24 hours or longer to set. Once the pieces are completely dry, glue the copper pipe fitting to the bottom of your ornament and set it aside to dry.

When your ornament has set, take it and your length of copper pipe outside. Push the pipe into the ground and attach the ornament by slipping the fitting on the bottom of the ornament over the end of the pipe. (You could also glue the fitting to the end of the pipe, but if you don't, it's easier to lift the ornament off the pipe and bring it inside for the winter.)

3 FINISHING TOUCH If you'd like, wrap some copper wire around the pipe. Twist one end of the wire and let it hang long, like a tendril from a vine, or string a few glass beads onto it. Then tuck in a candle for a warm glow or let it catch and play with the sunlight. □

— *Deborah Gruca*

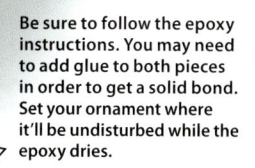

Be sure to follow the epoxy instructions. You may need to add glue to both pieces in order to get a solid bond. Set your ornament where it'll be undisturbed while the epoxy dries.

Turned upside down, fluted or flared glassware has a beautiful skirting effect.

A fitting gives the copper pipe a larger gluing surface, so your ornament will hold strong. Choose one that best fits your glass piece.

PHOTOS: Brent Isenberger (lead photo); Katie Downey (copper pipe fittings); Doug Appleby (dishes that bloom)

DISHES THAT BLOOM

For a fun twist on these glass ornaments, put together bowls, plates or cups to create pretty "flower" ornaments. Use the same epoxy to glue everything together. Then glue the flat part of the cap below to the back of the plate. When it's dry, attach it to the copper pipe using a fitting. (A 90-degree fitting will make the flower outward-facing; use the 45-degree one to make it more upward-facing.)

Glue ½-in. cap to back of flower.

45-degree fitting for up-facing flowers

90-degree fitting for out-facing flowers

the YEAR IN GARDENING

did you know...

Leave the plastic package on the suet cake so starlings and sparrows can't get to it.

Woodpeckers and nuthatches can hang upside down to eat.

Suet solutions
Jane Wetmore, Connecticut
Tired of feeding starlings and sparrows instead of the nuthatches, woodpeckers and chickadees that you're hoping to attract with your suet feeder? Jane uses suet in square packages. But instead of taking the suet completely out of the package, she tears off the front label and places the rest, stiff plastic back and all, in the suet feeder. Then she hangs the feeder with the suet side facing down. Check out the photo above to see what happens: The birds she wants to feed, such as woodpeckers and nuthatches, have no problem hanging upside down for their dinner, while the starlings and sparrows look for easier pickings elsewhere.

Easy-fill feeder
Elizabeth Smith, Michigan
Hungry birds mean feeders need to be filled regularly. So you want to do all you can to make this chore easy. The best place for Elizabeth's feeder was hanging from a tree branch, which made it a challenge to reach and fill. Here's her solution: She looped an 18-inch bungee cord over the branch and attached both of its hooked ends to the top of the bird feeder. Now when the feeder needs a refill, she pulls it down with her left hand, removes the lid and fills the feeder with her right. Then she replaces the lid and gently eases it back into position under the branch of the tree.

Good-bye geese
Diane Eaton, Georgia
Diane was tired of Canada geese damaging her garden, so she found a way to deter them. She took an old CD and painted a large circle in the center on both sides with black acrylic paint to make it look like a big eye. When the paint was dry, she drilled a hole at the top of the CD and ran a fishing line loop through it. Then Diane made others and hung them around the yard: on tomato cages, shrub limbs — anywhere the geese might be. The idea is that the shiny CDs look like big eyes and scare the geese away. It worked! Since she's hung the CDs, the geese haven't been back to her garden.

Keep the seed flowing
Denise Thompson, Illinois
Large bird feeders are real time savers — you don't have to fill them as often. But with extra space, the seed doesn't always flow to where the birds can reach it. And seed that sits can rot, causing problems for the birds. Denise found a way to keep the seed flowing and her birds fed. She places a clear 7-ounce plastic cup upside down in the center of the feeder. Then when she pours the seed, the

Place a clear plastic cup in the center of the feeder to keep seed in easy reach of the birds.

in the news

Birdfiles
Bird lovers have another Web site to bookmark. Dave's Garden now has Birdfiles, a database filled with photos and information. You can check it out at www.davesgarden.com/guides/birdfiles. Search by common or Latin names to find out where your favorite bird has been sighted and read the comments of other bird watchers. If you want to add a photo, bird information or post comments, you must be a member. But that's free and easy: Just choose a user name and type in your e-mail address on the registration page. Or you can buy a paid membership that gets you into all the forums on Dave's site.

When the pulp is gone, fill the orange with nectar for an additional bird treat.

Disposable feeder
Brenda Shafer, Illinois

Nothing beats the excitement of seeing colorful orioles and grosbeaks eating just outside your window. Commercial nectar feeders get sticky and they're difficult to clean. So Brenda feeds her orioles and grosbeaks oranges! The board in the photo at left has a nail sticking upright, and Brenda just pushes the orange onto the nail. The birds feast on the juice and pulp for a few days. When most of the goodies are gone, she fills the orange half with oriole nectar and lets the birds eat that for up to a week. She's never had a problem with nectar leaking out of the nail hole because the pulp tends to stop up any crevices around it. When the nectar is gone, she throws out the orange and starts the process over again.

cup directs the seed closer to the feeding area so it isn't wasted. Denise recommends pouring the seed slowly so the momentum doesn't move the cup off center.

Winter bird treats
Marie Sanborn, Oklahoma

Instead of squishing the bugs eating her garden, Marie turns them into a winter treat for the birds. In summer, she and her grandchildren collect cabbage loopers, grasshoppers, tomato hornworms and other pests and drop them into plastic containers with lids. Then Marie labels the containers carefully and puts them in the freezer. For containers with lots of caterpillars Marie adds a couple of tablespoons of cornmeal so they don't stick together. When winter kicks in, Marie can provide high-energy high-protein frozen treats for her feathered friends. Chickadees, nuthatches and woodpeckers are especially appreciative.

product picks

Easy-to-clean feeder

A dirty bird feeder can grow toxic mold that harms birds, but cleaning those long tube feeders can be a challenge. Here's a new feeder that makes this chore easier than ever: Aspects' Quick-Clean® Big Tube. It has its own unique quick-release base, making it easy to wash in warm, soapy water.

The top, base and perches are made of metal and the tube of clear UV-stabilized polycarbonate. This 18-inch-tall feeder holds 3½ quarts of seed and has six feeding stations, so you should have plenty of visitors to enjoy. It comes in the spruce finish in these photos or brass and includes a lifetime guarantee.

Bottom line A quick-release base helps you get back to feeding (and watching) the birds in a flash.
Source Nottawa Wild Bird Supply Store at 800-958-3520 or www.nottawawildbirdsupply.com
Price $49.99

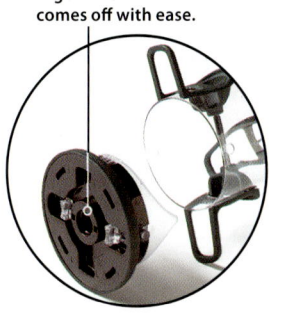

Squeeze the two tabs together and the base comes off with ease.

did you know... (CONTINUED)

Easy plant support
Our readers often come up with new ways to recycle old items around the house. Here are two great ideas you can use with your vines.

Marlene Whitacre, Vermont
When some of Marlene's clip-on holiday lights stopped working, she put the strands to use in a different way: as plant supports. She started by removing the bulbs so they didn't break. Then in a spot where she often planted tomatoes, beans, peas or squash, she wove the plastic-coated wire through a section of lattice mounted on the house wall. The flexible wires were easy to work with when she trained plants up the lattice. She used the clips (shown at left) to hold the plants that needed a little help attaching to the lattice. Marlene suggests cutting the plug off the end of the strand to keep it from getting caught in the openings.

Teddy Budy, California
Teddy thought it seemed like a waste to throw out an old wooden stepladder that had lost its support side. So he decided to use it as a trellis! He leaned the 6-foot ladder against his privacy fence and planted morning glories at the base in spring. As temperatures warmed, the seedlings twined their way up the sides and rungs of the ladder. Later that season, all you could see were the top two rungs and lots of beautiful morning glory flowers.

Remove the light bulbs before putting the cord in the trellis.

Use the clip to hold or direct the vine where you want it to go.

Quick clean up
Zinta Obal, Ohio
Clay soil is a challenge — both for your plants and for you, when you have to scrape it off your shoes after a trip out to the garden. Zinta found an easy solution to the dirty shoe problem — a wire grill brush. She uses the kind with a long handle and hangs it on a hook in the garage where it's easy to grab. The stiff wire bristles make short work of the sticky clay, even getting it out of heavy work-boot treads.

Sift compost easily
Debby Stagg, British Columbia
Whenever Debby wanted a wheelbarrow load of compost from the pile, she found it took too much time to pick out all the big chunks that hadn't yet decomposed. Then she noticed some black plastic nursery trays stacked in her garage and got an idea. Why not use the trays as sifters? Debby stacks two trays with grid-like bottoms on top of each other: One with 1½-inch triangles and the other with 1-inch squares. Finer pieces of compost fall through the openings. That leaves the big stuff to be tossed back onto the compost pile, and she's done with her chore in no time.

(1) Start with the loop. Hold the end of the fence post loosely in the vice. Bend and turn until the loop is finished.

(2) Put in the angle. Next, tighten the vice and put a single 90-degree bend in the post so it'll hold your tools up.

No more lost tools
Lois Lally, Washington
Lois was tired of losing her hoe when she laid it down in the vegetable garden. So she made a tool stand from an old electric fence post. You can find new ones at your local home improvement store for less than a few dollars a piece.

To make the tool stand, place the top of the post in a bench vice and with your hands form it into the shape you need. The photos above show the two-step process: First you bend the loop, then put in an angle so it'll hold your tools upright.

Lois leaves her stand in the garden all summer. Now she can get back to work and skip the search for her misplaced tools.

Lean long-handled tools in the loop so you can find them again later.

PHOTOS: Doug Appleby (lights, hoe holder); courtesy of Bogs Footwear (boots)

Add another layer of tape if one doesn't keep it upright.

Duct tape splint
Linda Steffy, Pennsylvania
Linda found a clever way to salvage some of her black-eyed Susans damaged by a summer hailstorm: The bent stems got a little splint made of duct tape. She cut a 2-in.-wide and 3- or 4-in.-long piece of tape off of the roll and wrapped it around the bend a few times. It worked! The stiff tape kept the flowers upright and Linda's flower garden looking good.

Easy tool storage
Roy Via, Tennessee
Tired of walking back and forth from your tool shed to the garden? Make a storage container like Roy did from a 3-lb. coffee can. Roy screwed the plastic can to a fence post in the middle of his garden. He put in some pruners, gloves, twine or whatever else fit, replaced the lid and everything stayed dry until the next time he was ready to garden.

Knee relief
Kathleen Ryan, New York
A kneeling pad is a knee saver when it comes to weeding. The only drawback is that you have to hop up and down to move it along a border. But Kathleen uses two kneelers to remedy this problem. As she works, she places both kneelers side-by-side in front of where she needs to weed. Then, as she moves onto the second kneeler, she jumps the first one ahead. Now there's no more getting up and down — weeding is one smooth operation.

in the news

Get your mower in shape
A lawn mower that's had regular tune-ups runs better, has 50 percent fewer emissions and lasts about 15 years longer. Get your walk-behind mower in shape with Briggs & Stratton's "Get in T.U.N.E." program. You'll learn how to do your own tune-up in four simple steps. Visit www.mowertuneup.com to find how-to videos and instructions. If you're not mechanically inclined and still have questions, call the Mower Tune-Up hotline at 800-274-4477. It's open March 1 to May 31 from 8 a.m. to 5 p.m. CST Monday through Friday. When you're finished, take the old oil to your local Briggs & Stratton dealer, and the folks there will recycle it for you — free! Click on "Find a Dealer." at www.briggsandstratton.com for help.

product picks

GardenScribe Plant Organizer

Pull all the information you have about your garden plants together — it's time to get organized! With the GardenScribe Plant Organizer, you can keep all those tags, notes and photos that you've collected over the years right at your fingertips. This D-ring binder is about 12 inches square and 3 inches thick, so it holds plenty of information. Each page is a form that includes the name and needs of each plant and a clear vinyl pocket for photos. Refill pages are $5 for a 10-page packet.

Bottom line Get organized and stay that way.
Source GardenScribe at www.gardenscribe.com or 516-554-9461
Price $39.95

Redesign your garden or plan a new one with a handy design template.

Plant detail pages help you keep track of what's growing where.

Garden boots

These waterproof and attractive rubber boots are perfect for slogging through a wet garden bed *and* for trudging through snow. The nylon jersey lining helps keep your feet warm in temperatures down to -40 degrees Fahrenheit.

This pattern, Mid Paisley, comes in blue (shown), orange, gray and port in women's whole sizes 6 to 11. Other women's styles and men's sizes and styles are available as well.

Bottom line Garden boots + winter boots = a smart (and good-looking!) investment.
Source Local retailers or Bogs at www.bogsfootwear.com
Price $86

did you know... (CONTINUED)

New use for old political signs
Mary Reavely, Iowa

When the elections were over, Mary found a use for a leftover plastic corrugated political sign. Since the campaign didn't want the 2½-by-6-foot sign back after the election, she laid it on the ground under her outdoor potting bench with the legs anchoring the corners. Then she covered the sign with a 3-inch layer of wood mulch. It's a great weed barrier.

The plastic is durable and lasts for years, especially if it's protected from UV rays by the mulch. And there are no seams for weeds to creep through. Policies on what to do with political signs after an election vary according to districts and even campaigns. Check with the candidate's campaign office after the election to see if you can keep the sign.

Catch you later
Donna Faber, Montana

To save every drop of water she can, Donna sets small, inexpensive pails from garage sales around the yard to act as mini rain barrels. The best places are those that don't really need water — bare spots, along a path, etc. When it rains or she has to set out the sprinkler, the pails collect the water. Later she can pour it onto the plants that need an extra drink now and then.

She likes colorful pails because they can double as garden accents. More utilitarian-looking ones can be set in less conspicuous spots.

Keep the fish safe
Lou Curnes, Vermont

Q *I'm building a small pond. Any tips on keeping the fish from becoming a meal for the raccoons?*
A Raccoons don't like to swim — their fur isn't waterproof. But they will wade into the shallow areas. And even if they decide to go for a dip, they can't catch fish while they're swimming. So, a pond that's at least 2 feet deep and 8 feet wide, like the one above, will give fish room to swim to safety. Also make the edges steep so the raccoons won't be tempted to wade into the water.

Include stone ledges like the ones below — fish can dart underneath and raccoons can't reach back to get at them. Raccoons don't like unstable footing either, so if possible, let the stones wobble a bit. Include a piece of PVC pipe in the bottom of your pond and the fish can swim into it when they're being stalked.

6- to 8-in. overhang so raccoons can't reach underneath
At least 8 ft. wide
At least 2 ft. deep
Steep sloping sides mean raccoons can't wade into the pond.

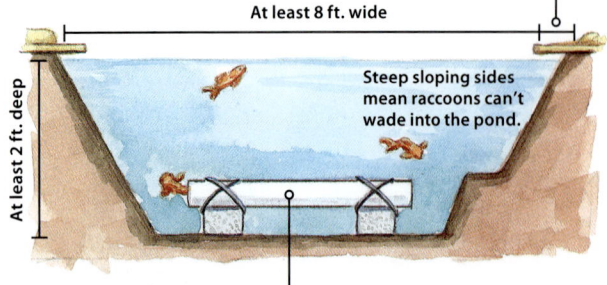

A 4-ft.-long piece of 6-in.-diameter PVC pipe tied to cement blocks will give even large fish a safe place to hide.

Keep the shredded paper from touching the base so insects won't make a home and feed on the stem.

Special delivery
Louise Herron, Missouri

Q *I shred junk mail and old bills. Is it OK to use as mulch in my vegetable garden?*
A Shredded paper makes great mulch and it'll break down in the soil, adding a small bit of humus. Even the colored dyes aren't made with toxic materials anymore and are safe to use around edibles. Coated shiny paper may take longer to break down, but it will over time. Before you shred, tear the plastic windows from billing envelopes and get rid of any other pieces that won't rot.

On a calm day, spread 2 or 3 inches of shredded paper around your plants and wet it down right away to help hold it in place. Like any mulch, keep it an inch or two away from stems. If you don't like the look of the paper, go ahead and spread some compost on top.

product picks

Super-slim hose

Watering sure gets to be a chore in summer. Make it easier on yourself with the Super-Slim hose. At only 3 pounds, this 25-foot hose is so lightweight you'll barely notice you're carrying it (the 50-foot hose is 6 pounds). Both ends have chrome-plated solid brass fittings to prevent leaks, and spring guards to avoid kinks. One thing we noticed about working with this hose: Make sure you attach a nozzle or shut-off valve before you turn the water on. The water pressure coming through the ½-inch-diameter hose is pretty strong and can surprise you or make a big mess. Want to use it indoors? Just hook it up to your sink faucet. The Super-Slim hose comes in two colors: violet (shown) and moss.

Bottom line This lightweight hose is easy to carry and a cinch to roll up and store.
Source Gardener's Supply at www.gardeners.com or 888-833-1412
Price $44.95 for a 25-foot hose; $64.95 for a 50-foot hose

Orbital 360° sprayer

To get rid of foliage pests, it's important to spray the undersides of leaves, as well as the top. But spray bottles stop working when you tip them to spritz beneath the leaves. Not anymore! With this new hand-held sprayer you can spray any way you want — even upside down or sideways — and you'll get a consistent and even spray. The nozzle is adjustable for a fine mist or a steady stream.

Bottom line Now you can finally get an even coating of whatever pest- or disease-control product you like to use.
Source Liquid Fence Company at 800-923-3623 or www.liquidfence.com
Price $2.49 for a 24-ounce sprayer; $2.79 for a 32-ounce sprayer

Gecko's Toes hose rack

Don't you hate wrestling with a tangled hose? The thing is, if you can keep your hose coiled neatly in the first place, it'll stay kink-free and last longer. Here's a new gadget that can help: Attach the Gecko's Toes™ hose rack with screws to any sturdy surface. The one in the photo at right is on a shed wall. To hang up the hose, start at one end of the rack and snap a loop of hose between two molded "fingers." Repeat, moving toward the other end of the rack. You can fit more than one loop per finger. The rack holds about 100 feet of hose and when you're ready to water, give a tug to release the hose.

Bottom line This is an easy way to keep your hose kink- and tangle-free.
Source Kinsman Garden at www.kinsmangarden.com or 800-733-4146 (Look for it under "improved hose rack.")

Molded "fingers" keep the hose organized, but pulling the hose off is easy, too.

did you know... (CONTINUED)

Recycled labels
Deb Reis, New York
Starting seeds saves you money on plants, but you don't want to spend the difference on plant labels! That cost can add up, especially if you're starting a lot of seeds. Deb found a way to keep her label costs down with the lid from a rotisserie chicken container. With a marker, she divides the dome-shaped lid into pieces like the one in the diagram below. Each of these labels is about 1½ inches wide but yours might vary, depending on the size of the lid. Deb trims off the rim of the lid with a pair of scissors and cuts along the marked lines. Now she writes the names of the seeds she's starting on the label with a black permanent marker before she sticks it in the seed-starting mix. Because the lid is dome-shaped, she writes on the arched portion of the tab, which curves back away from the plant. That makes it easy to see the writing, and she's recycling, too.

To be sure that the labels are the same size, draw lines on the dome with a permanent marker.

The arch from the lid makes it easier to read the label.

Easy pickings
Joyce O'Reilly, New Hampshire
Getting apples from the top of an apple tree can be a challenge. Susan gets double-duty from a tool she already has and saves money by not having to buy an apple picker: She uses a light bulb changer!

The 6-foot-long handle extends to 11 feet, allowing her to reach the highest fruit on the tree. The changer has two "basket" sizes for both standard and large bulbs. Susan found that the standard size fits the apples best. At harvest time Joyce extends the pole and places the basket around an apple. Then she gently pushes up or pushes to the side. If it's ripe, it drops into the basket easily. If there's resistance it isn't ripe, so she moves on.

Where's the seed?
Brenda Tripp, Illinois
Brenda had a large tilled area where she liked to plant seeds of her favorite herbs. But sometimes she lost track of where she'd planted the seeds. Her solution was simple. She gets a bag of potting *soil*. It's darker in color and has a heavier texture than the potting mix that's used for container gardening. After broadcasting the seed on top of the soil in the area where she wanted it, Brenda covered the seed right away with the soil from the bag. The dark potting soil was easy to see contrasted against the light brown clay of her garden. That made it easier to tell where she'd been. Plus, a quick glance lets her know where to keep an eye out for new seedlings a few weeks later.

Keep track of plant tags
Those plastic plant tags that come with your plants are helpful when you want to know which tomato you grew last summer or when that new perennial blooms. But tags are no help at all if you can't find them. Here are two great tips for keeping track of them:

Mike Kilts, Tennessee
The tags for Mike's veggies kept getting lost in the mulch or soil of his raised beds. That meant he couldn't figure out which veggie variety was growing where. To solve this problem, he made special tag holders. Mike glued a wooden spring clothespin, business side up, to the front of a raised bed like the one in the photo above. He used a waterproof glue, such as Gorilla™ Glue, so it wouldn't be washed away by the rain. Now he clamps the tag into the pin and he doesn't lose tags anymore. For in-ground beds, Mike found a different solution: He glued the clothespin to a pointed cedar stake and pushed it into the soil near the plant it identifies.

Use waterproof Gorilla Glue, so the clothespin stays in place.

Susan Langner, South Dakota
Susan often referred back to the tags that came with her plants. But as her plant collection grew, so did the pile of tags. What she needed was a way to organize them. So she came up with the system in the photo below. All it takes is a hole punch and a metal ring (the kind that opens in the middle — you'll find them in the school or office supply section of the store.) Then she punched a hole in the tag and placed it on

Cut tips off tags so they move more easily on the ring.

the ring. Be sure to check where the plant name and growing information is to avoid punching a hole through it. Susan likes to keep her tags in alphabetical order. That makes it easier to flip right to the plant she's looking for. She hangs the ring from a hook in her shed, so the information is always at her fingertips.

Keep garlic dry
Tom McInnis, Oregon

After garlic is harvested in summer, it needs to dry. As Tom's garlic harvest increased every year, it became harder to find a method that didn't take too much room, and still gave the heads the circulation they needed. An old circular wire tomato cage provided the inspiration for these garlic-drying towers.

You can make the towers from 5-foot-tall 14-gauge fencing. A 5-foot length will form a cage that's 18 to 20 inches in diameter. Hold each cage together with a few zip ties. Then attach the bundled garlic to the frame with S-hooks. The 2-by-4-inch squares provide room for air to circulate and let the garlic dry, or cure. Set the cages up in a sheltered place, such as a shed, where they won't get rained on. It usually takes 2 to 3 weeks for the garlic to cure. When you're finished, the panels are easy to store. Just cut the zip ties and store them flat.

Gotcha covered
Kathleen Ryan, Pennsylvania

Cabbage loopers and worms can ruin crops of broccoli or cabbage in no time. On a tour of the nearby chocolate museum, Kathleen noticed that the fabric of the protective hair cap she was asked to wear was similar to floating row cover she used to protect her veggies from these critters. So she took a few caps home and put them through the washer (but not the dryer, which would ruin them) Then she let them air dry and tried them on some broccoli heads in the garden. It worked! Kathleen noticed that the vegetables she covered didn't have nearly as much damage as the others. Now she leaves the caps on the plants all the time because they're light enough to let in sun and water.

Fortunately, you don't have to take a tour of a chocolate museum to get a cap. These bouffant caps are available at discount stores and restaurant supply stores. Just make sure the caps aren't lined with plastic so they don't hold moisture.

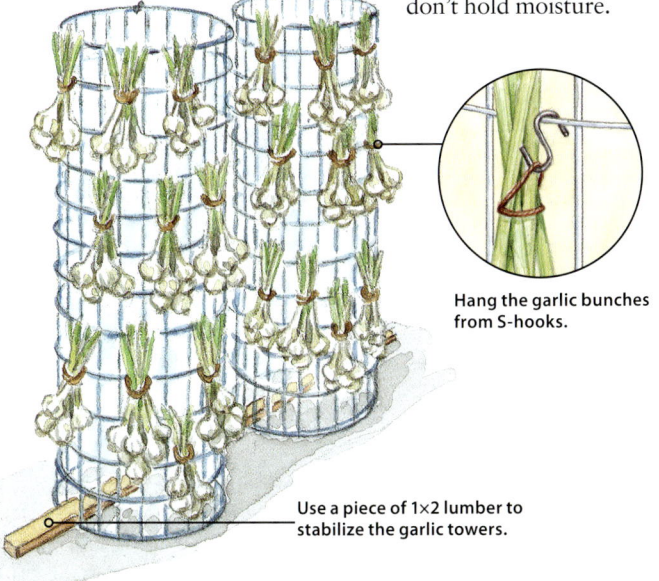

Hang the garlic bunches from S-hooks.

Use a piece of 1×2 lumber to stabilize the garlic towers.

Keep cauliflower white and tasty by fastening leaves around the head to block out sunlight.

White cauliflower
Steve Metheny, Oregon

Q *The label on the cauliflower seedlings I picked up in spring shows snow-white heads, but what I grew is yellow-green. What happened?*

A The heads received too much sunlight. While they are edible, they may taste bitter. However, "blanching" the heads will keep them white and tasty.

As soon as the immature head is about 2 inches in diameter, pull some of the side leaves up and over it. In the photo above a rubber band holds the leaves in place, but you can use twine or fabric strips, too. As the head grows, if necessary, tie more leaves up to keep sunlight off of the forming head. Depending on the cultivar and temperature, in a week or two it's time to harvest. The smooth, firm snow-white heads are ready to pick when they're about 6 inches across.

Wash day for row covers
Olive Weinberg, Florida

Q *My floating row covers get really dirty. Can I wash them?*

A Yes, and you should: Dirty fabric won't let as much light through as clean fabric does. Use the same detergent you use for your clothing and set your machine for cold water and a gentle cycle. Rinse with clear water, and hang the fabric outside to dry.

When row covers are not in use, store them indoors. Sunlight and long periods of being wet will eventually break down the fabric.

did you know... (CONTINUED)

product picks

The granules are actually coated walnut shell pieces so they're totally organic and break down in the soil.

Animal Stopper

We're always looking for methods to keep deer, rabbits, groundhogs and other animals from damaging the plants in our test garden. Animal Stopper is now a part of our arsenal of repellents. It did a great job last fall keeping groundhogs from gobbling up our lettuce and deer from munching the snapdragons at left.

Although critters don't like the scent, we didn't think Animal Stopper smelled bad, like other products do. Oils of rosemary, mint and cinnamon cover the smell of the putrescent eggs. Since it's granular, this repellent is easy to apply: Just shake the bottle around the area you want to protect — no messy sprays involved. Use it year-round; one application lasts 30 days and holds up to rain, snow and watering.

Bottom line It's organic, easy to apply and it works even in wet weather.
Source Home improvement and hardware stores and Messina Wildlife at www.messinawildlife.com or 888-411-3337
Price $19.99 for a 2.5 pound jug (shown), which covers 1,800 square feet; or $74.99 for 12 pounds, which covers 10,500 square feet

Deer-Resistant Landscaping

If you have deer nibbling your garden to the ground, add this book to your library. *Deer-Resistant Landscaping* is full of information to help you understand deer behavior and how to keep them out of your garden. What's really helpful is the section that includes a list of more than 1,000 plants that are deer-resistant. And since deer tastes seem to vary by region, each plant has a listing of areas where studies have shown it to be less than appetizing. But deer aren't the only wildlife that cause problems. With this book you'll get additional tips for dealing with a number of other pesky critters, such as raccoons, mice and moles.

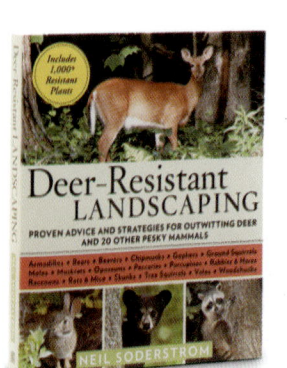

Bottom line Whether it's deer, raccoons or mice, this book will show you how to keep pests away.
Source Local and online bookstores and www.GardenGateStore.com
Price $23.95; softcover; 354 pages

Safer EndALL Insect Killer

EndALL™ Insect Killer may sound menacing, but it's a new organic pesticide from Safer®. This ready-to-use spray is the first of its kind to combine neem oil, horticultural soap and pyrethrin to take care of insects in all stages of life. The neem zaps insect eggs and soft-bodied larvae while the soap and pyrethrin get rid of adults. Spray EndALL every seven to 10 days as directed. You can even use it safely on your vegetables right up to the day of harvest.

Bottom line It works on insects in all stages of growth so you don't have to worry about timing applications just right.
Source Independent garden centers
Price $6.24 for 24 oz.; $7.82 for 32 oz.

How long will milky spore last?
Irene Barna, Vermont

Q I didn't use up all of the milky spore I bought this year to control Japanese beetle grubs. Will it still be good next year?

A Milky spore dust has an unlimited shelf life as long as it's stored in a cool, dry spot.

However, you probably don't need to keep a large supply on hand. Once milky spore is applied to the soil, it can be active for up to 20 years. But one application can take three to five years to give complete control. As the grubs feed on it, they will multiply the milky spore in their digestive tract, spreading it into other areas. If you live in a region with severely cold winters, frigid temperatures can shorten its longevity and you may see those hungry grubs reappearing after 10 or 15 years.

Fertilizer breakdown
Kay Burke, Iowa

Q I used slow-release fertilizer in my patio containers, but it doesn't seem to dissolve. Is it working?

A You're probably seeing the empty shells of the capsules that held the fertilizer. After the fertilizer is released, the capsules can last a long time, but eventually they dissolve.

These capsules dissolve and release fertilizer at different times. Even after they are empty, the capsules don't all break down at the same rates. The ones on the surface stay dryer than those mixed into the soil, so they often last longer. But in the photos below you can see the difference. Plus, empty fertilizer capsules will float when you water the container but full ones won't.

Full capsules are opaque and won't float when you're watering the soil.

You may not see a hole, but empty fertilizer capsules often have a translucent look.

in the news

Killer compost
Gardeners in the United Kingdom and the United States have recently lost plants due to compost contaminated with aminopyralid. It's a chemical found in the weed killers ForeFront® and Milestone®, used to treat pastures where cattle and horses graze. The problem for gardeners is that aminopyralid doesn't break down even if eaten and digested by an animal. As a result, some manures are laced with an unhealthy dose of broadleaf herbicide. The company that produces this chemical recommends that composted manure from animals grazing in treated fields not be sold for use in gardens. So next time you buy manure from a local source, ask if the field where the animals grazed was treated with aminopyralid.

Catnip keeps Asian lady beetles away
Scientists at the USDA Agricultural Research Service have been looking for an environmentally friendly way to keep Asian lady beetles out of homes. They've tested extracts of several plants. But so far, nepetalactone, a compound made from catnip oil, has worked the best. Research continues, but scientists expect that eventually combining a spray repellent like this with other strategies will encourage the beetles to stay out of your house and in the garden where they belong.

Keep those amendments dry
Dorothy Nixon, Vermont

Epsom salts, sulfur and potash often come in paper bags or cardboard boxes that aren't the best containers for storage — especially in a shed or garage. It's easy for moisture to ruin the contents. But Dorothy found that her empty plastic laundry detergent jugs were the perfect size to keep these powdered products fresh and dry. And the spout comes in handy, too. To get a jug ready to use, Dorothy rinses it thoroughly and lets it dry upside down for a couple of weeks just to make sure there's no residual moisture. Then she takes a permanent marker and writes the name of the product and the date on the outside.

Dorothy uses a pair of pliers to pull out the jug's spout so she can pour ingredients in easily. Finally, she puts the spout back and it's ready to use. If the spout in your container won't budge, you can always use a funnel.

did you know... (CONTINUED)

garden jargon

Ever seen a horticultural term and wondered what it meant? We can help!

CONIFER Mostly plants with needles or scalelike leaves. Many also produce their seeds in cones. Some of the best-known conifers are evergreens, such as spruce, pine, fir, juniper, yew and hemlock. However, larch, which loses its needles, is also a conifer.

Cankerworm control
Jon Sass, South Dakota

Q *What's the best technique to keep cankerworms from crawling into my trees?*

A Cankerworms "hibernate" in the soil until it's time to breed. Males have wings, but females have to crawl up into trees to lay their eggs. The caterpillars that hatch will feast on foliage.

Banding is a technique that uses a sticky material as a trap. To keep children and pets from getting to the sticky surface, construct the band about 5 feet off the ground. Start with a layer of batting. The one in the first photo below is about 15 inches wide. Next add a layer of tar paper. It'll hold up in wind and rain and offer a surface to hold the sticky trap

You'll find the best control, Tanglefoot, at most garden centers. It won't wash off and remains sticky. Wearing disposable gloves, smear a 1/16-inch-thick layer of Tanglefoot on the tar paper. To keep crawlers from finding alternate routes you'll also need to band trees, and even light poles, that touch the branches of a susceptible tree.

Scrape away the dead crawlers frequently. They can become a bridge for the crawling insects. Apply more Tanglefoot if the surface is no longer sticky.

Have the bands in place before the adults emerge from the soil (mid- to late March in most areas). But check with your local extension service to be sure of the timing. And remove the bands in mid-May to let the bark under the tar paper dry out. Then about the middle of September, you'll want to put them up again to catch fall cankerworms. Keep them in place until mid- to late October.

Here's a list of seven cankerworm favorites:
- Apple (*Malus* spp.)
- Ash (*Fraxinus* spp.)
- Basswood/linden (*Tilia* spp.)
- Elm (*Ulmus* spp.)
- Hackberry (*Celtis* spp.)
- Maple (*Acer* spp.)
- Oak (*Quercus* spp.)

Artillery fungus
Paul DiMaio, Ohio

Q *I spotted bubble-like stuff growing in the mulch around my shrubs. Is it harmful?*

A If it looks like the photo above, it's artillery fungus (*Sphaerobolus* spp.). Each bubble, less than 1/10 of an inch in diameter, is where the *peridiole*, a capsule that holds spores, has been ejected. Believe it or not, they can be projected up to 20 feet! While the brown capsules aren't harmful, they stick like glue and are unsightly on light-colored surfaces, such as siding.

Artillery fungus breaks down rotting hardwood, and is most active in spring and fall, when temps are between 50 and 70 degrees F. If the specks are affecting nearby surfaces, your best bet is to remove the mulch. Or cover your existing mulch with a mix of two parts mushroom compost to three parts cedar, redwood or cypress mulch. Recent studies have found these mulches, mixed with mushroom compost, are resistant to this fungus.

The capsule that holds spores is still in this artillery fungus.

This bulging fungus has just shot a peridiole, like the small brown sphere to the right.

Cinch a strip of fiberglass batting, at least 6 in. wide, with duct tape to keep insects from crawling under the tar paper.

Wrap a piece of tar paper, wide enough to cover the batting, around the trunk and hold it in place with two strips of duct tape.

Crawling insects get stuck in the sticky material, so smear a thin layer over the entire surface.

product picks

Paper ties

Keep your plants in place with these new paper ties. Made of 100 percent unbleached recycled paper and ½ inch wide, the material is strong enough to tie raspberry canes in place with ease. But the paper is soft and pliable, so it doesn't dig into plant stems, as twine sometimes does. Last year, they easily lasted all season at our test garden. And when we cleaned up beds, we simply tossed this natural material into the compost pile. You could also till it into your soil.

Bottom line It's easy to tie, gentle on plants and makes fall clean-up a little easier.
Source Lee Valley Garden Tools at www.leevalley.com or 800-871-8158
Price $4.20 for 33 feet

Hedge shears

Tired of aching hands, arms and shoulders after a big pruning job? Try these new hedge shears from OXO. What makes these shears different is that the nonslip handle grips rotate. With a twist of your wrist, reaching for high or awkward branches is a lot easier. The thing we loved most about these shears was how well-balanced and light the aluminum handles are. In addition, the blades are made of rust-resistant steel and have a nonstick coating.

Bottom line Good shears like these help keep aches and pains to a minimum.
Source Local garden centers or OXO at www.oxo.com or 800-545-4411
Price $29.99

The rotating handles move easily with a little pressure.

in the news

Moth trouble

There's a new pest causing problems in California: the Australian light brown apple moth (*Epiphyas postvittana*). This unobtrusive-looking brown moth has been found on more than 2,000 plant species, where the larvae rolls up into and munches leaves. It's difficult to identify because the moth and its larvae look similar to native moths. They're so close that an entomologist is probably the only person who could tell them apart.

It seems that the most significant route of this pest's spread so far is through live plants sold at nurseries. And since California is a major source of nursery plants, it's likely that without precautions, its range will grow. In New Zealand, an integrated pest management approach to treatment has been effective over a 10-year period. So far only 13 counties in California are affected, but researchers at the USDA and other industry professionals are working to find the best treatment plan for North America.

While there's not much individual gardeners can do yet, there may be soon. Be watching for updates on what you can do to help prevent this pest's spread.

Get connected

If you enjoy seeing what other gardeners are up to in your state, across the nation or even around the world, check out garden blogs. A blog is kind of like a garden journal, but it's available for everyone to read on the Web. There are hundreds of them out there and more are added each day. Fortunately, our friends at Cold Climate Gardening, a blog about gardening in New York, have developed a state-by-state or country directory, so you can find blogs specific to your region. Visit www.coldclimategardening.com/garden-blog-directory to get connected with gardeners everywhere!

did you know... (CONTINUED)

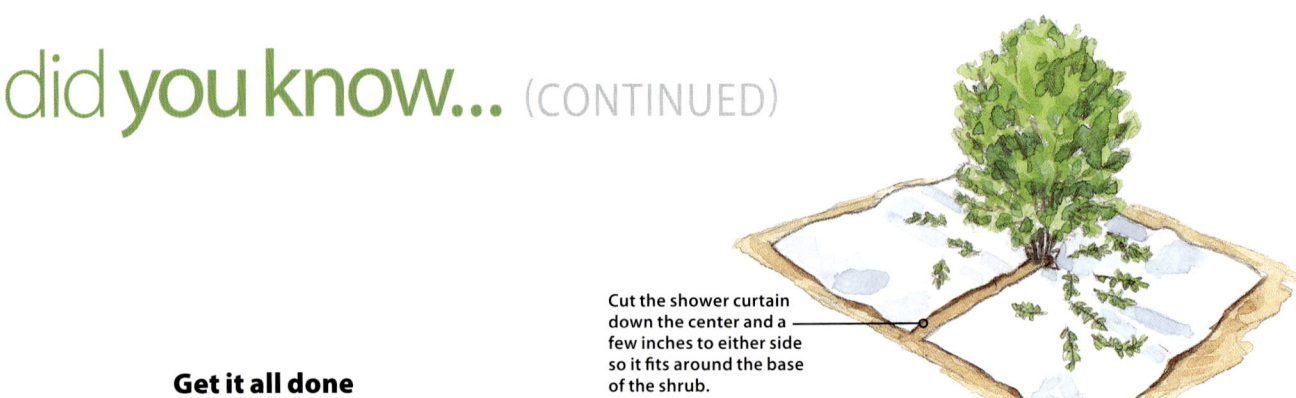

Cut the shower curtain down the center and a few inches to either side so it fits around the base of the shrub.

Get it all done
Carolyn Magnuson, Maryland

After a long work week, Carolyn's to-do list for yardwork used to be overwhelming. But now she has a plan: Before leaving for work in the morning, she thinks of one small task to do when she gets home. It's something that'll take five or 10 minutes and won't require a change of clothes. Then she packs whatever tools she'll need in her car. When she gets home, even before walking into the house, she goes right to the garden with her tools in hand and does that chore. Whether it's deadheading or pulling a few small weeds, Carolyn finds that it's a great way to decompress after work. And it makes her weekends more relaxing, too.

Tidy pruning
Barbara Smoak, South Caronlina

When it's time to prune her viburnums, Barbara gets out her old shower curtain and starts working. She's modified the heavy-duty plastic curtain to look a lot like a barber's cape: She's cut it up the middle and to either side like the curtain in the illustration above. That way she can easily place it around the shrub. As she prunes, she lets the twigs fall where they may. Cleanup is a lot easier when she just has to drag the prunings away rather than pick them out of the mulch.

Wear gloves and eye protection when using chemicals to remove lichen from surfaces.

Patio fungus
Terry Grinnan, Massachusetts

Q A fungus is growing on my stone wall and brick patio. How can I remove it?

A This is lichen, which is a combination of fungi and tiny plants. It forms on surfaces like stone, brick, wood, soil, metal and bark, but doesn't harm them. Some people like the aged look, but lichen can be slippery when wet. This is often a problem on patios and walks.

Unfortunately, there isn't a quick or easy way to get rid of lichen. But scrubbing it off with a soft-bristle brush and a mixture of one part bleach to 10 parts water is effective. Scraping it off with a plastic or wooden scraper or blasting it with a pressure washer works, as well. These methods will need to be done periodically, depending on how fast the lichen returns.

Garden centers also sell ready-to-use products, such as Moss Max® Moss Killer and Bayer Advanced™ 2-in-1 Moss and Algae Killer. These concentrates are applied to lichen with a hose-end sprayer. Rinse garden and lawn areas after applying to prevent damage. And carefully read and follow the directions on the package. Repeat the treatments every two weeks or as needed to prevent more growth.

Rain garden cleanup
Diane Rhodes, Iowa

Q *I put in a rain garden this spring. What do I need to do to get it ready for winter?*

A A rain garden is about the same as any other flower border. However, since it's a new garden or if it's been a dry fall, make sure to give it a good soaking before the ground freezes. Wait until spring to cut back your perennials and grasses. Many rain garden plants have interesting seedheads to look at or to feed birds. Next spring, when you're cleaning the rest of your garden, cut back the dead stalks to make room for new growth.

Don't get all worked up
Marge Kimm, WY

Q *Is it a good idea to deeply work the soil in my perennial border every year?*

A No, you may damage shallow roots and lose valuable moisture. Deep tilling also brings weed seeds to the surface, where they quickly germinate. And turning up the soil can kill organisms that help plants manufacture food. Only work the soil deeply when you're starting a new garden or in the spot where you're putting new plants into your established border.

product picks

New Encyclopedia of Gardening Techniques

You may have seen an earlier edition of this helpful American Horticultural Society reference book published in 2002, but it's been revised and updated. From pruning your wisteria to sowing onions, the topics covered are quite varied. But what makes it even more helpful are the 2,000 color illustrations and 200 photographs that show you, step-by-step, how to get things done in the garden.

This handy attached bookmark helps mark your place.

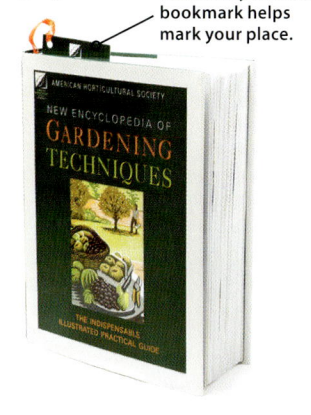

Bottom line Whatever garden topic you can think of, it's covered her
Source Local and onlin bookstores and www.GardenGateStore.com
Price $45; hardcover; 480 pages

garden **jargon**

Ever seen a horticultural term and wondered what it meant? We can help!

CULTIVAR This is a plant that a breeder has selected for a special trait, such as color, form or hardiness. It's usually propagated by division, cuttings or tissue culture. Seed gathered from a cultivar may produce the same traits, but most often plants will be different from their parents.

Echinacea purpurea 'Magnus'
Genus — Species — Cultivar

For example, the purple coneflower found in the wild is *Echinacea purpurea*, and each plant can look slightly different. A cultivar name, such as 'Magnus', in single quotes after the genus and species on a tag tells you each plant with that name will look the same.

Rainwater Harvesting System

There are a lot of rain barrels out there, but this new series from Fiskars® is better-looking than most. The one in the photo is Salsa but there are other styles, colors and sizes to choose from. Each barrel comes with the water diverter at left, which hooks up to your downspout so the barrel won't overflow, even in a heavy rain. With most other brands, you have to buy the water diverter separately. These barrels also come with a spigot and a tightly fitting lid. For installation details, how-to videos and tips, visit www.rain-barrel.com. It only takes .2 inch of rain running off a 500-sq.-ft. roof to fill a 52-gallon barrel. So you might want to buy the connector kit to hook a couple of barrels together.

Each kit has two diverters to fit the most common downspout sizes.

Bottom line These rain barrels save water, help the environment and look good while doing it.
Source Check your local home-improvement center or hardware store
Price $189.99 for the 58-gallon Salsa (shown). There are other styles that hold 48 or 57 gallons, and prices range from $129.99 to $189.99.

pests to watch

Cabbage looper
Trichoplusia ni

IDENTIFICATION Be on the lookout for a small green caterpillar with white racing stripes and a voracious appetite each spring in North America. The cabbage looper can eat three times its body weight every day! And with two to seven generations each year, depending on the length of your growing season, that's a lot of plant damage.

The moth has mottled brown wings with a single silver spot in the center and most often lays a single pale yellow to green egg on a leaf. But clusters of six or seven eggs aren't uncommon. Cabbage loopers' favorite egg hosts are cruciferous vegetables, such as cabbage, turnips, kale and others, but it's not picky. About three days after the egg is laid, a caterpillar emerges and starts eating.

DAMAGE Yes, a cabbage looper loves to eat cabbage, but it also munches on broccoli, cauliflower, potatoes, lettuce, tomatoes and cucumbers. Ornamental plants, such as mums, carnations, snapdragons, geraniums and hollyhocks, are also on the menu. Avoiding the veins of the leaves, the cabbage looper eats irregular holes and can defoliate a plant in no time. This can stunt growth or even kill the plant. Be sure to check the centers of broccoli and other plants, as a cabbage looper will sometimes bore its way into the heads.

CONTROL You can hand pick any caterpillars that you find. Or encourage predatory wasps and ground beetles to live in your garden by avoiding insecticides and leaving leaf debris or mulch around for hiding places. In turn, they'll do you the favor of eating these hungry caterpillars. For serious problems, try a spray product containing neem. This organic pesticide stops the caterpillar from eating and disrupts its growth so much the insect dies. ◻

Actual size: 1½ in. long

Actual wing span: 1½ in. long

Approximate size: 6 to 8 in. long

Eastern mole
Scalopus aquaticus

LOOKS AREN'T EVERYTHING Moles may look like rodents but they're actually related to bats and shrews. Eastern moles have a smooth gray coat, tiny eyes, a hairless pointed snout and big flipperlike front legs. These underground dynamos can excavate up to 18 ft. of tunnel near the surface in an hour. All that effort creates a big appetite. Moles can consume 45 to 50 lbs. of earthworms, grubs and other insects yearly.

TUNNEL KNOW-HOW There are two types of mole tunnels: foraging and runway. Foraging, or surface, tunnels meander, are generally shallow and fill in as the soil settles. These tunnels damage lawns by uprooting grass, creating unsightly ridges and soft spots. The deeper runway tunnels are where they spend more of their time in summer as the soil gets harder and in winter when the soil freezes. You'll probably never see evidence of these tunnels in your lawn.

MOLE CONTROL Not everything about moles is bad. They do eat pest insects and aerate the soil. Bulbs and plant roots aren't on their diet. But their tunnels are a problem. You can forget the vast majority of the "remedies" you hear for getting rid of moles. Here's why a couple of common solutions — eliminating lawn grubs and flooding tunnels — won't work. If you get rid of grubs, the moles eat other insects. And there's not enough water pressure from your hose to flood the tunnels — moles move quickly when they have to. To really get rid of these critters, keep watering to a minimum so the soil is harder, which discourages both insects and moles. The surest solution is a trap. Set the trap on a foraging tunnel and follow the directions carefully to ensure humane results. ◻

Botrytis blight
Botrytis paeoniae

IDENTIFICATION Having trouble with your peonies? Botrytis blight may be the problem. There are several species of *Botrytis*, also called gray mold, that attack a wide range of ornamental flowers, fruits and vegetables. In the case of peonies, you may notice a fluffy gray mold on new shoots in spring. Later, the botrytis damage you see above shows up on stems, leaves and flowers. Wet, humid weather gets this fungus going early in the year. A rainy summer makes things worse because the spores are spread by splashing water. Botrytis overwinters in the soil and on dead plant tissue. It can remain dormant for years waiting for the right weather conditions.

DAMAGE Botrytis blight shows up on any part of the plant that's above ground. Leaves and stems get large, irregular dark spots. Buds fail to open, then turn brown and rot, and sometimes flower petals are spotted. Often the rot is accompanied by the fluffy mold. The severity of infection can vary from year to year, depending on the weather, so botrytis blight doesn't usually kill the plants it infects.

CONTROL There are four things you can do to help your peonies avoid or combat botrytis blight: Don't water overhead, allow space between plants for good air circulation, clean up in the fall and, if things get really bad, use a fungicide. Watering at soil level prevents spores from being splashed onto the stems. Keep an eye on your peonies, especially in spring, and if you notice signs of infection, prune the affected stem down to the ground. Getting rid of spent foliage in fall is a must. Burn or throw away any debris, as this fungus can survive in compost piles. If botrytis keeps showing up, try using a fungicide with neem, such as Garden Safe Fungicide 3. It can be used as a preventative, and also after the infection has started. ◻

Botrytis blight turns leaves, stems and flowers brown.

beneficials to know

Septoria leaf spot
Septoria lycopersici

Did you notice dozens of small black spots ringed in yellow on the leaves of your tomato plant last year? It could be septoria leaf spot. Septoria is a group of fungi that causes problems for hundreds of agricultural and ornamental plants. But this particular species causes problems on tomatoes.

WHAT DOES IT LOOK LIKE? Right after the tomatoes begin forming in early summer, septoria leaf spot starts showing up on the leaves closest to the ground. These irregular spots start out yellow, age to brown and then turn black as they begin producing spores. Spots range in size from 1/16 to 1/4 in. in diameter.

WHAT DOES IT DO? Septoria thrives in warm, wet weather as wind and rain spread spores that settle in plant debris and soil. So the first problems you'll see are on the lower half of the plant — rain splashes the spores onto the leaves. As the disease moves up the plant, leaves turn yellow and fall off prematurely. Eventually, the plant is defoliated. Without leaves to shelter them, the tomatoes develop sunscald and may rot.

HOW DO I GET RID OF IT? To get rid of septoria leaf spot, clean up plant debris in the fall. Then spores won't have a place to spend the winter. During the growing season, try not to water overhead and make sure you get rid of weeds, especially horsenettle, jimsonweed and nightshade. (They are hosts for this fungal pest.) If this is a recurring problem, rotate your tomato crop every year, also avoiding other related plants, such as peppers, potatoes and eggplant. For a really large problem, use a fungicide such as Liqui-Cop, a liquid copper spray, according to label directions. ☐

Eastern firefly
Photinus pyralis

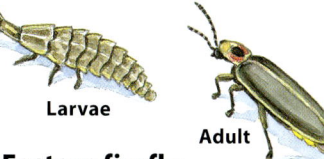

Larvae
Adult
Actual size: 1/2 in. long

WHAT'S THAT LIGHT? It's hard to miss these guys on hot summer evenings when they're flashing their tail lights over and over. Summer is peak mating season for Eastern fireflies (also called lightning bugs), and the flashes of light are their mating calls.

SEEN ONE LATELY? Adult fireflies are actually winged beetles, not flies, with two red spots on their heads. The wings are brown-black, edged with a light yellow stripe. During the day they seek out dark, damp places to rest, so you may not notice them. The larvae are segmented with six legs. The eggs and the larvae light up, too, not just the adults. Several species are found throughout the United States and Canada but the Eastern firefly is one of the most common. It's found east of the Rocky Mountains in open, grassy areas.

THE LIFE OF A FIREFLY In early summer, the adults surface after a year underground. Around dusk, the males begin to fly and flash in search of a mate. Females respond with flashes, mate and deposit eggs singly or in groups in the soil around grass roots. Both adults die shortly after mating. Eggs hatch in about three weeks, and the larvae overwinter underground, emerging in the spring to begin the process again.

INVITE THEM IN Both the firefly and its flightless larvae are good to have around. They eat aphids, slugs, earthworms, mites and pollen. Make your garden attractive to these bugs by giving them bark or mulch to hide under. Grow small trees and shrubs so flightless females have a spot to wait for their mates. Light pollution interferes with the mating process, making these insects harder to find in urban areas. So turn off the porch light to help them feel at home. ☐

Dark-eyed junco
Junco hyemalis

You know winter is here when dark-eyed juncos, or snowbirds, show up at your feeders. One of the most common is the slate-colored junco, in the photos at right.

IT'S A BIRD'S LIFE Most of these small members of the sparrow family spend their summers in coniferous forests in Canada, the western United States and the Appalachians, where they breed and raise their young. The females build nests in shallow depressions on the ground. Eggs are incubated for 12 to 13 days, and baby birds are ready to leave the nest in 9 to 13 days. Both the male and female feed the babies, whose diet consists exclusively of insects.

In late summer, dark-eyed juncos head to warmer climates. Females are the first to migrate and go as far as the Deep South. Males only travel as far as the Midwest. That way, they don't have as far to travel in spring and get a head start on establishing breeding territories.

FEED 'EM WHAT THEY WANT Dark-eyed juncos eat small weed seeds and any leftover flower seeds they find in your garden. If you're short on ragweed, smartweed or dried garden flower seeds, these little birds will happily eat millet, cracked corn and hulled sunflowers from a feeder.

Since they're mostly ground feeders scatter seed on the ground or set up a low platform feeder to attract them to your yard. A brush pile or shrub nearby gives birds a spot to rest or head for cover if something startles them. But keep plantings at least 10 ft. from any feeding area so the neighborhood cat doesn't find an easy place from which to nab a tasty bird treat. ☐

Male

Female

Approximate size: 5 to 6 in. long

6 weeds to know

Spiny sowthistle
Sonchus asper

Long unbranched stem with flower clusters at the top

WHAT IT LOOKS LIKE Despite its name, the spiny sowthistle is not actually a thistle but part of the sunflower family. Found throughout most of North America except northern Canada, this weed resembles a tall dandelion. It's a winter annual, sometimes behaving more like a biennial. In spring, an unbranched leafy stem grows from a basal rosette and can reach up to 6 ft. tall. Break the hollow stem and it releases a milky sap. The jagged-edged leaves clasp the tall stem and have prickly hairs that can cause an allergic reaction in some people.

Blooming from late June until frost, pale yellow flowers grow in clusters at the top of the stem. The seeds are a puff of fuzzy white and when fully ripe they float away on the wind. Seeds germinate in fall and overwinter as young plants.

WHERE TO FIND IT Spiny sowthistle prefers full sun. You may spot it in cultivated gardens, as well as in lawns and other undisturbed areas.

HOW TO GET RID OF IT Young seedlings can be cut with a hoe. However, some may sprout from roots left in the soil. A deep taproot and a weak stem make it hard to pull mature spiny sowthistle. However, young plants often come right out if you pull when the soil is wet. Just be sure to wear gloves and a shirt with long sleeves to prevent an allergic reaction similar to poison ivy. You can also mow the stem to prevent flowering and seed formation. In a lawn, a selective herbicide, such as Trimec®, is effective. ☐

Horseweed
Conyza canadensis

WHAT IT LOOKS LIKE Growing throughout North America, the first sign of this annual is a low rosette of broad leaves. A winter annual, or sometimes biennial, it'll be there in early spring. Growing quickly with no side branches, horseweed can reach 7 ft. tall. The leaves have bristly hairs and toothed edges. At the base of the plant they are broad, but get smaller further up the stem. Crush a leaf or break a stem and you'll pick up a slight odor of carrots. Near the top of the stem, small white to lavender flowers open in late summer. As the flowers fade, they're replaced by seeds with short tufts of bristles that help the seed travel by wind.

WHERE TO FIND IT Look for horseweed in sunny flower and vegetable gardens. It grows tallest in areas with moist, rich soil, but you'll find it in dry spots, too. Horseweed is a host to aster yellows disease, which can affect zinnias, coneflowers, asters and many other plants and is transmitted by insects. You'll recognize it by yellow veins in the leaves, as well as stunted and deformed plants. If you spot infected plants, send them away in the trash or bury them at least 3 ft. deep to prevent spreading it.

HOW TO GET RID OF IT Young horseweed plants can easily be hoed out. And even though they have a taproot, they can be pulled, too. However, be sure to wear gloves when handling horseweed — it can cause skin irritation. Herbicides are usually effective for large stands of this weed. But in some areas it has become resistant to glyphosate herbicides, such as Roundup®. And since it spreads by seed, a fall application of a pre-emergent herbicide is effective, as well. ☐

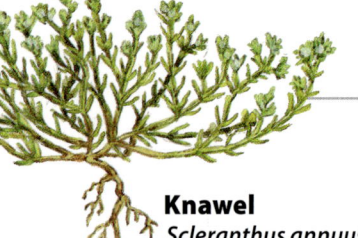

Knawel
Scleranthus annuus

WHAT IT LOOKS LIKE Low stems of this winter annual fan out from a taproot to sprawl over the ground. Where it has formed colonies, the 2- to 6-in.-tall plants mesh together, forming a dense mat. The ½-in.-long leaves are narrow, almost like those of a tufted grass or creeping phlox.

When it's ready to bloom, often starting in spring and continuing most of summer, you'll barely notice the tiny star-shaped flower. It's green and has modified leaves instead of petals. Seeds form from spring until fall, and can remain viable in the soil for several years.

WHERE TO FIND IT At home in sunny flower and vegetable gardens, as well as lawns, knawel prefers dry, sandy or gravelly soils. And it's most common in the eastern half of North America and along the West Coast.

HOW TO GET RID OF IT Since it's an annual and grows from a fibrous taproot, pull or hoe this pest out of the ground. Just make sure to get rid of it before it sets seeds. Selective broadleaf herbicides will kill it in lawns. Pre-emergents applied in fall or early spring before it sprouts will also keep it under control in turf areas. ☐

Ivyleaf morning glory
Ipomoea hederacea

WHAT IT LOOKS LIKE This annual climbing vine is easily identified by the funnel-shaped flowers in shades of pink, purple or white. Blooming begins in July and continues into midfall. The twining stem can grow up to 10 ft. long and is lined with three-lobed, ivy-shaped leaves. It runs along the ground or crawls up into other plants. Both the stem and the base of the flower are covered by soft hairs.

WHERE TO FIND IT Ivyleaf morning glory grows best in full sun and moist, well-drained soil. But it tolerates almost any soil, even dry. Look for it in gardens, especially where it has shrubs, perennials or a fence to wind into. And you'll find it at the edges of gardens, sprawling over the ground, even out into lawns.

HOW TO GET RID OF IT Seeds drop in summer and sprout the following spring. However, they can survive in the soil for many years, waiting for the right conditions to sprout. Apply a pre-emergent herbicide in spring to keep the seeds from growing. Even though ivyleaf morning glory has a taproot, it's slender and shallow, so pulling or hoeing is a good way to eradicate this weed. It won't resprout even if you don't get the entire root out of the ground. Just make sure to get rid of the stems before the flowers form seeds. And, as with most annual weeds, both selective and nonselective herbicides are effective. ☐

Each leaf is shaped like an ivy leaf.

Jimsonweed
Datura stramonium

WHAT IT LOOKS LIKE One of the best ways to identify this annual is by the 2- to 5-in.-long five-sided, trumpet-shaped flowers. They're sweet-smelling and either white or light purple, like the illustration at right. Each flower lasts one day, but there will be enough to keep the plant blooming from late spring into early fall. The egg-shaped fruit is covered with stiff prickles. In the illustration it's mature and splitting open into four segments to release dozens of small black seeds. These seeds, and all the plants' parts, are poisonous.

Growing 2 to 5 ft. tall with an upright habit, the hollow stems can be green to red-purple and covered with fine hairs. Large 3- to 5-in.-long leaves are triangular with deeply toothed edges. Crush or just touch one and it'll release a disagreeable odor.

WHERE TO FIND IT Typically you find this weed in cultivated gardens, as well as perennial and shrub borders. It'll thrive in areas where there's little competition and it has room to grow.

HOW TO GET RID OF IT Jimsonweed's roots are thick and dense. But they don't grow deeply into the soil, so you can pull them out easily. Repeatedly mowing or cutting the plant short is effective at keeping it from setting seeds. Systemic herbicides, like Roundup®, usually work well if you apply them to young, actively growing plants. However, jimsonweed is showing signs of becoming resistant to herbicides, so hoeing or pulling may be your best bet for control. ☐

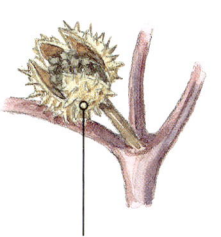

Five-sided trumpet-shaped flowers have a sweet smell.

Prickly egg-shaped pods split open to reveal small poisonous black seeds.

Hairy bittercress
Cardamine hirsuta

WHAT IT LOOKS LIKE Strolling through your garden in early spring, you spot a small, bright green mound less than 6 in. tall. It's up, and sometimes flowering, with the daffodils. That's hairy bittercress, an annual weed found throughout much of the United States and into Canada.

The leaves are small and rounded. Tiny white, four-petaled flowers bloom in early spring. However, in a cool, moist spot, you may find flowers blooming at any time of the year. Seed pods are narrow spikes that point straight up. When they're dry, they spring open to eject the seeds.

WHERE TO FIND IT Often hairy bittercress comes into a garden with new plants from a greenhouse or nursery, where it's a common pest. It'll grow just fine in sun or shade, moist or dry soil, and given time, will spread around your flowerbeds and vegetable gardens.

HOW TO GET RID OF IT In moist soil you'll find hairy bittercress has a taproot, but in dry conditions the roots tend to be more branched. Either way it's easy to pull. Or if you cut it off with a hoe it won't resprout. There's really no need to use a herbicide unless you're dealing with a very large stand of this pest. ☐

know YOUR zone

WHAT'S A ZONE AND WHY DOES IT MATTER?

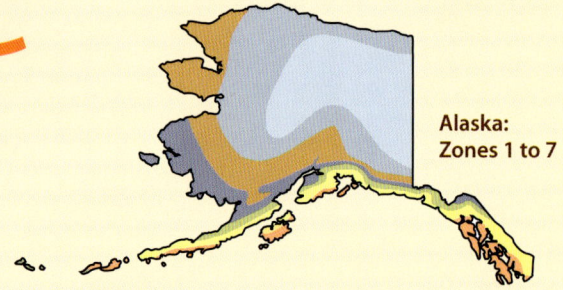

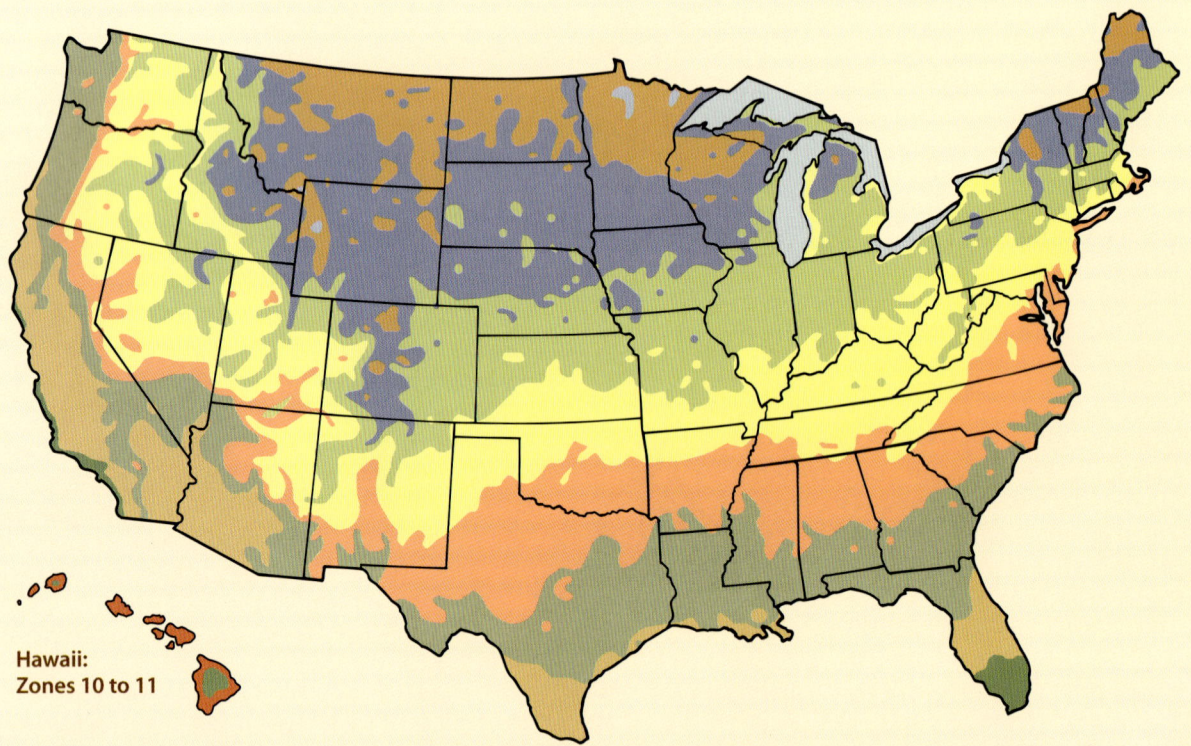

Alaska: Zones 1 to 7

Hawaii: Zones 10 to 11

COLD Hardiness

The USDA cold-hardiness map has long been the authority to help gardeners pick plants that will survive through the winter. It creates zones based on coldest average annual temperatures throughout the United States. A plant's cold-hardiness zone rating indicates where it's likely to survive the winter.

NOTE: For zones in Canada and Mexico, visit www.usna.usda.gov/Hardzone/ushzmap.html.

AVERAGE LOW TEMPERATURE	ZONE
Below -45	1
-40 to -45	2
-30 to -40	3
-20 to -30	4
-10 to -20	5
0 to -10	6

AVERAGE LOW TEMPERATURE	ZONE
10 to 0	7
20 to 10	8
30 to 20	9
40 to 30	10
Above 40	11

308 the YEAR IN GARDENING   www.GardenGateMagazine.com

Alaska:
Zones 1 to 2

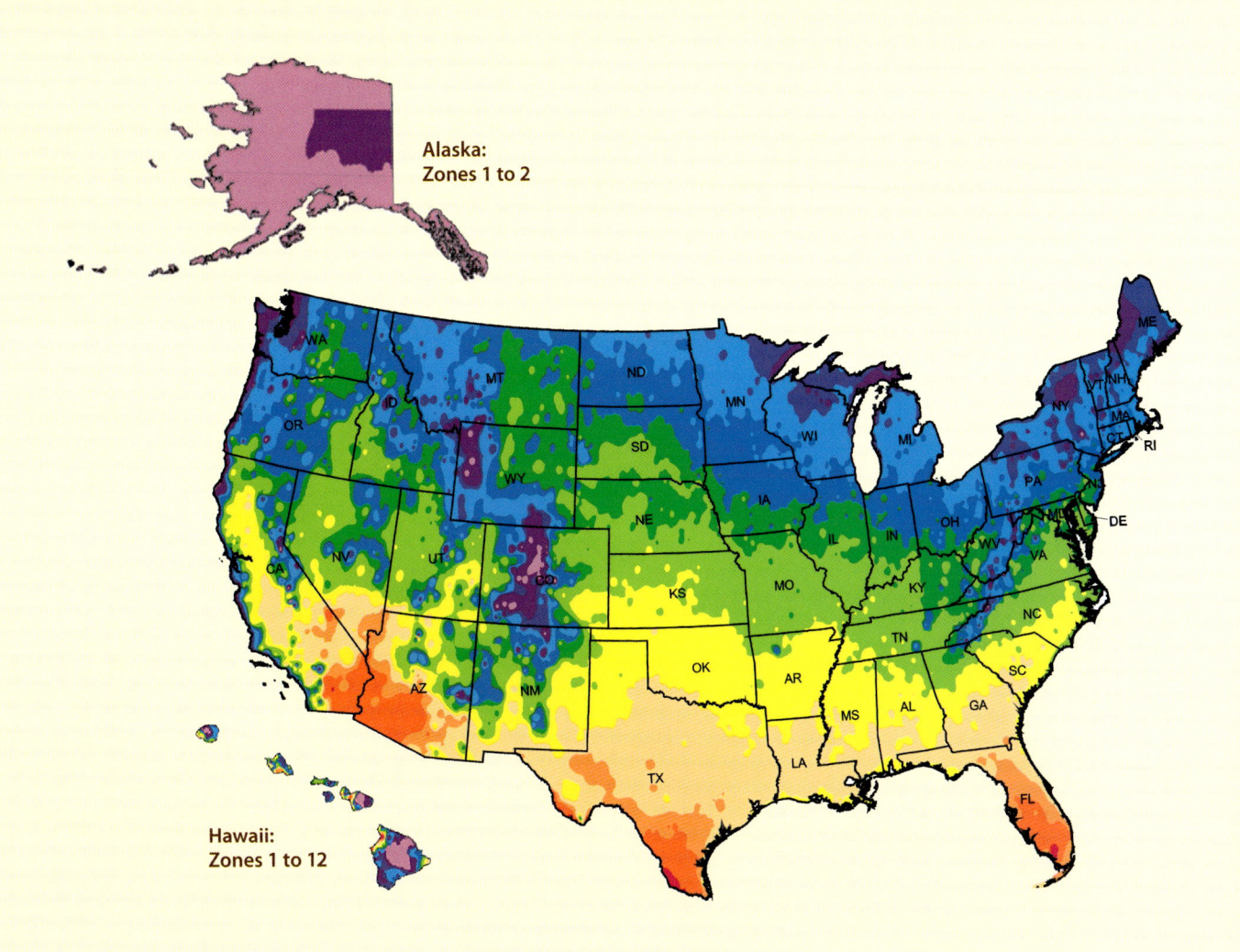

Hawaii:
Zones 1 to 12

DAYS ABOVE 86°	ZONE	DAYS ABOVE 86°	ZONE
Fewer than 1	1	60 to 90	7
1 to 7	2	90 to 120	8
7 to 14	3	120 to 150	9
14 to 30	4	150 to 180	10
30 to 45	5	180 to 210	11
45 to 60	6	More than 210	12

HEAT Tolerance

The American Horticultural Society's heat-zone map can help you determine how plants will cope with heat.

This map of the country is divided into 12 zones to indicate the average number of days in a year when the temperature goes above 86 degrees F. This is the temperature at which plants begin suffering and are unable to process water fast enough to maintain normal functions. Zone 1, the coldest zone, has less than one day. Zone 12, the hottest zone, has more than 210 days above 86 per year.

did you know...

Arbor Day Foundation changes zones

The National Arbor Day Foundation (NADF) has updated its hardiness zone map. Starting with the USDA zone map as a base, researchers examined 15 years of temperature information from the National Oceanic and Atmospheric Administration's 5,000 climatic data centers across the country. When everything was tabulated, the NADF decided to make some changes. Many areas of the country have moved up a full zone because of temperature changes over this time period. Check out www.arborday.org for the new cold-hardiness zone recommendations.

The YEAR IN GARDENING   Volume 16 INDEX

Acer
   dealing with leaves, 264
aconite, winter *see Eranthis hyemalis*
Aconitum carmichaelii
   for fall color, 26
Actaea simplex
   for fall scent, 137
Agastache foeniculum
   bird-attracting, 65
Alchemilla mollis
   chartreuse flowers, 147
Allium
   drying, 297
   fall color, 27
allspice, Carolina *see Calycanthus floridus*

Alstroemeria
   top pick cut flower, 94
alyssum, sweet *see Lobularia maritima*
Amelanchier
   top pick multiseason showoff, 108
Amsonia tabernaemontana
   top pick multiseason showoff, 107
Anemone
   top pick cut flower, 96
angel's trumpet *see Brugmansia*
annuals
   top pick multiseason showoffs, 107
   top pick new, 72

Antirrhinum
   top pick new, 79
   for perennial border, 173
aphids
   pest watch, 274
apples
   picking up high, 296
apricot *see Prunus mume*
Aquilegia
   cottage garden favorite, 153
   Editor's Choice, 18
arbor facelift, 187
arborvitae *see Thuja occidentalis*
Armeria maritima
   for high-altitudes, 68
Asperula orientalis
   plant profile, 69
Aster xfrikartii
   bird-attracting, 65
Astilbe
   top pick new, 74
autumn
   flowers for color, 26
   garden IQ, 264
   vegetables, 263
azalea *see Rhododendron*
back yard garden fixes, 174
Baptisia
   for perennial border, 173
   top pick multiseason showoff, 106
barberry, Japanese *see Berberis thunbergii*
bark
   mulch, 132
   winter appeal of, 168
barley, foxtail *see Hordeum jubatum*
bats, 281
beds
   island, 156, 196
   shaping up neglected, 124
bee balm *see Monarda didyma*
beetles
   Colorado potato, 276
   Japanese, 59, 299
beets, fall planting, 263
before & after
   curb appeal, 112
   entries, 120

   fantastic fall garden, 120
   front yard border, 116
   neglected bed, 124
   no space too small, 122
Begonia
   container makeover, 226
   monoecious, 69
beneficial creatures, 140, 277, 305
Berberis thunbergii
   Editor's Choice, 10
berries for birds, 109
Betula nigra
   top pick new, 78
birch *see Betula nigra*
birds
   attracting, 65, 200
   Birdfiles (database), 290
   feeders, 290, 291
   food, 109, 291
   geese, 290
   junco, 305
   woodpeckers, 280
bittercress, hairy *see Cardamine hirsuta*
blackspot on roses, 59
bleeding heart *see Dicentra eximia*
blight, botrytis
   pest watch, 304
blueberry *see Vaccinium*
bluegrass, annual *see Poa annua*
books
   Bloom's Best Perennials and Grasses, 186
   Containers Made Easy!, Volume 3, 223
   Deer-Resistant Landscaping, 298
   New Encyclopedia of Gardening Techniques, 303
   Succulent Container Gardens, 244
   What's Wrong With My Plant?, 63
borage *see Borago officinalis*
Borago officinalis
   cottage garden favorite, 153
border gardens, 170
   front yard, 116
botany
   conifers, 300
   cultivar, 303
   monoecious, 69

How to use your index

The index is divided by main topics with specific references following. All plants are referred to by botanical name.

For example, if you are looking for information about bleeding heart, the entry will look like this:

   bleeding heart *see Dicentra eximia*

Then turn to the reference for *Dicentra eximia*, which looks like this:

— Main topic (in this case, genus and species names)

   Dicentra eximia
      top pick long-bloomer, 98 — Page number

Specific reference to topic

You also might come across a topic that gives you specific references as well as an idea of other places in the index to look for similar information. For example:

   pests and pest controls
      see also names of specific pests;
         wildlife
      Orbital 360° sprayer, 295
      pesticides, 268, 298, 299

daisy

ILLUSTRATIONS: Mavis Augustine Torke

botrytis blight
  pest watch, 304
boundaries, fences and, 148
box, sweet *see Sarcococca confusa*
boxwood *see Buxus*
brick edging, 172
broccoli
  hairnets for protecting, 297
brown-eyed Susan *see Rudbeckia*
Brugmansia
  top pick big bloom, 87
Buddleja davidii
  cutting back, 66
  for fall scent, 137
bugbane *see Actaea simplex*
bugs, plant, 277
building projects
  glass ornaments, 288
bulbs
  among rocks, 127
  fertilizing, 266
  planting, 266
  spring combos, 182
  top pick new, 77
butterflies
  attracting, 196
  caterpillars, 198
  garden plan for, 194
  Monarch, 63
butterfly bush *see Buddleja davidii*
Buxus
  rootbound, 265
  shearing vs. plucking, 66
cabbage
  hairnets for protecting, 297
cabbage lopper
  hairnets for deterring, 297
  pest profile, 304
cabbageworm
  hairnets for deterring, 297
cactus, Christmas *see Zygocactus*
Callirhoe involucrata
  top pick long-bloomer, 100
Calycanthus floridus
  pruning, 255
Camellia
  for fall scent, 137
  pruning, 252
cankerworms, 300
canna leaf rollers, 63

Cardamine hirsuta
  weed watch, 307
caterpillars, feeding, 198
catmint *see Nepeta*
cauliflower
  color of heads, 297
cedar *see Cedrus atlantica*;
  Chamaecyparis; *Cryptomeria japonica*
Cedrus atlantica
  blue-green foliage, 169
Ceratostigma plumbaginoides
  for fall color, 29
Cercis
  propagation from seed, 67
Chaenomeles japonica
  pruning, 253
chafers, rose
  pest watch, 276
Chamaecyparis
  colored foliage, 169
chipmunks, 281
Christmas rose *see Helleborus*
clay soil, 172
Clematis
  for fall scent, 137
  top pick long-bloomer, 101
  top pick new, 77
coleus *see Solenostemon*
color
  accessorizing your garden, 165
  chartreuse, 145
  choosing scheme, 133

evergreen foliage, 169
  long-lasting, 138
  season-long, 170
columbine *see Aquilegia*
compost and composting
  contamination, 299
  sifters, 292
concrete patios, 131
coneflower *see Echinacea*
conifers
  definition of, 300
  undercutting low-growing, 127
  winter appeal of, 169
containers
  see also garden plans
  Containers Made Easy!, Volume 3, 223
  cork "feet", 242
  old boats, 242
  recycled wet vac, 243
  removing big plants from, 240
  squirrel protection, 243
  two-tier plant hanger, 244
  watering pouches, 242
  windowsill planter, 244
Conyza canadensis
  weed watch, 306
Coreopsis
  top pick new, 79
  for perennial border, 173
  top pick long-bloomer, 103
Corneliancherry *see Cornus*
corner gardens, 112, 178

Cornus
  berries for birds, 109
  pruning, 253
  winter appeal of, 168
Coronilla varia
  perennial weed, 271
Corylopsis glabrescens
  winter-bloomer, 167
Corylus avellana
  winter appeal of, 168
cottage gardens, 152
cowslip *see Primula*
crabapple *see Malus*
cranesbill *see Geranium*
crown rot, 260
Cryptomeria japonica
  chartreuse foliage, 169
cultivar, definition of, 303
culver's root *see Veronicastrum virginicum*
Cupressocyparis leylandii
  chartreuse foliage, 169
cut flowers
  preservatives, 97
  readers' top picks, 92
cypress *see Cupressocyparis leylandii*; *Taxodium distichum*
cypress, false *see Chamaecyparis*
Dahlia
  easy planting, 68
  top pick big bloom, 86
  top pick cut flower, 95
daisy, gloriosa *see Rudbeckia*

www.GardenGateMagazine.com *the* YEAR IN GARDENING **311**

Daphne

Daphne
   pruning, 253
   for winter scent, 137
Datura stramonium
   weed watch, 307
deadheading
   10-minute task, 173, 302
   shrubs, 252
deer
   Deer-Resistant Landscaping, 298
Delosperma nubigenum
   for high-altitudes, 68
Delphinium
   plant profile, 20
   top pick big bloom, 89
design
   see also color; garden plans; *names of specific plants*
   accessorizing your garden, 164
   back yard gardens, 174
   elements, 142, 176
   from scratch, 130
   tips for fall, 29
   trial and error, 173

design challenge
   birds, welcome, 200
   bring in butterflies, 194
   perennials and shrubs for easy gardening, 190
   shady haven, 208
   tame big space, 204
Deutzia gracilis
   pruning, 252
Dicentra eximia
   top pick long-bloomer, 98
Digitalis
   cottage garden favorite, 153
diseases
   artillery fungus, 300
   blackspot, 59
   botrytis blight, 304
   milky spore, 299
   septoria leaf spot, 305
dogwood *see Cornus*
dryer vents, planting near, 186
earwigs
   pest profile, 276
Echinacea
   bird-attracting, 65
   plant evaluations, 65

economics
   of gardening, 67
   plant shopping, 214, 249
Edgeworthia chrysantha
   winter-bloomer, 167
edging, 132, 172
Ellisia nyctelea
   biennial weed, 273
Eranthis hyemalis
   winter-bloomer, 166
Eremurus
   dividing, 267
   top pick big bloom, 89
Erodium pelargonium
   top pick long-bloomer, 99
Eschscholzia californica
   bird-attracting, 65
Eucomis bicolor
   chartreuse flowers, 147
Euphorbia
   plant profile, 24
Eustoma grandiflorum
   top pick cut flower, 95
fences
   to deter deer, 209
   materials for, 131

   uses for, 148
   for vegetable gardens, 131
fern, Boston *see Nephrolepis exaltata*
fertilizer and fertilizing
   bonemeal, 266
   bulbs, 266
   homemade, 268
   over fertilizing, 245
   slow-release, 299
   storing, 299
   tips for, 173
Filipendula rubra
   for perennial border, 173
fireflies, eastern, 305
fish, protecting, 294
flag *see Iris*
flowers
   chop stick stem extenders, 64
   long-lasting bouquet, 65, 97
foamflower *see Tiarella cordifolia*
focal points, 176
Forsythia xintermedia
   pruning, 253
Fothergilla gardenii
   pruning, 253
foundation gardens
   new home, 112
fountain grass *see Pennisetum alopecuroides*
fountains, low, 140
foxglove *see Digitalis*
fragrance, 136, 175
fringe flower *see Loropetalum chinense*
front yard gardens
   borders, 116
fungus
   artillery, 300
   fungicides, 268
   on patios, 302
Gaillardia
   plant profile, 12
Galanthus nivalis
   winter-bloomer, 166
garden plans
   see also before & after; design; design challenge
   border gardens
     drive-by, 154
     low maintenance, 192
     spring bulb combos, 182
   container gardens
     begonias, 228
     for butterflies, 199
     colorful combos, 221
     exuberant, 238
     flowery fall, 239
     focal point, 216
     for gaps, 218

grouping, 220
hot and sunny, 219
pansies, 236
shade, 225
shade combo, 223
for steps, 217
sunny, 224
vase basics, 97
whimsy, 225
wonderful whites, 222
corner gardens, 211
with big blooms, 91
Mailbox planting, 155
front-yard gardens
peony welcome, 52
spring bulb combos, 182
getaways
cozy retreat, 135
nearly no-care, 180
island beds
butterfly bistro, 196
nearly no-care plants, 156
patios and decks
bird-attracting, 202
shade gardens
pretty primroses, 54
showy palette, 210
woodland, 37
woodland retreat, 206
windowboxes
best tips, 230
Editor's top pick, 224
spring, 219
windowless, 232
gardeners
Barbara Damrosch, 262
Jeff Gillman, 268
Duane Hoover, 142
Carol Lindsay, 178
Lucy Tolmach, 136
Stephen Westcott-Gratton, 152
Gardenia jasminoides
pruning, 254
garlic, drying, 297
Gazania splendens
top pick new, 72
Geranium
'Rozanne' vs. 'Jolly Bee', 65
top pick long-bloomer, 99
geranium, ivy *see Pelargonium peltatum*
getaways, 134, 180
Geum
top pick multiseason showoff, 106
top pick new, 75
Gladiolus
easy lifting in fall, 64
top pick new bulb, 77

grasses
Bloom's Best Perennials and Grasses, 186
Hakonechloa macra
bright green foliage, 146
sun requirements, 141
Hamamelis x*intermedia*
pruning, 255
for winter scent, 137
winter-bloomer, 167
hanging baskets
frost protection, 243
lining, 242
Harlequin bugs, 277
Harry Lauder's walking stick *see Corylus avellana*
Helianthus
fall color, 27
The Great Sunflower Project, 63
top pick big bloom, 90
Heliotropium arborescens
for summer scent, 137
Helleborus
plant profile, 34
winter-bloomer, 166
herbicides
aminopyralid, 299
spot treatment, 248
heronsbill *see Erodium pelargonium*
Hesperaloe parviflora
top pick long-bloomer, 102
Hesperis matronalis
biennial weed, 273

Hibiscus moscheutos
top pick big bloom, 88
Hordeum jubatum
perennial weed, 271
hormones
thidiazuron (TDZ), 65
horseweed *see Conyza canadensis*
horticultural terms *see* botany
hoses
Gecko's Toes™ rack, 295
Super-Slim, 295
Hosta
bright green foliage, 146
for Southwest, 65
house plants and pollution, 63
Hyacinthus orientalis
for spring scent, 137
Hydrangea
chartreuse flowers, 147
as mum shelter, 68
top pick big bloom, 90
top pick new, 78
hyssop *see Agastache foeniculum*
ice plant *see Delosperma nubigenum*
Impatiens
plant profile, 38
indigo, wild *see Baptisia*
insect repellents, homemade, 268
Ipomoea
bright green foliage, 146
for fall scent, 137
top pick new, 79
weed watch, 307

Iris
plant profile, 44
for spring scent, 137
island beds, 156, 196
Itea virginica
top pick multiseason showoff, 108
Jacob's ladder *see Polemonium*
Japanese beetles, 59, 299
jimsonweed *see Datura stramonium*
journals
blogs, 301
Juglans nigra
black walnut decline, 67
Juniperus
foliage color, 169
Kalmeris pinnatifida
top pick long-bloomer, 103
Kalmia latifolia
pruning, 254
Kerria japonica
winter appeal of, 168
Knautia macedonica
top pick long-bloomer, 102
knawel *see Scleranthus annuus*
Kniphofia uvaria
for high-altitudes, 68
kudzu *see Pueraria montana lobularia*
labels
saving plant tags, 296
seed starting, 296
lady beetles, 277, 299

lady's mantle

lady's mantle see *Alchemilla mollis*
Lantana
   top pick new, 79
Lathyrus odoratus
   top pick cut flower, 93
laurel, mountain see *Kalmia latifolia*
Lavandula
   for summer scent, 137
   top pick cut flower, 96
lavender see *Lavandula*
lavender cotton see *Santolina chamaecyparissus*
lawn mower maintenance, 293
lawns, low-maintenance, 265
leaf spot, septoria, 305
leafhoppers
   pest profile, 275
Lepidium virginicum
   annual weed, 272
lettuce, fall planting, 263
light and lighting
   street lights and plants, 62
lilac see *Syringa vulgaris*
Lilium
   for summer scent, 137

lily see *Lilium*
lily, blood see *Scadoxus multiflorus*
lily, foxtail see *Eremurus*
lily, Peruvian see *Alstroemeria*
lily, pineapple see *Eucomis bicolor*
linden see *Tilia*
lisianthius see *Eustoma grandiflorum*
Lobularia maritima
   for summer scent, 137
locust, black see *Robinia pseudoacacia*
Loropetalum chinense
   pruning, 254
love-in-a-mist see *Nigella damascena*
lungwort see *Pulmonaria*
Magnolia xsoulangiana
   for spring scent, 137
mallow, poppy see *Callirhoe involucrata*
mallow, rose see *Hibiscus moscheutos*
Malus
   for spring scent, 137
maple see *Acer*

maps and mapping, 130
Mentha
   keeping contained, 64
metal edging, 132
mint see *Mentha*
mockorange see *Philadelphus*
moles, 304
Monarda didyma
   top pick new, 75
monkshood see *Aconitum carmichaelii*
monoecious, definition of, 69
moonflower see *Ipomoea*
morning glory see *Ipomoea*
moth, Australian light brown apple, 301
mountain laurel see *Kalmia latifolia*
mulches and mulching
   corrugated plastic sign, 294
   fall-planted perennials, 264
   with fertilizer, 140
   one-time, 172
   save on broken bags, 248
   shredded paper, 294
   trees, 266
   types of, 132

Narcissus
   top pick cut flower, 93
   for winter scent, 137
narrow beds, 122
Nepeta
   Asian ladybug deterrent, 299
   for high-altitudes, 68
Nephrolepis exaltata
   dividing, 62
new plants for 2010, 72
Nigella damascena
   cottage garden favorite, 153
ninebark see *Physocarpus opulifolius*
nodding ladies' tresses see *Spiranthes cernua*
nurseries
   plant shopping, 214, 249
olive, tea see *Osmanthus fragrans*
ornaments
   accessorizing with, 164
   DIY glass, 288
   Tuffits™, 186
Osmanthus fragrans
   for fall scent, 137
Oxalis stricta
   perennial weed, 271
Paeonia
   plant profile, 50
   supports, 68
Papaver somniferum
   top pick multiseason showoff, 107
paper bush see *Edgeworthia chrysantha*
paperwhites see *Narcissus*
Parietaria pennsylvanica
   biennial weed, 273
parsley, overwintering, 62
pathways
   creating depth with, 177
   design, 159
   inviting, 140
patios
   fungus on, 302
   makeover, 284
   materials pros and cons, 131
   roomy, 176
pea, sweet see *Lathyrus odoratus*
Pelargonium peltatum
   anemic, 69
pellitory see *Parietaria pennsylvanica*
Pennisetum alopecuroides
   Editor's Choice, 30
pennycress see *Thlaspi arvense*
Penstemon
   Editor's Choice, 48
peony see *Paeonia*

pepperweed *see Lepidium virginicum*
perennials
  bare-root, 258
  for the birds, 65
  Bloom's Best Perennials and Grasses, 186
  borders, 170
  for easy gardening, 190
  for high-altitudes, 68
  top pick new, 79
  snow as insulation, 69
  soil cultivation, 302
  spring fluffing, 251
  starting from seed, 249, 256
  top picks, 74, 98, 104
  winter-blooming, 166
pergolas, 131
Perovskia atriplicifolia
  for perennial border, 173
pests and pest control
  see also names of specific pests; wildlife
  Orbital 360° sprayer, 295
  pesticides, 268, 298, 299
Petunia x*hybrida*
  top pick new, 73
Philadelphus
  pruning, 255
  for summer scent, 137
Phlox
  top pick big bloom, 88
Physocarpus opulifolius
  pruning, 255
Picea
  blue-green foliage, 169
  training, 66
Pieris japonica
  winter-bloomer, 167
pincushion flower *see Callirhoe involucrata*; *Scabiosa columbaria*
pine *see Pinus wallichiana*
Pinus wallichiana
  blue-green foliage, 169
plans, 130
plant combinations
  spring bulbs, 182
plant markers
  potting soil as, 296
  tags, 296
plant shopping, 214, 249
plumbago *see Ceratostigma plumbaginoides*
Poa annua
  annual weed, 272
Polemonium
  top pick multiseason showoff, 104

Polygonatum
  top pick multiseason showoff, 105
poppy, California *see Eschscholzia californica*
poppy, opium *see Papaver somniferum*
potato beetle, Colorado, 276
potting soil
  reusing, 248
  save on broken bags, 248
prairie gardens, 138
praying mantis, 277
primrose *see Primula*
Primula
  easy to grow, 54
privacy fences, 151
pruners and pruning
  cleanup, 250, 291, 302
  OXO hedge shears, 301
Prunus mume
  for winter scent, 137
Pueraria montana lobularia
  fungus for control, 67
Pulmonaria
  top pick multiseason showoff, 105
queen-of-the-prairie *see Filipendula rubra*
quince *see Chaenomeles japonica*
rabbits, 280
raccoons, 294
radishes, fall planting, 263
rain gardens, winterizing, 302
rainwater collection, 294, 303

raking, spring, 251
record keeping
  GardenScribe Plant Organizer, 293
redbud *see Cercis*
red-hot poker *see Kniphofia uvaria*
repellents
  Animal Stopper, 298
  insect, 268
Rhododendron
  pruning, 254
Robinia pseudoacacia
  bright green foliage, 146
roots
  bare-root stock, 258
  crown rot, 260
  pot-bound, 215
Rosa
  top pick new, 79
  low maintenance shrub, 56
  pruning Labrador, 127
  for summer scent, 137
  top pick cut flower, 94
rose, Christmas *see Helleborus*
rose, Japanese *see Kerria japonica*
rose chafers
  pest watch, 276
rose mallow *see Hibiscus moscheutos*
row covers
  for fall crops, 263
  washing, 297
Rudbeckia
  bird-attracting, 65
  for perennial border, 173
  plant profile, 32

sage *see Salvia*
sage, Russian *see Perovskia atriplicifolia*
Salvia
  for fall color, 28
  for perennial border, 173
Santolina chamaecyparissus
  for high-altitudes, 68
Sarcococca confusa
  for winter scent, 137
  winter-bloomer, 167
Scabiosa columbaria
  top pick long-bloomer, 101
Scadoxus multiflorus
  top pick big bloom, 87
scale (insects)
  pest profile, 275
scale (size) of accessories, 165
Scleranthus annuus
  weed watch, 306
screens, fences as, 151
sea thrift *see Armeria maritima*
Sedum spectabile
  top pick new, 76
seed starting
  labels, 296
  perennials, 249, 256
septoria leaf spot, 305
serviceberry *see Amelanchier*
shade gardens
  top pick multiseason showoffs, 104
shears, OXO hedge, 301
shoes
  Bogs garden boots, 293
  cleaning clay off of, 292

shrubs

shrubs
  deadheading, 252
  for easy gardening, 190
  top pick new, 79
  pruning, 252
  thinning, 254
  top pick multiseason showoffs, 108
  top pick new, 78
  winter-blooming, 167
slugs, 278
snake, garter, 281
snapdragon *see Antirrhinum*
snow as insulator, 69
snowball, Chinese *see Viburnum*
snowdrop *see Galanthus nivalis*
soil, replacing clay, 172
Solenostemon
  for perennial border, 173
Solomon's seal *see Polygonatum*
Sonchus asper
  weed watch, 306
sorrel, wood *see Oxalis stricta*
sowthistle *see Sonchus asper*
spiderwort *see Tradescantia*

spinach, fall planting, 263
Spiraea xvanhouttei
  pruning, 255
Spiranthes cernua
  for fall color, 28
spirea, false *see Astilbe*
sprayer, Orbital 360º, 295
spring (season) cleanup, 250
sprinklers, 282
spruce *see Picea*
spurge *see Euphorbia*
squash bugs, 277
squirrels, 243, 281
stakes
  holiday light strands w/clips, 292
  make your own, 249
  paper ties, 301
stems, winter appeal of, 168
steppers, Tuffits™, 186
Stewartia monadelpha
  winter appeal of, 168
stone
  edging, 132
  mulch, 132
  patios, 131
  placement for casual look, 117

storm damage
  duct tape splint for, 293
straw mulch, 132
strawflower *see Xerochrysum bracteata*
succulents
  Succulent Container Gardens, 244
sunflower *see Helianthus*
sweet alyssum *see Lobularia maritima*
sweet box *see Sarcococca confusa*
sweet pea *see Lathyrus odoratus*
sweet potato vine *see Ipomoea*
sweet rocket *see Hesperis matronalis*
sweetspire, Virginia *see Itea virginica*
Syringa vulgaris
  pruning, 253
  for spring scent, 137
tatsoi, fall planting, 263
Taxodium distichum
  fast-growing shade tree, 67
tea olive *see Osmanthus fragrans*

thinning shrubs, 254
Thlaspi arvense
  annual weed, 272
Thuja occidentalis
  burgundy foliage, 169
Tiarella cordifolia
  top pick new, 76
Tilia
  fast-growing shade tree, 67
tools and equipment
  co-ops, 249
  invest in best, 248
  kneeling pads, 293
  last used in fall, 265
  lawn mowers, 293
  light bulb changer as apple picker, 296
  OXO hedge shears, 301
  temporary garden storage, 293
  tool stand, 292
  totes, 249
  for watering, 282, 295
Tradescantia
  top pick long-bloomer, 100
traffic control and fences, 150
trees
  fall-planted, 266
  fast-growing for shade, 67
  mulching, 266
  top picks, 78, 108
  with winter appeal, 168
trellises
  recycled patio umbrella, 187
trenches as edging, 132
trimmers, 301
Tulipa
  plant profile, 85
  planting depth, 267
  top ten picks, 80
Vaccinium
  top pick new, 79
vegetables, cool-season, 262
Veronicastrum virginicum
  for perennial border, 173
vetch, crown *see Coronilla varia*
Viburnum
  Editor's Choice, 16
  pruning, 255
Viola
  top pick new, 74
  for winter scent, 137
  winter-bloomer, 166
walnut *see Juglans nigra*
water and watering
  and chlorine, 283
  collecting, 294, 303
  pouches, 242
  tips for, 173, 245
  tools for, 248, 282, 295

Zygocactus

water gardens and raccoons, 294
waterpod *see Ellisia nyctelea*
weeds and weeding
   10-minute task, 302
   biennial, 273
   neglected bed, 127
   perennial, 271
   spot treatment, 248
   spring, 270
   winter annual, 272
wheel bugs, 277
whiteflies
   pest profile, 275
wildlife *see names of specific types of wildlife*
willow blue-star *see Amsonia tabernaemontana*
window boxes
   see also garden plans
   gadgets for, 235
   quick change, 234
winecups *see Callirhoe involucrata*
winter color, 166
winterhazel *see Corylopsis glabrescens*
Wisteria brachybotrys
   for spring scent, 137
witchhazel *see Hamamelis* x*intermedia*
wood sorrel *see Oxalis stricta*
woodruff, blue *see Asperula orientalis*
Xerochrysum bracteata
   Editor's Choice, 60
yucca, red *see Hesperaloe parviflora*
Zelkova serrata
   fast-growing shade tree, 67
Zinnia
   chartreuse flowers, 147
   for perennial border, 173
   top pick new, 73
Zygocactus
   blooming, 245

Want helpful garden advice delivered EVERY WEEK?

Then you'll LOVE our weekly e-notes. They're filled with:

- At-a-glance plant guides
- Pests and weeds to watch (and how to eliminate them)
- How-to videos and projects
- Practical tips that make gardening easier

Visit **www.GardenGateNotes.com** to become a member today!

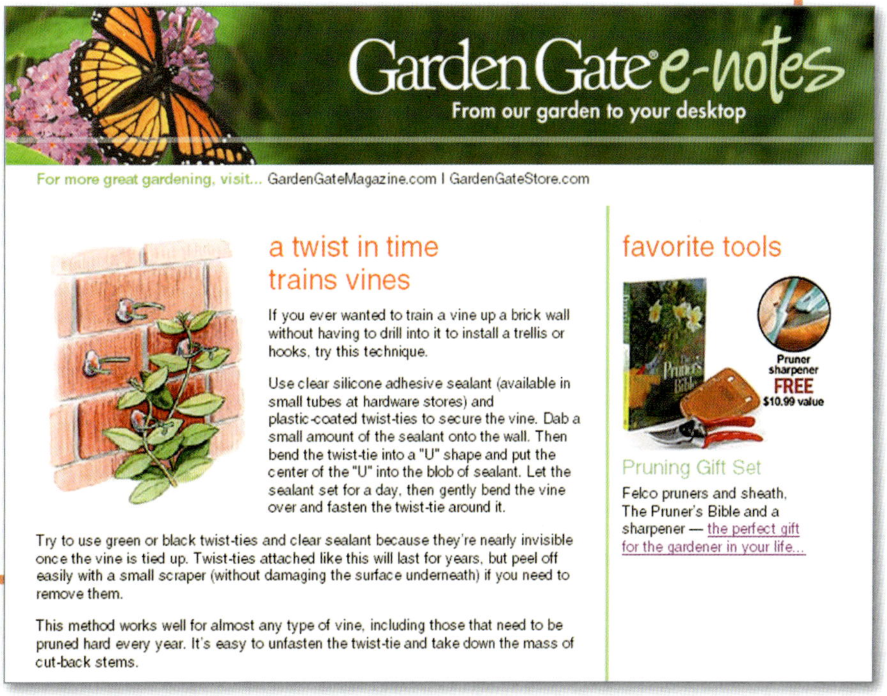